BEVERLY HILLS DETECTIVE

BEVERLY HILLS DETECTIVE

Memoirs of a former

Beverly Hills Detective

Robert E. Downey

Library of Congress Number:		99-91283
ISBN #:	Hardcover	0-7388-0728-1
	Softcover	0-7388-0729-X

This book was printed in the United States of America.

To order additional copies of this book, contact:
Xlibris Corporation
1-888-7-XLIBRIS
www.Xlibris.com
Orders@Xlibris.com

CONTENTS

DEDICATED TO MY WIFE, DIANA
There are not enough superlatives
to fully describe the type of woman she is.
Through each of the joys and sorrows, pain and elation,
anxiety, disappointments and heartaches,
she was always there with just the right support and encouragement.
God bless her and all the cop's wives like her.

PROLOGUE

Books are written for many reasons. Notoriety, wealth, fame, immortality, desire to inform, and ego, are but a few of those reasons. I started this book with a fervent hope that I could impart to the general public the knowledge that the vast majority of police officers are a credit to their profession, and to the people and agencies that employ them.7

The Rodney King case and the O.J. Simpson case are aberrations. Contrary to some opinions it has not always been that way. In the last fifteen or twenty years we have continually witnessed the vilification, denigration, maligning and castigation of people who have devoted their lives to the profession of providing safety for their fellow man. Whether you believe it or not, most Police Officers want to help, and feel a deep sense of accomplishment and satisfaction when they can. By no means would I presume to argue that all officers are devoid of the frailties of other humans. I will argue, that from my personal experience and observation, the people of the law enforcement profession have a far fewer ratio of bad to good than do most other professions. With the odd exception of New Orleans at the present time.

I often wonder if the way police officers are portrayed by some writers today, could be adding to the growing perception that all cops are oversexed, drunken, uncouth misfits, and generally uneducated slobs.

This book starts in the late fifties and runs through the mid sixties. When William Parker was Police Chief of Los Angeles and Clinton Anderson was Chief of Police of Beverly Hills. They were both the right man for the right job, at the right time.

People like Daryl Gates, a rising young Parker protege, was

about to be promoted to Lieutenant and the legendary Thad Brown was the Los Angeles Chief of Detectives. Our first encounter with Daryl Gates would be in the LAPD Intelligence Division.

You will witness the genesis of the Los Angeles Police Department Special Investigation Unit (SIU) which was initiated by a small group of burglary detectives from a couple of local departments. They were becoming increasingly frustrated at chasing the same shadows, knowing who was committing the burglaries, but being unable to gather enough physical evidence to charge the suspects. Information was available from various sources, but knowing it and proving it were vastly different.

This pick up unit evolved into a highly efficient surveillance and investigative unit that still operates to this day, on a much wider scale. The only problem now is that they have become too efficient, according to some detractors. The phrase, "Damned if you do and damned if you don't", comes to mind most readily.

Some who have read the preliminary drafts of this book have commented that there is not enough sex and violence. It's hard to get across to people that every time an officer puts on his gun and leaves the office that he doesn't get into a high speed chase or a gunfight. You didn't then and you don't now. Although gunfights today are a much commoner occurrence.

It's also hard to get people to understand that every third word out of a cop's or a suspect's mouth was not a four letter word. We weren't saints by any means but we were not foul mouthed, sex crazed, trigger happy, drunks that had no respect for people. For the most part, you gave what you got.

All the stories in this book are true. A couple of names have been changed to prevent embarrassment, and because I just couldn't remember every name.

I've been told by some who have read the first drafts that while the book is interesting, no one is really interested in the life of the ordinary detective. That although there are many celebrities and personalities in the book, there is no inside stuff like who's sleeping with whom, what politician is a cross dresser, things like that.

Some of these stories involve celebrities in their more vulnerable moments. Those times when they are just victims like many others. I have been criticized for not "dishing the dirt", if there was any, on these people. It may seem strange, but revealing demeaning or derogatory personal information obtained while in a position of trust just isn't and wasn't honorable. Working in Beverly Hills you had to have the personal integrity to know just what was and wasn't "grist for the mill".

Lt. B.L. Cork, later Beverly Hills Chief of Police, Sgt. Frank Gravante, Los Angeles Police Department, Special Agent Peter Meaney, FBI, Detective Jack Mourning, among many, many, others are an integral part of this book and are typical of the type of dedicated officers that represent you.

Jack Webb, actor, director, producer, writer, and, above all, an in-his-heart cop, said it best in the Feb. 9, 1967 episode of his "Dragnet" T.V. series on NBC, when a rookie officer got unhappy with his Department and "Sgt. Friday" was enlightening him on;.

"WHAT IS A COP ?"

It's awkward having a policemen around the house. Friends drop in. A man with a badge answers the door. The temperature drops twenty degrees. Throw a party and the badge gets in the way. All of a sudden there isn't a straight man in the crowd. Everybody's a comedian, "Don't drink too much," somebody says, "or the man with the badge will run you in." . . . Or, "How's it going Dick Tracy? How many jaywalkers did you pinch today?" . . . And there's always the one who wants to know how many apples you stole. All at once you've lost your first name. You're a "cop," a "flatfoot," a "bull," a "dick," "John Law," You're "the fuzz," "the heat," . . . you're poison, you're trouble . . . you're bad news. They call you everything, but never a policeman. It's not much of a life . . . unless you don't mind missing a Dodger game because the hot shot phone rings . . . unless you like working Saturdays, Sundays, holidays . . . at a job that doesn't pay overtime. Oh, the pay is adequate. If you count your pennies, you can put your kid through college. But you'd better plan on seeing Europe on you television set. Then there is your first night on the beat. When you try to arrest a drunken prostitute in a Main Street bar and she rips your new uniform to shreds. You'll buy another one . . . out of your own pocket. You'll rub elbows with all the elite: pimps, addicts, thieves, bums, winos, girls who can't keep an address and men who don't care. Liars, cheats, con men, the class of skid row. And the heartbreak: underfed kids, beaten kids, molested kids, lost kids, crying kids, homeless kids, hit-and- run kids, broken-arm kids, broken- leg kids, broken-head kids, sick kids, dying kids, dead kids. The old people that nobody wants, the reliefers, the pensioners, the ones who walk the street cold and those who tried to keep warm in a three- dollar room with an unvented gas heater. You'll walk the beat and pick up the pieces. Do you have real adventure in your soul? You'd better have. You'll do time in a prowl car. It'll be a thrill a minute when you get an "unknown trouble" call and hit a back yard at two in the morning, never knowing what you'll meet . . . a kid with a knife . . . a pill head with a gun, or two ex-cons with nothing to lose. And you'll have plenty of time to think. You'll draw plenty of time in a "lonely car" . . . with nobody to talk to but your radio. Four years in uniform and you'll have the ability, the experience and maybe the desire to be a detective. If you like to fly by the seat of your pants, this is where you belong. For every crime that's committed you've got three million suspects to chose from. Most of the time you'll have few facts and lots of hunches. You'll run down leads that dead end on you. You'll work all night stakeouts that could last a week. You'll do leg work until you're sure you've talked to everybody in California . . . people who saw it happen but really didn't. People who insist they did it, but really didn't. People who don't remember, those who try to forget. Those who tell the truth, those who lie. You'll run the files until your eyes ache. And paperwork . . . you'll fill out a report when you're right, you'll fill one out when you're wrong, you'll fill one out when you're not sure, you'll fill one out listing your leads, you'll fill one out when you have no leads, you'll make out a report on the reports you've made. You'll write enough words in your lifetime to stock a library. You'll learn to live with doubt, anxiety, frustration, court decisions that tend to hinder rather than help you: Dorado, Morse, Escobedo, Cahan. You'll learn to live with the District Attorney, testifying in court, defense attorneys, prosecuting attorneys, judges, juries, witnesses. And sometimes you won't be happy with the outcome. But there's also this: There are over five thousand men in this city who know that being a policeman is an endless, glamorless, thankless job that must be done. I know it, too. And I'm damned glad to be one of them.

BARRICADE

It was one of those absolutely perfect, defies description, Southern California days. Sun shining, not too hot, cloudless, a good gentle breeze blowing from the ocean, and the long shadows of the palm trees lining Sunset Blvd. making shade breaks along the street. Such a day mandated a leisurely return to the office from the meeting with the Hollywood Division Detectives. Crossing from West Hollywood into Beverly Hills on Sunset was like moving from one world to another. From the jumble of businesses, buildings, and crowds of people, to the treelined, divided streets, with manicured lawns in front of immaculate residences.

Even the meeting went well. Whether because of the day or in spite of it, didn't matter. Cork and I were both deep into our own thoughts when the radio popped and tore a ragged hole in the entire mood.

"Car four, car fourteen, ambulance follow up at the Livingston residence in the 600 block of Rodeo Drive, shooting. Approach with caution. Suspect is the son of the victims and is believed to still be in the house and armed."

"Car four, roger. Car fourteen, roger." As each car responded.

Car four was the beat car for that particular area of town. Car fourteen was the patrol sergeant for the day.

Automatically my foot crunched down on the accelerator as Cork and I both sat upright in our seats and started watching traffic anxiously. Cork had already started reaching for the microphone. We had been working closely together for a couple of years. Closely enough that we both knew instinctively what the other would do in a given situation. No wasted motion, no wasted conversation. Cork has an outward appearance that belies the intensity within him. Without the slightest thought or hesitation we both knew we were going to respond to that call. Still, Cork is an enigma. Still waters run deep doesn't quite fit. To know him is to understand him certainly doesn't fit. Whatever it is, we work well together.

"Car seventeen one and two, responding from Sierra and Sunset." Cork said into the microphone. Seventeen being the numerical designation for the detective bureau cars. Numbers one and two identify the detectives.

"Roger seventeen, be advised that the suspect is believed to be barricaded inside the house with two firearms."

"Seventeen, Roger."

"Christ," I said, "what a day for it," as we steadily increased our speed. As we passed Mountain Drive we were bouncing between 60 and 65 MPH.

With the red light and siren going we cut off Sunset onto Beverly Drive and cross it to Lomita then turn south on Rodeo. Even with a red light and siren, being in an unmarked car has it's disadvantages. If people do hear the siren they're looking for a black and white or an ambulance. A plain car is usually upon them before they know it and it startles them. You can never tell then what they're going to do. You just keep driving. And praying.

A block from the house we saw the ambulance in the driveway of the two story stucco house and a couple of people in the front yard. A black and white patrol car was pulling into the curb in front of the house. At Elevado we cut back across to the wrong side of the divider and pulled to the curb just north of the ambulance.

We learned from the beat car that songwriter Jay Livingston and his wife had been shot. Apparently by their 20 or 21 year old son who was probably still on the second floor of the house. Mr. Livingston was in the ambulance being treated for a bullet wound through his elbow. His wife however had been shot in the chest and was lying in the back yard being treated by two ambulance attendants. Her prognosis was unknown.

While Cork headed to the ambulance to interview Mr. Livingston I went to the back yard to check on Mrs. Livingston. I rounded the corner of the house and saw an attendant bending over her as she was lying on her back near the center of the yard. I got closer and could see she was wearing a white sweater with a very large, bright red, stain high up in the center of her chest. It was the brightest red I could ever remember seeing.

My first thought was if that bullet was centered in the red area of the sweater, this could be a very major wound. As I got closer and began to speak to her she immediately started to implore me not to hurt him.

"Who?", I asked.

"My son", she said, "he's not well. He didn't mean to do it. He just got upset at his father." Her voice was clear and her eyes were bright and attentive. Her arms were moving with no apparent difficulty. The attendants were about to put her on the stretcher. It was only then that I noticed that we were all in full view of several windows on the second floor. If he was up there, and still angry, we were sitting ducks. I motioned to the ambulance attendants to look up, and then jerked my thumb toward the side of the house. They understoodd and with no hesitation she was put on the stretcher and we were on our way out of there with me watching the upper windows.

As we started back around the house I encountered two uniformed officers. and told them to take up positions on either side of the rear yard and stay under cover until we could get more information on the suspect.

As I got to the ambulance Cork was coming out.

"Kid's name is Gary. He has a 12 gauge shotgun, a .22 rifle, and a .22 pistol. And plenty of ammo." Cork said as we moved toward the open front door. The uniformed officers had formed a semicircle around the front of the house keeping the curious at bay.

"Father says he doesn't know just what set him off today. He says the kids' been troubled for a while. Under a doctors care."

“Yeah, mother told me he didn’t mean to do it. Just got upset with his father. I’d hate to think what the hell he would have done if he had meant to do it. She looks like she’s hit pretty bad but she’s alert and attentive.” We each took a side of the open front door and cautiously peered inside. Across about 12 feet of foyer we could see part of a hallway with a large living room on the left and a staircase leading up to the right of the hall. About eight stairs were visible between two banisters before they disappeared between two walls. Nothing else was in sight.

We had a problem. The son had been located on the second floor when the shooting happened. Since the arrival of the ambulance he had plenty of opportunity to move anywhere in the house. No one had been in the house since the shooting. Cork and I decided to make sure the downstairs was clear before concentrating on the upstairs. Just in case.

Before spreading out we had motioned one of the uniformed officers to cover our backs from the front door. We quickly headed out in opposite directions to check and clear each room on the ground floor. We locked the basement door as we passed. Returning to the front door we set out trying to locate a friend or neighbor who could describe the upper floor of the house for us. We located a next door neighbor who said she had been a guest in the house many times.

“Can you give us a rough diagram of the
second floor. That seems to be where Gary is located.” Cork took a piece of paper from his pocket as he questioned her.

“I’ve never been on the second floor.” She said. “We’re not that close. I’ve been in the house many times but never upstairs.”

“Do you know of anyone out here that knows the house.” I asked as I looked at the crowd that had gathered.

“No. The servants are gone. I just don’t see anyone that can help.” she said. We turned her over to a uniformed officer and asked another officer to poll the crowd to see if anyone may know the layout of the house. No one could help us.

Cork and I re-entered the house and took up positions on

either side of the staircase. There was a blank wall at the top of the stairs with apparently a hall off to either side.

We started to work our way up the stairs to see if we could figure out the layout. When I was in the backyard I had seen several uncovered windows coming to a corner at the rear of the house. That room was to the left of the stairway, but how far? Any room between it and the stairway? From the vent pipes through the roof we could estimate the location of a couple of bathrooms. We guessed the adjoining windows were in bedrooms. How big ? How small? Closets? Half baths? Little things like that were swirling around in our minds.

We were almost to the top of the stairs when we heard it. A shot. Certainly not the shotgun, probably the .22. The heat index just went up about 20 degrees and the sweat popped out. Now what. Had he shot at us? Had he shot himself? Or had he fired out a window? No one outside reported taking any fire. O.K. We knew for sure now he was upstairs. But where ?

"Gary. Can you hear us ?" I asked loudly.

No answer.

"Can you hear us Gary ?" Louder.

Still no answer.

"Gary, if you can hear us, we want you to know that your parents are all right and on their way to the hospital. They're very worried about you." Cork said. "Did you hear me Gary ? Did you hear what I said ?"

We looked at each other and shrugged. We heard a noise from upstairs but nothing like a voice answering. More like the muffled sounds of movement. But where ?

There we were. Sitting near the top of the stairway, guns drawn, not knowing whether our suspect was to the right or the left. Also knowing that if he decided to stick that shotgun around the corner and pull the trigger there was no way he could miss either one of us. It was getting warmer, much warmer.

We backed down the stairs to reevaluate our position. And the hair was standing up on the back of our necks. You could see just as much from the bottom of the stairs and less of a chance of a blind shotgun blast taking off your head.

We radioed for tear gas and shotguns, and a few more men to block off the streets and move the gawkers back. In a few minutes the streets are blocked and the equipment arrived. Along with Chief Clinton H. Anderson, Car 11, and Detective Captain John Hankins, Car 18.

While I was outside Cork had been trying to talk to Gary. When I went back in to fill Cork in we heard another sharp report. Still not the shotgun. We were even more concerned that Gary did not believe that his folks were going to be O.K. and may take his own life. We wanted to take him safely and unharmed, if possible. If he was shooting at anyone in particular we couldn't determine who.

Joe Head of the Record Bureau brought the tear gas to the doorway as Cork and I went back outside to confer with the Chief and Captain Hankins. They seemed perfectly content to leave the situation in our hands. Thanks a lot. We had left Detectives Wayne Rutherford and Tom McCarthy in our spots at the bottom of the stairs.

In a few seconds I was lobbing tear gas shells through shuttered, draped, windows from the barrel of a gas gun while Cork covered me. Because of the shutters and drapes we had decided to use the three inch barricade shells. As each shell entered the house you could hear the muffled POOF as it exploded to release its teary contents.

After launching four shells into various windows on the second floor we settled back to wait for the gas to take effect. The shotguns had been loaded and passed out to several officers. When Cork and I returned to the interior of the residence tear gas was flowing freely down the stairway. We concluded that sufficient time had passed with no results so we went back outside and sent two more shells through two other windows closer to a wide windowless portion of the second floor.

As we started to return to the doorway we heard shouting

coming from inside the house and a few seconds later Rutherford and McCarthy came out the front door with a pajama clad, handcuffed, Gary between them. They were all crying and coughing copiously.

They were loading Gary into a car when one of the firemen noticed smoke coming from an attic roof vent. The firemen, who had been standing by, donned their gas masks and entered the house. They found a small fire starting to burn in the attic, apparently started by one the tear gas shells that had pierced the bedroom ceiling and lodged in the attic. It was quickly extinguished and the firemen set up their fans to evacuate the gas and smoke from the house.

A quick search of the second floor turned up the guns and the ammo. We discovered that the gas had taken a while to reach Gary because he had been in a dressing room without windows and had closed both doors virtually isolating himself from the gas. It did eventually have the desired effect and he was taken into custody without injury. Cork and I were discussing the situation with the Chief and the Captain when a very loud shotgun blast went off just a few feet behind us and to our right. As we turned to see what happened, another blast went off.

That time we could see what happened. The officer attempting to unload his shotgun was apparently unfamiliar with the gun. He had kept his finger on the trigger as he tried to eject the ammo by moving the slide back and forth. The Winchester Model 12 firing pin came down on the shell each time the slide was pulled forward discharging another round.

Our nerves had only come half way down before the shotgun went off. We sat down on the lawn near the two large holes the shotgun had made while the patrol Sergeant took the gun and unloaded it. It took a few deep breaths for our hearts to slow down again.

The Chief told us to go to the UCLA medical center to check on the victims while Capt. Hankins took care of booking Gary and transporting him to the County hospital for evaluation. I think he knew we needed some settle down time.

On the way to the hospital we didn't say a hell of a lot to each other. It took the ride time for us to unwind a little. Besides, what was there to say? What seemed like a week had only taken about 45 minutes. And every instant, every movement, every sound, was vividly clear. What causes that? Several times during the ride Cork and I glanced at each other without saying a word. We both knew that those two shots we heard could just as well have been Gary poking the shotgun around the corner of the stairway and just squeezing the trigger. Even then, just thinking about it sent a slight shiver up my back. We both knew how we felt but there was no way you could explain it to anyone.

Once at the hospital we asked several people just where our victims were. It was a big place. The more we walked around the more we realized people were shying away from us. Then we remembered that our clothes were permeated with tear gas and we were leaving a trail of tears every where we went.

We located Mr. & Mrs. Livingston in the Emergency room area. Mr. Livingston was still on the treatment table and she was in the recovery room. The doctor told us Mrs. Livingston's wound had not penetrated into her chest cavity and that Mr. Livingston's wound was a through and through wound at the elbow. Both would recover. We told them that Gary had been taken into custody without harm and was being transferred to the county hospital for observation. She was very grateful and relieved, with tears in her eyes.

Mr. Livingston was still being treated and the doctor said the next procedure was to draw an antiseptic piece of gauze through the wound from one side to the other. I wasn't anxious to stay for that. Mr. Livingston told us he had told Gary to get out of bed and straighten up his room and that's what set him off. He said Gary had been upset before but never to this extent. We filled him in on Gary's disposition and started to leave the hospital.

It was about time. The hospital staff was about to gang up on us and throw us out. We had left a trail of tears throughout the building. The ride back to the station was made with all the windows open. There was hardly any conversation. We had gone through another situation that could only bring more understanding of each other. We were just parking on the ramp when Capt. Hankins and Det. McCarthy were escorting Gary out to a car for the trip to the hospital.

We headed for the shower and locker room and took off the reeking clothes. We all kept extra clothes in our lockers. We had to drop the gas clothes outside the door where we could get them later for the cleaners.

We filed our incident reports in record time and headed for home. When we got to the parking lot we suddenly realized this was still the same beautiful day we had started with. What the hell had happened to it in the meantime ?

While waiting for our respective rides we just stood looking at each other for a couple of minutes.

"Did all this really happen today ?" Cork asked.

"How can the day turn upside down so damn quick ?" I responded.

We were both shaking our heads as we headed for our separate rides home.

I was sitting in my recliner draining my second large vodka and tonic by the time Diana drove into the garage. When she opened the door her face changed a little. She'd seen me in this mood before.

"Do you want to talk about it ?" she asked as she sat down on the couch.

"I don't know what to say. I can't figure out how everything can go to hell in a hand basket in just a few minutes." In a couple of minutes she'd gotten the whole story, including the part about the beautiful, glorious ride back from Hollywood.

"Honey, you've got to feel good about the fact that he was taken without anyone else getting shot. Think how much better his mother feels knowing that he wasn't hurt. There's no way you're going to be able to change human nature. The best you can hope for is to keep it from going wild and hurting too many people."

She had a point. It was time to methodically dissect the whole incident, pick out the good points for future reference, and vow to correct any mistakes. Like giving a shotgun to someone who's not familiar with it. We decided to go out to dinner and I was still trying to sort out the day in my mind.

"Remember how you felt when you first started on the Department ?" she asked. "Remember how we spent so much time talking when you'd get home ?"

"Yeah, we talked about a lot of things. I
don't know which one you're talking about."

"You used to talk about how good you felt after you could help someone that really needed it. Those were the times you would feel the best about your job. O.K. think back about today. You and Cork had a chance to help someone that really needed it. Remember how the mother felt when she knew her son was safe. Tomorrow you may have a chance to do the same for someone else. Hopefully no guns involved, but each day is the beginning of another chance." That said, she settled back in her seat and watched traffic.

Now she really had me thinking. She was right of course. Damned few times that she wasn't.

By the time we were being seated at Whittinghills' the gloom was gone and it was time for a good prime rib. The day was ending as beautifully as it had started.

And, tomorrow was the beginning of another chance.

CHAPTER 1

"Do you, Robert Downey, swear to honestly and faithfully uphold and enforce the laws of the State of California, and the City of Beverly Hills to the best of your abilities?"

"I do"

"Congratulations Officer Downey, welcome aboard. Sergeant Peterson will take you around and familiarize you with some of our routines and show you where every thing is. "Sergeant, be sure you go by the firing range and get him qualified with his revolver." Peterson nodded and turned for the door.

"Thank you Captain Smith", I said as I followed Peterson.

"Don't try to remember everything right away Downey, it'll all come as routine pretty soon. You'll be working the four to twelve shift during your training period. Your training officer will be Officer James Bolander.

Each day after your classroom training you will spend the rest of the shift riding with your training officer. There will be three of you rookies attending the classes. The other two have been aboard for a couple of weeks and now we have enough for a class. After the sergeant completes your tour, your first written test will be on the names of the City's streets from the map I gave you last week."

"O.K. sergeant, introduce him around and bring him back here when you're done"

"Right Captain, let's go. Peterson is my name, what do you prefer to be called?"

"Bob. Nice to meet you sergeant. How long have you been with the Department?"

"Eight years. Have you been in law enforcement before?"

"Not in civilian law enforcement. I spent a year with Oakland

P.D. as a dispatcher before I got recalled to the Air force during the Korean `conflict'. While I was back in the service I spent a year as an Air Policeman and five years as a criminal investigator. I had given some serious thought to staying in but I had reached a dead end. I was frozen in rank because we were overstaffed in our Command, and I couldn't get a transfer because we were declared critical personnel. They had me coming and going so I opted to get out.

I've been waiting for this opening for nearly a year now. I've taken enough police department tests preparing for this one. Huntington Park, South Pasadena, LAPD, LASO, Inglewood. I was starting to worry that I would have to take one of the other departments before Beverly Hills opened up. I've been working for a finance company as an assistant credit manager while I was waiting. Really a glorified title for a skip tracer and repossessor. My wife still works for the parent company as office manager".

"We'll go over to the range first." He said. "Let's go down this way so I can show you the locker room and roll call room. The training room is just off the roll call room. The locker room is to the right at the bottom of the stairs, and across from that is the door to the basement garage.

That elevator at the end of the hall goes to the jail floor and will also stop at the central office level. If you are taking in a prisoner, take them up in the elevator and stop at the desk to get the key to the jail floor. Then take them on up to the booking desk on the jail floor. That way you can maintain the security of the suspect as well as keep them out of public view. Sometimes, when we're shorthanded, we have to book them at the desk in the business office. But we try to avoid that if we can."

"O.K. this will be your locker, the showers are in the other room. We'll go out past the roll call room to the parking area. Roll call begins 15 minutes before your shift starts. Be sure to check the bulletin board daily for any special lookouts or suspect information from the other shifts or the detectives."

"Each day when your shift begins you be sure you inspect

your assigned car for any damage or deficiencies. Also give the car a shakedown. We don't want any abandoned weapons, evidence or dope left from prior suspects."

"Sometimes in the heat of arresting someone you may overlook searching them as well as you should and they get to dump the loot or other evidence in the car. That's when you or some other officer can get hurt really bad either in court or by some weapon another suspect has found. It only takes a few minutes but it's well worth it."

"Here, lets take this car. If you do see any damage let your shift sergeant know about it. If some of the equipment is not working, like the red lights or siren or headlights, take the car to the shop and get it fixed or get another car from the sergeant until yours is fixed. The firing range is located in the basement of the city garage."

"You'll fuel up your car near the beginning of each shift. Check the oil each time you fill up. You always try not to let your vehicle get below half a tank. Just in case something unforeseen happens."

"Our beats are so small that you probably won't ever use a tank of gas during a shift but you never know. Whenever you leave your car for any reason other than a traffic stop or whenever you will be away from your car you always take the keys with you. Nothing will be harder to explain than having your car stolen by some wise guy while you are shaking some door or making a pit stop."

"We'll park here on the street and go through that door to the range. To stay qualified on the range you must shoot a minimum score of 210 out of 300 each payday. Marion Davies, the movie actress, sponsors a shooting competition each year. The best Department shooters receive individual and team trophies. Load five rounds of wadcutter and I'll run you through the course on single action. Keep the gun pointed down range at all times."

There was no problem qualifying. Sgt. Peterson was quite pleasant and supplied a wealth of information about procedures, customs and organization of the department. We went back to the office where Capt. Smith recorded my shooting score and took me to the training room located just off the roll call room.

"This will be the test about the city streets that I told you about. Start at the west city limits and moving east, write down the north / south streets in order, to the east city limits. When you've done that, start at the south city limits and list the east/ west streets, in order, up to Lexington."

"With the streets north of Lexington just write them down without trying to keep them in any specific order. They wind in and around so much you can't really tell which direction they run. It's sufficient that you know them and where theyare located".

"In a couple of weeks, during training sessions, you will be given a street address and asked the most direct route to respond from a given location. Our beats are small and we pride ourselves on our response times. Usually less than two minutes to any call. O.K. start your list. Bring it up to the desk when you are finished and we will get you with your training officer. Good Luck".

Well, alone in the City of Beverly Hills Police Headquarters. That was what I had been working toward. It was the time to start proving to myself and the Department that I had what it took to make Law Enforcement my profession. First though, I'd better quit daydreaming and work on the test. Don't hurry, and write legibly. What good was the list if no one could read it. Nothing was said about any time limit but surely it will be a consideration. Here we go.

CHAPTER 2

"Excuse me Captain, Here is the test paper". It would seem that a Captain of the Beverly Hills Police Department would have a somewhat more impressive office. One 10 x 12 room with two windows overlooking the basement driveway and part of the police parking lot. One old wooden desk, two bookcases, and two wooden side chairs for company. The Captain leaned back in his vintage wooden swivel chair, a toothpick in the corner of his mouth. He and his surroundings all seemed to go together.

"O.K. Downey we'll have the desk call in your training officer. Here is a list of subjects to read up on from the Penal and Vehicle Codes that you got. Some of them you will need to know from memory, especially the laws of arrest. That little red book, written by the Judge on California Criminal Law and Court Procedure, is your basic guide to arrest and procedure. Be thoroughly familiar with all of it as soon as you can. Your classroom training will be from two PM to six PM daily and then you will go into the field. Your days off will be the same as your training officer, but all that can change depending on the circumstances.

Walking me from his office to the main business office he pointed out the various offices and locations and briefly described what duties each person performed. At the bend corner of a long ell shaped service counter he introduced me to the dispatcher/switchboard operator and general information clerk. This particular individual was Bert Sloane.

"This is what we call the Desk, and is the nerve center of the office. That lighted board on the wall up there lets the dispatcher know what units are in service and which ones are out. The Watch

Commander's office is located in that room to the left of the dispatcher."

"Here's your training officer. Bolander, I'd like you to meet your new recruit, Officer Downey".

"Yes Captain, we know each other. My sister in law and her husband are friends of Bob and his wife. We met a couple of weeks ago at a bar-be-cue".

"Well take him around and show him the City and brief him on some of our procedures. I'll have the desk keep you off calls as best we can for a couple of days until he gets the lay of the land. Good Luck Downey. Welcome aboard".

"Thank you Captain".

We went down the back stairs to Bolander's car which was parked on the ramp. Bolander was an all business person. The few times I had met him at social functions it was hard to imagine him as a cop in the city of my dreams. About 6 feet tall with a sort of gravelly voice and eyes that kept moving every minute we were on the street. As my training went on I found I couldn't have had a better training officer. Patient but insistent. The only room for error was in hypothetical situations. And he dreamed up plenty of those.

The rest of the shift was spent riding up and down streets and alleys and Jim pointing out call boxes, city limit lines, beat limits and a zillion other things. All the time asking me questions about "What street did we just cross? Which way is north from here. What hundred block are we in?"

I was convinced I didn't have enough brain cells to store all the random information I needed just to find my way around in the City. Even if it was a small city. All during that time he kept telling me not to worry about it now, it would all come naturally in time.

I learned that the City was divided into six beats, three north of Santa Monica Blvd. and three south. Even numbered beats 4,6,& 8 from west to east North of Santa Monica and odd ones 5, 7, & 9 west to east south of Santa Monica. These were regular patrol car beats. Traffic enforcement beats were numbered the same way, with the letter "T" preceding their call number. Traffic 11 was the accident investigation unit, IF we had enough manpower to field one. Car 14 and Traffic 14 were the shift sergeants. Car 16 was the Watch Commander.

Most important however was Car 11. The Chief. He didn't call often but when he did, pay attention.

Car 12 was the Captain and 17 the detectives. More often than not we didn't have enough people to fill all the posts so we ended up with Cars 5,7,9, 4 & 8 and traffic 4 and 5 or 9. All were one man cars. Very seldom was there a two man car. And not because we had enough manpower. Usually it was because several cars were broken down at the same time.

Each shift was usually headed up by a Lieutenant/Watch Commander and a patrol sergeant. Roll call took place 15 minutes before each shift change. In order to read the bulletin board and change into your uniform you needed to be in the locker room at least 30 minutes before the shift began. And even then that was cutting it pretty fine.

Each shift you checked the 'special watch' book. When a resident was going to be out of town he could call the desk and request a 'special watch'. A special list was kept, by beat, of houses that would be unoccupied for a specific length of time. During each shift the beat officer checked each house for security. Sometimes the officer was so busy he couldn't make all the checks. When that happened the next shift made a special effort to check the place. No house went more than a day without physical security check.

By that time I had numbers spilling out of my ears. I was given a list of call box locations and a list of "Codes". Code 2, for dinner. Code 6 for coffee being two of the more popular. Those two you never forgot or got mixed up. Day and evening shift, 10 minutes for coffee once a shift, and 30 minutes for lunch. Midnight shift you get the bonus of one extra coffee break. Of course you couldn't take any of them within the first or last hour of your shift, or while someone else was on a break. Incidentally, if you were on a call and missed your chance for a break, that was life. Code one, return to station. Code One R, return to the parking ramp and wait. Usually to provide transportation for someone.

Several places would insist on giving you coffee or halving your lunch check. In those cases you didn't argue with them or embarrass them, you just left a tip more than enough to pay for the coffee as well as a tip. As for lunch, you avoided going there. In one of the places you were requested to sign the back of the check if you received a half priced lunch. I don't know why, but I never felt comfortable signing my name to what certainly could have been classified a gratuity.

Of course avoiding the same coffee shop was extremely difficult when there were only one or two open after certain hours. One of the many DON'Ts passed on from Command (Chief) was, don't frequent any of the bars or nightclubs in town when off duty. "To much opportunity for trouble if they get to know you too well". Eventually you would find out that there were those who liked to live on the edge and ignored those "guidelines". But not so much so that they would flaunt it to the Chief or his pipe lines. For the most part the great majority of the officers adhered to the "rules".

Jim also explained that we frequently got 'silent' burglar and robbery alarm calls. 'Silent' meaning the alarm sounded only in the office of the burglar alarm company. They in turn telephoned the alarm location to the police desk. At the same time they dispatched one of their technicians or patrolmen to the location with keys or other pertinent information. Those alarms were installed and monitored by various companies like ADT, Morse, Bel Aire, etc.

Quite a few years ago, Jim told me, all the alarms used to be wired directly to the police desk. With the growth of the city, the monitoring task became overwhelming and had to be discontinued. The alarm business was taken over by private enterprise. Besides the silent alarms in the businesses and many residences, there were many audible alarms on businesses.

While these alarms were loud bells or sirens, the silent alarms are heard only in the monitoring office. In many of the residences where silent alarms were present, there was usually what was termed a 'panic' alarm located near the bed of the residents. Jim went on to tell me that frequently alarms were set off by the resident either to show off to their guests, or just to time how long it took for the police to arrive. He said it didn't take long to figure out what the resident was trying to do. After the first couple of 'false alarms' the resident was advised that if it continued, the police department would no longer respond to their call. They usually got the message very quickly.

"I'm going into detail about this so when you start answering these calls you'll know what to expect. On some shifts you'll think that's all you do is answer alarm calls. Especially on windy nights. Windows and doors shake and rattle, and the alarms start going off. Businesses and residences. Silent and audible. All kinds. It's the nature of the beast. Handle them all like they're the real thing. You never know when a burglar or robber will be using the wind to cover their activity. Contrary to some opinions, they're not all stupid".

He finished his sermon as we were turning into the parking ramp. Midnight already. I was back in the locker room putting away my gear and meeting a new group of people whose names I seemed to forget almost as fast as I heard them. I just couldn't remember any more. There's not room for all that information.

My shift couldn't have been over so soon. I was up. Wound tighter than a cheap watch. What do I do now. I was wide awake and my brain was working a mile a minute. Whoa. Time to take a deep breath and wind down. Get in my car and just sit for a few minutes, then go home. Take that pent up energy and use it to read some of the things you needed to learn.

I talked to Diana when I got home and tried, just tried to explain how I was feeling. Was it going to feel that good all the time? Would the high wear off and you get indifferent, calloused, and unfeeling after a while? God I hope not. It couldn't have gotten much better than this.

If I could feel that way after only one night on the job what was the rest of my career going to be like? I was already looking forward to coming to work the next day. I'd worked lots of jobs since I started in a factory at 14 but I couldn't remember ever wanting to be anything but a cop.

I could remember working on the assembly line at Chrysler, San Leandro and daydreaming about being a cop in Beverly Hills. I had no idea then how it was going to come to pass but I could always imagine. While I was in the Air Force during the Korean War, I got a large dose of the aspects of law enforcement, but nothing that could have given a hint of how it would actually be when it happened.

Even during that period it was a gratifying experience to know you had the opportunity to make a difference for somebody who maybe was unable to help themselves. It's a heady experience to realize that even though you are the same as every one else, because of your position, people EXPECT you to be able to do more, or take some action that will relieve their situation.

The drive home was totally lost in the memories of what had taken place in the past few weeks. Now came the ultimate challenge. Everything up to this point had been preparatory, preliminary. From now on it was all for real.

You couldn't lose your concentration. You must consider the consequences of every move you make. What effect it will have on all parties concerned. You have a commitment and responsibility to the public, to the City, and to yourself, to give your best efforts to every aspect of your profession. Now it was time to wonder if you're ready to accept that responsibility. You realized later that this was the point where you first began to play the "what if" games in your mind.

CHAPTER 3

"Come in and sit down Downey"

"Thanks Captain" I took my seat in one of the wooden chairs in the office as the Captain opened a file folder in front of him. The everpresent toothpick in his mouth.

"This is your first months review and evaluation. We'll discuss your training and any questions you may have. Your classroom work is going well and your test scores are good. Your training officer tells me you are picking up things easily and are eager to learn more. That's good.

"You and Bolander made a nice pinch the other night with those two burglars. They had already hit an office on South Western Ave. In L.A. and were planning to hit Bekins Van and Storage when you got them. This just points out what I always stress to the troops. Good observation will always pay off on patrol"

"It felt pretty good, Captain. Once we spotted them coming down that alley behind Paganos Beauty Shop without lights, it didn't take long to figure out they were casing some place. It was pretty funny when Jim asked the one what he did for a living after we saw the typewriters in the back seat. He said he was a business machine repairman and those were his tools on the floor. I don't know if I would want him working on my machines with a 12 inch screwdriver, a 24 inch pinch bar, a 50 foot coil of 2 inch rope, and two pairs of cotton gloves. Sgt. Polakov told Jim and I the next day that they had been turned over to LAPD for their burglary".

"Well Downey your progress reports seem fine. Next month your training will include several classes at UCLA put on by the California Peace Officer Standards and Training."

"You'll work the 4 to 12 shift and the classes will be in the morning or early afternoon. When you finish those classes, which only last for two to four weeks, we will review your training and then decide when to put you in a car by yourself. Bolander advises me that you have completed most of the field training with flying colors so it should only be a formality before you're on your own. I'll get you a schedule of the classes to be taught a UCLA. There are a couple that we want you to take but a couple can be your own choice. O.K. catch your partner and get on patrol."

"Thanks Captain."

Jim picked me up on the ramp after Dispatcher Bert Sloane gave him a Code 1R on the radio.

"Well how'd it go?"

"Fine I guess, he didn't say too much other than I am to attend some classes at UCLA next month."

"Yeah, most of us take some of those classes each year. Helps to keep up with some changes in the laws and some procedures. Nobody bothered to tell you that you volunteered for those classes on your own time did they? I'll bet not. Don't worry too much about it though, it's only once a year. For two to four weeks."

"Well Bob, it's been a month now, how do you feel about the job?"

"I don't know just how to explain it. I look forward to coming to work more and more each day. The more I do and learn the more I want to do and learn. I tried to tell Diana that I get buggy and antsy on my days off wanting to get to work. I suppose that will wear off eventually but right now it feels weird. I've had jobs where I didn't mind going to work, but I actually look forward to working now. I hate to imagine anyone who goes to a job they don't like. I don't think I could do that any more".

"Yeah, this job gets in your blood. It's

always something new and different. Some aspects could get boring if you let them but there is always something new coming around the corner.

No matter how many times you perform the same general function they will all be different in some respect because people are individuals and react differently. When they all start seeming the same to you that's the time to start worrying. Look for something else to do, because that's when you will start to get careless. In this job, you just can't afford to get careless."

I'd never heard him so solemn.

"At the next shift change you will be going out in a car alone. Your shift will be from midnight to eight AM and you'll probably work Car 8 'til you get some whiskers. The shift sergeant will spend quite a bit of time with you checking your procedures and understanding of the laws of arrest. You have a years probation and whatever shift or beat you pull, the sergeant will spend some time with you.

"The midnight shift gives you time to orient yourself and get to relax a little. It also offers a chance to make good pinches if you keep your eyes open and are aggressive in following through on your hunches. If you get the slightest feeling that a certain situation needs more attention, do it. It's a lot better than saying to yourself I should have."

"Eventually you will work Car 4 on the midnight watch. Car 4 has the detail every night of going to the West L.A. station and picking up the "hot sheets". You usually go out there after 1:30 AM. Somebody will take you out there and show you the procedure before you're sent out by yourself."

"That's also your chance to get your first coffee break while you're crossing out the recoveries and adding the new stolens to the list before you bring them back to the office. You will get to where you look forward to the trip if only to break the monotony on the slow nights. Believe me, there will be some S L O W nights."

"O.K. lets pull in behind Litton and we'll go over some of the fundamentals again". Our '57 Chevy turned into the railroad right of way behind Litton Industries and we parked beside one of the loading docks. The next half hour we spent practicing come-alongs, car stop procedures, car searches and shake down searches. All the time reciting laws of arrest, definitions of legal terms and Penal Code sections. The formal classroom training had ended and now it was up to you to take the initiative to learn as much or as little about the law as you thought would serve you and the City. Obviously, the more you knew the better.

Many things, you realized, would have to be studied over and over again because you would be dealing with them routinely. You had already determined that while you will seldom need many of the statutes it would be advantageous to have an understanding of them. This of course meant more and more study. Well, that was the profession you had chosen so if you're going to do it, do it right.

CHAPTER 4

"Car eight, Code five, Sierra and Sunset, have another unit meet me here"

"Roger car eight, car four meet car eight at Sierra & Sunset"

As I approached the car I had just stopped, I could see there was only one occupant. The driver turned to his left in the seat and extended his cupped left hand into the top of a cardboard box just behind the seat. He immediately pulled it out with the fingers partially extended. As I got to the drivers door the driver rolled down the window with his right hand, having turned a full 90 degrees in the seat to face the window.

"Please turn off the car. May I see your drivers license and registration please?"

"What's the problem officer. What did I do?" as he shut off the engine.

"I'll explain it to you as soon as I see your identification."

He presented his license and told me the registration was in the glove box. As I shined my flashlight into the car for the driver to reach into the glove box, Officer Lampe, in car 4, arrived and pulled in behind my car. He turned on his red lights and flashing caution lights to warn traffic of our presence. That really didn't seem necessary at that time in the morning. What traffic there was, was spread out pretty well and coming off the highly lighted stretch of Sunset Blvd. Getting into the subdued lighting of the quiet treelined streets of Beverly Hills tended to slow it down perceptibly.

"Is Thomas Harris your true name?" I asked as Lampe approached and joined me at the side of the car.

"Yes it is. What the hell is wrong, what did I do? I'm just on my way home from work. I'm a musician and just got off work at 2 o'clock. I'm surely not being stopped just because I'm in Beverly Hills at 2:30 in the morning".

"No Mr Harris, that's not the reason I stopped you. You say you are on your way home from work? Is this your correct address?"

"Yes, I'm on my way home."

"Well Mr. Harris, the reason I stopped you is that you are westbound on Sunset on the wrong side of the construction barriers and are no longer on any paved roadway. Have you been drinking tonight?"

"No I haven't. I must have gotten confused with the signs."

"What time is it Mr. Harris ?"

"About 2:30 Am. I'm on my way home from work"

"Please step out of the car Mr. Harris. You seem to be somewhat confused, its 4:20 Am and your residence is in the opposite direction. What did you have in your hand that you put in the box as I approached?"

"Nothing. I must have dozed off in the car after work and just made a wrong turn. Look I know where I'm at now so I'll just turn around and head for home".

"Not quite yet. Lamp, keep an eye on him while I look in the box."

I reached into the car through the open front door and lifted the flap on the cardboard box just behind the drivers seat. Located on top of some clothing in the box was a king sized Excedrin bottle full of a green leafy material. Taking the top off the bottle the strong odor of marijuana immediately filled the air. I turned and showed the bottle to Harris and said "Maybe this explains your lack of direction and loss of time. You are under arrest for possession of narcotics"

"Turn around and place you hands behind you. Lamp, let's shake him down and put him in my car while we search the rest of the car and wait for the tow truck"

"You don't have to search any farther officer, that's all there is.

I just got it tonight and had a little before I left the club. What are you going to do with my car?"

"We're going to impound it ", Lampe said, "The State of California has a forfeiture law for vehicles used to transport narcotics"

"What do you mean forfeiture? Are you telling me I'm not going to get my car back?"

"That's not up to us now, it's up to the State. We notify them of the impound and they take over from there. Fooling around with narcotics can get to be expensive."

Harris was placed in the back seat of my car with his hands cuffed behind him, to wait as his car is thoroughly searched.

Harris was right, nothing else was found. The search was finished just as the tow truck arrived. We waited for the truck to hook up and Lampe parked his car on Sierra just off Sunset while we transported Harris to the station.

Lampe seated Harris in the business area while I explained the arrest to Lt. Colford, the watch commander.

"And that's it Lt. I couldn't figure for the life of me why he was turned around in that seat so strangely. When I saw his hand coming out of that box the hair stood up on the back of my neck. I sure didn't expect an empty hand to come out of there."

"O.K.Downey, nice pinch. You and Lampe take him upstairs with Sloane and book him in then you can make out your report. You are doing all right for your third night out by yourself."

After Harris was booked and locked in his cell Lampe was taken back to his car by the sergeant. I proceeded to make out the arrest report. By the time the report was done and approved there was just time left for the car to be gassed up before end of shift.

It had been a long night but a good one. I was on my way home, a short talk with Diana before she went to work, a long hot shower and a few hours sleep before it started again. I wondered why I couldn't sleep more than four or five hours. At least I had a routine then where I slept until about one PM, got up and worked around the apartment or did my studying while I waited for Diana to come home. Then I got a couple hours rest in the evening before I headed back to work at about 10 PM. God, It was still feeling good.

"Downey, pick me up on the ramp about two o'clock and I'll ride with you a while"

Lt. Colford has just concluded roll call and Sgt. Grey had informed me he would be riding with me for a while. It wasn't unusual for a probationary officer to have the Sgt. ride with him during the shift just to find out how you are progressing. I still wondered just what I may have been in for. Did I forget to shakedown my car, turn in my citations? Did I mess up an arrest report?. Aside from the apprehension of what I may have screwed up most of these supervisory checkups are friendly, cordial, and informative.

For some reason I was unable to explain, I got a strange feeling whenever I had any contact with Sgt. Grey. We had never had any adversarial contact or any confrontation that would give rise to any negative feelings. It was just an intangible something that caused my self-preservation instincts to go on alert. Not a full blown alert, just a heightened awareness. I'd had ride-alongs with Sgt. Peterson, Sgt, Crowder, Sgt. Pierce, Sgt. Paez and some of the lieutenants and had nothing but good feelings about those contacts.

Well, maybe it was just a personality clash. Even if we've had no reason to clash. Whatever it was I had to shake it and approach it as I was sure it was intended. A routine check-up and interview to assess my progress. In the meantime go out on patrol on beat 8 and see what the beat looks like. Most of the guys I worked with take the first half hour of their shift to make a complete tour of the beat to get the "feel" of the beat for the night.

That's of course if you don't catch a call right away. Most of the time the beat will not have had any major changes from your last tour. It's just that one time that you haven't made your tour that you're on an emergency response and suddenly find that part of your route is blocked for some reason. Aside from feeling stupid for getting hung up you may have further escalated the emergency because you didn't get there timely.

Well, the beat had been secure. Usual cars in the usual places. Notations made of street lights out. Notes made of cars to be checked on later to see if they are violating the 2AM to 5AM no parking on the street ordinance.

When you first heard about that ordinance you wondered just what purpose it would serve. Later you found out all the streets were washed every night and without cars parked everywhere the job is much easier and the streets look better. It also helps a hell-of-a-lot in keeping track of the cars that are supposed to be in the area and those that are not.

There are many little things about this City that set it apart from other affluent cities in the area. All addresses painted on the curbs, street signs on all four corners. Little things that make life easier. God, I loved that town.

I guessed I had better start making my way back to the station. It was almost 2AM and I didn't want to be late. Didn't need to make any bad impressions. I'd just pull up on the ramp and wait. Still a couple of minutes before two.

"Car eight code 1R"

"Car eight, on the ramp" Huh, that didn't take long, it's only 2:10 am.

Here came the Sgt. He had his briefcase and notebook so it looked like a long night.

"Where have you been? I thought I told you two o'clock." He placed his brief case in the back seat as he got into the passenger side, putting his flashlight on the seat between us. I had never been able to be comfortable with my flashlight on the seat beside me. It was always sliding off somewhere when I wanted it most. At night, when I would need my flashlight most, I put it on the seat between my legs and sit on it just a little. I knew where it was all the time and I never forget it when I got out of the car. I guess it was all in what you got used to.

"That's right. I've been sitting on the ramp since three minutes 'til"

"Why didn't you let me know you were there?"

"I thought you'd know I'd be there. You told me to be there."

"Well next time let someone know you are there"

"Right" That didn't start out right.

"Let's head up to Lomita and Beverly, we've just gotten a call from ADT about a silent alarm from the Robert Wagner, Natalie Wood house. They haven't moved in yet and are still remodeling."

The house was on my beat, and as we headed that way the dispatcher sent car four to assist. In less than a minute we were drifting up to the house quietly, with our lights out. As we carefully closed the car doors, car four pulled up from the opposite direction.

Bob Devich, working car four, started walking down the driveway to the rear of the house. Grey and I made our way to the front door of the residence. When we found that secure, we started around the house looking for a possible entry point. When we reached the back, Bob was waiting near an open back door. There was no sign of forced entry and it didn't look like the door had even been locked.

We began our sweep of the interior and eventually found ourselves in the bedrooms of the second floor. Whatever remodeling they were doing looked great. As we finished our search we ended up in the master bathroom. We looked around momentarily when I spotted my first bidet.

"So that's a bidet." I remarked.

"Haven't you ever seen a bidet before?" Sgt. Grey asked with a strong sound of sarcasm in his voice.

"No, I can't say that I have."

"Well they're simple fixtures. Here, I'll show you how they work." As he said that, he stepped in front of the fixture and lowered his head slightly to reach the faucet handles. He turned the hot water faucet as he started to turn his head to look at me. He didn't figure on that much water pressure. At that precise moment, several sprays of water rose from the bowl of the fixture and sprayed him in the face and upper chest.

"What the hell," he yelled as he jumped quickly away from

the fixture. He turned off the faucet and brought out his handkerchief to begin drying himself off.

The alarm man had arrived and reset the alarm as we left the house. There was not much conversation.

Sgt. Grey and I returned to the car and signed back in service.

"Take me around the perimeter of your beat. How many citations have you written tonight?"

"None yet, but I'll probably write the first good violation I run into".

"You should find a stop light or stop sign and stake it out till you get a ticket or two. Then you don't have to worry about getting one"

"Maybe so, but if I'm sitting in one place then I'm not getting around my beat often enough. Besides that, I usually see a violation or two while I'm cruising so I can always write one then."

What the hell was I doing? It was sounding like I was arguing with him.

"Yeah, but remember, citations are income for the city and the more they get the better it looks for the Department."

"I guess I got the wrong idea. I always looked at citations as safety warnings. More like a reminder that the violator did something dangerous and the fine was the shock that would stick in their mind for the next time they contemplated doing it. Do all the cities look on citations as money makers or is this the only one?"

"Well hell it's not recognized City policy but you don't have to be a genius to realize that the city coffers could use anything it can get."

We were westbound on Sunset and turning north on Foothill Road toward Doheny. As we neared the intersection there seemed to be the headlights of a car on Doheny making a U turn. Now why the hell would someone be making a U turn up there at that time of night, unless they wanted to avoid being seen.

I punched the gas a little and at the intersection saw a blue Chevy making the final part of the U turn and taking off at a high rate of speed. There were at least two people in the car. As I turned on the red lights the suspect car really speeded up.

"Oh boy, here we go" I said as I picked up the radio mike and announced "Car eight in pursuit, east on Doheny passing La Alturas, Blue Chevy, two passengers, turning left on Schuyler"

As we turned left onto Schuyler we saw the Chevy, with it's front end wrapped around a large Eucalyptus tree on the west side of the street. The doors were open and two figures were running through the open gates of the estate at Schuyler and Doheny.

"Car 8, subjects have crashed at Schuyler and Doheny and have fled onto the estate at the northwest corner. Request assistance for a grounds search. Two suspects, both with blue trousers and dark jackets, one with long blond hair, could be female, we're entering the grounds now."

We entered the grounds and swept the area with our flashlights. Laid out in front of us was about two acres of lawn, pool with pool house, tennis court with dressing room, and what looked like a gardeners building. Not to mention the large circular concrete staircase leading up to the second level of the lawn and ultimately the house. To the west side of the house was a triple garage with living quarters above.

"Jesus, this is going to be a job rousting them out of here. I hope we get some backup before they have a chance to find their way out of here. I'm going to work my way over to the staircase and down to the pool house. sergeant, sergeant, where are you?"

He must have gone down to the left around the tennis courts. The sirens of the backup units were getting closer now. I got back to the gate to direct the units in surrounding the estate.

As I approached the gate several officers were being dispatched by Lt. Colford with Sgt. Grey at his side. As I hurriedly approached, Sgt. Grey exploded in a loud voice,

"Where the hell are the car keys? What the hell is the matter with you taking the keys like that. Don't you think someone might need to use the radio?"

"No, I didn't as a matter of fact, I had broadcast all the info we had and we both left the vehicle and . . ."

"Well dammit you should have known that your partner may have needed to use the radio to direct the other cars into the area".

"Just a minute Sergeant," says Lt. Colford, " Downey was just following procedure. You always remove the keys to your car when you leave it, especially on foot pursuit. I know you're upset but he did what he was trained to do. Now lets find these suspects."

Well what do you know, the Lt. pulled the sergeants chain. Maybe I hadn't pulled such a big boner after all. Although I didn't even think about it at the time, it was just reflex, taking the keys with me. After all isn't that one of the cardinal rules the Captain laid out in those training sessions?

Shortly after the search teams fanned out on the grounds one unit located a female juvenile hiding in the bushes next to the pool house. As she was being brought to the gate another unit spotted a male suspect and after a short foot chase he was apprehended and brought to the gate. She was sixteen, he was eighteen. The car was stolen from Santa Monica, where they both lived. He was on probation for car theft and they were just out for a joyride. After all the paperwork, she was released to her parents for a later appearance in Juvenile court and he was locked up pending arraignment or bail whichever came first. All in all, a pretty good night.

Fifteen minutes 'til quitting time. I'd gotten my equipment and papers from my car for the next shift. It would have been a real pleasant night if I hadn't gotten cross- threaded with the Sgt. Oh well, there are days like that.

After checking out in the roll call room, we were leaving for the locker room, Capt. Smith pulled me aside and congratulated me on the good pinch.

"I also hear that the Sgt. got on you pretty hard for taking your keys out of the car. Don't worry about it, you did what you were trained to do and that's all there is to it".

"Captain, can I make a suggestion? I don't want to be out of line but couldn't we eliminate that problem if we had the dealer key all the cars the same and issue one set of keys to each officer? It may have some drawbacks that I haven't thought about but it seems feasible"

"Yes, that's a possibility. I'll give it some thought. See you tomorrow".

CHAPTER 5

What a beautiful day it was. Another evening shift and a different beat. Well, that kept it interesting. Some people would think I was nuts, getting to work an hour earlier than I needed to. At least that way I could take my time dressing and then read the bulletin board thoroughly and make what notes I needed. Whoa, the Chief was coming out of the roll call room. I wondered what was going on, he very seldom went in there.

"Good afternoon, Chief"

"Humpf, good afernoo . . ."

What do you know, he spoke, I thought.

After dressing I went into the roll call room and noticed a 4x6 white index card in the middle of the board with the following message.

"Any officer wishing to live on an estate in town in exchange for light security duties contact the Chief"

Well that sounded all right. I knew that there were a couple of officers living on estates in town in exchange for some light maintenance duties and they were doing fine. I would talk with the Chief and then call Diana and see what she thought. It could be a real break. Could save a lot of rent money.

"Hello Vi, could I see the Chief about this notice on the board?"

Vi Renquist, the Chief's secretary and a policewoman, went into the Chief's office returning a few seconds later to usher me in.

"Yes officer, What can I do for you?"

That was the first time I had been in the Chief's office. I don't know what I expected but it wasn't that. Red clay tile floor, an old, worn, pine office desk with two wooden chairs and two glass fronted bookcases along one wall. A flag in the corner and the Chief sitting in an old high backed leather swivel chair with wooden arms.

I didn't know it then but that setting said it all about the man. No pomp, no window dressing, no nonsense. An all up front cop with one job to do. I was to find out later that there were many more facets to the man but basically he was what you saw. His manner had a way of misleading people into thinking he didn't have much depth. To assume that was a sad error. I was to frequently see indications and examples of his depth.

"Chief, I came to see you about this notice on the board. I would be interested in finding out more about this. "

"You're Downey aren't you"?

"Yes Chief"

"Here's the address of the place. A man named Robert Campbell lives there and is looking for an officer to live there in return for security while he's away, which I gather is quite a lot. Go talk to him and let me know what happens. He's a retired stockbroker and has lived in town since the twenties."

"O.K. Chief, thanks a lot"

After calling Diana at work and explaining everything to her she told me to call her back after I see him and let her know if we would be moving. I told you, she was the greatest. It's not like we hadn't discussed this possibility before, but until it comes up it's all supposition.

Before we ever got married she knew I wanted to join the Beverly Hills Police and accepted it without hesitation. If there were ever any qualms about my career choice she never gave any indication of it.

The question of her worrying came up once after a particularly hairy incident involving gunfire. Her response to my questions about her worrying was; "Of course I worry, but it is your career and I have to believe you can take care of yourself. What good does it do for me to worry about something I can't change? And wouldn't want to change if I could. You're happy doing what you do and not many people can say that." One in a million. Ten million.

It was getting close to roll call so I'd wait 'til after roll call to go see Mr. Campbell. I was sure the Watch Commander would let me have a few minutes to go see him. As we started to get settled in the roll call room the Watch Commander entered and took his seat behind the desk on the podium. After reading the reports and notices he called the roll. Hey, what happened? He called Franklin for car 4. As we were leaving the room I asked him,

"What about me, I thought I was working car 4, Lieutenant?"

Looking at his schedule, he said "What are you doing here, this is your day off" and he continued to look at me like I had two heads. I quickly looked at the calendar and then at the schedule on the board. My God, he was right. It was my day off. How in blazes did I do that. I knew I was wrapped up in that job, but to come to work on my day off would surely get me the dum dum award.

Well, I was here now, so I might as well see if I could use a car to go see Mr. Campbell and then volunteer for a few hours of work. When I laid my request before the Lt. he looked at me like I had a screw loose but agreed to my working Car 6 until ten o'clock, after I went to see Mr. Campbell.

I found the beat 6 car and took off for 1003 Cove Way. It was a fine location, two blocks behind the Beverly Hills Hotel. As I turned into the driveway which was guarded by two Spanish columns and a stucco wall I saw the driveway was lined on both sides with tall palm trees.

You couldn't see the house from the street. The driveway was slightly curved and about 200 yards long as it wound it's way up the hill and slightly to the right. Near the end of the driveway it opened onto a large triangular shaped parking area in front of a stucco, Spanish style, single story residence with red Spanish tile roof. Further up the hill, beyond the parking area, was a driveway to a large double garage on the right and to the left of the driveway was a small two story stucco building with a double garage on the bottom and what appeared to be an apartment on top. There was a stairway on the outside of the garage winding around to the back of the building and assumably to the door.

Mr. Robert Campbell answered my knock at the door of the main house. Had this gentleman not been a success as a stock broker he certainly could have had a career doubling for President Eisenhower. And both about the same age. His shoulders were slightly stooped and his hands seemed thin but his eyes and voice were sharp and clear.

Mr. Campbell proceeded to show me around the estate after I introduced myself and informed him the Chief had given me his name and address. He explained in a matter of fact manner that he traveled to his ranch in Hemet a lot and wanted someone to oversee the estate and forward the first class mail for him. We quickly reached a mutual understanding of what my duties would be and proceeded to the garage apartment which would be Diana's and my new home for the next seven years.

The apartment consisted of a small living room, equally small bedroom, kitchen and bath. Not expansive by any means but quite adequate for a young couple without children.

Returning to the station I went to the Chief's office and informed him that Mr. Campbell and I had reached an agreement. He acted almost like he didn't know who I was or what I was talking about. Strange man. As I was leaving his office he called after me "take that notice off the board when you go down".

"Yes, sir" I didn't think I needed to tell him that I had removed the notice before I ever went to his office the first time. No sense pushing your luck too far.

Back in the business office I informed Lt. Cao, the Watch Commander, that I was returning to my beat. He asked me to wait a while and called Mort McIntire over to the counter. Mort was the Identification Officer and attached to the Records and Identification Division. His duties included fingerprinting and photographing arrestees and crimes scenes and classifying fingerprints among a myriad of other tasks.

"Mort, Downey will go with you to process that guy that was brought in on that warrant." Cao said as he handed Mort the jail and elevator keys.

McIntire took the keys and headed for the elevator door. We rode up the one flight to the jail floor and got the guy out of the cell block and took him to the processing room. Watching Mac work you realized he wasted no motion. While he chatted amiably he moved with efficiency. The subject was being booked for several major traffic warrants that Roy Garrett, our warrant officer, had served on him after hunting him for several days. Roy loved his warrant job but didn't enjoy having to chase these guys around for too long.

Roy's reputation was such that some local L.A. Divisions and other departments referred to him as "The Phantom". He had a knack for appearing in town with his warrant in hand and disappearing with his subject before most people knew he'd been around. He very seldom asked for or needed help or back up.

The story went that one morning about 4:30 AM our desk got a call from one L.A. Division wanting to know if "The Phantom" was working that night. When informed that he was, the caller stated he thought so. He went on to relate that some lady had called to complain that some man claiming to be a police officer had slipped into her house and jerked her husband out of bed claiming he was being arrested for several traffic warrants. She said they were out of the house, into the car, and gone before she could get out of bed and find out who it was. She wanted to report a kidnapping because she didn't believe a cop would go that far just for a few traffic warrants. She didn't know "The Phantom". Roy was built like a fire plug with a grip like a large vise.

Now here was Mort and I finishing up another Garrett capture. I didn't know what Garretts capture ratio was but I wouldn't have been afraid to match it against any warrant detail in the State. With Roy, it was a matter of honor. You just didn't shirk your responsibilities when there was a warrant against you. Mort and I put the miscreant back into the cell block and returned to the business office.

Back on the street it had gotten dark. Only a couple of more hours to go. Beat 6 was a relatively small and quiet beat so it should have been an uneventful evening. Sure.

Part of covering your beat was picking an advantageous spot to watch traffic and people. On a busy beat in a very active city many cops don't ever get this luxury. Even in this city there are long stretches where you never seemed to have the time to just sit and look. Luckily this was one of those times when you could zone in on the activities around you.

I sat right there at Park and Beverly and watched the world go by. Rolls Royce, Cadillac, Mercedes, Lincoln, Jaguar, Limos. A crazy quilt of the best, the worst, and the in-between. How many are owned? How many are dodging repossession? Which ones are flash only and running on empty? Which ones are borrowed or rented to impress the girlfriend, agent, casting director? Which drivers don't fit in which cars? Which license plates are old plates on new cars? Are there any rear plates with mud covering some of the numbers? Do the front plates match the back plates? Is one of the plates missing? Are any of them backfiring? They do that sometimes when the hot wiring is not secure. Who looks nervous? Who's avoiding the lighted streets. Who spots you and turns their head away quickly? Are there clean plates on a dirty car? Visa Versa?

Observation pays dividends. So said Capt. Smith. Must be so because he said it often enough. Something like that Ford station wagon heading north on Beverly from Santa Monica. My God what a load he had in that thing. The rear bumper was about dragging the ground. It Looked like only one person was in the car but it had large load of something in the back. I'd known heavy safes to make a car look like that but they would be in the trunk not in the back of a station wagon.

I had pulled up behind him and I could see the stuff in the rear was covered by some kind of blanket or cloth. He obviously made me for a cop, he'd slowed to exactly the speed limit and was making every move just right. Unfortunately his load seemed to have interfered with his light wiring because his license plate light and right tail light were out. A good place to talk to him would be at Lomitas and Beverly Drive.

As soon as my red lights came on he headed for the curb.

Damn. I had misjudged that one. He'd pulled over so quick we hadn't reached Lomitas and the street light yet.

Good grief, I didn't even have my car stopped and he was getting out and coming back to my car. What was it he didn't want me to see? Care, Bob, care. The hair started to bristle a bit. The air started to get a little charged. If you were a little lethargic when you started that stop it was gone now. Maybe he was just super nervous about being stopped by a cop. Maybe he'd had bad experiences before. What If . . . .again.

"Hi Officer, what'd I do?" He was pleasant. Dressed in working clothes. Dirty hands. he stopped at the front end of my car.

"Nothing really, I wanted to inform you that your rear end lights were out. What ever you have in the back may have knocked the wires loose. May I see your license please? What do you have in the back end? I don't see how you can see out the rear with that load in there".

He reached to his right rear pocket and produced his wallet and handed me his license.

"Thank you Mr. Dandholder, where are you headed?"

"Home, from work. I live up in Hollywood.

I work for the City, in West L.A. In the Public Works Department".

Now the nervousness was creeping into his voice. We were getting close to something in that conversation that he didn't want to discuss.

Walking backward to my drivers door, I used the radio to call for another unit. There was something that was not quite right about this.

At the front of my car I shined my flashlight into the back of the wagon, "What'd you say was in the back?"

"Just scrap wire. Our shop was throwing it away so I thought I could find some use for it". He opened the window of the tail gate and pulled a part of the blanket off of the pile of wire. It was pretty obvious now why he was so nervous.

"Is all this wire copper?" I asked as I pushed back the insulation.

"I guess so, I didn't really pay any attention. It was just in the scrap heap when I loaded it." His hands were visibly shaking now and his voice had raised about half an octave. Dick Clason drove up to the rear of my car and walked up to join us.

"What's up Bob?'

"Mr. Dandholder was just about to tell me the truth about where he got this load of copper wire he says was being thrown away by the Public Works Department in West L.A.?" I Informed Dick as I walked to the side of the station wagon.

Dick laughingly replied, "Oh sure, I know L.A. has lots of money but no city has enough money to throw away several hundred pounds of copper at todays copper prices. You don't suppose he was going to store it for the city do you? Nah, I guess not". Answering his own question.

"Mr. Dandholder, You can see how your story sounds. I'd ask you for another explanation but I know it wouldn't be any more plausible than the first one. Where exactly did you pick up the wire?"

"Where I told you, at the Public Works Department yard in west L.A." His voice has a sound of futility or finality about it now.

"Did anyone there know you were going to take it?"

"No," he said after a short pause and a deep sigh.

"Are we right then, in assuming you took this stuff without permission?"

"Yeah, It's been in the yard for a long time and I didn't think anyone would miss it now. What's going to happen to me?"

His whole body seemed to have shrunk then. He leaned heavily against my car and his head was hanging on his chest. Sometimes you get the feeling that what you do just destroys a person. Then again . . . .

"I don't really know. Of course you're under arrest for suspicion of burglary and grand theft. We'll turn you over to L.A. in the morning and what charges are filed will be up to them. Dick, will you put the cuffs on him while I call for a tow truck?"

"Sure, Bob." He put the suspect in his car as I finished shaking down the car. In a few minutes the tow truck arrived.

"Jimmy, this one has to be stored in the locked garage area. It's full of evidence and has to be secured"

Jimmy was one of the several tow truck drivers that usually responded to police tow calls. "No problem", he replied over his shoulder as he crawled under the front of the wagon to hook up the chains.

"I've got just the spot for it. When will you be in to get the tow tag and secure it?"

"As soon as we drop this guy off for booking. About fifteen minutes."

Dick dropped us off at the ramp and went on to the impound lot to pick up the impound slip and seal the evidence. He got back to the station just as McIntire and I were coming back down from the jail floor to begin work on the arrest report.

"We weighed a couple of those rolls of wire and estimated the rest. It'll come out to between 350 and 400 pounds of wire.", Dick said as he handed me the paper work. "Did he say anything else?.

"Yeah, he said he was going to burn off the insulation and take the copper to a junk yard in Long Beach on Saturday. Said he'd get about .30 cents a pound for just the wire. Hell of a lot of risk for a hundred bucks".

Sgt. Bowers, the evenings patrol sergeant, came to Mort's desk where we were gathered to work on the report.

"Here's a copy of this guys record. L.A. records just called it back to us. Seems like he's not a virgin after all. He's done county jail time twice for receiving stolen property and grand theft. Got a record going back eight years. I'm surprised he has a job working for the city. Then again maybe he doesn't. Well, we'll know to-morrow".

So much for feeling sorry for somebody. "Downey, give me your keys and we'll get

someone to bring in your car while you're doing the report".

Bowers added, "Just look at what happens when you come to work on your day off."

That did it. Dick and Mort looked at me with a quizzical stare.

"Say you didn't", said Clason. "Nah, you couldn't have."

"Did you? Never mind, I don't really want to know". He headed for the stairs shaking his head. As I turned to McIntire, he was looking at me over the top of his glasses with a half grin on his face. I don't know what he was thinking but you could sure see the wheels turning.

By the time all the reports were done, my self appointed shift was over. As I wound my way through the streets of Hollywood and Glendale on my way home I had lots of time to consider just what had happened that day. It just kept getting better.

Diana was waiting when I get home. It was then I remembered I hadn't told her what happened with the house yet.

"Well honey, when do you want to move?"

"Anytime I guess. How's the place. Where's it at?"

The next half hour was spent telling her about the estate, the apartment, the location, and then telling her that I had gone to work on my day off.

She just stood there looking at me and shaking her head, with just the hint of a smile on her face.

"I guess you do like that job. Of course I can't say much, I didn't remember it was your day off either. When do we move?

"I figured next Monday. That'll be the first of the month and our rent here will be up then. O.K.?"

"I guess so. I'll have to work out my drive to work. Now comes my time to get up earlier to get to work. I figured there was a method to your madness."

CHAPTER 6

"Captain Smith, may I speak to you for a minute?"

"Sure Downey, come on in, what's on your mind?"

"Well Captain, It may sound crazy but I thought I would talk it over with you and see what you thought. We've had three fur store window smashes and two jewelry store window smashes in recent weeks. Wilshire Division, Hollywood, Pasadena have all had fur store window smashes within the last two months In a couple of cases a sports car, probably a Corvette was seen fleeing the area right after the smash. I don't know exactly why, but I have a hunch I have talked to the suspect and I filed a Field Interrogation card on him several weeks ago. When I was working beat 9 morning watch a couple of months ago I stopped a guy walking near the fur store at Willaman and Wilshire at about 1:30 AM. While I was talking to him I ran a record check and he was out on appeal bond for a conviction of auto theft. Corvettes were his trademark and he was an up and coming sportscar racer in the California Sports Car Racing Association. He was apparently on foot and walking through town at the time so I just F.I.'d him and turned him loose.

A few days later that fur store was hit. What I would like to do is talk to the Detective Bureau about this and if they don't have the time or inclination to work on it maybe I could volunteer my off duty time to follow up on it at least until it fizzles out or turns into something. It'd take me a while to identify him and pull the F.I. card, but I think it would be worth it".

"Well Downey, if you feel that strongly about it I can't see any harm in it, come on and I'll introduce you to Capt. Hankins in the Detective Bureau. You can tell him about it."

The two of us left Capt. Smith's office and proceeded down

the hall past the front desk to the Detective Bureau where we went into Capt. Hankins office.

"John I want you to meet Officer Downey, he has an idea he wants to talk over with you. It doesn't sound like a bad deal to me and may even ease some of your case load".

"Yes Capt. I know Downey, He's had quite a few good felony arrests since he joined the Department. He's testified on several of our cases. Sit down Downey, what can I do for you?

"Downey, you talk it over with Capt. Hankins and let me know what decision you come to." With that he turned and left the office.

"O.K. Capt., thanks".

Capt. John Hankins could only be described as an imposing presence. Even in his large old fashioned swivel chair his corpulence was obvious. His voice, face and manner were filled with sparkle and friendliness. His white hair and moustache lacked only a flowing white beard to turn him into the living embodiment of Santa Claus. His suit was well tailored and he presented himself as a man entirely comfortable with his stature and surroundings. His manner and direct look had the effect of putting a person at his ease. Comfortable was the word for it. He had been Traffic Commander until recently.

The former Detective Commander, Capt. Ray Borders, and Hankins had been flip flopped after Borders and the Chief tangled, big time. There was still a lot of tension in the Department about the transfers and most officers were guessing about the final outcome. Whatever happened, Hankins was the man to deal with.

"Well Downey, what can I do for you?'

I filled in Capt. Hankins about my feeling that the guy I stopped several weeks ago may be connected with the window smashes.

"I can't really explain why I feel like I do about him but when I look back on it he could have been casing that fur store at Willaman. Hell, He might even have had a Corvette parked somewhere around there. I kept an eye on him while he walked out of town on Wilshire but he still could have left a car somewhere.

Like I was telling Capt Smith, I know it was real slim for anyone to put in much time on. If he didn't mind I would gladly volunteer my off duty time to check it out, either to eliminate him, or get enough information to make him a suspect. I was working graveyards so I could put in some time in the mornings after I get off shift. I didn't ever get to bed before 1 or 2 o'clock anyway so I won't be missing any sleep".

"Do you know Sgt. Cork?"

"Yes Capt., I do. We worked the same shift a couple of times"

"O.K. let me get him in here and see what he thinks. Have you had any investigative experience?"

"Yes, as a matter of fact I had quite a lot while I was in the Air Force. I was a criminal investigator for several years".

Sgt. B.L. Cork entered the office in response to the Captains phone call, and took a seat. Sgt. B.L. Cork was an enigma of a police officer. He was about 6 feet tall with a flat top haircut. His slight stoop belied his height. He was known as "B.L." and don't bother to ask what B.L. stood for.

He was a quiet individual but exuded an intimidating presence. His reputation was one of a no nonsense cop that set a goal and doggedly pursued it. If you underestimate the man you will eventually learn to regret your assumption. You learn from him just the things he wants you to, either professionally or personally. "Still waters run deep" does not quite describe him. Complex better described the man.

"Hi Downey, how are you? Yes John, what's up?

"Downey here has a "feeling" about a possible suspect on these fur and jewelry store window smashes we've had. He wants to volunteer his off duty time to run it down and either prove or disprove his hunch. I'm thinking about letting him do it but under your supervision. If he keeps you advised of everything he's doing and how it's going. What do you think?"

"I don't see any problem with it, except I won't have time to be of much help. Downey and I have worked together in the field so I don't think we'll have any problems"

"O.K. Sgt. take him into the office and introduce him to the men and explain to them what he'll be doing. Good luck, Downey."

"Thanks Captain, I appreciate it."

Cork and I left the Capt's office and entered the squad room of the Detective Bureau. The room was about 12 by 25 feet with five wooden desks aligned along the outer wall. Talk about austere surroundings. It was a good thing no one had heard about depressing work environment then. The whole Detective Bureau must have been elbow deep in paper work for they were all in the office.

Cork proceeded to introduce me around. I knew who they were of course but had only been introduced to Cork and Jim Bolander, my training officer, who had since moved into the Bureau. Sgt. Valentine, checks & forgery, Sgt. Polakov, burglary & theft, Les Britton, juvenile officer and B.V.Moe, robbery.

As I later found out, no one worked anything exclusively. The assignment schedule merely meant that's who was responsible for the paper work or who was the point of contact for the department.

Jim Bolander worked burglary & theft and anything else he was assigned and Cork oversaw all the investigations and worked the major cases. Everybody worked everything, which I was to come to realize was an excellent idea. You got experience in all investigative fields and were able to step in on any case and carry on for someone else with very little lost momentum.

Five wooden school teacher desks, a small table, eight chairs, four telephones and two file cabinets. All windows along the north end long wall and the east end short wall. None of them shaded or draped in any way. Not exactly what one expected to find in the Detective Headquarters of the Beverly Hills Police Department.

Red clay tiled floors and four florescent lights hanging from the acoustical tile ceiling. The short wall at the west end of the room held a few wanted posters, a calendar and several mug shots of known criminal suspects. It didn't have the ambiance of a gym locker room but at that time, to me, it was Shangri- La. I then knew that this was where I was destined to work. It didn't take an hour or two or even 15 minutes, it was instantaneous. It felt like I had walked into a world that had been created just for me to look for, and find, and when I did, know that I had climbed the mountain.

"Guys, listen up a minute". Cork leaned against the door frame as he told the group what my purpose was. A couple of them looked at me like I was two bricks short of a load but went along with the program when they realized I would be doing work they wouldn't have to do.

"Look Downey, we don't have enough phones or desks so you will just have to find room when and where you can. When do you figure to start your project?"

"Tomorrow morning if it's O.K. I'll have to search all my notebooks first to locate his name and then pull the F.I. card before I can really get started on him. Once I've found him I'll need to talk to the officers and Department that handled him on his auto theft arrest."

I was doing my best to hold down the excitement that was churning my guts around. I knew it must have been showing on my face. It just wouldn't seem appropriate to get so worked up over volunteering to put in countless unpaid hours of my free time just to catch some burglar. Even I was starting to wonder about me.

"O.K. We'll see you in the morning."

"Yeah, I'll be in as soon as I get home and change clothes"

I went down the stairs and out to the ramp to wait for Ken McHuin in car 4 to pick me up and drop me off at home. Diana and I had moved into town a couple of weeks before. Ken and I started to work about the same time and had lockers next to each other. We'd worked some of the same shifts and seemed to have the same feelings about the job. I explained my project to him and he announced that he would like to give me a hand if I needed it.

"Kenny, I don't have the slightest idea if this will pan out. It's only a hunch. I don't know if anything will come of it or not. I just have a feeling".

"Yeah, I know, if you do need any help let me know. What post did you have on the presidential detail the other night?"

"I was working the lobby and the front door for a few hours before I had to leave to make roll call. How about you?"

"I was working the parking lot entrance most of the time then I was sent to the roof.", he said as we turned into my driveway.

"You know Ken, I got a real charge out of the President when he came down to go to the meeting. He came across the lobby and started toward the Grand Ballroom, looked over at me at the door and came all the way over and stuck out his hand, shook mine and said "thank you for your time and trouble". He's the kind of guy that gives you a different attitude about politicians. Most of the other candidates never even see the cops around, and some don't want to see them. Maybe he got his approach from having commanded troops during the war. Whatever it is, he gives you the feeling that you're appreciated. I know they don't know that it's extra duty and that you still have to put in your regular shift, but you get the impression from some of them that you're a necessary evil."

"Remember when Johnson was here with his daughter?"

"Yeah, that was real fiasco"

"He sure wanted all the uniforms around when he wasn't having his picture taken. He sure got bent out of shape when he was leaving or going into the hotel if a uniform was anywhere in sight. It gave you the feeling that you were good enough to get your ass shot off for him but not good enough to be seen in his company".

"Yeah, he did seem like a cold fish. He is a big sucker though. I didn't realize he was that tall until he came out the side door to get into the car. Hell, I'm 6-2 and he was 2 or 3 inches taller than me. His daughter is tall too. Well, we'll probably get a chance to see Kennedy and Nixon pretty soon. They'll all make it through here before long. I talked with the Hotel desk manager last night, and they are both scheduled to come in before too long."

I had a chance to talk with the Secret Service supervisor for a while. That job is a real mankiller. The personal security detail. Those guys are on the go all the time. They have two or three advance parties for setting up communications and liaison with the local law and the local Secret Service Office. Then, if they are going someplace where there is no local office, they have to arrange for additional agents to move in for support."

Hell, the logistics of just a couple of moves has to be a nightmare. I guess I can see where the whole thing can get to be routine and overlooked by the one they are protecting. I wonder if any of the politicos really understand what goes on behind the scenes. Well Kenny, I'll see you in the morning. I'll start my project then."

"O.K. Bob, take it easy. What time's the wife get home?"

"About 6 o'clock. I think I'll catch a few hours sleep before she gets home. I'll have to talk this project over with her. She gets a little upset if she thinks I'm not getting enough rest. She knows when I'm working midnights that I don't sleep worth a damn during the day. I'll see you later"

"Right", Kenny said as he headed down the driveway.

I climbed the steps to the apartment and got the main house key and checked it out. I needed to stay up a while so I could get the mail forwarded for Mr. Campbell. Some days just seemed to have more hours in them than others. I wondered why this never seemed to be the case when you needed more time?. Well I'd get a few hours in before Diana got home.

Mr. Campbell's mail was stamped and ready for forwarding. The house was secure and the gardener was due today so I'd have to stay awake till I gave him his check. I wouldn't get much sleep today after all. I would just settle in the recliner and read a couple chapters of my school books or the Penal Code and wait.

"Bob, . . . Bob, . . . how long have you been in that chair? Did you get any bed sleep today?"

"Good grief, what time is it? I was just resting my eyes waiting for Fernando to finish the yard and give him his check. I guess he didn't come today. At least I didn't hear him."

"Oh he came all right" she said as she came back into the living room from the bedroom, "He left a note that he didn't want to wake you so he'll collect on Saturday. You must really have been zonked out. What time did you get home?"

"About 10:30 I guess. I had a talk with Capt. Smith and the Detective Bureau Commander about my putting in some of my own time trying to run down a possible suspect on all those window smash burglaries. They both thought the idea was O.K. so I start tomorrow. After I come home and change clothes and wake you up of course."

"How many hours a day are you going to put in. You don't get enough good sleep now. Why don't you go to bed now for a couple more hours and I'll wait to make a light dinner before you go to work".

"O.K. Honey but don't worry about it, I won't get any more involved than some wives I can think of. I don't know too many wives who take a hot sheet to work with them and have their husbands set their car radios and house radios to police calls".

"Well I have to do that in self defense. I wouldn't know what you were talking about if I didn't keep up on the activities and the jargon. I've got most of the codes memorized now and have gotten the hang of reading the hot sheet quickly. You just wait, I'll find one of these hot cars for you on my way to work one of these days. I thought I had one at the liquor store on Sunset on the way home yesterday but the number was two off. I'll get one yet though."

"Listen honey, you be real careful about where you look for hot cars. If you spot one in a liquor store or grocery store parking lot, don't hang around waiting for the law. get away from there and then call in. I don't want you involved in the middle of an armed robbery. If you spot a rolling stolen for God's sake don't try to follow them. Get the direction and then call it in. It's too easy to get caught up in the excitement and end up in the middle of an accident somewhere, or worse."

"O.K., O.K., don't worry. You lay down for a while and I'll wake you about 10:00. Will that give you enough time?"

"Yeah, that'll be fine. Thanks" I went into the bedroom and laid down knowing I was too wide awake to sleep. I'll just stretch out and rest for a while.

"Honey, it's ten after ten. You'd better get up and shower.

Breakfast will be ready in about 15 minutes. You were really sawing away. I was going to let you sleep a little longer but thought better of it. Hurry up and get washed and dressed".

"Holy cow, I didn't think I would get to sleep at all. Just goes to show you what a clear conscience can do for you".

At ll:00 PM we had finished eating and I had called the station for my ride. Diana was ready for bed and so the circle started over again.

CHAPTER 7

Well, here goes. The last years work schedules in one hand and a pile of my personal notebooks in the other. The notebooks were small 3 inch by 42 inch tan covered paper notebooks the department supplied on the roll call desk. Depending on the beat you worked, or how active you were on your beat you could fill one of those in a week. Or a month if you had a slow beat on the midnight watch.

On any beat, however, you could be as active as you wanted to be. I found out early that any shift goes faster the more active you were. To say nothing of the possibilities of making a good arrest or two. Anyhow, after a few months of even moderate activity you filled many books.

Suspicious vehicle license numbers, victims and witnesses names, F.I. card information, suspect information and wanted notices given out at roll call, along with a hundred other items that could be of interest in the future. There is never really a lack of stuff to put in your notebook. As soon as you picked up a fresh book from the roll call desk you put the date along the top border. Then when you finished the book you entered the closing date next to the beginning date. It certainly cut down the search time when you were looking for information about or around a certain date.

The Bureau was almost empty with only Bolander and Polakov in residence. At least I didn't feel like I was walking the gauntlet on the first morning.

"Will anyone mind if I use this table for a while"

"No, no one will be using that today" Polakov said, "Most everyone will be in court for the best part of the day. Didn't you work the midnight shift last night?"

"Yeah, I went home and showered and talked to my wife before she left for work."

Jim Bolander came over to help move some of the books and other odds and ends left on the table.

"How's your project going Bob?", he asked as he stacked everything on one corner of the already crowded table.

"I don't really know yet. I have to go through the work schedules first to pinpoint the times I was working Car 9 on the midnight watch. Then go through my notebooks and see if I may have made any notes that will single out this one guy from the others that I have filed Field Interrogation cards on. I have a feeling I made some notes about his Grand Theft Auto conviction. I always make a note of the location when and where I interview someone. I just hope I didn't slip up on this one."

"O.K. Bob, let me know if I can help in any way"

"Thanks Jim".

Now to the work schedules. Luckily I hadn't been working here too long. I only had fourteen months of schedules to go through. The only thing that would really trip me up was if the Watch Commander switched beats around during a schedule. The only way to circumvent that possibility is to go over the whole months notebooks for that particular schedule. The fact that I volunteered for steady midnights at that time was both a blessing and a curse. I wouldn't have too many schedule changes but I'd have a hell of a lot more notebooks to search.

By about noon I'd narrowed down the number of notebooks to 14. Before I started going through them I would retrace my steps on the work schedules just to be sure I didn't overlook something. By then it was about time to knock off for the day and go home and get some sleep. My eyes were starting to droop anyway. It felt good though. Finally I was getting my teeth into something and had a direction that gave me the feeling of real accomplishment.

Not that patrol work was any slouch at providing feelings of accomplishment. The feeling of gratification you can get from any number of assignments. Like the call I got the last day watch I worked. See the lady on south Elm Drive, unknown trouble. When I got to the door, apprehensive and a little cautious, the resident, a tiny, grey haired, 76 year old widow, met me at the door.

She took me into the house and down the hall to her major problem. The bathroom light bulb was burned out and she couldn't reach it. Could you please change it for her? Now you could spend a lot of energy explaining why changing light bulbs is not really a police matter and getting hot under the collar about wasting police time.

But, give it some thought. Your five minutes of switching light bulbs had given you a needed break from the norm. It had also given a lonely lady someone to talk to. It's also given her the assurance she has someone to call on for much needed assistance. That kind of glow stays with you for a while.

"O.K. guys, I think I'll knock off for the day and pick it up tomorrow morning. I'll be needing to prop my eyelids open pretty soon"

Howard Polakov responded, " O.K. Bob we'll see you later".

Howard is a friendly outgoing individual. He dressed well and always seemed to be going somewhere with a purpose and determination. It was hard to tell whether he preferred a pipe or cigar. One thing was for sure, whichever it was, it was the best. It was well known that Howard was a gourmet and his wife, Lois, was a gourmet chef. It's nice to know you could ask him anything at any time and not feel you're intruding.

It was 1:30 when my ride dropped me off at my driveway. By the time I walked up the drive to the house I was ready to drop on the couch and nap until Diana got home. I stayed upright long enough to sort and restamp the first class mail for Mr. Campbell, that I had picked up on my way up the drive. Rather than lay on the couch I'd just stretch out on the bed. I would take off my clothes when Diana got home.

"Bob, honey, come on get up. It's ten fifteen. You just have time to take your shower and eat before you go to work. What time did you get home to bed?"

"Why didn't you wake me up when you got home? I laid down about two or 2:30. I figured you'd wake me up and I'd go back to bed later"

"Yeah, wake you up. I called you twice and shook you once. When that didn't do it I figured you needed the sleep worse than the talk".

I could hear her rattling around the kitchen as I prepared to get into the shower.

We had a new face at roll call tonight. I didn't recall having seen him at any time earlier. As the watch commander came in he introduced me to Jack Egger, my partner for the next few nights. It seemed Jack had been on the department before and took leave to go to work for the District Attorneys Office as an investigator. I was to work Car 5 that night and Jack was riding with me to refamiliarize himself with Department policy and procedure since he left. A short time later we hit the road.

Jack was a friendly outgoing type of person with a quick smile and a ready comeback for the usual wisecracks heaped upon "rookie" cops. As we made our initial rounds of the beat we become more comfortable with each other. Among other things I found out about Jack was that he spent some considerable time working on Howard Hughes personal security detail.

Hughes had been living in a bungalow at the Beverly Hills Hotel for some time now. I found that out by accident. When I was working car 4 I noticed a light blue '56 Chevy 2 Door sedan parked on Hartford just north of Sunset. That car was parked there all night, almost every night.

Naturally, I would hang an overnighter ticket on it every night that it was there. Some nights it was gone. I was to find out later that this was one of Howard Hughes several '56 Chevys. He would sneak out at night and drive around. It seemed strange that in all the time I worked that beat I had never seen him driving the car. Almost like the man was invisible. Jack didn't talk much about his experience with Hughes.

No matter how much experience the other person has, you

find yourself verbally sparring and probing to attempt to establish just where you can categorize this new and unknown element in your life. What happens when it comes down to push and shove. You both recognize what you're doing but you also know that no amount of talk will give you the real answer. It was going to take a situation or an incident before either of you will feel totally comfortable with each other. We were to have our situation within three hours of having met.

Westbound on S.Santa Monica Blvd. at 2:45 AM. The cleanup crew was still at La Scala and traffic had dwindled to a trickle when a Chevy 4dr Sedan turned west on S. Santa Monica from Rodeo. The car was occupied by four young males and the driver got one look at our black and white and the chase was on.

Tromping on the gas and grabbing the radio mike at the same time the call went out, "Car 5 in pursuit, West on Santa Monica from Rodeo, Grey Chevy 4 Door. 4 male occupants". About the time all that was put out the suspects had reached Wilshire Blvd. They made a hard left turn and headed East on Wilshire. As we braked to make the turn I glanced at the speedometer to see the needle coming down from 55 MPH. As I picked up the mike again to give the new direction the vehicle turned right on Linden Drive.

"Pursuit now south on Linden from Wilshire. Crossing Charleville, still south, exceeding 60". Jack said, "The way they are driving they won't keep this up for long, they'll crack up or roll over"

"Yeah, if they do Jack, you take the right side, I'll take the left."

By this time we were making a left onto Olympic in time to see the other car starting back north on McCarthy. Even as this was going over the air the suspects started into a right broadside skid. About 200 feet north of Olympic they plowed into the left side of a nice white Cadillac Coupe DeVille parked at the curb.

"Suspects cracked up at McCarthy and Olympic, request assistance" went over the air as Jack and I were exiting the patrol car which had barely managed to stop a few feet short of the drivers side of the suspects car. All the doors of the Chevy seemed to burst open at the same time with arms and legs flailing in a frantic attempt to depart the area.

Jack went around the back of the car and up the right side. He grabbed one of the young suspects exiting the rear door as he reached for the kid coming out the front door.

As I got to the driver he was trying to scale the left front fender of the Chevy where it met the left rear fender of the Cad. He came down in my arms. With a little help from my jerk on the rear of his jacket. I had managed to grab it as he vaulted onto the trunk lid of the Caddy. I caught sight of the fourth suspect running across the hood of my car and jumping to the ground in a dead run toward Olympic. Not much chance of dragging the driver with me while I went after the other one.

So there I was, my first night with a new partner and he got both his suspects and I only got one. We had laid to rest any lingering questions we may have had about how each of us would act or react in a highly charged situation.

All the subjects were 16 years or younger, but we had no way of knowing that until after the situation was defused.

The driver was 16. A 165 pound, 5'10" juvenile on probation for a prior auto theft. The two Jack got were fifteen and both with long prior juvenile records. The one that got away temporarily was later determined to be 14 and an escapee from the juvenile detention center.

As the stolen car was towed away we tried to locate the owner of the Cad without success. We put a note on the windshield for the owner to contact the Department for information about the damage to his car. By the time the routine details and paperwork was finished, it was shortly after shift change.

Jack and I approached the business desk to turn in our paperwork and check out with the watch commander. We noticed a somewhat heated conversation going on between the watch commander and an unknown civilian. It didn't take to long figure out that he was the owner of the damaged Cadillac and he was hopping mad about his car. As Jack and I tried to explain how his vehicle got damaged the subject turned his wrath on us.

"Why the hell did you have to chase them anyway? They were probably only joyriding and would have dumped the car when it ran out of gas. No, you guys got to be heroes and catch the bad guys. Who the hell is going to pay for my car? I ought to sue the city".

Unknown to Jack and I, as this tirade was going on, Chief Anderson had come up the stairs and was standing off to the side of the business area watching the activity. Our "citizen" was continuing his verbal abuse as Jack and I looked at each other. We arrived at the same resolution to this distasteful situation. As I stepped directly in front of the distressed citizen Jack pulled his citation book from his pocket.

"Sir, are you the registered owner of the Cadillac?"

"Of Course I am, why do you suppose I am so damned mad?"

"About what time did you park on McCarthy last night?"

"Sometime after eleven, but what the hell difference does that make?".

"And you found our note this morning?"

"Yes, about 7:30 and I came right over here, so?"

As he was making this last statement, Jack stepped forward and handed him a citation for overnight parking on the street.

"What the hell is this?. What are you guys trying to do?"

"That sir, is a citation for parking on the street in excess of one half hour between the hours of Two AM and Five AM in violation of the city ordinance. It would seem that if you had been obeying the law your car would not have been where it was and would not have been hit by the stolen car."

"Good morning, Lt. We're going end of watch". As Jack and I started down the stairway we both noticed the Chief walking toward his office shaking his head slightly.

"How long had he been standing there"? Asked Jack.

"I'm damned if I know but apparently he wasn't too upset with our solution". I replied as we reached the bottom of the stairs.

"Or maybe we won't hear about it until tonight."

We're almost into the locker room before the shock wore off of Mr. Citizen and he started stuttering and sputtering. Sometimes there was no pleasing anyone.

How do you explain to anyone, especially Mr. Citizen, in that frame of mind, that the last thing you need in your life is a high speed chase. How do you describe the emotional pressure that begins at the instant you spot the car and the flood of adrenaline hits your system.

With each movement, turn, corner, headlight, tire noise and slight skid, your pump pushes harder and harder. Mind racing in superfast speed while you're trying to out think your adversary and making "what if" plans to handle and control the ultimate conclusion, whatever it may be.

Make no mistake about it, this individual had gone from what ever his status was, to being your adversary. He had instantly placed his life, your life, and untold others in dire jeopardy, intentionally or otherwise. And all the time you were making every move you can muster in your mind to keep from making that one error in judgement that could terminate your existence or someone elses.

How can you tell someone how it feels to have every nerve ending standing on edge and being massaged with a wire brush. Your entire surroundings are brighter and more vivid, and the sounds are louder and sharper than anything you've ever experienced or imagined. Then thrust that massive, overwhelming experience on your body and mind, unexpectedly, in varying degrees, dozens and dozens of times during your career. The pump you get while you're walking down the darkened alley checking back doors and one knob that isn't supposed to, turns in you hand.

Climbing to the roof of a building on the outside metal stairway. As you near the top, still in the deepened nighttime shadows, your entire sensory system on full alert. The resident tom cat launches from his concealment just behind you with all the attendant and prerequisite noises. As your nerves start to ravel up again after unraveling in an instant, you realize you are standing in a half crouch. Your flashlight low and away from your body and your gun two thirds of the way out of the holster. As you start to regroup you remember that this is the second time that damned cat has gotten your attention like that.

Don't tell me that cats don't have a sadistic streak.

CHAPTER 8

That morning was going to be one of those days in the Bureau when it would be hard to find a place to work. Most of the Detectives were at their desks pouring over paper work or on the telephone. I laid down my pile of notebooks on one of the file cabinets as Cork looked up and remarked, "I hear you had a short, hairy one last night".

"Yeah, it didn't last very long but crossing all those intersections at that speed keeps your jaws tight and your pucker string pulled. Bunch of juveniles apparently joy riding."

I started going through my notebooks right on top of the file cabinets until a desk or table opened up.

"Les and Howard just finished talking to the driver. He named the one that got away and we've notified LAPD Valley Division to watch out for him at his home. One of the other kids gave us another place where the kid is staying so Valley Division is going there to see if they can bag him up and put him back in the Hall. How much longer are you going to be on morning watch?"

"I haven't given it much thought. I volunteered for it at least until I can chase down this theory of mine. I don't know how long that will take. I didn't have much trouble getting on morning watch but I don't know how easy it will be to get off when I want to." I was into my first notebook when Capt. Hankins came walking in and announced that the fourth kid had been picked up by West L.A. walking on Wilshire Blvd near Beverly Glen.

Cork said, "We'll be working together on morning watch for a few weeks. I'll be working vacation relief for a while"

Bill Valentine rose from his desk and as he walked out the

door he said, "You can use my desk now, I'll be gone for a couple of hours".

"Thanks, I'll do that", as I shifted my load onto the desk.

Once settled at Bills' desk I started pouring through my notebooks.

Before long my eyes were starting to droop. The names and notes in the book were starting to run together. I guess I was finally winding down from the tension of the chase and arrest. You never cease to be surprised just how much an active night drains your system. It's not the kind of draining that leaves you feeling dull and beaten. It's a relaxed draining that leaves you wrung out and weary but alert and satisfied with yourself.

I was about to close my fifth notebook, and my eyes as well, when I came across the notes I'd been looking for. What happened to the drowsiness? As I reread my entry, I announced to one and all (in a very reserved voice of course) in my best Stan Laurel imitation, "By golly Ollie, I think I've got it."

Since Cork and Polakov were the only ones in the room at the time it didn't set off any rockets or whistles.

Howard asked, "Who is he?"

"Name's Andrew T. Porterfield, and he allegedly lives down in Westchester. I'm sure this is the guy I was thinking about. Now I need to pull the FI card. He was out on appeal for GTA of Corvettes. Now I can start running same real information on him. I think that will about do it for today though. It doesn't look like he will be caught before tomorrow. Good night guys, or good morning whichever way you see it".

"O.K. Bob, We'll see you Monday"

"Good Grief, this is Friday, I forgot. And aren't I lucky. Tomorrow night is when we move the clocks back one hour. We get to donate an extra hour to the City. Well I'll pretend tonight is one hour shorter to make up for it. See Ya."

As I left the parking lot in my little putt-putt Studebaker I started to realize I had to formulate a plan to direct my efforts to gather the most information I can and the most relevant to proving my theory. Or disproving it, as the case may be. On Monday I'd start with a short list of things I must know to determine if it's worth while wasting anymore time on it.

Does he have a steady job? How much does he make? What hours does he work? What are his days off? Does he own a car? Does he have any charge accounts? How much does he owe? What kind of cars does he have access to? Does he actually live with his parents or does he have an apartment somewhere? That and a hundred other things were going through my mind when I turned into the driveway at home.

After the ritual of forwarding the mail and checking out the security of the main house I dropped on the bed thinking I'd fade out right away. Wrong. The hundred things balloon into several hundred then all melted together into one thought. I could be spinning my wheels for a couple of months if I don't make the right moves at the beginning. I woke up a few hours later with that thought on my mind just as Diana was coming in the door with her arms full of grocery bags.

"Hi, I hope you're hungry tonight. I stopped at the market at Canon and Dayton and got us some filets and salad makings. As I was in the checkout line Groucho Marx was in front of me and handed me his green stamps. Said he didn't collect them. It's not like he would need them."

She was busy unloading her bags while I was rubbing the sleep out of my eyes.

"You were almost out of Cognac so I stopped at the liquor store at Crescent Heights and Sunset and got another bottle. O.K. what is it? You're just looking and not saying anything, what's happened?"

"Oh, nothing really." I imparted with my usual Cheshire cat grin, "I just narrowed down my search to one individual and now I can start running him to ground. If he is the right guy of course?"

"That's great. Are you sure this is the one you thought it was?.

"Yeah, I'm sure this is the one I was looking for if only it's the guy who's hitting the fur and jewelry stores."

By the time we got done with dinner and the small talk about her job and the people at Stout Motors in Glendale, I still had time for a short nap before going back to work.

For a Friday night/Saturday morning it had been a pretty slow night even for Car 8. Usually the flow of cars from West Hollywood on Sunset or Santa Monica would keep you busy but that night seemed like the traffic flow stopped at the City limits. Of course Car 8 was the biggest beat when there was no car 6 working.

From Santa Monica Blvd on the south to the north city limits including the fairly new development of the Trousdale Estates. From West Hollywood on the east to Beverly Drive/Benedict Canyon on the west. At that time there were only about 40 houses in Trousdale but it was filling up fast.

Beautiful, long range, city views from almost every lot. Pacific Ocean views from some of them on a very clear day. I understood most of the property came from the old Doheny Ranch.

Greystone, the former Doheny Estate, bordered Trousdale on the west. A formidable brick fenced, iron gated entry way, guarded by a fortress like, brick gatehouse. Hardly any activity there with the exception of some movie companies using it for location shooting. It hadn't lost any of it's grandeur. It was these very late hours of the early morning that you get time to pay particular attention to the little details of your beat.

What lights were usually on in the house? What cars were normally in the driveway? As I coasted slowly down the curb lane of Schuyler to Mountain with my lights out, I caught sight of a car parked in the shadow of a tree just north of the driveway of 601 Mountain Dr.

As I drifted a little closer, two figures came from the lawn of 601 Mountain and entered the driver and passenger side of the car. If I was going to take them I needed do it before they got the car rolling. As I turned on my headlights and redlights I could see both individuals shoulders slump and heads droop. I stopped about 6 feet behind their car and approached the drivers side very slowly with my hand on my gun and my flashlight away from my body.

When I shined my light into the car I caught a glimpse of two metal statues on the back seat of the car. The two occupants were both males about 18 to 20 years old and neatly dressed.

I got them out of the car and after a very short period of questioning, the two very nervous, obviously scared, individuals told me that they had just taken the two statues from the pedestals on the porch of Dean Martins house. They said they were both fans of Dean Martin, and had gotten his address from the Hollywood star maps that are sold on some of the street corners just outside of town. They wanted to have a souvenir of their adventure. After running a record check on them and convincing myself they were telling the truth I had them get the two statues and follow me up to the door of the residence.

After a few rings on the door bell several lights came on in the house and someone opened the curtains slightly. The door was then opened by Dean Martin. Standing somewhat behind him to his right was his wife Jeanne. Both of them were dressed in casual clothes so It didn't look like I had awakened them.

After I apologized for the lateness of the call they advised that they had been in the den watching T.V. I explained the situation to them and had both the young men come to the stairway and place the statues back on the pedestals.

They both apologized profusely for their conduct. So much so that it was hard to shut them up. Here were two young college kids who could just see themselves spending an undetermined period of time in a very hostile environment for a very foolish prank.

After listening to the story, the Martins drew me aside and indicated they didn't wish to press any formal charges on the two. They did agree to go along with a short period of putting on the pressure so that the two would think twice about their actions in the future.

When they finally realized that the Martins were going to let them off the hook, they beat a very hasty retreat yelling their thanks all the way to their car. Mr. and Mrs. Martin and I discussed the incident briefly and I returned to my car after declining their very gracious offer of a cup of coffee.

One more note to make about your beat; the lights of the Martin den cannot be seen from the street. Little things. Filed away somewhere in the brain. Probably never to be called up again but there none the less.

What happened to all those notes. Where were they stored. What triggered some mechanism to call them up from their depths to usefulness again? Whatever it was, I just hoped it didn't break down at the wrong time.

"Car 8, Code one" the radio popped. For a couple of seconds you're startled when the radio comes on when it's been so quiet.

"Car 8, Roger", as I turned onto Rexford from Sunset.

A few minutes later I was standing at the dispatch desk talking to Lt. Bowers, the Watch Commander.

"Downey do you know where the actor, Louis Jourdan lives on Camden?"

"Yes, Lieutenant."

"Well, car 4 is on another assignment so you'll have to handle this. We just got a call from Santa Monica Hospital. They have a female out there in the Emergency Room that was brought in by the police.

She's apparently in a coma and they can't figure out why. The only thing she has on her for identification is her Social Security card with her name, and the name and address of Louis Jourdan. They want us to go up there and talk to him and see if he knows her or anything about her. Her name is Margaret Wilkins. She's about 45 years old. Find out what you can and come back here and call the Hospital.

"O.K. Lt. I'll be right back", as I headed down the stairs.

A few minutes later I was ringing the doorbell of a beautiful two story French Colonial house on Camden Drive. I'm not surprised it took a while to get a response at this time in the morning. After about five minutes, a light went on in the foyer of the house.

A male voice asked, "Who is it?" A very smart move. Find out who's there before you start to open any door.

I told him who I was and then stood in front of the lighted window next to the door as the curtain moved and eyes peered out. He must have been satisfied because he opened the door.

I've obviously awakened Mr. Jourdan. He was still rubbing his eyes and brushing his hair with his hand as I walked into the foyer.

"What's this all about", he asked.

"Do you know a lady about 45 named Margaret Wilkins ?" I asked as a lady I presumed to be Mrs. Jourdan came into the room.

"Yes we do. She worked for us until a week ago. Why, what's happened ?"

"I'm not sure. Santa Monica Hospital called us to contact you. The police brought in a woman apparently in a coma and they can't figure out what's wrong with her. Her Social Security card has the name Wilkins, and she had a piece of paper in her pocket with your name and address. They asked us to find out what we could about her. How long did she work for you, and if you don't mind, why did she leave ?"

"She only worked for us a short time as a maid and cook. It was strange. Shortly after she came to work our grocery bill jumped dramatically. We noticed that every time we saw her around the house she had a large cup of coffee in her hand, and there was always a pot of coffee brewing.

We noticed that we were always running out of coffee. We usually used a couple of pounds a week. We were now using two or three pounds a day. We spoke with her and told her that she would have to curtail her use of coffee because it was interfering with her duties. She agreed to cut back. A few days later we had to speak to her again. Finally, when she didn't comply with our wishes we had to let her go. We haven't heard from her since."

"Did she ever mention any illnesses she may have suffered from ?" I asked.

"No, we didn't get to know her that well. She was only here a few weeks."

Having gotten all the information I felt was available, I thanked them for their help, apologized for the lateness of the hour, and left.

Back at the station I related all the information I had obtained to the Lt. Bowers. He instructed me to relay it to the hospital. A short time later I was talking to Dr. Spooner at the Emergency room of the Santa Monica Hospital.

As I was passing on the information I had obtained from the Jourdan residence, the Doctor suddenly remarked,

"Of course, that's it. Hold on a second officer,"

I could hear voices in the background at the hospital that indicated a sense of urgency. After about five minutes, Dr. Spooner came back on the line.

"Thanks officer, that did it, she's starting to come around already."

"What did what?" I asked, thoroughly confused.

"The information about the coffee. This lady is addicted to caffeine. When she didn't have her usual source, it took a few days for her money to run out and to go into withdrawal. She must really have it bad. I've never seen anyone go into a coma from it before. I've just given her an intravenous shot of straight caffeine and she started to come around almost immediately. Thanks officer, we appreciate your help." He hung up.

After digesting this information, I filled Lt. Bowers in on the final aspects of our inquiry. We were both impressed with the fragment of knowledge we'd just acquired. Makes you look at coffee drinking, especially on the morning watch, a little differently.

By the time I'd finished my report it was almost time for end of shift. It would be interesting to see Diana's response to the information about the coffee.

CHAPTER 9

"Hey Honey, what time is it?"

"A little after ten. Did the noise wake you up?" She came into the bedroom and turned on the light. Sitting on the edge of the bed while I tried to keep my eyes open, she told me that the James Masons, next door, were having a large and pretty noisy party.

It seemed our home was located rather strategically above the parking area and main entrance of the Mason house on one side of our house, and the Glenn Ford home on the other side. All in all a very nice neighborhood. Fred Astaire lived about a block up the street, with Janet Leigh and Tony Curtis just a little further on. Of course Mary Pickford and Buddy Rogers on Pickfair, across from them.

The Beverly Hills Hotel, our polling place, was only three short blocks away. With Milton Berle, Rita Hayworth, Clifton Webb, Jimmy Stewart, Lucille Ball & Desi Arnaz, Jack Benny and Jack Palance within two or three blocks in any direction. Historically the estate we were living on was the second or third one built in this area when Beverly Hills became a city. I was to find out while we were living here that our landlord, Mr. Campbell, was one of the founding fathers of the City.

He was also one of the charter members and founders of the Los Angeles Country Club, which bordered the City on the west. Yes, a lovely neighborhood.

"I guess I can get up and start getting ready for work. How'd your work go today?"

"Oh fine. You know that place, always seems to chugg along without too many problems. Until the end of the month. Then we have to figure out who's going to pay for what and how much each salesman is going to kick in for supplies. Then comes the dodging and shifting to see who can avoid the most costs. It would be funny if it didn't happen every month. But it all goes away in couple of days and everything is back to peace and harmony. The whole crew is a good bunch to work with. What do you want to eat tonight?"

"Lets try some creamed beef on toast for a change. When I eat sausage or bacon it seems to come back to haunt me about three o'clock in the morning. We'd better start giving some thought to where we want to go on our vacation this year. Because of my low seniority I'll have to go early in the year, probably April or early May at best."

She may have answered but the shower drowned out whatever outside noise that may have existed. A good close shave and a lingering hot shower seemed to set things right with the world, at least for a little while. All combed and polished I went into the kitchen to the aroma of breakfast and fresh coffee.

"Did you hear what I said? How many pieces of toast do you want?" As she was pouring a cup of fresh coffee.

"Two will be plenty, I'm going to try not loading myself up at the start of a shift. Maybe my gut won't get so upset if I eat lighter. Where do you think we should go on our vacation?"

"Let's just do like we did last year. Start up the coast with no place special in mind and stop where we want to. It was a nice trip last year. Besides that, going in late April up to mid May keeps us out of the vacation rush season."

"What about going to Seattle to see your Mom? We could always pick her up and bring her back with us. She could go back on the bus when she's ready. Have you got the police calls on again? What's been going on?"

The background noise of the party was suddenly crowded out by LAPD radio calls about a liquor store robbery in Hollywood Division.

"Not much, that's the first robbery call this evening. Most everything else has been routine calls. Parking complaints, drunk calls, prowlers. For Hollywood that's pretty quiet. Want any more coffee?", as she picked up my plate and put it in the dishpan and began washing it.

We were standing on the back porch looking at the jumbled mass of cars and people coming and going from the party. Must be pretty warm in the house. All the windows and doors were open and the music and voices were drifting over the neighborhood. I hoped it would get quieter before I went on shift that night. One of the calls I disliked most was to go tell people who are having a good time that they have to quiet down. For the most part, people in that town were tolerant of their neighbors parties and respectful of their privacy.

As with all towns though, there are always the chronic complainers and non-compliers. The usual procedure was to drive into the area of the complaint and judge for yourself if the noise is beyond reason. If it is, then you ask the resident to tone it down. Usually they cooperate. Like I said, nice town. Nice people. Once in a while you have to make a return call that requires a little more insistence on cooperation. Failing that, shut them down and cite them for noise violations. Usually the only time that's necessary is when the resident is overly impressed with their own importance.

"Here's my ride. Get some rest and don't listen to calls all night"

"What better way to keep track of you? It isn't often a wife knows exactly what her husband is doing while he's at work. It's O.K. until one of those scary calls starts. Then I imagine all kinds of things. And knowing you, you're probably right in the middle of it. I tell myself I'm going to quit listening when that happens but I can't. As long as I can hear you on the radio I know everything's O.K. See Ya".

Leon Snow was driving my ride. Snow was a Motor Officer and not on his bike! Must have taken a major emergency to get Leon off his bike. I didn't suspect he knew how to drive a car given his preference for motorcycles. One would think from his manner that he didn't know cars existed. Except as receptacles for drivers who deserved citations for endangering civilization by aiming their motorized projectiles at innocent bystanders. In simpler terms, he just had no use for cars when it came to doing his job. "Where's your bike Leon?"

"Broke down earlier so I'm finishing my shift in a car. Takes some getting used to. I'm working Traffic 6 'til two AM. if I don't cut some corner too short and take off the side of the car. I guess I'll survive a couple more hours".

"Thanks for the ride, Leon"

"O.K., take it easy".

After a routine roll call held by Sgt. Chuck Mann, who was acting Watch Commander, I took my unit and headed for my beat and the usual beat tour. About half way through the tour I got a code 1R call. When I got to the ramp I found Leon standing there waiting for a ride. As he got into the car he explained that he had to assist in the transport of a suspect and had to leave his car at Hillcrest and Elevado and was now going back to retrieve it.

We were at Maple and Elevado when the call came out, "Car 6 in pursuit, south on Canon from Lomita, 3 white male robbery suspects driving white Oldsmobile 4 Dr. Approaching Santa Monica". By this time Leon and I were headed south on Hillcrest toward Santa Monica, with my foot in the carburator.

Car 6 was being operated by Clint Brickley working the 6 PM to 2AM shift. What unwritten rule dictated that if you're going to get involved in something like this it happens shortly before you are due to go off shift? Another hour and Brickley would have been on his way home. Now, no matter what happens he'll be writing reports 'til at least 4 AM.

"East on Santa Monica from Rexford." Brick's call tightened the tension as Leon and I begin to slow as we neared Santa Monica.

"Here they come" says Leon, "like a bat out of hell. Clint's right behind them"

"I'm going to lay back here to let them pass Beverly Blvd. before I pull out and try to force them to the curb" I didn't want them to see me coming from the side and force them to turn right onto Beverly Blvd. Once past Beverly they couldn't turn right again for six blocks. Plenty of time to force them to the curb.

"Here we go Leon". As the suspects committed to pass Beverly I punched our Ford, at the same time turning on the red lights and turning east on Santa Monica. Timing was everything. In Police work too. We had chosen, with the guidance of whatever Saint watches over cops, the perfect time to enter Santa Monica. Brickley was close behind and slightly to the left of the Olds virtually eliminating a left turn.

As we entered the street we took an angle toward the south curb that instantly narrowed the escape route of the Olds. The driver of the Olds wisely chose to brake hard to avoid trying to climb the 18 inch curb along the south side of Santa Monica Blvd. As we all came to an abrupt stop everyone in both cars started to bail out.

Of course the "what if" mind games started the instant the chase started. What if they go south? What if they crash the car rather than stop? What if they get stopped and want to fight it out? What if they split in different directions, which one will I go after? And on and on. Did you ever stop to wonder how your mind covers so many topics in so short a period of time?

Until I got into the profession I didn't understand the theory of everything appearing to go into slow motion at a particular time, and the surroundings being so vivid and distinct at the time. In the last few months I had experienced that phenomenon frequently. Natural protective mechanism? Instinctive defense mechanism? Subconscious mind adjusting to record simultaneous actions in an orderly fashion? Whatever it was, it was real.

We were all out of the cars at the same time. As the front seat passenger of the suspect car started around his door, I saw a dark object leave his hand and land over the three foot hedge that parallels the street. Leon has exited my passenger door and has crouched by the door, weapon drawn, and is directing the driver to raise his hands.

The driver bolted toward the rear of the car and Leon body slammed him against the rear fender. By the sound of the collision, that fight was over. Brick had taken a position at the right front of his car as the rear seat passenger lost his footing as he attempted to get traction of the concrete. Giving direction to his momentum, Brick unceremoniously draped him over the hood of his police car.

My man decided to follow whatever object he threw into the hedge area. He must have thought he had seen an opening I didn't. As he attempted to jump the hedge he spread his legs like a high hurdler. With a high pitched, piercing scream my anticipated foot pursuit came to a brick wall halt.

The thick, freshly trimmed hedge, had been let grow at that point and was three feet high, and nearly six feet wide. As I was applying my handcuffs to my uncomfortably impaled suspect, I asked him what he had thrown into the bushes.

"You're seeing things cop, I didn't have anything to throw. You fuckers don't know what you're doing. Why are you chasing us, we didn't do anything? Get me out of these bushes. I think I'm bleeding."

"Well, since we don't know what we're doing, maybe I'd better wait for the ambulance to arrive. I wouldn't want to inflict any further damage to you. It'd be a damn shame for us to do anything to interfere with your procreative abilities."

"Hey, you can't leave me like this. Get me off of here. I can't use my hands and arms to get myself off with these handcuffs on."

"O.K., but remember, if your trolling gear for your victims gets damaged, you'll have to give up your robbery career".

As the three of them were loaded into a transportation car Brickley told us that the weapon used was a black handled hunting knife. When it wasn't found in the car an organized search of the brush area turned it up in the same area I had seen it thrown by our distinguished high hurdler. So much for truthfulness. Sort of shatters your faith in the honesty of some of our youth.

As we were finishing up our booking reports Clint got a call from one of his contacts on Post 12, which was a walking beat south of Wilshire and west of Beverly Drive. After a short conversation he hung up and returned to our gathering which had now increased with the presence of Sgt. Cork and Sgt. Mann. "Chuck, that was a janitor I know on So. Beverly Dr. He's told me before that there are some pretty big crap games held in the rear of Puccinis Restaurant. He says there is a big game going on now, and has been since the place closed tonight"

"Does he know how many people are involved and who they are?"

"No, He just says there are several people involved. He can't see them but he can hear them."

"Isn't that Sinatra and Lawfords place?" Leon asks.

"Yeah", says Cork, "but neither one of them are there very often. I doubt seriously that they would know about or condone something like that knowing how much adverse publicity that would cause".

"O.K.", said Mann, "the five of us should be enough to handle it. John, have cars five and seven call in, then have them move to El Camino and Charleville, and Reeves and Gregory, and standby in case we do need backup"

John Wright, a very efficient clerk/dispatcher, moved immediately to the radio console where he put out the call, "Car 5 and Car 7 code 4."

"Lets take two plain cars and one marked car so we don't have too big a parade in the street before we enter", said Cork. "Don't know how many cars we'll need for transportation"

"Yeah, we don't know how we're going to get in first. I can't remember if they leave any doors unlocked at night or not".

Brickley provided an answer to that.

"They usually leave the front door unlocked until after the cleanup crew leaves. They get done about 4:00 or 4:30. If we get right down there we can probably just walk right in".

As our three cars are pulling to the curb in front of the restaurant Sgt. Mann broadcast to Car 5 & 7. "Take up a position in the alley between Beverly Dr. and Reeves and cover the rear in case someone tries to go out the back"

Sgt. Mann, Sgt. Cork, Snow, Brickley and I quietly approached the front door and heard loud voices coming from inside the restaurant. From the conversation it was pretty obvious that a heated crap game was going hot and heavy. With all the noise and activity going on, the participants didn't notice our entry until we had gone completely through the restaurant and were standing in the doorway of the kitchen. Crouched and standing around a large stainless steel steam table were eight restaurant employees and one visitor shouting bets and imploring the dice to do their bidding. As we spread out to encircle the room, Sgt. Mann brought their revelry to a sudden stop with the command:

"Nobody move, you're under arrest. Don't touch the money or the dice. Raise your hands and line up against the wall over here. Cork, call the other guys inside, we're going to need more handcuffs. Downey, you and Brickley start gathering the money and dice, Leon start getting their I.D. Don't you just know we'll be writing reports 'til it's time to come to work today", lamented Chuck. We herded our group out the front door and into waiting vehicles.

"How much money was involved Downey?"

"Right around a thousand dollars, Sergeant. Tips around here must be pretty good".

Our arrest reports were just being finished as the Chief came up the stairs. He picked up his stack of reports for the previous nights activity, took one brief look at the haggard faces around the office and beckoned Sgt. Mann into his office. A short time later Chuck came out of the Chiefs' office with a subdued grin on his face. The Mighty One was pleased.

Four of our gamblers had long felony records and had not applied for or obtained the City required "Liquor and Food Service Handlers Card" before going to work in an establishment serving alcohol in the City limits.

In order to obtain the "card", the applicant had to submit to being fingerprinted and fill out an application form. After a record check, a card was issued, if no derogatory information was found.

The procedure, although controversial, was quite effective in keeping track of possible trouble areas as well as identifying wanted felons and a couple of prison escapees.

By the time we submitted our paperwork, closed out our activity notebooks, and changed clothes it was arraignment time in court.

As Cork and I walked across the hall to the courtroom, Al Grevelding, the jailer asked us for a hand with the prisoners.

"What did you guys have to do, lock them up in bunches". Al asked. "One of us will have to stay with them 'til I can bring the rest of them down".

A few minutes later, most of our prior nights arrestees were seated in the jury box of the courtroom. All of a sudden, with the sunlight pouring into the courtroom, the hallway heating up, and the jury box full of arraignments, the wait no longer seemed worth it. Weighing our curiosity with the need for rest and sleep, Cork and I opted for the latter.

"How's your investigation of Porterfield coming, Bob?."

"Pretty slow right now. I need to talk to the two L.A. dicks that handled him before and I can never seem to catch them in the office."

"Get in touch with Howard and see when he's going down to LAPD next time and get him to take you along and see if you can connect with them in person. Sometimes when they don't know you they just won't talk to anyone on the phone. They want to get to know the people they are sharing their careers with. Try it, see if it works. O.K. Bob, see you tonight".

CHAPTER 10

Even at roll call that night the atmosphere was strange. Then again you couldn't call it exactly strange. Nothing at all like your usual Saturday night. Sgt. Pierce was acting watch commander and Sgt. Cork was the patrol sergeant. Even before roll call everything seemed spooky quiet. Bert Sloane had worked the evening shift on the desk and was relieved by John Wright. John mentioned that the swing shift log was one of the shorter ones he had seen in a long time. The "log", of course, was a compilation of the Departmental activity that transpired on a shift. All calls for service, all complaints, accidents, arrests, and any other fact worthy of notation.

As we took over our cars from the previous shift there was little small talk or chatter between the men. They just gathered their equipment from the cars and entered the basement to check out for the night. There seemed to be an aura of quiet apprehension.

If you asked anyone what it was, you might get some nervous laughter out of them. Mostly you would get a smart ass remark about hob-goblins or fortune tellers or intuition. But you noticed none of them were standing around to analyze it or dissect it. No, they were going inside and checking out a bit more hurried than usual, and a lot quieter.

Cork and I talked briefly on the ramp and agreed to take our coffee break together at about 2:15 Am. Not much choice where to take it on the morning watch. Biff's on Wilshire, the back of the Luau on Rodeo or the kitchen of the Hilton Hotel. Maybe the drive-in at Robertson and Wilshire depending on who was doing the cleanup after closing. Like I said, not many places.

You could always go to the coffee shop of the Beverly Wilshire Hotel if you didn't mind all the after midnight hoods that came and went after their apparently obligatory meeting with Mickey Cohen, his girlfriend Sandy Hashhagen, and his current entourage of henchmen.

Currently Joe DeCarlo seemed to be the rogue of choice and the favored one. One thing for sure, you don't have to look very far for any of the 'connected' crowd after midnight. For whatever reason, they seemed to have anointed the Beverly Wilshire Pharmacy Coffee Shop as their home away from home after the sun was way down.

Not too long after midnight Mickey arrived in his Cadillac with Sandy driving, followed closely by Joe DeCarlo in another Caddy. Somehow the corner booth was never occupied when they arrived.

After settling in the booth they begin to hold court with DeCarlo hovering nearby. As if responding to Pavlov's bell the 'undesirables' began to arrive and pay tribute or homage to the runt. After their pilgrimage most of the 'in' group hung around the corner in front of the Pharmacy entrance, passing the time of day, or rather, night. At times there would be as many as ten of 'them' hanging around. It was not unusual to see the casual citizen heading for the Coffee Shop suddenly realize what he was seeing and abruptly change course and seek some other source of refreshment or relaxation.

Bookies, pimps, muscle, con-men, extortionists, they ran the gamut. Some strutting, some just strolling around in circles. Some leaning against paper racks or poles but all with the same identifying characteristic habit. Turning their heads, moving their eyes and shifting their feet, as if to take flight at the first unfamiliar sight to reach their eyes. You couldn't exactly call it nervous. Just an overly obvious attempt not to appear nervous.

Must be a hell of a way to live. Never knowing who is after your string of girls, who's skimming the book, who's past-posting in your organization. Never being 100% secure in the feeling that your 'friends' aren't working some angle to ease you out and take over your operation, insignificant as it may be.

Of course they know the feeling. They should. They're doing the same damned thing. Always figuring the angles to grab a little bigger piece of the action. Without stirring the smoldering embers into a full flame, of course. Or causing enough heat to have their associates get the feeling that they may prove to be more of a threat than they want to tolerate. What a way to live.

At roll call that night Sgt. Pierce put out the word that DeCarlo was supposed to be carrying a gun. As an ex-con that was a no-no. LAPD Intelligence had gotten the word from someone in the Parole Division that since the shooting at the restaurant out in the valley, Cohen had Joe sticking closer, and packing. Of course there was lots of feeling among law enforcement types that the shooting of the bookmaker was probably ordered by Cohen. Or at least condoned. The fact that Cohen was in the restaurant at the time the shooting took place may have contributed to that feeling.

The guest list at his table that night was a who's who of minor local thugs. Of course none of them could describe or identify the shooter. He just walked into a mob hangout, picked out his victim, shot him several times and walked out unhindered. Some lucky assassin.

Naturally by the time the police arrived none of the restaurant patrons could help in the identification and none were armed. It is said, however, that the busboy's dishpan was unusually heavy on his first trip to the kitchen after the shooting. As is the case in most situations like that, the next few days were a flurry of newspaper stories about the lack of suspects. And many stories listing the victims long career of criminal activities and his total uselessness to the world.

One would be led to wonder if all that was known about the guy before he got whacked, how the hell did he stay out of jail? For a few days after the shooting the usual crowd around the Pharmacy was diminished. Those that did show up displayed very subdued attitudes and didn't hang around long after their respects were paid.

Working car 5 made the corner of Rodeo and Wilshire one of

my priority locations. That night was no different. By the time I could make my beat check and handle a routine call or two, the anointed one had arrived and was ensconced in the corner booth with Sandy. DeCarlo was wandering around the corner like the ever vigilant centurion.

While looking around the parked vehicles in the local area there was one that warranted a little closer scrutiny. It was tucked pretty discreetly in the back of a few cars parked on Rodeo just north of Wilshire.

When the windshield was backlighted by a car coming down Rodeo there seemed to be two people sitting in the front seat but slid way down with only the top of their head showing above the dashboard. From the look of the car and their location it was a good shot they are some type of law enforcement.

With what ever it was that was in the air I didn't feel quite like bracing them headon. It had only been a few days since the valley shooting and it was not out of the realm of possibility that someone may want to even the score.

After parking my car on Dayton Way and signing out on the radio, I walked back to Rodeo and took up a doorway position for a period of observation. As Capt. Smith was so fond of saying on his commendations "Observation Pays Dividends". It also makes damn good sense if you don't know exactly what you're facing. It doesn't take long to determine that these individuals were on some kind of surveillance. Now the question was, who was it, and why weren't we notified that the would be there? Well, we'd just see if we could find out who they were without burning them.

Of course if it was the FBI and I did burn them, the Chief would probably give me a Departmental Citation. It was no secret to anyone that the Chief and the FBI had lost no love for each other. I understood it dated back to when the Chief attended the FBI Academy and locked horns with J. Edgar himself. It must have been a doozy of a fight because it filtered all the way down from Hoover to the local offices.

The unwritten rule was, the FBI is not welcome in or around

Beverly Hills unless requested, and then very grudgingly. With all the highpowered movers and shakers in town and all the mob connected people who live there it made inter- agency cooperation pretty near impossible. But for now, we took things as they came.

By staying close to the street side of the two cars behind our inquiring guests I was at the side of their car just as they became aware of my presence. At the same time they held up an LAPD badge, I noticed the light of their radio control head in the glove compartment. Opening the rear door I slipped into the seat and slid down.

"How you doing guys? Sorry if I burn your stake out but I wasn't notified anyone would be out here".

"That's O.K. I'm Jones and this is Unland. we're from L.A. Intelligence. We didn't know we would be here so we didn't have time to tell anyone yet. We were cruising Hollywood when we saw Cohen and DeCarlo playing tag along on Sunset and decided to see where they were headed. After that fiasco out in the valley the other night things could get pretty touchy in some corners of their society."

"The car that DeCarlo is driving is registered to the guy who got killed at the restaurant. It hasn't been around for a while. It was gone at the time of the shooting and just turned up tonight. Have you guys been told that DeCarlo is supposed to be carrying a gun now?"

"Yeah, it was put out at roll call tonight. Apparently came from the parole office. I would imagine quite a few of those guys are walking pretty nervous about now. Is there any speculation on why the guy was taken out?"

"Not for sure. He'd been stepping on a few toes for a couple of months now but nothing that would appear to cause his sudden departure. Hell, who knows what these guys do to each other. In their circles it doesn't take much to offend somebody".

"O.K guys, I'll get the hell out of here and leave you to your fun. I'll notify the desk that you're around so you don't get burned again".

"O.K., thanks. We'll probably be gone before long. Just want to get a look at who all shows up. Nite".

By the time I got back into my car and signed on, it was time to meet Cork for our coffee break. Traffic was very thin for a Saturday night and the overall atmosphere hadn't changed much. As car 8 signed back on from his break, I pulled into the lot at the back of Biff's and signed out. Corks car was already there so I imagined he was holding court inside. He must have gotten there while I was out of the car. Well, it was as good a place as any for a sergeant to meet and talk with his troops. As I slid onto a stool next to Cork at the counter, Shirley put a mug of coffee in front of me.

"I just left a couple of LAPD Intelligence guys on surveillance at Rodeo and Wilshire. They followed Cohen and DeCarlo from Hollywood. If I didn't know better than to have premonitions, with this spooky feeling tonight, I would say something's about to happen".

"Yeah, Bob, there's something in the wind. If there was a wind. Nights like this can get to you. You keep waiting for something to pop and break the tension and the longer it takes to pop the tighter the tension gets. Before long you're as tight as a guitar string".

"It doesn't sound like there is much going on anywhere tonight. Not a hell of a lot on the radio and traffic seems about half of normal. Nobody is saying much but it's pretty obvious that most of the troops are feeling something". Cork said.

I waved off a refill and got ready to leave. Ten minutes goes pretty fast. Then came the usual dance about paying for the coffee. Department policy said you wouldn't accept free anything. Most of the restaurants wouldn't accept payment.

Especially on the morning watch. They welcomed the comfort and security of policemen coming in and out at various times. So it boiled down to leaving a tip large enough to pay for the coffee and compensate the waitress.

After a quick tour of beat five to note the cars parked on the street I had drifted back into the business district. As I slowed to a stop at Brighton and Rodeo who should pass in front of me northbound on Rodeo but Mickey Cohen in his black Cadillac with Sandy at the wheel. As expected, about a half a block behind them came another Cadillac with none other than Joe DeCarlo driving.

Well, there would never be a better time to find out if Joe was carrying a gun. He was driving a dead man's car that hadn't been seen for several days. It'd be interesting to get his story on how he got the car. As Cohen turned right on Park Way, I dropped in behind Joe and prepared to stop him at Beverly Drive and Park Way.

I notified the dispatcher that I was making the stop at the same time I turned on the red lights. It was pretty obvious he knew I was behind him. My red lights hadn't started to get warm before he had pulled to the curb. As I got out of my car I saw the L.A. Intelligence car, lights out, pulling to the curb under a tree a half block behind us.

On the other side of Santa Monica Blvd. I saw the front of one of our black and whites easing out from behind the hedge just far enough to have a full view of the intersection. One thing was for sure. I didn't need to look far for backup should anything go wrong.

Joe was getting out of the car as I got to his left rear fender. Flashing my light quickly into the interior of the convertible as I walked by the drivers side had assured me that there were no other passengers.

"Morning Mr. DeCarlo, let's step onto the sidewalk. May I see your drivers license please?"

"Sure officer, here it is." That's one thing nice about dealing with a professional. No stupid questions about "What did I do wrong?" or "Did I run a stop sign or something?" They knew just by virtue of being who they were subjected them to a little closer scrutiny that the usual citizen. No games. No feigned innocence. No false indignation. Extending a little respect never cost you anything and usually came back many times over. Throwing your weight around may get you reluctant cooperation but no respect.

As he reached for his wallet, I kept a very close watch on his waist and under his arms for any signs of a weapon. He got his license out and handed it to me. No telltale indications of any gun so far. His license was valid except for an address that everyone knew was for show only. You would be old and grey waiting for him to show up there if you wanted him very badly. Not much can be done about it. He did get some mail there and the manager said he paid the rent on time. His parole officer knew it was just a cover address but couldn't do anything about it until he was bagged doing something wrong. Until then, we all went along with the charade.

"Who is the car registered to, Mr. DeCarlo?" as I was filling out a field interrogation card.

"You know it's registered to Jack Saritone. That's why you stopped me isn't it?", he answered. No sarcasm, just resignation in his voice.

"No, not really. I am interested in how you got the car but there is one other thing on my mind"

As we stood talking, Cohen's Caddy kept slowly circling the two block area. Always within sight of us. Carefully stopping at all the stop signs and signals. Sandy never took any chances about her driving. Mickey must have been a little nervous about going home alone. As they passed for the third time I give Mickey a friendly wave. This was not the first time I had wished I could read lips.

"What's the other thing?" Joe asked. Now it sounded like his voice is a little more strained.

"Well, it seems someone has put out the word that after that shooting you have gone to carrying a gun again. If that's the case you know that would break your parole. Are you carrying?" As I gave him back his license I put away my F.I. card and notebook.

"Hell no, I'm not about to put myself back in the joint. How stupid do you guys think I am?"

"Well Joe, I don't really know. You know as well as I do some guys never learn. The only thing we can do is go on the information available to us. Place you hands on the hood of the car please while I pat you down."

Shaking his head in disgust he turned and placed his hands on the car and stepped back and spread his legs. As I ran my hands over his body I noticed the doors of the L.A. car open about half way. They closed as I finished my search and Joe stood up.

"Mr. DeCarlo, I'm going to shake down the car so please stand by the right front fender and don't move or wander around. I'll have you on your way as soon as I can."

"O.K. but I'm telling you, I don't have a gun. But I guess my telling you is not going to stop you".

"Yeah, you're right about that. This won't take long". I guess I lied a little bit. By the time I had gotten done with the car about 30 minutes had passed and I had car seats, rugs, air cleaners, jacks and other sundry items piled on the sidewalk.

Not once during the search did Joe make a sound of protest. Yes, it's nice dealing with a professional. When I had finished I was totally sure of one thing. There was no weapon on Joe or in the car.

"I guess you were right Mr. DeCarlo. No guns or weapons of any kind. Sorry about the delay. You can be on your way anytime. Thanks for your cooperation". As I turned to go to my car he sputtered a little.

"Hey, what about all this shit on the sidewalk. Are you just going to leave it there?" His voice was sounding more and more agitated now.

"Yes, but I guess if you don't put it in your car you are going to leave it there. I really don't have the time right now, I've been out of service too long. I really appreciate your cooperation. Good night".

As I left the area Mickey's car pulled up beside Joe and he approached the car as the window went down. That conversation would have been interesting.

As I made a wide circle of the block I saw the L.A. car leaving the area. By the time I got about six blocks away the black and white that had been staking us out pulled in behind me. We went into a parking lot, making wide circles, we pulled up beside each other, drivers door to drivers door.

"Well, how'd you do?" Cork asked as we both turn down our radios.

"Not very well. Obviously he was totally clean. Damned polite though. I can't say I would be the same if I was left with all that stuff on the sidewalk".

"Yeah, I noticed. He's got it pretty well under control not to get upset with all that. Were you trying to piss him off?"

"No, I wasn't. I just didn't want to miss anything. Did you see the L.A. Intelligence car parked on Park Way?. They left as soon as I had finished".

"Yeah, I saw them. Did you talk to Polakov about taking you to L.A. to meet some of those people you need to see about your case?"

"We're going to go down Tuesday morning. Howard has court on Monday and I'm off Monday night so I'll have some rest before we go. He's said he will take me to central burglary/auto theft and then we'll go to Hollywood Division and meet some of the burglary detectives. He wants to talk to them about something anyway. Should be interesting. Damn, I'll sure be happy when this nights over. I still can't shake this feeling that the air is thick and about to bust open."

"It gets that way sometimes. Just don't lose your concentration. That's just when something will happen. I'll see you later." He drove out of the lot heading for the north end of the city. I pulled out of the lot and started making my rounds and writing my overnight parking tickets.

I'd gone only a few blocks when the radio crackled, "Car 5, 4-5-9 silent, J.J. Haggerty's, Rodeo and Wilshire. 10 minute delay on the man." "Enroute" I responded.

A silent burglary alarm at J.J. Haggerty's. Not your usual call. The alarm there doesn't usually misfire. The alarm company response man would be delayed ten minutes. Time for me to go around the building and check the doors. When the alarm man got there we could go inside and check the office, then the roof. Check the cars parked in the area too. This may be a trial run just to see how long it takes for the police to respond.

Once the company man got there it only took a few minutes to check out the building and find nothing wrong. No reason for the alarm, no explanation. Just something else to add to the tension. It was about 4:30 AM when I went north on Beverly Drive and started to cross Wilshire when a new Buick passed, going west on Wilshire. The driver just looked like he was not at ease behind that wheel. When I pulled in behind him I saw there were no plates on the car. He acknowledged my red lights and pulled to the curb at Camden.

I radioed for another unit as I got out of my car and approached the drivers door. His face was ghost white as my flashlight cast a light in the front of the car. He looked to be about 18 or 19 years old. "Would you step out of the car please?" As he opened the door it became apparent there were no keys in the ignition. The car was still running!!

"Good morning. Where did you steal the car?"

A slight hesitation, and then, "At the Buick dealer a couple of miles down Wilshire. I've got to be back to my ship by six AM and didn't think I was going to make it."

It took a few seconds to soak in that this guy had already confessed to Grand Theft Auto after only one question. I didn't know if it set any record but it served to remind me not to be surprised at anything. Hoping that I didn't display my amazement, I responded with, "It's pretty obvious you're not going to make it now. Where is your ship docked? "

"Long Beach. I'm supposed to go on duty at 6 AM. I don't want to be AWOL." He didn't seem to comprehend that his main problem right now was a stolen car, not being AWOL.

"If you got this car a couple of miles back, what are you doing out this way? Why didn't you go south toward Long Beach?".

As I turned him around to shake him down he replied, "I thought that now that I had a ride I didn't need to hurry. So I thought I'd go through Beverly Hills on my way back. I guess I should have gone right back".

"I guess so. Let's get these cuffs on and you can have a seat in the back of my car." As I was putting him in the back of my car, K.O. Mchuin arrived driving car 7, and parked his car to help transport the suspect. A tow truck arrived in a few minutes and hooked up the new Buick after disconnecting the hot wire job under the dash.

Enroute to the Police station I realized that from first sighting to towing the whole incident had taken only twenty minutes. Even the booking report went like greased lightening. The whole incident was over in less than an hour, including the impound sheet from the tow truck.

By the time I got back into my car I started to realize that the oppressive atmosphere of the night seemed to be dwindling away. What broke it? Nothing dramatic had happened. It felt like a plug had been pulled from a barrel and the tension was running out of the hole at a rapid pace. It was not all gone but it was definitely softening up.

It was obvious at end of shift roll call that I was not the only one to feel that way. There was a lot more relaxed feeling in the air. The horseplay and wise cracks had returned. That feeling was gone. Whatever the reason, it's gone. Thank God. I could do without that feeling very often.

CHAPTER 11

"Well Bob, your smash and grabber hit again last night" was Howard's greeting as I had entered the Detective Bureau on Tuesday morning. "Are we waiting for him to build up his retirement nestegg before you bust him?" As he not so gently inserted the ribbing needle.

With just the right amount of contritness I asked, "Where'd he hit?"

"Got a jewelry store on Wilshire just east of town about four o'clock in the morning. A maintenance man a few doors away heard the noise and saw a sports car speeding away down the side street. You can call Wilshire Division and talk to Howard or Chapman this afternoon and see if they got anything else on a description. As soon as I make a couple of calls we'll head on downtown and meet the guys at Burglary/Auto theft".

I got my case folder out of the file cabinet and proceeded to make my notes on the inside fly leaf. Date, location, type of store, leaving blanks for the information I didn't have yet. It's quite possible this was not my man.

Smash and grab is not a crime of high technical skill. Almost anyone can do it. If it was him, it's the first time I have known him to go after a jewelry store. Maybe he's branching out. Counting this one, I had 21 unsolved cases in this folder already, from all over the Metropolitan area.

Maybe I was chasing shadows. I'd hate like hell to think I'd convinced my people that I had pinpointed the right guy and find I'd blown it. A cold chill went through me from top to bottom. I didn't even want to think about that.

"O.K. Bob, let's go. We'll go downtown and then stop by

Hollywood Division on the way back. Unless you really need it, leave the folder here. This is a shakedown cruise just to meet the people. If we talk specifically about any case it would be only superficially".

We went out the back door and got into one of the detective cars. Really undercover. Plain four door sedan, black wall tires, small hub caps, no good time radio and a whip antenna. Also no heater or defroster. At least we got new cars every year. I still hadn't figured out the logic of no heaters or defrosters yet, but maybe it'd come to me. "When we get there Bob, try not to say to much. They'll be sizing you up so they will ask a few pointed questions just to see how and what you answer, and how much. Keep your answers short and don't say too much. Part of their feeling you out is to find out if you shoot off your mouth or tell everything you know.

Just be reserved and on your guard. Look and listen but don't volunteer anything. They'll warm up after they figure you're not out to be a bigshot and milk them and impress them with your wisdom. Most of these guys have been burned a few times by hot shots and now they are cautious as hell. As a whole, they are damned good people."

"I figured on feeling my way along very slowly. Do they have any idea what it is we're working on?"

"Yeah, I told them you were interested in Porterfield, so they may offer the information right away or they may hold back waiting to see what you're like. We'll stop by the shoeshine stand and get a dime shine while we're there. The jail trustees operate a shine stand in the basement and give a damn good shine for a dime. Also gives you a chance to look at who's coming and going while you're sitting there."

A half hour later we had pulled into the basement of Parker center and found a parking place as close to the elevators as we could. Of course everyone else figured the same thing.

It was almost ten o'clock so a good many of the cars were already on the street. When we got to the shine stand all the chairs were full and a couple of guys were waiting so we went directly to the elevators.

As we got on one of the elevators, four suited behemoths, wearing wide brimmed felt hats, stepped in with us. For some untold reason you just seemed to want to give them more than the average amount of room. They are obviously detectives. At least two are carrying two guns. One shoulder holster, one belt rig. They nodded, superficially acknowledging our presence and one of them spoke to Howard. As they stepped off at the second floor and turned right, Howard and I went left.

"I would hazard a guess that those four are representatives of the famous, or infamous, "hat squad". I remarked to Howard as we approached the door to Burglary/Auto.

"Yeah that's a few of them. Funny how just a few of them seems like a big crowd, especially when you're in a small place like an elevator. They have quite a reputation. You don't stay in that group very long unless you can earn the rep you have."

We entered the ante room and then the squad room of the Burglary/Auto Theft Division. The room was a large open area fitted with grey metal desks and tables grouped together in varying numbers, in strategic areas. Along the walls and between some of the table groupings were a few grey metal file cabinets. Along one side of the room were a couple of glass enclosed offices. Along one wall was a row of windows overlooking part of downtown Los Angeles.

Howard headed toward one group of tables where three men were seated, one on the phone. As we approached they looked up and one rose. "Hi Eddie" Howard said.

"What's up Howard? What brings you downtown?"

"Just showing one of our new men around and introducing him to some of the people he will be talking to eventually. Going to check a few records while we're here. Eddie Levold, meet Bob Downey, and this is Pete Bishonden." As we shook hands, the third man hung up the phone. "Bob Downey, Ed Barr".

"Hi Bob, welcome to the squirrel cage. How long have you been aboard" asks LeVold.

-DOWN

Before I could answer Howard responded "Bob is working on a special project of his own for the time being. He's getting a file together on this fur store window smash burglar. We came down to see Carpenter and Hayes. They handled the guy for auto theft and we're here to pick their brain about him".

Barr looked toward a couple of men seated at a table near the center of the room and said, "Yeah, they're here, over at that table" pointing.

"O.K." With a `see ya later' Howard headed toward the table where Carpenter and Hayes were pouring over their paperwork. Holding out his hand as we approached Howard said,

"Hi guys, I'm Polakov and this is Downey. We're from Beverly Hills. I called yesterday about getting together with you about Porterfield."

"Yeah, pull up a chair", after handshakes all around. "What can we do for you? Here is his file if you want to look at it. It took a while to nail him but we finally convicted him of Auto Theft".

Hayes opened the file and spread out some paperwork. The packet had several mug shots. After looking at them I started to recall him more vividly. A pleasant cherubic looking face. As I thought back, a likable soft-spoken fellow. He obviously had what I thought were all the right answers at the time because all I did was F.I. him and turn him loose.

"He's out on appeal bond now. It'll probably be another six months before he comes up for sentencing. There are some indications he might still be active in Corvette thefts but we haven't had time to concentrate on him. What makes you think he might be good for those window smash jobs? You can keep those mug shots if you want. There are plenty in the files".

"Thanks, I was going to get some from records today". I told him as I pulled a couple of photos from the stack. "It'll sound crazy I know, but it's only a hunch at this point. A couple of months ago I FI'd him on Wilshire near Willaman at about 3 in the morning. A few days later the fur store on the corner was hit by the window smasher. The only person in the area at the time was a janitor who heard what sounded like a sports car speeding away. I don't even know if the sports car was involved in the burglary or not. Like I said, just a hunch"

"Well, knowing Andy he could very well have branched out. He's got a quick mind and quite an imagination. He could have switched his M.O. for a while knowing we were still interested in him. There is a pretty big market for Corvette engines in speedboats at the marina. We figured him for supplying some of them as well as torching some Corvette bodies for insurance. Like I said we're still looking at him but don't have time to concentrate on him right now." Carpenter said as he handed me the 510 sheet from the package.

The 510 is the suspects personal history sheet that's filled out by the detectives when they are interviewing him. This innocent looking and sounding sheet of paper has come back to haunt many a suspect later in his career. Full of innocuous questions that can provide lots of direction later in a follow-up investigation. Credit accounts, bank accounts, relative phones and addresses, associates and a plethora of other information.

"Do you guys mind if I copy some of this information?".

They both answered to go ahead and I began transferring information that I didn't already have in my notes. After a few minutes we thanked them for their trouble and information. "Give us a call if there is anything we can do for you here that may save you a trip downtown." they said as we were going out the door. Seemed like that intro meeting went pretty well. The only time we'll know for sure is when we call or come back the next time.

Before we returned to the car, we took a brief tour of Parker Center, the record bureau, photo lab, and of course the cafeteria. This day was not one to be spent in the cafeteria for lunch. On the way out of the garage Howard informed me we were going to have lunch at "Phillipe's"

For the uninitiated, "Phillipe's" was the local lunch Mecca of the City Hall and Police Department. At any time close to lunch, four door, black side- walled, no hub capped, whip antennae equipped sedans, can be seen parked in every available space within a block of the place. The inside of the place can only be said to have "atmosphere". A sawdust floored deli, with seven or eight lines of mostly city employees, lined up for a wide variety of excellent sandwiches and various accompaniments. Not to be forgotten of course, is the wide assortment of beverages. Especially a good cold draft beer to wash down a professionally built sandwich. Put together with the speed that can only come from long experience.

Along one wall was a series of stand up tables, with a foot rail, that would accommodate up to six standing eaters. Through a narrow doorway was an alcove fitted with several picnic type tables. A quick glance around the place let you know that there are at least six different police departments represented at that time. The majority plain clothes, but a few uniforms.

If you were so inclined you could stand and philosophize about all the encounters with life that those people have had. All the experiences with exaltation, desperation, exhaustion, futility, exasperation. Co-mingled with feelings of accomplishment, satisfaction, strength of purpose, confidence of ability and knowledge of personal weaknesses and frailties.

Buried deep inside was the constant knowledge that there are those situations that will wrench your guts out, bring a bucketful of never to be shed tears to the back of your eyes. Or bring you to the brink of that terrible abyss that separates you from the parasites you pursue.

On the surface though, they give the overall appearance of aloof self confidence with no external signs of the myriad of desperate situations they have confronted and resolved. Some, only short hours before. Where do they find the space to store those memories and experiences? How do they keep them from creeping back into their consciousness and impacting every action they take. Would I develop that ability? How long would it take? Had I started already?

"Huh?, Oh yeah Howard, Pastrami will be fine. And a Coke. I'll find us a spot over here at this back table".

A few minutes later Howard came to the table with two mammoth sandwiches and two Cokes. We downed them without the proper reverence for the skill needed to assemble such a repast. Nor the time needed to reflect on the subtle flavors of the meat and it's accompaniments. It filled the empty spaces. It was also another demonstration of Howard's skill at finding great places to eat.

Thirty minutes later we were pulling into a parking place at the Hollywood Division. The second floor detective division was quite a contrast from the Burglary/Auto Division at Parker Center. It was an old building with fixtures and furniture to match. Wooden desks and files cabinets crammed into every available space. There were a couple of windowed offices near the top of the stairs for the command officers. Otherwise, everyone else worked out of the "Bull Pen".

From the number of desks, telephones and in and out boxes scattered in the room, it would seem that quite a few people worked here. I began to wonder where everyone would fit if they were all in the room at the same time. We headed toward two shirt sleeved men engaged in conversation at a desk near the back of the room. They both sported crew haircuts and shoulder holsters.

As we got closer they looked up and Howard began the introductions,

"Toomey, Turner, I want you to meet Bob Downey." They stood and we shook hands all around exchanging the obligatory pleasantries.

Chet Turner was a large, well proportioned man with a quick grin and firm handshake. Jim Toomey was somewhat smaller with the hint of a twinkle in the eyes and an equally firm handshake. A no nonsense, get it done, handshake must be an unwritten requirement of police officers. After a quick assessment of the many introductions to policemen I had had in the last few months, I can't recall any that weren't firm, solid, and short. "Have a seat guys. What can we do for you today?"

"Nothing really" Howard says, "I'm just showing Bob around

and introducing him. He's working up a special file on this window smash burglar and may need to call on you in the future for background. I wanted you to meet him so you would know who you were talking to".

"Have you got a suspect yet, Bob?" Turner asked.

"Not really, just a strong hunch. There's still a lot of loose ends to pull together". I remembered not to ramble on or talk too much. At the same time I didn't want to appear too secretive. These guys had a basketful of their own cases to worry about. They didn't need me trying to impress them with my `brilliance'. Howard asked, "can I use your phone, I have to call the office"

"Sure go ahead, you don't need to ask", chuckles Toomey. "You've been around here enough to know where the phone is."

While Howard was on the phone we chatted aimlessly about cars, guns, and other pointless matters. We were all making an effort not to be specific about anything. After a while it was obvious we are all trying to say something without saying anything. It was close to being laughable when Howard got off the phone and returned to our circle.

"Bob, we have to get back to the office. Capt. Smith wants to see you when we get back." He said.

"O.K. Nice to meet you guys. I'm looking forward to doing some work with you." I shook hands with both of them as I rose from the chair and headed for the stairs, Howard right behind me.

As we were getting into the car I asked, "Any idea what P.R. wants?" "None" he said, "he just left a message in the bureau for you."

It was pretty quiet on the twenty minute ride back to the office. Howard filled me in on some of the background of the people we had met today. Some of it pretty colorful. Bishonden, LeVold and Barr, are recognized far and wide as experts on safe burglaries and burglars. Toomey and Turner are known for their tenaciousness and connections in the Hollywood underworld. As I listened to Howard talk, I realized that he has a memory akin to a recording machine. Many of the things we learned today he is repeating verbatim. How did he do that?

We parked in the traffic circle and I headed directly for Capt. Smiths office. I didn't know what I was preparing myself for but I'd mentally prepared myself for most of the perceived situations. I'd passed my probation so it was probably nothing like that. I'd had several good arrests on the morning watch lately so it shouldn't be anything about my activity reports.

Well I'd know pretty soon. Waiting again.

I ran into the Capt. at the front desk as I got to the top of the stairs. Toothpick in the corner of his mouth.

"Oh, Downey, come into my office", he said. I followed him down the short hall to his inner- sanctum.

"I wanted to talk to you about your schedule" as he rounded his desk and sat down. "Have a seat. I know you have volunteered for the morning watch for the past few months and you've done well there. Starting next month though you're being reassigned to the Detective Bureau, if you have no objections." He said rather smirkingly. "Since you're spending so much time in there I suppose you won't object too much". He said with a small smile on his face, rolling the toothpick around.

"No Capt., I won't mind at all." I replied, trying not to smile too broad a smile, or jump up and down. "I didn't expect this. I've been trying to figure out what I may have screwed up to prompt this meeting but I didn't think about this. I do have one question though, you say this is to be effective on the first, I'm due for vacation from the first to the fourteenth. Should I cancel that or not? I'll work it out either way."

"Why don't you talk it over with Capt. Hankins. He'll be your supervisor then. You can work it out with him. Good luck," he said as he got up and headed for the door.

He was gone several seconds before I suddenly woke up and realized what had just happened. I'd had high hopes of getting into the Bureau for some time but never expected it to come so soon. Less than two years on the Department. Sure, I'd been putting in a lot of time in and out of the Bureau on this case, and I've gone along with them on some of their stakeouts and arrests but it was still a welcome shock to be given that assignment. It was also a source of great pride but full realization didn't come until later.

As I walked into the Detective Bureau I ran into Cork and Howard coming out the door. "Congratulations," they said in unison "welcome aboard. We'll see you when we get back."

"Thanks guys. I'm still in shock. I have to see the captain now." I turned and tapped on the captain's door frame. Seeing that he was on the phone, I leaned against the wall and began to analyze what had just happened. I didn't get much time to reflect when Capt. Hankins called for me to come in.

He stood and offered me his hand as he said, "Congratulations, have a seat. Well, how do you feel about it? Are you ready for this assignment?"

"Yes Capt., I think so. Capt. Smith suggested I talk to you about one thing. I'm due to go on vacation next week. If you'd rather I postpone it, I can do that without to much trouble. My wife would just have to reschedule hers"

"No, don't do that, just take your vacation and report in here when you're due back. We knew you were set for vacation when we made the selection. Just be ready to work like hell when you get back" He said. "You'll be working a weekend schedule with one of the Sergeants until you get some experience. Also, you'll continue to work your windowsmash case. How's that coming?"

"Pretty slow right now Captain. I did get some new information on the guy from the people at Auto Theft that Howard introduced me to today. I've got some phone numbers to check on and some bank information. I'll get on that tomorrow".

"O.K. keep me advised of what's going on. We'll look forward to seeing you when you get back. Welcome aboard"

"Thanks Capt." as I left his office and went into the squad room, picked up the phone and dialed Diana's number.

"Stout Motors" she answered with that ever present smile in her voice. The kind of voice that lets you know there is a warm and friendly person on the other end of the line. And in her case, beautiful too. How'd I get so lucky?

"Hi, honey." I tried to sound normal and not indicate I'm about ready to bust a gut. "If you're ready for it why don't you meet me at the Saratoga on your way home. We can have a drink or two and an early dinner".

"Oh, that sounds good, we can listen to Ronnie Brown at the piano bar. We haven't done that in a long time. What's the occasion" she asked, with that hint of suspicion that follows any unexpected deviation from the routine.

"Nothing really." I lied. "I just feel like having dinner out. That's O.K. isn't it?

"O.K. I'll see you there about six." she said with that knowing sound in her voice that said she knew better but she'll play along anyhow.

"I'll probably get there about 5:30 so I'll be at the bar. Make it sooner if you can I don't want to get too far ahead of you. I'll catch a ride from here with someone and ride home with you".

As I got off the phone, Cork and Howard returned. I asked Howard if he would give me a ride to the Saratoga a little later and he said yes. As a matter of fact he wanted me to go with him to interview a theft victim now and then he will drop me off. We were walking out the back door to the parking ramp when we saw Al Grevelding, the jailer, coming from the side of a parked car with a man he was holding by the arm with his left hand. In his right hand is what appeared to be .32 cal semi- automatic pistol that he was holding by the trigger guard.

He called us to come over. As we got there he handed me the gun and said, "This man just stopped me as I was going home, and told me he had just shot his wife at a Medical Center in Santa Monica. He says he used that gun. Will you guys take it from here?"

Al seemed to be very anxious to pass this one to us in a hurry. Although Al was a policeman, it'd been a long time since he'd been on the street.

"Sure Al, we've got him, go on home." Howard and I got on each side of the man and headed for the elevator. Getting off on the business office floor, I asked the desk clerk to call Santa Monica and see if they had a shooting near a medical center today.

We went into Capt. Hankins office and Howard asked the Capt. to step out in the hall where he explained what we had and that we wanted to use his office for the interview because he had a tape recorder rigged up in his desk. He agreed and said he will coordinate with Santa Monica P.D. We got the man's identification and the name of the shooting victim, his estranged wife, and gave it to him for Santa Monica.

When we sat down to interview the man we introduced ourselves and told him we were recording the conversation. He didn't seem to care. He seemed more than anxious to tell his story.

As we were about to start the interview, Capt. Hankins knocked on the door. When I got to the door he told me quietly that Santa Monica did have a shooting about an hour ago, and the female victim is dead. When I got back into the room I signaled Howard that the story was true and the victim was dead.

We started the conversation with the shooter, Mr. Spindler, and asked why he had shot his wife. He proceeded to tell us they had been having trouble for some time and she finally left him. He began to get the feeling she was 'playing around' with a therapist or doctor in Santa Monica. He felt this guy was keeping her from getting back together with him. He'd followed her today and found she went to the doctor's office in Santa Monica.

That was too much for him. He decided to kill them both. He drove back to his house and got his gun from the bottom bureau drawer. He put the disassembled gun together and then went to buy some ammunition. He kept the gun disassembled because he didn't want any accidents at home. He went to the sporting goods store, bought a box of ammunition, went back to the car and drove back to Santa Monica to wait.

While he was waiting in the parking lot he loaded the gun. When his wife came from the building he confronted her and exchanged a few words, then shot her several times. He didn't feel he knew which doctor to kill so he left the area.

When he got to Beverly Hills he knew he had to pass the police department so he decided to turn himself in.

He identified the gun he had given Al as the weapon he had used to kill his wife.

We briefly recapped his story for verification, then obtained the information for the booking sheet. While he was being finger-printed two Santa Monica Detectives arrived and requested his release. Howard and I both tried to fill them in on what he had said but they didn't seem to want to have any of the details.

While they were handcuffing him, I went to get and package the tape for them. By the time I returned from the office they had left the building. Howard and I marked the tape for identification and booked it as evidence. It took only a few minutes to complete the arrest report.

It was too late to interview Howards' victim so he called her and reset the appointment before he drove me to Hollywood. We had an in depth conversation about the suspect, and Santa Monica's attitude, on the way. We had solved nothing by the time I got out at the Saratoga. At ten minutes to six we were ordering a drink at the piano bar and waiting for Ronnie to start playing.

"O.K. what's up? You look like you are about to split your sides holding in what ever it is". She asked with the assurance of a wife that knows her husband pretty well. She does as a matter of fact.

I quickly related the days activities up to the point of meeting with Capt. Smith.

"Well" she said, "whatever it was couldn't have been too bad or we wouldn't be sitting here".

"You're right. Beginning after our vacation I report for duty in the Detective Bureau, how about that?"

"Congratulations. We'll probably have to cut short our vaca-tion so you can get to work sooner", she said with a smiling, all knowing, smirk on her face.

"No, I've talked with Capt. Hankins and he isn't expecting me 'til after our vacation. I guess the assignment will be there when we get back".

"Great, then this is a night to celebrate. There may not be much of an opportunity to do this once you start working in the Bureau."

"It may have already started." I took about ten minutes to fill her in on the homicide arrest and the surrounding circumstances.

"You better hope they are all that easy", she said.

As our drinks were served, we settled back for some outstanding piano playing, excellent food, and some time to share special moments. After we'd listened to some great music, we moved to a booth and enjoyed a leisurely steak. If it got better than this, I don't know if I could take it.

Some months later Howard and I were subpoenaed to testify at the trial of Mr. Spindler. When we arrived at the Santa Monica Courthouse we found that Spindler had been charged with second degree murder. We tried to talk to the Deputy District Attorney before the trial began but he was "very busy." During the lunch break we asked him why the charge was second degree. He told us they didn't have any evidence of premeditation. The shock waves set in.

We set about explaining about the taped confession we had and how Spindler had taken the time to go home, get his gun, put it together, went to the sporting goods store and bought ammunition, drove back to the Doctors' office, sat in the parking lot and loaded the gun, then confronted her and shot and killed her. I then handed him the tape, sealed, and initialed.

The Deputy D.A. looked ashen. He stammered for a few seconds then asked "Why didn't the Santa Monica Detectives have this?" We explained what had happened and he immediately headed for the conference room calling the Santa Monica Detectives to follow him. They emerged a few minutes later with the DDA looking like his face was on fire. The Detectives approached us and asked,

"Why didn't you tell us you had this tape?"

"We did" Howard said, "But you guys were too damned busy rushing off with the prisoner. Bob had even packed and initialed the tape for you but you left before he could give it to you."

"Well, it's too late now," said one of them. The D.A. says we have to go with the second degree charge now that the trial is almost over."

Howard and I went into the courtroom and got the Deputy District Attorneys permission to leave as he would not need our testimony any more. We left the building shaking our heads.

We were later told that the subject had been found guilty of second degree murder but sentencing was postponed. We were never advised of the final results.

CHAPTER 12

"Well, how was the vacation . . . Detective? All refreshed and ready for duty are you? Have a seat."

"Yes Captain, ready to go. I didn't know exactly what time to report so I came in at seven-thirty if that's O.K."

"Yeah, that's fine. we have a saying around here, if you come in after seven-thirty or leave before five we will presume you have resigned. It's said in jest but that's pretty much the way things work around here."

"We have a relatively small Detective unit so there are no specialists. Everybody works everything as it comes along. Of course certain people are responsible for certain categories of cases so there is some accountability."

"Bill Valentine works robbery and checks with Moe. Britton is responsible for juvenile but helps out in other things. Polakov has burglary and theft with Bolander helping him. Lt. Cork supervises all categories and pitches in whenever any unit needs help. That way every one in the Division is kept up on everything that is going on. It seems to make for more well rounded investigators. It defeats that old excuse "the right hand doesn't know what the left hand is doing". It wasn't designed that way, it just works out that way because we are so small."

"When anyone is working weekends or nights they are up to date on all the cases and don't have to say call back tomorrow, I don't know anything about it. It makes a better impression on our citizens. When people call the police department they expect answers not delays, and being shunted around waiting for someone to answer their questions."

"You'll start out with Wednesday and Thursday off and work

weekends with Valentine. You'll have to work on your windowsmash case whenever you have any free time. You have to stick pretty close to town when you're working weekends because there are all kinds of calls that require a detective. You'll get the hang of it pretty quickly. A lot of reports we handle should and could be handled by the patrol officers but we just seem to handle all the preliminary investigation reports. It makes for a heavier work load but that's the way it is."

"Well Captain, what happens when no detective is available?"

"Patrol makes the preliminary report but we make a quick follow-up the next day. The case is assigned to a detective working that category the next day and he usually makes the follow-up. We try to get a finished follow-up report submitted within three days.

"Working weekends you will probably be going to court on your days off. As you know there is no such thing as paid overtime. We handle court time the same as when you were in patrol. $20.00 for up to the first three hours. After that you're on regular hourly pay. You get lucky sometimes if the case is continued shortly after you show up. You still get the $20.00. Of course, more often than not, you wait around for half a day and then it's continued.

By the time you put in 4 to 5 hours you are losing money at regular pay. They say it evens out over time but it just doesn't seem that way. We get very few 'special jobs', like premiers or parties. Most of those jobs call for uniforms."

"When plain clothes are asked for, we rotate so that everyone in the Bureau gets a chance. Pay rules are the same as court pay. You can see if you do catch a special job, you hope it's a short one. If you have any other questions, ask anyone. Find the corner of a desk to work on and get together with Sgt. Valentine. It's good to have you aboard".

Going from Capt. Hankins office into the general work area of the Detective Bureau was an entirely different feeling that day than it'd been for the past several months. Then, I was an interloper. Now I worked there. What gut busting pride can come from such a small occurrence.

Imagine, a detective in one of the prestige police departments in the country. It can't get much better than that. The room didn't seem so drab and cramped anymore. After a few hellos and handshakes I found a seat next to Valentine's desk located against the back wall, and sat down.

"The Capt. tells me I will be working weekends with you, Sgt."

"Yeah, don't worry about it, we can handle it." He said as he picked up the phone and started to dial. Bill was a heavy featured man with a gruff manner. His husky build and height was disguised by his stooped shoulders and leaned forward gait when he walked. His slump made it appear that his suit didn't quite fit. His eyes, however, were quick and sharp belying the general appearance of inattention or carelessness.

His voice on the phone was loud and brusque, imparting a no nonsense approach to whatever subject he was addressing. You began to get the feeling that even if he didn't know what he was talking about he would have you convinced he did if you let him talk long enough.

Cork motioned me to follow him into the hallway. "Let's go get a cup of coffee and a bagel. I want to talk to you about your windowsmasher"

We walked down the stairs and out the side door and started walking toward the drug store and coffee shop at Canon and So. Santa Monica Blvd. It was one of those glorious southern California mornings when the sun was shining and the air was clear and just the right temperature. It just keeps getting better.

"Where do you stand with this guy? Are you any closer to wrapping him up?"

"Yeah, I think so. I got some of his creditors off of his 510 and started with them. He had some pretty miserable credit until shortly after the burglaries started, then his payments started picking up. Some of his accounts were paid off in full shortly after some of the jobs. I got his bank info from his credit report. His bank records show a definite pattern of rather hefty cash deposits within a few days after most of the smashes. He doesn't have a regular job so he's not getting any salary to account for the money and not many jobs would pay the kind of money he's depositing."

"I asked L.A. Burglary/Auto to get a recovery record on Corvettes recovered since the burglaries started. If I get a pattern on the area of recoveries I'll start looking in that area and see if I can put him there for some reason. Maybe he dumps the cars in the area where he has a cool pad or stash pad. He's about due to hit again so I'm trying to work out a stake out plan and see if the Capt. will authorize some manpower for a couple of nights."

By that time we had ensconced ourselves on a couple of counter stools and put in our order. This little drug store was a bonanza for someone who liked to watch people. Business executives, bank employees, lawyers, secretaries, actors and actresses and would be's and wanta be's. And a lot of won't ever be's.

They all passed through the door making those last minute or just remembered purchases that are mandatory to make their day a success or at least bearable. Some with the obvious painted on pleasantness that covers deep sadness.

Some looking detached, with thoughts a thousand miles away only to be returned to reality when the cashier announces the price of the item for a second or third time.

Spaced among them was the truly enthusiastic, bright-eyed dreamers with the whole world ahead of them and the sure knowledge that nothing can defeat them if they try hard enough.

"How much manpower are you going to need and for how long?"

"I figure myself and at least two others. Three would be better but I know we don't have many people to spare," I answered as I took my last bite of bagel and cream cheese. Was it my imagination or did everything just taste better that morning?

"Where would you put them?"

"Well there haven't been any repeat hits on any of the fur stores so there are only five left in town that haven't been hit yet. Two of those can be covered from one spot. I figure that any we can't cover we can ask the owner to cut back on his in window display for a couple of nights just to reduce temptation. If one of them put too many furs in the window it would look like a baited trap so we'll just let them keep the normal stock in the windows. We can work it so we have three likely targets. I would like to stake out the store at Linden and Wilshire, the one on Bedford just north of Wilshire and the one in the 400 block of Rodeo.

They all have good concealment points fairly close to them and I just have a feeling our guy cruises the area just shortly before he hits. If he does, it would give any stake out time to get prepared."

"Sounds O.K. When would you want to set it up?"

We paid our bill and stood on the corner for a few minutes looking around. I understood more every day what Capt. Smith meant when he said "observation pays dividends." I was beginning to realize just how much I didn't see before I became a policeman. I could walk by a bank or jewelry store and never think about the person standing at the curb near the entrance looking around. Never glancing in to see what's going on inside. Never look for a running car parked at the curb a short distance from the entrance. Or pay any particular attention to an individual who was looking too intently into parked cars, especially luxury cars.

You begin to realize that instinct was largely the exercise of good training, observing your surroundings, and processing that information logically.

Trying to be aware of everything that was going on around you seemed overwhelming initially. Then you realized that when you sped up your thought processes to equal what your eyes were seeing it got a little easier. It went in fits and spurts at first. Visual shorthand.

Then slowly, after repeated honing, it started to happen naturally, without effort. You begin to have fewer and fewer times when you drew blanks. You don't find it necessary to jerk yourself back to alertness. Alert becomes a common state of mind. Before long you don't even notice that "Alert" is a primary part of your existence.

After a few moments observation time we crossed Canon and strolled back to City Hall.

"I'll talk with Hankins and see if we can find the manpower to try a stakeout. When do you want to begin?"

"I figure on Tuesday, Wednesday or Thursday night. He's never hit on the weekend and only twice on Monday night so we stand a better chance during the week. If he doesn't hit this week we have a real good shot at next week. It's been a pretty long dry spell for him."

"O.K. get your plans together and we'll see about it. By the way, tonight most of us from the Bureau will be going over to Frascati for a happy hour. It's really a wetting down for a new guy in the Division. Give you a chance to buy the old timers a toddy or two by way of introduction. Any problem with that?"

"No, no problem at all."

On the surface that is. From what I had gathered by going around to other departments I would presume this was my time to be looked over by my own department. I guessed the same ground rules would apply here as with the other departments. Answer questions briefly, listen well and don't volunteer anything.

It was going to be a little different here though. There'll be liquor involved. Now the first priority would be to figure out what the pattern would be. How subtle would the encouragement be to "have another drink". We'd find out in a few hours. That was going to be an interesting evening.

Les Britton was coming out of the Bureau as we approached the door. He waved for me to follow him as he started down the stairs. As we were getting into the car he said,

"We got a call from the Gramaphone Shop on Beverly Drive about some guy in there trying to buy some records with an account closed check. They're stalling him waiting for us. He's described as a white male about 25, 6 feet and about 180. Grey slacks, white shirt and blue sweater. Hell, look at the traffic. We probably should have walked over. We may just have to double park when we get there."

As we turned onto Beverly we pulled into the red zone across from the Gramaphone Shop. We crossed the street as a clerk from the store was standing in the window pointing at a man just leaving the store. He had a package under his arm and was heading south on Beverly Dr. Les and I quickly caught up to the man and took up a walking position on each side and slightly to his rear.

As we approached an open area in the pedestrian traffic and near a recessed doorway Les said,

"Excuse me sir, may I talk with you for a moment. We're police officers . . ."

His head turned toward Les and at the same time he reached toward his back and under his sweater with his right hand. As I grabbed his right arm at the elbow and the wrist, his head turned toward me just as Les grabbed his left arm and executed a leg sweep with his left leg, taking both legs from under our suspect and sending him face down on the sidewalk.

Both of us were holding onto his arms so his meeting with the sidewalk was relatively soft. With little trouble he was quickly handcuffed. As we stood him on his feet we saw we had attracted a small crowd. Reaching under the right side of his sweater I removed a bone handled, 6 inch bladed, hunting knife from a sheath stuffed inside his trousers.

Having gotten his wind back he started protesting such treatment.

"You're under arrest for suspicion of issuing bad checks and carrying a concealed weapon." Les advised as we started back to the Gramaphone Shop.

Once inside, the owner presented the check our suspect had given him. By now our suspect had gotten his second wind and was really telling all that would listen what a big mistake had been made. That he had just picked up the wrong checkbook when he left home this morning and that it was a simple mistake. It could happen to anyone.

"The bank says the account has been closed for three months" Mr. Simonson said. "They say they have been returning checks on this account daily. They estimate about three thousand dollars worth by now".

We returned the four records the guy had bought with the bum check and thanked Mr. Simonson for his help. His smile diminishes somewhat when we told him he will have to appear in court when our suspect makes his appearance.

On our way back to the office we were treated to a tirade of reasons that this terrible error has occurred, including but not limited to, our misguided behavior. By the time he was booked in and Valentine had begun to question him, we were about to hang our heads for our shameless conduct. Going down on the elevator Les said "God, let that guy go on long enough and he'll have you believing you wrote the damned checks".

As we were turning in the completed arrest report, Valentine came down from the jail. He told us that our man had admitted writing a large number of bad checks for several months but insisted that the bank was at fault. They had failed to recall all the extra checks they had given him when he opened the account. He had merely lost track of his balance. He couldn't explain why he hadn't stopped writing checks when he was notified that the account was closed.

We told Val that we had run a record check on the guy for the arrest report and it came back with four prior arrests. He also had two convictions for checks and fraud in the past six years and was still on parole from his last conviction.

"It's getting so you just can't rely on anyones word. Sorta destroys your faith in mankind", Val laughingly replied as he handed the jail keys to the dispatcher and we headed back into the Bureau.

Shortly after five we were threading our way through the stopped traffic on S. Santa Monica Blvd. towards Frascati. Cork, Polakov, Valentine, Bolander, Britton and I. As we entered the bar area I excused myself and headed for the men's room. I caught a waiters eye and fortified myself with four pats of creamery butter. This was one test I was not going to blow. Joining my companions I found that the first round had been on me.

And so it went for a couple of hours. The buying honors going around the table of course. And each in his turn, without being to obvious about it, had elicited some morsel of information from me about my family, my background and my philosophy of law enforcement. I demonstrated what I thought was just the right amount of reluctance about answering too many questions. The drinks were starting to show on some of the celebrants.

Either the butter is working well or the waitress had caught on and is weaning the liquor in my drinks. Whatever it was, the evening seemed to be going quite well. Without any discernible signal the happy hour had been called to a halt. Everyone was downing their last drink and heading for the door. All in all it was a pleasant experience. Certainly not the adversarial confrontation your imagination could conjure up if it ran away with you.

Stopping by the desk to catch a ride home, I picked up a message from LA Auto that they had the info I requested and please return their call tomorrow. There goes another day off.

As I climbed the stairs to the chauffeur's house we were occupying on Mr. Campbell's estate, Diana opened the door saying,

"So, you got through your initiation O.K. How was it?"

"Not bad at all. Why don't we go somewhere for dinner?"

"That sounds good, I haven't started anything yet. Where do you want to go?"

"What about Whittinghills, we haven't been there for a while."

"It couldn't be that you want to see if Julie London is going to be there".

"Who, me? You know how I like to listen to Bobby Troup. If she happens to be there it's an added incentive. Besides that, they have good food. Let me change my shirt and we can get going."

We drove over Coldwater Canyon to Ventura Blvd. and to a comfortable, friendly, eatery, with a make you feel at home atmosphere. The owner, Dick Whittinghill, was a very popular disk jockey with radio station KMPC.

During a perfectly cooked and served dinner of prime rib, I recounted the days activities for her.

"Sounds like you enjoyed yourself"

"Yeah, I guess I have to admit that. By the way I have to go in tomorrow and do some work on the smash and grab. L.A. got me some info on Corvette recoveries I need to correlate. I've got to see if I can fit any pattern of the car thefts, recoveries and burglaries together. If I get a chance I'll come by your office and we can maybe go to lunch together".

"O.K. that's fine. Just remember to try to take some time off in the next couple of days. I guess we aren't going to hear Julie or Bobby tonight."

"Hell, I forgot, it's Monday night. They're hardly ever here on Monday. Lets go."

The drive back over the hill and the lights of L.A. stretched out in front of us capped off an excellent day and evening.

CHAPTER 13

"What are you doing here today, I thought you were off?" Howard asked as I sat down at an empty desk and reached for the phone.

"I am, but I have to get some info from L.A. that I ask them to look up for me. I don't want them to think I didn't need it by making them wait for my return call. Besides, the captain said I'd have to work on this case in my spare time."

I finally got through to Hayes and after exchanging a few remarks he started to read off the dates and locations I had asked him to look up for me. A few minutes later I had the dates and locations of 24 stolen and recovered Corvettes in the past six months. I thanked him profusely, hung up, and began to sort out the dates and locations I had just written down.

I determined that I was going to need a large surface to lay out all the paper I'd be working on. I got my notes and files gathered up just as the other detectives came in the office and spread out to their assigned desks. I got the captain's permission to use the small conference/interrogation room next to his office.

It was a room just a little too big for a one man office and too small for two. There must be a reason no one used it for an office but I didn't know what it was. Yet.

First, date & location of Corvette thefts. Second, date of windowsmash occurring shortly after theft. Third, location and date of auto recovery. Combine this information with the dates of suspects cash deposits. It became pretty obvious that not all the car thefts are associated with the windowsmashes. That was to be expected. Certainly this suspect couldn't be the only Corvette thief in the L.A. area.

It was pretty well known that many in the boating community were swapping their inboard engines for the much hotter

Corvette engines. It was also well known that the origin of the engine was not of great concern. Many Corvettes were recovered as a pile of melted fiberglass without engines. Didn't take a great thinker to figure what was happening to the engines.

A pretty strong pattern was beginning to emerge as Cork came in the room and sat down across the table.

"The Captain has approved your stake out for Tuesday and Wednesday of next week. It'll be you, one other Detective and a volunteer from Patrol. See if you can dig up a volunteer from the midnight shift then clear it with the Watch Commander. How are you coming with your chart coordination?"

"Well it's coming out better than I thought. I've been able to tie in 16 of the car thefts to 16 of the windowsmashes."

"The cars were stolen just one day before the smash and recovered a couple of days afterwards. They were stolen from a pretty large, general area. Eleven of them were recovered within an eight block area of that huge apartment house complex at Jefferson and LaCienega. Five other of the stolen Corvettes were recovered just a few blocks outside that general area. It's interesting that this location is on a direct route toward Westchester. If I were a jumping to conclusions type of person I'd conclude that our man is heading for home after one of his jobs."

"Yeah, that does start to tie a lot of threads together"

"Sure, but there is one thing that still nags at the back of my mind. If I let it sneak through too often, I start to shudder. I REALLY don't have anything solid to tie this guy to any of the windowsmashes, or the car thefts. I've certainly got a lot of coincidences. And they tie in pretty well with my gut feeling."

"I sometimes get to wondering if I'm trying to find ways of supporting my theory. Or if my findings are holding water because I may be bending or twisting them a little. I still don't have anything to put him in the fur stores or in any of the stolen cars".

"That's right, but if we don't keep wondering about such things there wouldn't be any checks or balances in our system. Questioning yourself helps keep your perspective. It keeps us from rushing into situations that are not supported by good background work and solid techniques."

"I guess when you're on patrol you play your `what if' mind games to keep yourself prepared for any eventuality. In here you do it to find where the holes are in your case. Where the weaknesses lie. Just a wider variety of `what if's' than in the patrol car."

"Yeah, they never end." As he got up to leave, "Don't forget to see the midnight Watch Commander for your volunteer".

If I got a move on I could make it to Glendale in time to take Diana to lunch. I gave her a call first to make sure she waited a little while. By the time I finished making arrangements to meet her, half the guys in her office had invited themselves along. That's fine. She has the good fortune to work with a great bunch of people.

Working for Stout Motors she was working for one of the oldest trailer and mobile home dealers in the L.A. area. The sales and maintenance people were there because they wanted to work for a company with a good reputation.

You wouldn't think this was a multi- million dollar operation from the way the employees treated each other. This was the near perfect example of a 'family' operation. Before I married Diana I had to pass muster with Ray.

Ray Humphrey was the General Manager and father figure of the 'family'. On one of my visits to the office before our marriage, Ray managed to isolate me from the group and proceeded to conduct a "prospects" inquiry. When it had run it's course I got up from my chair and, flashing my biggest grin, I told him, "and I've got most of my teeth too."

When I walked back into the general office area most of the staff were sitting around like they had been waiting for school to let out. I must have passed, because shortly afterward, we were married.

After a good lunch at Casa Gonsales, across the street from Diana's office. I made my way back to the office and had time to make a few phone calls to my suspects creditors. It was time to pack it in for the day. As we were leaving the office, Valentine took a call from the Hilton Hotel.

Hotel security was reporting they had a couple of young men checked into the hotel using a stolen Carte Blanche credit card. It seemed they were running up some pretty considerable charges at the better shops in the hotel. The card had been reported stolen in Texas. As he hung up Bill said "Well you might as well get your feet wet and come along. Security said they are in their suite now and they are keeping a watch on them for us."

"Suite yet" I said as we were heading down the stairs.

"Why not" Bill answered, "it's not their money".

We took Santa Monica Blvd. and pulled in the back way to the hotel. Half way across the lobby we are met by Bill White, a retired Beverly Hills Police Captain, and now Chief of Security at the hotel.

"They're up in 808. The card is a definite stolen. They also have a Cadillac parked in the basement with Texas plates. They are registered as Arnold and Karl Steiner. One of them's in a wheel chair".

"Wheel chair! For Christ's sake, what's the criminal world coming to?" Bill replied as we looked over the register and sales receipts held at the desk to be charged to the suspects rooms.

Judging from the charges they had made at the restaurants and gift shops they were living very high on the hog. That much activity on a credit card would draw attention even if it wasn't stolen.

"They certainly aren't trying to keep a low profile. A Texas Cadillac, a suite, a wheel chair, and spending like they were going to jail, which they are. It seems like they are looking to get caught. 'Course, the wheel chair could be a cover of some kind."

"O.K." says Bill, "what's the layout of this suite". The desk clerk brought out a room diagram and laid it on the counter. The suite consisted of a large sitting room with an adjoining bedroom, one half bath just inside the main door to the left, and a full bath off the bedroom, which is to the left past the half bath door. The diagram indicated there was a large balcony off of each room. There was also a door leading to the hallway from the bedroom.

"Bring your pass key and lets go do it". He said as Bill lead the way to the elevators.

"My man is in a room down the hall. We can get him on our way" said White. Hotel security was not armed so they would be stationed at the second door to prevent anyone from leaving and keep out of the line of any possible gunfire. As we exited the elevator on the eighth floor White's man came out of his room and met us. "They're still in there", he said.

Without instruction, White handed the passkey to Bill and he and his partner stationed themselves on each side of the bedroom door. Bill silently slipped the passkey into the lock and turned it. The door opened about three inches and was stopped by the night chain. Instantly, we both hit the door with our shoulders and the chain parted with a loud snap.

As we charged into the room with our guns drawn we saw our wheelchair man turning toward us from the open balcony door. As Bill was shouting "Police Officers, Don't Move" he was heading toward the wheel chair. I looked to the left as I got past the half bath and saw a young man standing in the doorway to the bedroom.

He was attempting to pull his right hand out of his right front pants pocket but was having great difficulty due to the extremely tight pants. As I ran toward him I could see the outline of a gun in the pocket but he couldn't get it out with his hand around the butt.

For an instant the story of how some Pacific Island natives trap monkeys by placing food inside a coconut with a small hole in the top and tie the coconut to a tree. When the monkey reaches in to get the food he clasps his hand around it and is too greedy to let go, and with the food in his hand it's too large to extract from the hole and he is captured.

It was hard to realize that so much can run through your mind in the short time it takes to cover about 15 feet in a hurry.

He was still trying to pull the gun from his pocket as I reached him and he started to retreat into the bedroom. His left hand started to come around in a full swing as I raised my gun across my chest to my left side and come down with a slashing left to right swing. My gun barrel crashed down on his right arm just above the wrist. The sound of my gun connecting with his wrist was almost as sickening as the screeching howl he let out. His hand came out of his pocket, empty, as he fell back on the bed. He'd lost his combative mood and I rolled him over and applied the handcuffs. Not without some degree of wailing about the pain in his arm.

When I rolled him back over I reached into his trousers pocket with two fingers, because that's all that would fit, and pulled out a chrome plated, plastic handled, .25 caliber automatic. Fully loaded. Bill was standing in the doorway as I unloaded the gun and ejected the round from the chamber.

"God Bob, you'd think these guys were serious about hurting someone the way they act. Bring him in here with his buddy."

As we headed for the living room White and his partner come into the room. The wheel chair suspect was sitting with his head down and handcuffed to the chair. I seated my suspect in a straight back chair facing the window. He was still complaining loudly about his "broken arm". Hell I didn't hit him that hard. I didn't think.

We found the stolen credit card in the wallet of our wheel chair man and other identification in the name of the credit card victim. A quick search of the room turned up several brand new credit card purchases from some very exclusive shops in town. They're not yet taken out of the store bags or boxes. It certainly wouldn't be hard to find out where they had been using the card.

White and his partner quickly packed the newly purchased suitcases as we stacked up the obvious recent purchases. We had to call a patrol unit to assist in transporting the suspects and the property to the office. Before leaving the hotel we located and searched the Texas Cadillac. It was determined to be a rental from

San Antonio, rented with the stolen credit card. We made arrangements with the hotel security for the car to be towed and impounded as we left to book our suspects and inventory the property.

After the booking process, Val and I took both subjects into the interrogation room. Tight pants was still complaining vociferously about his "broken arm". In response to our phone call Dr. Laurion assured us he would come by the jail shortly and give our man an examination.

After a few minutes of verbal sparring the suspects insisted on disclaiming any knowledge of a stolen credit card, any forgeries, and any stolen car. Tight pants even denied I took a gun from his pocket. He said I broke his arm just to set him up for the gun charge.

By now it was eight P.M. and they had succeeded in bringing us to the brink of outright anger. Bill and I conferred and decided to put them in separate cells until morning and start fresh then. When we advised them of our intent they both become quite agitated and started asking that we sit down and talk a while. When we were convinced they were serious about really conversing, we settled in for some prolonged conversation.

By 11 o'clock we had learned they were really brothers named Robert and William Steifer. Both were ex-cons recently released from Texas prisons. The credit card they were using was stolen from a man in a bar in Fort Worth. They used the credit card to purchase the gun in an Arizona gun store. For their full cooperation they requested that they not be returned to Texas for prosecution.

William claimed he would be killed if he returned to Huntsville prison. He stated that he was in a wheel chair from a beating he received while in Huntsville. They both said that they feared for their lives if returned to Texas. The Texas Rangers did not like them.

We said we would have to determine just what charges were pending in Texas before we could give them any definite information. We left it at that as we placed them in a cell and turned in our arrest report.

As we were leaving the building to go home, Bill advised me that he would not be in the next day so I would have to handle getting the complaint from the D.A. and making the necessary phone calls to Texas. And so went another day off.

CHAPTER 14

After filling the Captain in on the prior evenings activities, I spent the next couple of hours finding out just where our suspects stood with Texas. Texas advised me that if we were going to prosecute in California they would waive their charges in favor of our cases. Now at least I had a basis for making some commitment to our defendants.

I discussed with Howard the advisability of contacting the FBI and inquiring about prosecution for Interstate Transportation of a Stolen Motor Vehicle. He suggested that I call Special Agent Pete Meaney of the Santa Monica office.

Both Howard and I were well aware of the animosity that existed between our Chief and the FBI. When the Chief had attended the FBI Academy, he'd tangled with J. Edgar Hoover face to face, and lost. I could imagine both of those monumental egos clashing. But then again, it was pretty obvious that some of the Bureaus policies created very strained relationships between the FBI and local law enforcement.

I contacted Pete Meaney and after introducing myself, filled him in on the situation at hand. We agreed he would come by the P.D. and we would re-interview our suspects. I then contacted Bill Ritzi, Asst. District Attorney in Charge of the Santa Monica Office and brought him up to date on the case to that point. Now if Pete and I and the U.S. Attorney could agree, I would be able to talk with the Steifers and lay out our course of action.

By one PM, Pete and I were sitting in Biff's having lunch and discussing our alternatives. It was pretty obvious Pete was not your typical FBI agent. None of the stiff formal approach and certainly none of the holier than thou attitude. Pete is soft spoken and friendly.

He exhibits a real interest in helping me accomplish my purpose as well as fulfilling the FBI mission.

I told Pete that the Steifers had agreed to plead guilty to Interstate Transportation in Federal Court and two forgery of credit card charges in local court, if they can go to Federal Prison rather than return to Texas. Pete said he will have to contact the U.S. Attorney after we talk to the Steifers but it seemed like a workable solution.

After lunch we returned to the P.D. and interviewed the brothers again. Pete made the necessary calls to complete the Federal end and I again talked with Bill Ritzi to formalize our case. We both returned to the Steifers and finalized the agreement.

They would plead guilty to the local charges, be turned over to the Feds to plead guilty to the federal charge. They will serve their time, 3 to 5 years, concurrently with local charges, in the Federal Pen at Terminal Island.

They were very pleased that they wouldn't be going back to Texas and requested we expedite the paperwork so they could begin serving their time. City and County jail time awaiting trial or hearings is usually "dead time" which doesn't count toward their sentence.

Pete and I shook hands on the first of our many future undertakings and headed for our respective offices to put together the paperwork for submission. All in all everything had worked out pretty well. We had our cases cleared and the property recovered. A plea bargain that will eliminate unnecessary court time. The Feds get to open and close a case on the same day with a conviction. And the crooks get something out of it too. They don't have to return to Texas. Whatever happened to them down there certainly made believers out of them.

While I was finishing my complaint request, Cork told me that I had only gotten one volunteer for the fur store stakeout the next week. I'd have to decide which of the three stores I wanted to leave off of the list. I told him I'd get back to him.

Jack Thomas from Patrol had volunteered for the job and I was just not as comfortable with that as I would have liked. Jack had a reputation for inattention and imbibing a little to heavily. I suppose I should have been thankful for any help considering how boring and uneventful stakeouts usually are. I'd have to give some deep thought to which stores to cover.

By quitting time all the necessary paperwork was done on the Steifers, and I'd decided on the fur store at Linden and Wilshire and the one in the 400 block of North Rodeo to be staked out.

By Tuesday I'd worked out the details of the stakeout with the midnight Watch Commander. Shortly after midnight Jack and I and our shotguns were dropped off at our pre- arranged locations. Mine was the lobby of an office building on the south side of Wilshire across the street from the store. Jack's was a parking garage under construction at the southwest corner of Rodeo and Brighton.

With a small thermos of coffee, the night began. Before too long the boredom started to set in. The "what if" thing started again. What If he came from this direction, or that direction? What If a car came from the other direction just as you started to cross the street? Mentally plan for each "What If".

Have you considered all the "What If's?" What if he doesn't stop when you challenge him? What If the shotgun misfires?. On and on. Finally you just settle into alert boredom.

Which cars had passed before? Does your guy cruise the area with a different car before he uses the Corvette? And so it goes. Minute after minute, hour after hour.

By five or five-thirty in the morning your eyelids start to weigh a ton. Shake your head, walk around.

At six-fifteen Sergeant Grey stopped in front of my position and motioned me out. At least he was only 15 minutes late. We were scheduled to call it off at six AM. After locking up the lobby I got into the car, placing the shotgun on the back seat.

"Boy that was a long night" I said as I settled into the passenger seat.

"Yeah I bet it was. Why did you stay out after the guy hit.?"

He said with just a small hint of snideness in his voice.

"What the hell do you mean?" I was wide awake then not really wanting to hear his reply.

"Hell, he hit the store on Rodeo at quarter to four. I don't know what happened to Thomas, he got off only one shot and the guy got away with three furs. He went north on Rodeo and turned east on Santa Monica Blvd. Nobody saw him after that."

"Is Thomas at the office?"

"No, he left about five o'clock".

"Why the hell didn't someone come and get me after the guy hit? He sure as hell wasn't going to hit again tonight".

We pulled into the ramp and I bolted up the stairs, shotgun in hand. While I was putting the shotgun away in the Watch Commanders Office, Lt. Colford came in and sat down.

"Lt. what happened? We couldn't get much luckier." Fred Colford was one of your more relaxed people. He seemed to take everything in stride without getting heated up in any instance.

"I don't really know Downey. I have my suspicions though. When we brought Thomas in he smelled like he had had quite a few. I couldn't tell if it was fresh or just residual. My personal theory is that he fell asleep and woke up when the guy hit the window. He got out in the open with just enough time to get off a shot as the guy was driving away. I ask him how the guy busted the window and he said he didn't see it. Claimed he was coming out of the garage when the window was broken.

We found the shotgun wadding right in the intersection so he didn't get very far out of the garage before he shot. Stands to reason if he had seen the guy driving up he could have gotten a lot closer before he had to shoot. We won't get any more chances like that."

"That's for damn sure. By the way, why did it take so damn long to come and pick me up?. Surely we weren't waiting for him to hit again tonight?"

"I don't know. I told the Sergeant to pick you up about five o'clock. I thought you had been picked up and gone home. I guess

I should have known better when your shotgun hadn't been turned in. I'll ask him when he comes in for shift change."

"Don't bother. Seeing who it is, it's not hard to figure what happened. We have no great love for each other and he had his chance to demonstrate that. Next time, my turn".

By the time I got home I'd cooled down some. Talking with Diana before she went to work and I went to bed gave me time to realize I was ready for a few hours sleep. Working a beat car at least gives you a change of scenery and activity. Stakeouts are a test of patience and perseverance.

At one o'clock McHuin and I were enroute to the apartment house area at Jefferson and LaCienega. I needed to test my theory that our man must have a cool pad or stash pad in the area. I don't really understand what McHuin was doing at the station so early that day. He was not due to work 'til midnight. I don't understand all I know about him. Whatever his reasons, he was always willing to help.

Block after block of apartment houses was going to take a while to cover. We each took a map and each picked a block to start with. We agreed to return to the car after each block to compare notes. We also started out with a recent mug shot of our man and began contacting apartment house managers.

We'd marked our map with the locations of the recovered Corvettes. We picked what is the apparent center of the recoveries and worked out from there.

When we met back at the car the first time we'd had no luck. We'd each had one apartment house where the manager wasn't home. Starting our list of must return addresses. We started out on another block.

By the time we returned to the car the second time we each had located one apartment house where our guy had lived in the past couple of years. Nothing recent enough to explain why he was dropping his cars in this area after his jobs. By five-thirty in the evening we had located another place he'd lived more recently. Still no indication where he might be holed up now. Enough for today. I'd get back on it next week.

Funny how none of these addresses where he'd lived appeared anywhere in his credit record or applications. He'd managed to keep a pretty low profile for some reason, even before the windowsmashes started. Back at the office it dawned on me to check the dates of his staying in the apartment house area with the dates he was suspected of stealing all those Corvettes before he got into the fur and jewelry business. I'll have to check with Hayes and Carpenter and see how those dates line up.

By the time I had gotten home Diana had a salad on the table and a steak in the broiler. She told me Mr.Campbell called and asked if I would come over to the main house when I got home.

As I approached the back door, Miss Lee, the housekeeper, opened the door. Inviting me in, she said, "He's in his bedroom. I'll be taking in his dinner shortly".

"Thanks Miss Lee. I won't stay long." I walked through the house to his bedroom. He was getting along in years and spent a good deal of time in his bedroom. He called for me to come in, in response to my knock. After exchanging a few pleasantries he asked if I could repair the dripping faucet in his bathroom. He escorted me into the bathroom and pointed out the faulty faucet.

The house, having been built in the 20's, was fitted with some unusual and unique fixtures. I told him I'd give it a try and left to get my tools. When I returned, a giant stroke of luck made the faucet repair routine. I made a right guess at un-screwing a part that didn't look like it came apart.

My luck didn't hurt my credibility with Mr. Campbell.

Before I left he had asked me to take on a couple of other maintenance chores at my convenience. Rehang a wooden gate and run a call buzzer from his room to the housekeepers quarters. We settled on a time for these projects and I went home and settled down to my steak and good company.

Being able to perform a service or two for Mr. Campbell gave me the feeling that I may in some small way be repaying him for his continued hospitality. He certainly was not a demanding landlord. Whoever coined the word "gentleman" most certainly had Mr. Campbell in mind.

Having put away a generous portion of sirloin steak and an outstanding salad we settled back on the couch for an evening of "Dragnet" and "Wagon Train". Every time I see Wagon Train I'm reminded of running into Ward Bond and his wife on a vacant lot at the top of Trousdale Estates, watching the Benedict Canyon fire roaring up the canyon.

Earlier in the evening I had begun to chase a car along a dirt road at the ridge on top of Trousdale Estates. Very shortly after leaving the paved road, flames began to leap from under the hood of my car. As I had jumped out of the car and started around the open door I lost my footing and rolled about 30 feet down the embankment. I scrambled back up, raised the hood and threw dirt on the engine to put out the fire. I radioed the Sergeant and he came and pushed my car back onto the paved road. With Sgt. Pierce breaking the way for me I managed to coast my car all the way to the traffic circle behind the Police Station.

I picked up another car and went home to change clothes and patch up some minor cuts and scrapes. When I returned to the Trousdale area, I pulled onto the vacant lot at the top to take stock of the progress of the fire. When I pulled onto the lot my lights picked up the Bonds standing near the edge of the lot. I parked my car and walked to the edge of the lot standing beside them and watching the fire glow further and further up the canyon. Mr. Bond asked me how the officer was who had fallen down the embankment a short while before. I told him that had been me and we both chuckled a little. He then said he had wanted to see how I had managed to keep my hat on. He said he had seen many movie fights and falls where the hero never lost his hat and didn't think it was realistic. Now he realized it could be done. Until that time I hadn't thought about it but he was right. My hat hadn't come off. How did that happen?.

A few minutes later I departed the area with the warm feeling that I had just met two very nice people.

About time the muscles start to relax and the brain begins to sag, the telephone rang. Cork was on the other end warning me that the first thing tomorrow morning I was set to interview Colonel Tom Parker, Elvis Presleys' manager, up on Maple Drive. It seemed he had returned home a couple of hours before and found his house burglarized. To put it mildly, he was quite upset and ready to bust a seam.

Well, so much for a relaxed evening. My follow-up appointment is for eight A.M. At least I'd have time to read the primary report. I was to take someone from the I.D. section with me to do the crime scene search for prints and such. Between 5,000 and 10,000 dollars worth of property is missing. Colonel Parker would have a partial list ready for me. Well, at least I wouldn't be looking for something to do in the morning. Not that any Detective ever has to look very far.

After spending half the night looking at the ceiling, I called for my ride at 6:45. By 7:30 I'd read the preliminary report, twice, reviewed the patrol activity log and the evenings teletypes. Since coming into the Bureau I had been delegated the duty of reading the previous days teletypes, separating them by crime category, and distributing them to the detectives handling that category. It kept me abreast of what was going on in the surrounding cities and who has arrested who and for what. It's better than waiting for some phone calls that never come.

Some Departments, it seems, are reluctant, for whatever reasons, to call other departments and spread the word about their arrests and recoveries. I have never fully satisfied myself about the reasons, but considered many. I know there are personality clashes between officers but find it hard to believe they exist between whole departments.

By the time I gathered up Sam Bottleman from the I.D. Bureau and got to Colonel Parker's it was exactly eight. Colonel Parker met us at the door and the introductions were made.

He showed us to the patio door in the den where the apparent entry was made. Sam set about taking photos and dusting for prints while I discussed the missing property with the Colonel.

He was naturally quite upset about the burglary and the property that was missing. He was most upset however, by the fact that a set of seven handcarved tobacco pipes, in a padded presentation box, given to him by Elvis, are among the items that were missing.

He explained that while he certainly would miss the other items that are gone he would miss the pipes most. When Sam finished and I had gone over the list of missing property I assured him we would do our best to recover his property and find the burglar. Throughout our conversation he gave me the impression that he was a thoughtful, considerate person.

Back at the office I completed my follow- up report and composed the teletype of stolen property to be sent out that day. The entry had apparently been made using a small bladed screwdriver. A small piece of the blade had broken off and fell into the channel of the sliding glass door. It'd be useful if we can find the right screwdriver.

Sam told me he hadn't had much luck with prints at the point of entry or in the bedroom where most of the property was taken. I called West L.A., Hollywood, and West Hollywood detectives and advised them of the burglary and missing property just in case they turned up anything from any of their suspects or informants. When a thief takes off someone famous, or in the limelight, they often have a tendency to brag about it to their confidants.

Many a criminal solution turns on just such misplaced trust.

It was just about 11:30 when I finished the reports and got the teletype sent out. As I started back into the office Cork met me at the door and told me we were headed to Roseati's on Pico in West L.A. We were in for lunch and introduction to some of the West L.A. Detectives we work with. Up to now I've met only the people in Central Burglary, L.A.S.O. Burglary, and Hollywood burglary. West L.A. of course, has a large area demographicaly similar to Beverly Hills and is a magnet for a wide variety of criminals.

On the way, we again went over the guidelines for building a rapport with these people. It was even possible that I might be plied with alcoholic beverages to uncover possible character flaws.

When we arrived and walked in the door it was immediately apparent who and where the police were in that establishment. At the curved end of a fairly long bar on the right, were seated or standing six suited, serious looking, individuals that could not be mistaken for anything but cops. As we approached, Cork began the introductions.

"Guys, this is Bob Downey, Our newest addition to the Bureau"

I started down the gauntlet and met, Jack Hooper, John Eggenweiler, Andy Anderson, Frank Gravante, Buzz Donnell, and Little Andy Anderson.

As it turned out Eggenweiler was from Central Burglary.

Questions were coming from all directions as we slid up to an open space at the bar and ordered. Cork was deftly separated from my side as I started to answer some of the questions that are getting more and more specific. The more specific they got the shorter and less specific my answers became. After drinking two drinks, nursing another, and turning down three others, we all adjourned to a couple of tables put together near the rear of the room.

Almost suddenly the mood had changed to one of joviality. The questions had stopped and the subject had changed to everyday conversation. An excellent lunch was enjoyed with friendly, relaxed, conversation. We all pitched in for the bill and began to walk out the door when we were hit in the face by the bright glare of the afternoon sun. We said our good-byes as our eyes are adjusting.

Having watched all the martinis being consumed in the last hour and a half I'm everlastingly grateful I held my consumption to three drinks.

As Cork and I went back into the Bureau, Capt. Hankins called us into his office.

"There's a plainclothes special job tomorrow night at Bob Cummings house if you guys want it. They're holding a party to celebrate a new television series kickoff. Nothing to indicate any trouble is expected, just general security. Suit and tie. They'll have valet parking. Party starts at eight, they want you there at seven. Expected to last till about midnight. About 150 guests. What do you say?"

"Fine with me" Cork says, looking at me.

"Me too, I'll meet you here at seven PM."

We rode up to the party with the beat car. There would be too much traffic for parking our own car. We introduced ourselves to the host and made our obligatory initial inspection. By the time we had become familiar with the catering staff and household help, the guests had started to arrive. It was quite a turnout. Many of the acting and producing community had come. The party was a well orchestrated affair with a buffet and champagne. The required showing of the first episode of the new show was had and after numerous polite and enthusiastic comments the group started to break up and head for home. A very well managed gathering. No rowdiness. No drunks. No trouble. And we were back at the station by twelve-thirty AM. All in all, a very nice night.

While we were checking out Lt. Don Barnes told us about being notified that Lana Turner's daughter Cheryl, had escaped from El Retiro school. She had been placed there by the court after having stabbed, and killed, John Stompanato, her mother's current boyfriend. Stampanato was known to be connected to the 'Mob', and had a reputation as a tough guy. It seemed Cheryl had been defending her mother and had used a kitchen knife to stab John once in the chest. It couldn't have been better placed. One wound, almost no blood, with the blade tip cutting the Aorta. John was dead almost before he hit the floor.

Cheryl's escape from the school posed some unusual problems. Stompanato had quite a reputation and was well liked by his 'associates'. Rumor had it that Cheryl might very well have an 'accident' if the right circumstances presented themselves. It was imperative to find her soon.

Her grandmother lived in town and the watch commander

had set up a stakeout of her house.

Since there was nothing we could do at that point, we went home. At quarter to six in the morning the phone rang and Bert Sloane, the dispatcher, told me that Cheryl and another girl had been arrested at the grandmothers house.

"Why the hell are you telling me? I'm not the juvenile officer."

"Lt. Pierce said you wanted to be notified if she was caught. He's out of the office right now but I'll check again when he comes in."

"Don't bother. I'll ask him myself. I'll be there in a half hour."

When I got to the office the Lieutenant told me that he had been instructed to call me by Lt. Cork. Oh great. Now we're going to start playing games. A few minutes later Cork came into the Bureau with a mile wide grin on his face.

"Didn't have to set your alarm today, Huh?"

"Not quite. But it's nice to have a long memory, you turkey."

Capt. Hankins was already interviewing Cheryl and her friend. After about an hour he joined us in the Bureau. He had met with open hostility and had finally given up. He assigned me and Policewoman Irene Grim, to transport the girls to Juvenile Hall.

The ride to the Hall was long and quiet. On one hand you could see Cheryl covering her fear and confusion by her false 'tough' attitude. Yet she was caught up in something she didn't really understand yet. At least she will have a good lawyer and good support. She had had her share of ups and downs already and didn't need anymore.

We dropped them off at the Hall and wound our way back to the office without saying much. Irene and I both felt like we had just delivered a whipped puppy. It leaves a bad taste in your mouth.

CHAPTER 15

What a wonderful day it had been. When I came to work that morning it was just any other day. Most of the day had been relatively boring. Phone calls, paper work. No hot information to work on and almost everybody out of the office most of the day.

At two-fifteen PM the phone rang and since I was the only one in the office I answered it. Clever huh?

"Detectives, Downey."

"Come in here when you can", click.

God forbid you wouldn't know who was calling or where "here" was.

He may have said when you can, but he meant now. When I headed for his office I let the desk know there was no one in the Bureau. When I got to Vi's desk she said "he's waiting for you."

In that thirty feet between Vi's desk and the Chief's desk I had time to think of several hundred things that may or may not have happened or was about to happen. I knocked on his door and went in when he responded.

"Yes Chief?"

"You know we're one Sergeant short since Elias' accident. Effective tonight at midnight you'll be promoted to Sergeant and take over as Patrol Sergeant on the midnight shift. Here's your badge. Do you have anything that will interfere with starting tonight ?"

"No sir, not a thing. Thank you Chief." I turned and walked out the door. No formality, no hoopla. Here it is. Go to work. As I passed Vi's desk she was smiling. She had known. I asked her who else knew. She said "no one". That was like him. Kept his own counsel.

I went back to my office and just sat for a few minutes taking many deep, deep breaths.

I had taken the Sergeants exam a few months before but had no thought of making it for a long time. Anyone that had passed their probation was encouraged to take the exam because they didn't want to have to go outside the Department for eligible candidates. There were plenty of candidates.

Apparently I had done pretty well on the written because I was notified about the oral board a few weeks later. By the time the process was over I had found out I was second on the list. Which really meant nothing. The Chief could and would select whoever he wanted. And I certainly didn't conceive that I would be that someone. I barely had three years on the job.

The Chief chose Ted Elias. And a good choice it was. Ted had come out first on the list. He also was a well liked and respected Police Officer. I personally hadn't done much work with him but I knew him and his reputation. A few months after Ted made Sergeant he had taken a trip and while on the trip had been involved in a serious traffic accident. Due to his injuries, he had to retire from the Police Department. This was the vacancy the Chief had referred to.

While I was sitting in my chair in a stupor, Cork came into the office. I must have looked like hell because he said, "What's wrong?"

When I rose from my chair I walked over to him and held out my hand, with the Sergeants badge in it.

"Well I'll be damned, congratulations. When did this happen?"

"A few minutes ago. I start as Patrol Sergeant tonight at midnight. I'm still not sure it happened. I sure want the promotion but I hate like hell to leave the Bureau."

"You probably won't be gone long. The Chief likes every new Sergeant to have some field supervisory experience right away. Believe me, he'll know every thing you do. He'll put you back in here before long."

"I guess I'd better get some stripes sewn on my uniform before I go to work tonight. I'd better take my uniform shirt over to the shop and have them put on right away. Jeez, I'm still not sure this is happening".

"It is, so enjoy it."

I went down to the locker room and got one of my clean uniforms out of the bag and headed for the uniform shop. In a half hour I was back in the office where I was met with congratulations from the other detectives. About that time Hankins came in and asked what all the fuss was about. When he was told, he seemed puzzled. He congratulated me and headed for the Chief's office.

When he came back he shook my hand and told me I may as well go home now so I could get some sleep before I came back tonight. No mention about who to turn my cases over to. Nothing said about briefing anyone on my cases. I thought I was beginning to understand. The old fox in the corner pocket figured he was going to get two bodies for the price of one.

And, damn it, he was probably right.

I was drinking a cup of coffee when Diana got home. I'd hung my uniform on the bedroom door so she could hardly miss it.

"What are you doing home so soon ?" she said as she headed for the bedroom to hang up her coat. "What's this doing here." as she passed the doorway. "Did you run out of locker space . . . ..Oh God, do these stripes mean what I think they do?"

"They sure do. I start as Patrol Sergeant tonight at midnight. I had to get the stripes on the shirt before I really believed it. The stripes, the gold badge, and the gold hat braid,,, it must be true."

"How long are you going to be in uniform?"

"I don't know. Cork doesn't think it'll be too long."

"I suppose you'll still go in on your own time to handle some of your cases ?"

"I sort of have a hunch that's what the Chief thinks too. I'll have to see what happens."

"Yeah, sure. I can see it now. No sleep again."

"No, I don't think so this time. I'll have to take it a little easier this time. Maybe a couple of days a week but not nearly like it was before."

"I'll believe that when I see it."

"Well, I'm going to get some sleep before I go in tonight. Wake me about ten o'clock will you?"

"Sure. You want some breakfast when you get up?"

"Something very light. My stomach's going to have butterflys tonight anyhow. There will be some guys who won't be very happy to have me for a supervisor and I'll have to deal with that right away. A few of them were on the Sergeants list too. Besides that I've got Tom Pierce for a Watch Commander. He's a good man but he has some strange philosophies about police work. I'll just have to deal with that as it comes."

Even though I was laying down, I just knew I would have too much on my mind to fall asleep. Two and a half hours later Diana was shaking me awake. So much for too much on my mind.

I called for a ride at ten thirty and Dick Clason picked me up and I was at the station by ten forty five. The handshakes and congratulations were coming from everyone. It felt good. I finished getting into the rest of my uniform gear and headed for the watch commanders office. I knew from prior observation what the patrol sergeant's duties were so I just repeated them. So far, so good.

Lt. Pierce came into the office and shook my hand saying "well sergeant, let's get to roll call." That was it.

After a rather lengthy roll call, Lt. Pierce asked me if I have anything I wanted to impart to the watch, seeing as how I was the 'new' sergeant and this was my first night.

"Yes, Lt., as a matter of fact I do. Gentlemen, if you figure I'm going to be spending my time trailing you around trying to catch you goofing off or having an extra coffee break, forget it. I'm going to be too busy trying to make arrests. If you are going to goof off or shirk your duty I'll find it in your activity reports. There will be time enough to handle it then. Aside from that, I'll be there to give you all the help I can. Now let's go to work."

As the men were leaving the office Lt. Pierce called me aside.

"You shouldn't have told them that. They'll take advantage

when they know that you won't be checking on them."

"That may be true Tom, but they don't really know if I meant it or not, do they? Of course I meant it. But they don't know that.

I think I'll be able to tell if they are not taking care of their job. Let's try it and see."

"You're the field supervisor." He said as he headed up the stairs. A short time later we were all in the field. It felt different. Better. It'd take some getting used to. But I loved it. I had a tough time keeping from howling and jumping up and down. Time for a little professionalism and restraint.

The night went without incident and..fast. As I was checking out the paperwork of the crew, Hankins came into the Watch Commanders office and asked me to come into the Bureau when I got a chance. Here it comes.

"Say Downey, do you think you could stop in here in the mornings after your shift and brief some of the guys on the cases you have open? It'll only take a couple or three hours each day for a few days to catch them up to speed."

His voice and eyes were so innocent looking. He did have that slight smirk at the corners of his mouth. He knew I was going to do it. He just wanted me to say so.

"Yes, Capt., I'll be glad to. But not this morning. I'm ready for some sleep right now. I'll see you tomorrow morning, O.K.?"

"Sure Downey, whenever you can." he said with a knowing smile on his face.

I'd made it home before Diana had gone to work and spent our entire time together filling her in on the nights activity. It was a good thing she liked to hear it. When I think back on it, it sure could have been boring for her. I also got the chance to tell her I had run across and had a talk with Jimmy Stewart. He had been for a short walk near his house on North Roxbury Drive and was just getting home.

Our conversation led to the information that he was coming to the office in a few days to be fingerprinted again. It seemed he had just been notified that he was being promoted to the rank of

Brigadier General in the Air Force Reserve. I told him I would be honored to fingerprint him for his promotion if he wanted to come to the office at about 8:00 AM any of the next three mornings. He said he would see me in a couple of days. He was a very pleasant gentleman.

After she'd gone to work I just sat and rethought the night. All in all, it went well. I fell asleep with a smile on my face. I must have been satisfied with myself because I didn't wake up till Diana got home around seven o'clock.

After a nice dinner and a couple of hours good conversation, I was ready to try it again. In fact I was looking forward to it.

At roll call Lt. Pierce reminded us of the continuous complaints we had received from the residents around Doheny and Elevado about the wild and noisy parties going on 'til all hours at the house on the north west corner. I hadn't been in uniform for a while but everybody on the department knew about the complaints.

It seemed the house was being rented or leased to the owner and operator of a large, popular nightclub on Sunset Blvd., in Hollywood. He had a habit of bringing a bunch of friends and acquaintances home from the club after it closed. Having boisterous parties in and around the pool area, until the very wee hours of the morning. The neighbors had complained about nude swimming parties and had gotten to the Chief. He was getting very tired of being on the receiving end.

Although the midnight crew had responded to the house several times and contacted the occupant, it didn't seem to do any good. He had been warned incessantly without appreciable results. The Chief was NOT happy and was really putting pressure on the Watch Commander. Lt. Pierce was not one to take pressure well. Bob Devich was working car 8 that night and was told to keep a close eye on the location.

We all broke for our patrol areas but I had been called to a meeting with Lt. Pierce. He wanted me to know how concerned he was with the noise complaints from the Doheny house and asked me to check on it frequently. I assured him I would.

-DOWN

All went well and quietly until about 3:30 am. A call came from the dispatcher about a loud party coming from Elevado and Doheny. Car 8 (Devich) and Car 14 (me) handle.

By the time I got there Devich had parked on Elevado and was standing on the corner. When I pulled up you could hear loud talking coming from the back yard and pool area of the house.

As Bob and I approached the front door we noticed bright flashes of light coming from the side of the house. We delayed our knock until we found out what was going on. As we got near the window where the flashes were, we began to hear voices. From the conversation going on and the flashes, we were convinced that there were pornographic photographs being taken inside. And from the conversation it was possible they were for commercial purposes.

With that information, I returned to the car and requested two more officers respond. Upon their arrival I assigned them to the rear of the house while Bob and I made entry to the front.

With everyone in place we knocked loudly on the front door. It was opened in short order by a man who said he was not the renter or owner. We followed him into the house as he quickly retreated toward the rear. As we passed down the hallway we saw two partially clad young ladies in one of the downstairs bedrooms. As we reached the rear door the man called to someone in the back yard and opened the door. As he did, our two men at the rear entered the yard and followed people into the house.

I advised the tenant that we had reason to believe that felonious activity was taking place at the house and that everyone was in custody until we sorted out the activity. Everyone was held in the living room of the house while a search was conducted. Three men and three women.

We began our search in the room where we had seen the young ladies. We found a Polaroid camera and a 35mm camera.

We also found a large supply of Polaroid negatives but no Polaroid pictures. Strange. Everyone denied any knowledge of pictures. Very Strange.

The two girls had been sitting on the bed when we entered the room. And they had not been anxious to move. Bob and I went to the bed and lifted the mattress. What Ho. A large pile of Polaroid photos. The photos showed four of our arrestees engaging in various forms of lewd and lascivious acts. Now we were starting to get protestations of innocence from everyone in the place. No one would believe they were in the pictures.

As we continued to search the house we found a chrome plated .38 revolver that no one would claim, with a bank bag that held a large amount of cash. There were conflicting stories about the gun and the bag. We decided to take them all in and sort it out at the station. I called for two more cars for transportation. While I was on the phone Lt. Pierce got on the line and very nervously wanted to know what had happened. I told him we'd be in in a few minutes and I'd explain then. He didn't sound happy but he knew he'd have to wait. We locked up the house and headed for the office.

Once in the office I gave the Lieutenant a quick rundown of who was under arrest and why. I got the distinct impression he was not comfortable with the whole thing. He walked nervously between people who were being booked looking at the paperwork as it was prepared.

By about 6:30 am we were tagging and listing the evidence when the Chief came up the stairs. He looked briefly at all the people in the office and picked up his copy of the paperwork and headed for his office. A few minutes later the switchboard lit up and Bert Sloane answered it. He turned toward the Lt. and said, "the Chief wants to see you."

Tom turned around in the same spot about three times before he headed for his office. He was only in there for a few seconds when the switchboard lit up again and Bert turned to me and said, "he wants to see you too."

I picked up the evidence, the photos, the gun, and the bank bag, and headed for his office.

As I went through his office door I could see the slight grin on his face.

"Did you bring the evidence ?" he said as he held out his hand. From what I'd heard about him, I handed him the pictures first. I had guessed right. He closely scrutinized the whole lot of them first. He then looked at the gun and bank bag.

"What are you going to charge them with ?" he asked.

"Lewd and lascivious conduct on three of them, two on suspicion of armed robbery, all of them on disturbing the peace. We're still checking out the ownership of the gun. The money is probably from the nightclub, but it needs to be checked. Other than that, that's it."

"All right Sergeant. Lt., you stay here." I took the hint and got the hell out of there.

A few minutes later Tom came out of the office with a very broad smile on his face. All he would say was, "he's very happy."

I had just distributed the last of the reports and was leaving the Watch Commanders office when Mr. Stewart came into the office and said "Good Morning, Sergeant" as he handed me his fingerprint cards. I took his cards as I said "Good Morning" and we walked to the fingerprint table. We chatted quietly as I took his prints and he cleaned the ink from his fingers. The office staff had grown quiet and were just mulling around, looking, yet not looking. As he headed out the door I said "Good Bye, General", and his back seemed to straighten as he waved goodbye. Then I had to explain to everyone that we had made the appointment a couple of days earlier and that he had just been promoted.

By ten o'clock, The money had been cleared and the robbery charges dropped. Three people were arraigned on disturbing the peace charges. There were no charges filed on the rest. The gun had not been reported stolen and was being held until proof of ownership was produced.

A few days later, the house on the corner of Elevado and Doheny was vacant. The Chief seemed to be in a better mood. Lt. Pierce didn't have anything to say about the morning watch activity for quite a while.

In a few days I was settling into this Patrol Sergeant stuff quite comfortably. I was keeping my word. I was trying to make arrests, and not following my people around. The whole watch seemed more relaxed. We were making some good arrests.

A week before my first month was up, I got called to the Chief's office just before I left for home.

"You'll be going back to the Detective Bureau at the next shift change." That was it. His tone of voice told you the conversation was over. Before leaving the building I stopped by the Detective Bureau to tell Capt. Hankins the news. Another surprise for him, and me. Cork just smiled.

Not long after the shift hit the street that night I got a radio call of a DB report at an address on South Palm Drive. DB meaning dead body. Nobody, but nobody, looks forward to these calls. The way the call is dispatched you can pretty much be assured that it's at the request of a mortuary. The mortuary had been called and when they arrived they found that there had been no doctor in attendance at the time of death so they had to wait for an official pronouncement of death. In the great majority of these cases you find that the victim is a Christian Scientist and the family and a reader/ practioner is present. Once at the scene you make a thorough preliminary investigation to determine there is no indication of foul play then make the formal declaration. The mortuary then removes the body. As I said, no one looks forward to these calls. You go back to the office, make your report, and then try to spend the rest of the shift shaking the feeling that has crowded around you.

Most of the officers have drawn this assignment at one time or the other but it never got any easier.

Suicides and attempt suicides were another call that made your heart stand still. What is the scene going to be? Who is the victim? What's the method. When someone is committing suicide they can pick some pretty bizarre methods. You have all that time from getting the call to arriving at the scene to contemplate what you'll run into. it's hard even to imagine what you could find.

On the next to the last night on morning watch I was dispatched to an apartment on South Tower Drive, "possible suicide, ambulance follow-up" Car nine was sent too.

The apartment was on the second floor and as I got to the top of the stairs I saw the open door to the bathroom. Directly across from the door was the bathtub heavily splattered with blood. The floor had two very wide trails of blood leading out the door toward the front of the apartment.

A quick look in the tub revealed a Shick injectable razor blade floating on top of a large pool of blood. I headed for the front of the apartment. More heavy blood trails. I was thinking nobody could lose this much blood and survive.

As I entered the living room I saw a straight backed dining room chair with arm rests, in the middle of the room with a female seated in the chair and facing the balcony windows. On the floor, beneath each arm, were large puddles of blood.

I went around to the front of the chair fully expecting to find a corpse. Instead I found a very weak young lady with very grotesque, deep, gashes on the inside wrist area of each arm. The gashes had bled dry and were now puckering with an ugly greyish white color to them.

She moved her mouth but no words came out. I was shocked to find her alive, now she was trying to talk. I quickly got two towels from the bathroom and tied them tightly around each wrist. I could hear the ambulance attendants coming up the stairs. Thank God. I thought I was going to have a little trouble holding down what ever I had eaten. It passed though.

She was hurried to the ambulance and taken

to the hospital. I learned later that she had survived and I was amazed that she could lose all that blood and live. God has his own plan.

CHAPTER 16

"I assume you guys have been listening to the news or read the paper this morning." The Captain said as Cork and I entered the Bureau. "Milton Berle's house got hit."

"Yeah, we heard about it, Bob and I were talking about it. Why is it that celebrities feel the need to call their press agents before they call the police when something happens?"

Cork and I went into the Captains office and sat down. "I guess it's newsworthy because they had been down to the presidents ranch at one of his famous "Bar-B-Ques".

"I can't figure out whether they are upset about the burglary or just wanted the world to know they were at the "Ranch", I said as I picked up the follow-up report Cork had just finished.

"Pederson and McCarthy did the initial investigation and Egger and Haas did an immediate follow-up. From their reports it would seem that it was an inside job and there are plenty of suspects. You two go up there and see if you can sort out who did what to whom and when. There are several domestics, one fired driver who still hangs around, and a nephew that was there while they were gone.

Howard Polakov and Merv Pederson had come in while we were talking and things started to settle into a normal process when the phone rang and Howard answered. He was still saying a few "Yeahs", and "O.K."s as he was rising from his chair, hanging up the phone and waving for me to follow him.

"Lets go. We've got a silent 211 alarm at The Beverly Wilshire Pharmacy. Two suspects, both armed with an automatic. "

As we headed down the stairs Cork said he and Pederson would cover the Pharmacy and Howard and I could cover the area for possible suspects. The Berles would just have to wait.

The dispatcher yelled at us as we're going down the stairs that there were two white males inside the office and at least one in a getaway car in the alley. A maroon Chevy was the only description of the car. The driver had short curly hair. The two inside the office had worn masks and had a blue steel automatic.

Howard and I followed Cork and Pederson out of the driveway and as they turned right on Little Santa Monica, Howard pointed to a maroon Chevy with a two white males and short hair crossing in front of us onto Burton Way, followed closely by Motor Officer Jimmy Smith. Smith waved for us to follow him on Burton Way. We swung onto Burton behind the motor officer and the suspects car.

As we were about to approach Doheny, Smitty began to pull the car over. As I swung our car alongside the Chevy, Howard held up his badge and yelled to the driver to pull over. We were less than five blocks from the station when we pulled in front of the Chevy as he pulled to the curb. Smitty pulled his motorcycle in behind them and dismounted drawing his gun. We both got out of our car with our guns down beside our legs.

Howard approached the passenger side as I walked slowly up to the drivers open window and Smitty covered the back.

As the driver started to say something I saw Howard raising his left arm and pointing toward the seat of the car, between the driver and the passenger. Howard's gun was now pointing at the driver and I raised mine and told the driver to keep his hands in sight and slowly get out of the car. Howard had opened the passenger door and was getting the passenger out. As the driver raised from the seat, a newspaper on the seat beside him slipped to the floor to reveal a cocked .45 caliber automatic on the seat.

While I was putting handcuffs on my man and telling him he was under arrest for suspicion of robbery, Howard was hooking up his man. Smitty was unloading the gun and searching the rest of the car. No other evidence was found.

While we were booking our suspects we got the story of the robbery from the beat officer. Two masked suspects entered the offices of Milton F. Kreis, operators of the Beverly Wilshire Pharmacy.

Their office was located down the alley behind the hotel, near Charleville. The suspects had entered through the back door and held three employees at gun point while demanding the weekends receipts. The suspects wore stocking masks and seemed to know where and how much cash was supposed to be in the office. Between $4000 and $5000 had been taken. The suspects made the employees lie on the floor when they left and got into a maroon Chevy driven by a white male with short curly hair. The latter information came from a janitor who had been outside when the robbers came out.

Within the hour we had arranged a lineup for the victims and the witness to look at the guys we had nabbed. Howard and I had been talking to them while we were waiting for the lineup to begin. They adamantly denied any knowledge of any robbery. One did admit being in possession of a concealed weapon but claimed it was only for personal protection. He also claimed he had only been in town from San Gabriel for a short time looking for a job. He couldn't say just where he had looked or exactly what kind of job he was hunting.

His story was obviously a phony but he certainly wasn't going to give us anything. The other one claimed he was just along for the ride and didn't know about the gun.

The line up was about what we had expected. The employees hadn't seen any part of a face they could identify and they hadn't seen the car or driver. The janitor said one of our suspects had the same kind of hair as the driver of the getaway car but he didn't see the face well enough to identify. He looked at the car and said it was the same color and kind of car but couldn't say for sure it was the same car.

We put our suspects back in the cell and started to complete the paperwork to charge one with carrying a concealed weapon. Cork and Pederson were checking on the car and the suspects background. The car was not registered to the suspect but was not reported stolen either. Teletypes were sent describing the robbery and the suspects descriptions.

By the time we settled back to evaluate just what has taken place so far we started to realize just how quickly we had run into a stone wall. It was hard to accept that we had made an arrest so soon after the robbery with a description of the car, partial of the driver, and a gun fitting the description of one used in the robbery, and it was possibly all a coincidence. All our leads seemed to be fizzeling at one time. That was just not normal. Now it came down to backtracking to see if we had missed anything. From here on it was up to Pederson and Cork for investigation. The rest of us would revert to our regular assignments until we were needed to help out on other parts of the case. In the meantime we needed a complaint from the D.A's. Office to arraign one guy on the gun charge in the morning. We had to cut the second one loose with nothing to tie him to the robbery or the gun.

By the time we got back from Santa Monica with the complaint we found out our remaining suspect had been writted out on a writ of habeas corpus. Now that was enough to make you stop and think a little. Getting a writ of habeas corpus that quick was no simple task. It requires two things. Knowledge of who, why, and where the guy was, and a lawyer prepared to move in a hurry. Now our man certainly didn't seem to be connected that well, but maybe we had missed something.

Obviously we were looking at more than a mere concealed weapon charge. Maybe if whoever hadn't moved so damn fast and let this die a natural death we may not have become so much more inquisitive. Maybe, but probably not. Well, he didn't have to show up in court for a couple of days so we would have more time to dig a lot deeper.

Cork and I were discussing the turn of events with Capt. Hankins when he answered the phone. After a couple of "O.K.s, Yeahs, and Wheres'", he hung up and his shoulders seemed to sag a little when he said, "It just keeps coming. You two had better get going up to Milton Berle's house. They're bent out of shape because no one has been there yet this morning. The news media is there again and are having a field day. Get up there and see what's going on. More publicity, that's all we need."

On our way out of the building we contacted McIntire at the front desk and asked him to bring the print and photo equipment.

As we were pulling up top the front of the Berle house we saw a couple of newscars leaving. The beat car was still parked in the driveway. Approaching the front door Officer Carden came out to meet us.

"I just stopped by to try and keep the news cars from blocking the street. The Berles are not happy, as I guess you will find out when you talk to them. Well, they're all yours." And he got into his car with a big grin on his face.

Just inside the open door Milton Berle put out his hand and said, "I don't understand what's going on. You'd think in Beverly Hills you could leave for a few days and expect to find everything in tact when you get back."

By the tone of his voice you could guess that this was not going to be a friendly encounter. We introduced ourselves and followed him into the den where he introduced us to his wife, Ruth. She couldn't understand why they couldn't have better protection especially in Beverly Hills. I guess they had a right to complain.

They advised us that they had not notified our office that they would be out of town so their house could be placed on special watch. We also found out that the housekeeper, Alice Cole, was on the premises during their absence as was the maid, Shirley Brown. Cole had been with the Berles for several years as a live-in housekeeper.

Shirley Brown was day help and had Thursdays off. There had also been a friend of Cole's visiting the house several times while they were gone. The friend had been a driver for the Berles but had been discharged several weeks before. The house had also been occupied by the Berle's child and his nurse.

The Berles took us to their bedroom and dressing room where

the missing property had been kept. While Cork checked the area, I looked over the outside of the house for signs of forced entry. Mac had arrived and was taking photos of the closet and bedroom area. The original investigating officers had done the same thing of course, but a display of activity helps calm the nerves of some victims and puts them in a better frame of mind.

After finding nothing that faintly resembled a possible point of entry to the house, I drifted into the kitchen area where Alice and Shirley were seated at the table holding cups of coffee. Alice offered me a cup of coffee which I gratefully accepted having not had time for lunch or coffee this day. Our conversation started out stilted and strained. It's obvious they were not comfortable.

We discussed the normal household activities and the things they had told the officers the evening before. Everyone's comings and goings, especially while the Berles' were away, were discussed, in detail. They were both cooperative and forthcoming about the household activities and service people who had been to the house.

It was becoming more and more obvious they both wanted to say something but for some reason were reluctant. It was also obvious neither one was going to say anything in front of the other. Without trying to push the matter, I finished my coffee and told them I would stop back later if I thought of any further questions and left each of them my name and phone number.

When I rejoined the Berles, and Cork he was just completing the list of stolen items. One full length sable coat, a diamond necklace, a diamond pin and two rings, amounting to $35,000 or more. The coat had "Ruth Berle" embroidered on the lining.

Asked if there had been any other visitors to the house besides staff while they were gone, they looked at each other, hesitated, then mentioned that their nephew, Marshal, had been at the house once or twice while they were gone.

The housekeeper had told them about it when they had called from Texas. When asked where we could contact Marshal they both said they didn't know just where he was staying at that time but he had been living with his mother on North Sweetzer in

Hollywood. Mrs. Berle got the address for us from her directory. They said they were sure he could have had nothing to do with the theft.

We advised them that there appeared to be no forced entry into their home and no ransacking, which frequently indicated some inside information and knowledge of the premises.

We told them that it was entirely possible that some acquaintance of Marshals' had overheard conversation that the house was unoccupied or something about the premises which had been passed on to someone not so trustworthy.

That's not usually the case but we felt since they were so adamant in their attitude, it didn't hurt to hand them some straw to hang on to. They were certain however, that our efforts would be better directed toward identifying the 'real' suspects.

We told them that we welcomed their advice and left the house with a full head of steam. We had both received our total ration of thinly disguised disappointment and intolerance at the inefficiency of our department. Neither of us could speak for several blocks.

By the time we got to the office we had cooled off enough to knock out the report and get out the teletype in record time. I placed a call to Pete Meaney to let him know of the burglary. Also to Frank Gravante who worked residential burglary in West L.A. When I had finished that, it was too late to call Hollywood. It was time to shut it down for the night.

By the time I got to the office the next morning I was braced to meet the events of the day. Diana and I had spent a delightful evening over a salad and sirloin and quiet piano jazz on the radio. No news, no commercials and no interruptions. Some nights, life is very good.

By noon the next day Toomey and Turner in Hollywood had been filled in on Berle as well as the Parker burglaries. I asked them particularly to tap their sources to turn up any information on Marshal Berle.

Shortly after lunch Cork told me to pick up line two, He had a somewhat puzzled look on his face. I picked up the receiver and said "Downey, can I help you?" and sat on the corner of the desk. When I heard the voice, I motioned to Cork to stay on the line.

"Yes, I think you can. You know who this is

don't you?"

"Yes, I think so, didn't I meet you yesterday?.

"That's right. Can you come up to the house pretty soon?"

"Certainly, if that's what you want. Is everybody gone?. Or would it be better for me to meet you somewhere away from the house?"

"No, it's all right. They'll all be gone from the house for the afternoon. You can come here if it's pretty soon".

"I'm leaving right now. O.K.?"

"Yeah, that's fine", and I heard the click as she hung up. I hung up and looked at Cork who had been on the other extension.

"What do you think B.L., you want to go along?"

"No, it doesn't sound like she wants any one else around. You must have struck some kind of cord with her yesterday. Which one is it, the housekeeper or the maid?"

"It's the housekeeper. They both acted like they had something to say yesterday. The housekeeper seemed to be the one in charge and the other one knew it. We'll see."

A few minutes later I pulled into the driveway toward the kitchen side of the house. The kitchen door opened as I pulled up and Alice was standing there with a cup of coffee in her hand. When I got into the kitchen there was another cup of coffee sitting on the table with a pitcher of cream and bowl of sugar next to it.

"I couldn't remember just how you took yours", she said.

"Black is fine", I said as I sat down at the table.

"What can I do for you Alice?" I said as she pulled up a chair and sat down. She still appeared almost as nervous as she had yesterday but there was also an air of resignation and determination about her.

"Well" she starts, "you know when you asked us about people coming and going in the house while the family was away?"

"Yeah".

"We really weren't sure just whether to mention it or not but the more we thought about it the more we thought we should. You know about the nephew visiting once in a while. Well, this time when they were gone he came much more than usual and a couple of times he had a floosey looking girl with him. In fact he came the same afternoon they left. He said he came to play with the little boy but that didn't make sense.

The girl just didn't look or act like a regular girl, the way she dressed and all. Beside that, she acted like she owned everybody and bossed everybody around. She reminded me of a call girl or a street walker. Hard. Older than he is and many more miles on her."

"I don't know whether they had anything to do with the missing property or not but the way she acted she sure could have."

"Did you ever get her name by any chance?"

"Not really. He called her Barbara once."

"Has he been around lately?"

"No, I don't even think he has called since they have been back. He never was around that much but he was around more this time when they were gone".

"O.K. Alice, we'll start working on her right away".

After getting as much of a physical description as possible from Alice I asked her about Bill Roberts. The Berles had told us that they had employed Roberts as a houseman and driver for a while but had let him go a couple of years ago. They said he had visited Alice several times since then.

Alice advised that Roberts was her boyfriend and often came to see her. She said the Berles were not aware that Roberts came as often as he did and she did not want to upset them by telling them. I got Roberts' home address and phone number as well as his work address, thanked her, and headed back to the office.

Now comes the part of an investigation no one likes. Scut work. Call him. Talk to her. Check this record or that. What kind of work does he do? Where does he work? Who's he work with? Find that thread and follow it. With Marshal it shouldn't be that hard. After all he's the nephew of a very famous man. Lots of people should know him. With the others, Roberts, Cole, the maid, the nurse, it could take a while.

By the time I got back to the office I learned that we had gotten a phone call from San Marino P.D. to tell us they had an informant who was talking to them about the Beverly Wilshire Pharmacy robbery. They wanted to check a few facts with us to validate their informant.

According to their informant, we had arrested the getaway driver but he had only driven them a couple of blocks and they changed cars. They would get back to us as soon as they squeezed their informant.

By late afternoon Roy Garrett, the warrant officer, and I were enroute to San Gabriel to pick up our previous suspect. This time to charge him with robbery. Cork and Pederson were headed to El Monte to search for two other suspects. They would stop by Pasadena P.D. and question a fifth suspect who was being held for us. Once it started to fall together it moved fast.

It seemed there were five men that pulled the robbery. Two had entered the premises, one had stood lookout, one drove one getaway car and one had driven the second getaway car which had been parked a few blocks away. According to the informant one of the gunmen was a brother to the driver we had arrested and had part of his left thumb missing.

We each had several possible addresses to check out for our suspects.

Garrett and I located our San Gabriel address just before dusk. We asked San Gabriel P.D. to stand by while we made entry to find our man. It was a small house located to the rear of a large house. Roy and I took up positions at each side of the doorway. My knock was answered by a young woman who opened the door about eight inches.

Before I could say anything I saw our man seated at a table in the kitchen. As he saw me he started to rise and lean toward the back door. I pushed the girl aside and entered as I drew my gun telling the guy to stop. He seemed to freeze in mid stride, looking over his shoulder at the barrel of my gun leveled at his head. Roy quickly followed me into the room and moved the girl to the kitchen table as I was handcuffing Mr. Fleetfoot. I asked Roy to check the rest of the house while I finished cuffing my man.

The house was obviously small and only had room for a bedroom and bath. The kitchen and living room could be seen from where we were. Roy started across the living room as I sat my man down at the table. A few seconds later Roy came back into the kitchen and said,

"There's another guy in the bathroom who looks like he's bleaching his hair. His left thumb is cut off."

"Roy, put the hooks on him quick. He's one of our inside men".

Roy bolted back to the bathroom to find the guy trying to get out the bathroom window. He pulled him back in and put the cuffs on him. When he brought him into the kitchen I recognized him as the passenger in the car we had stopped the day before.

A few questions now and we found the two were brothers. Obviously they had false I.D.s the day before. The plot really thickened. I called San Marino P.D. and filled them in on our arrests and that we had the one with the amputated thumb. San Gabriel P.D. stood by with the brothers while Roy and I searched the house for any property taken in the robbery.

When nothing else was found we put our suspects in the car, thanked San Gabriel P.D., and started back to the office. We left the woman and her child at the house. She said she was the wife of the missing thumb brother.

Just before leaving the house we had to take him back inside and stick his head under the faucet. When he tried to go out through the window he hadn't rinsed the peroxide from his head and it was starting to burn. He had gotten the desired result, it was white.

We got back to the office about eight o'clock to find we were the last ones back. By the time our people were booked and the arrest reports done, it was going on ten.

After a short discussion with the rest of the crew in the office it was time for home. All in all, a damned full day.

CHAPTER 17

Three days of backed up teletypes had greeted me when I got in that next morning. A quick check at the dispatch desk let me know that everyone arrested the previous evening was still resting comfortably in our jail. If we had many more it was going to be hard to separate them. We kept the brothers together, and put one each in the juvenile section, the female section, and the other side of the main section. With a couple of overnight arrests our little jail was starting to bulge.

I was scrolling through the teletypes over the writing leaf of my school teachers desk that I'd inherited from someone, when the rest of the crew started shuttling in. The conversation centered around each of our experiences in picking up the guys in jail and whatever they may have said. It was decided that Cork and Pederson would do the interrogations for continuity. The rest of us would write out our statements and pass them over to Cork.

Pederson, McCarthy, Egger, Mourning, Estill and Haas had come into the Bureau to replace Valentine, Britton and Moe. Howard Polakov had gone back to Patrol and Bolander had left the Department. Egger and Estill had come from patrol, Haas had been on three wheeler traffic control and Mourning, McCarthy and Pederson had been on motors. They were all enthusiastic and eager. God knows you needed both. The city's reputation was that of peace and tranquility and the police department's was one of invincibility. The Chief had succeeded in perpetuation of the myth that Beverly Hills was sacrosanct. We had been existing on that reputation for a long time. That reputation had proven invaluable frequently, even if it was somewhat mythical.

Tearing off teletypes for distribution around the Bureau. I

stopped at one from Santa Monica P.D. which listed stolen property recovered from an earlier arrest. The description of some of the property started to ring bells. A call to Santa Monica P.D. Burglary Detail got me a little more general description on several pieces of jewelry and other items taken in two or three burglaries in our town. Including some from Col. Tom Parkers house. If I wanted any more information though I would have to come to Santa Monica.

I gathered up my case folders for the past three months and headed out the door after telling the Capt. where I was headed. On my way out Santa Monica Blvd. I stopped by the West L.A. Station to talk with Frank Gravante about the property in Santa Monica only to find out he was already on his way there.

When I arrived at Santa Monica P.D. I was shuttled from pillar to post until I finally ended up with Detective Katt who was handling the case. Katt lead me to a group of desks in one corner of the large open area of desks which I presumed to be the Detective Bureau. I spotted Frank in a group of people and waved as I began my talk with Katt. It seemed a burglary suspect had been arrested in Illinois and had some stolen property with him that had been identified as coming from the Santa Monica area as well as West L.A. and Beverly Hills. The suspect, a male in his twenties, was from Illinois, but had a girl friend and an apartment in Santa Monica.

When Santa Monica was notified of his arrest they went to the apartment, talked with the girlfriend, and searched the apartment.

The property they had, was displayed in an adjoining conference room, and was merchandise they had recovered from the apartment. I began to get a funny feeling at the back of my neck when I asked where the apartment was and what the was girls name? Katt offhandedly told me they were not releasing that information because they were still working on it.

I must have jerked my head around or let my chin drop or something that let him know I was startled because he warmed up a little and laughingly said "we'll put it all out when we're ready".

I knew I was fairly new to the Detective Bureau but I had never run into this kind of sidestepping before nor had I heard of it. I tucked it into the back of my head and chalked it up to experience. After Katt and I had discussed the suspects method of operation and the type of property taken and recovered I asked if I could look at the property. Katt escorted me to the doorway of the conference room where the property was laid out on the conference table and on the chairs around the room. As I started to step into the room one of the officers in the room stepped in front of me and putting his hand on my chest said "no one comes into the room". I was about to respond when Katt informed me, "You'll have to view the property from the doorway. We haven't inventoried it all yet."

"How the hell can I tell from here whether the smaller pieces match any of my missing property lists", I said with no small amount of irritation in my voice.

"Well, you'll just have to see if you can recognize anything from here then give us a list of your missing property and we'll check it against what we have. If it looks close then you can bring your victims out here and they can look at the items that seem to fit the descriptions of their stuff".

After a few more exchanges along the same lines it began to dawn on me I wasn't making any progress with them. I resigned myself to looking into the room from the doorway.

I immediately recognized a large, unusual jewelry box sitting on the table nearest the doorway.

"That jewelry box on the corner looks like Mrs. Hallstrom's. It was taken about two weeks ago from her home on Linden Dr. Is there any property that was found in it?"

"What did she report missing?"

"Quite a bit of jewelry including a 32 carat diamond ring that was hidden in a secret compartment in the box."

"Do you know how to find the compartment?"

"Yeah, you slide both sides of the middle trey toward each side of the box and a small lid flips up." As I had finished describing the compartment the officer in the room stepped in front of the box and with his back toward us appeared to place his hands into the box. Almost immediately I heard a faint `snap' and the officer appeared to take his clenched right hand away from the box as he turned to his right keeping his right hand out of my sight. As he turned away from the table the box was again exposed, this time with the compartment open.

Katt stepped over to the box and looked inside saying, "well he, (meaning the burglar), must have found it 'cause it's empty now."

As he came back to the door, the other officer pressed past him and walked across the room and disappeared down the hallway, still appearing to have his right hand clenched. The hair was really standing up on the back of my neck now. I asked Katt who the guy was and Katt replied "That's the Lieutenant", and began to sort through my case reports.

"When you're through with your inventory how's about getting a copy and then I can go through by crime reports and try to match up some of the property" I asked.

"Naw, that'll take too much time, we'll have a showing for the victims day after tomorrow. Just bring your victims out between 1:00 and 4:00 and they can see if they recognize anything"

"Whoa, wait a minute. I'll have at least ten victims I'll want to look at the stuff and they may not all be able to be here then. And, are you planning for them to view the merchandise from the doorway?."

"Yeah, that's the way we do it here. It'll have to be done on Thursday. We want to wrap this up before the weekend."

"I'll try to have as many as I can here. By the way, what is the guys name that's in custody?".

"We'll put all that in a general teletype when we get it wrapped up. Get us a list of all your missing property on these burglaries and we'll go over them as we inventory the property. See you Thursday". He walked away after closing and locking the conference room door.

I guess I had just been summarily dismissed. As I was leaving the building I almost walked past Frank at the bottom of the stairs.

"Sorry Frank, I'm so pissed I'm not focusing very well. Did you get the same fast shuffle I did up there?."

"Yeah, that's not unusual. Makes a person wonder just what the hell goes on around here. I never did get to see what was in that room. They were still `inventorying'. It wouldn't surprise me if they never got done with their inventory. I don't know what the hell we can do about it though." He said as we headed for our cars.

"Just chalk it up to experience and file it for future reference. Of course, don't file it too deep. With a situation like that you want to keep your experiences close to the top of the file".

As we got into our cars Frank said, "Lets have lunch at Roseati's tomorrow. I'll see you there at noon."

"O.K. I'll see you there".

Frank was one of those guys you just knew would never forget an affront. His eyes narrow a little and the corners of his Italian mouth tightens. But the memory of his eyes stick with you. He was a snappy dresser with curly greying hair and an easy laugh. In the next few years he and I would work very closely together and get to know just what each of us will do next. You get very comfortable working with someone you trust instinctively.

I was still trying to figure out just what had happened as I parked my car on the ramp at the station. As I entered the office Cork got up from his desk and joined me as I headed into the captains office.

"How'd you make out" he asked as I sat down across from the Capt.

"I'm not really sure. My head is still spinning from whatever happened out there."

"Did you find any of our property?" Hankins asked.

"That's the weird part". I said as I went about explaining just what had taken place.

By the time I'd finished, we were all shaking our heads.

"What do think their reasons were for keeping you away from

the property." Cork asked.

"Oh it wasn't just me, Frank ran into the same problem. We discussed it shortly while leaving the building but couldn't come to any conclusion."

"Do you think that ring was in the box?" says Hankins.

"I didn't see it, and I couldn't swear to it, but my gut tells me it was in there. It was a well concealed compartment and I don't think the burglar could have found it. And damned sure Santa Monica didn't know about it until I told them. I don't know, I just don't like to think such things. Maybe I'm just too suspicious. So many other things happened that none of it seems to make sense."

"I do know that I have to dig and find out who this guy is that's in custody and talk to the department that's holding him." I remarked as I rose and left the office.

Back at my desk I sat for a few minutes staring at the wall trying to figure out the best and quickest way to find out who this guy was and where he was at.

Cork came in and sat down next to my desk. "You know it seems funny, they have more burglaries and robberies than we have and yet we have done very little business with them".

We were just trying to figure out who we knew out there and we couldn't really name anyone we could call and talk to. "Lets call around and see if anyone we know has had much contact with them. When you come to think of it, they keep a pretty low profile".

"Yeah, I'll do that, but first I want to get started on identifying this burglar. You know, I may have to be a little cagy going about this. I don't know who's Ox I may be goring. It really doesn't make any difference, we have every right to know who he is and what information he's passing out. Especially where our victims are concerned. If Santa Monica gets upset about it we'll have to chew that bone when it falls off the table".

I started pretty tentatively dialing the phone. Close to two hours later I was hanging up after talking to Lt. Terrell of the Danville, Illinois Police Dept.

"Well now, that's a little better. This guy is quite cooperative and hasn't the slightest idea why anyone would be holding out on information." Cork leaned back in his chair as I filled him in on my telephone marathon.

"I finally talked to Lt. Phillips of LAPD Intelligence who put me onto a Lt. in the Illinois State Police Intelligence Unit.

He called me back about a half hour later and gave me the name and phone number of the department handling the guy, and an officer to talk to. I caught him just getting ready to go home but he filled me in on everything. They are going to prosecute for two burglaries back there but would appreciate an out of state warrant just to hold the guy in case he can make bail. I told them I would get a complaint tomorrow morning and teletype our hold. He seemed very pleased.

He said he thought Santa Monica was going to do it a couple of days ago but nothing has happened yet and did I know what the holdup was."

"I told him I didn't know."

"What's the guys name?" Cork asked.

"Harold David Brown. I've got his vitals here to check for local records. The girlfriends name is Sally Sheldon and she lives on the outskirts of Culver City. Frank and I are having lunch tomorrow. I'll see if he wants to go with me to talk to her."

For about an hour we picked apart the

Berle case and put it back together. Each time from a different angle. Regardless of which way we approached it, we come up with the same conclusion. We need to locate and talk to Marshal first. Neither of us can explain it but when we get to the point in the case where we have to consider Marshal we both had that creepy feeling. We ultimately agreed on a course of action and started to pick up the papers and put them back in the file.

As we were putting the papers back, we found that we were the only ones left in the office. We must have both realized it at the same time because we both started for the door. What happened to the day?. By the time the police car dropped me off and

I walked up the long palm tree lined driveway my bones felt like they'd turned to mush. You begin to wonder just what it takes to keep the adrenaline pumping just enough to put you on the edge all day. And just when does it get the signal that it's O.K. to let up now.

Not amounts large enough to make you jumpy or fidgety, just enough to keep your brain firing on all 8 and your nerves standing at attention just under the skin. And when the brain sends the signal to ease off, does it also send a message for the muscles to turn to mush, the shoulders to droop, and the brain to drop back to idle.

Diana was already home from work and if she hadn't started dinner yet it may just be a good night to go to the Saratoga for dinner and listen to a little Ronnie Brown before bedtime. Provided she drives. She did.

I put a call in for Frank at 7:30 AM the next morning and should have known better. I'd call him from the D.A's. office when I got there.

I parked my city car in the garage next to Bill Ritzi's "E"Jag., and went upstairs to the office. There were already a couple of L.A. Detectives there to get a complaint. Bill took them into his office and I went with DDA Chuck Weidman. I used the phone in Chuck's office to call Frank and arranged to meet him as soon as the complaint against Harold Brown was issued.

After laying out our case on Brown to Chuck, he authorized a complaint for Burglary and Grand Theft and gave the paperwork to one of the secretaries for typing. I made arrangements to pick up the complaint later in the afternoon, and got to W.L.A. Division by 10:30AM.

Thirty minutes later Frank and I were face to face with Sally Sheldon at her house, which was half of a small duplex. She asked us in after we explained why we were there. She seemed to be more than cooperative, trying to answer questions that weren't even asked yet. Her story about her association with Brown had some obvious omissions and some rather glaring little white lies but for the most part she answered frankly and without hesitation.

She proceeded to tell us about her encounter with the Santa Monica people and was less than complementary in her assessment of them. She said she was under the impression from what they had told her she would not be hearing from any other department. She then added that given her feelings about the way they had treated her, she was reluctant to call them and tell them about two other boxes that Brown had stored with a friend of hers. She said she had just remembered them and wasn't sure about calling them.

Frank and I assured her that she could take us to where the boxes were stored and we would handle any contact with Santa Monica. She took us out through the back yard and down two doors from her house. She told the young lady who answered the door why we were there and they led us into a bedroom where a wooden footlocker and a medium sized cardboard packing box sat in the corner of the room.

The box was taped and the footlocker had a small lock on it. They both said they had no key for the locker. We opened the box and found a couple of cameras and furs on top and several paper wrapped packages down further in the box. The lock on the footlocker popped with little effort to reveal an assortment of stolen merchandise. Cameras, radios, another fur coat, and fur trimmed cashmere sweaters.

We carried the boxes out to our car and put them in the trunk and back seat. We gave the girls a receipt for the two boxes and headed back to Beverly Hills. After securing the boxes in our evidence room Frank, Cork, and I went to Roseati's for lunch. After a good lunch and a toast or two to our good fortune, I went on to the D.A.'s office while Cork took Frank back to W.L.A. in the car he had brought.

By three thirty in the afternoon I had filed the complaint with the Court Clerks office and had obtained the warrant. When I returned to the office I teletyped a message to Lt. Terrell that a copy of the warrant was in the mail and requested a hold be placed on Brown.

I was settling back contemplating just how I would notify Santa Monica P.D. about the rest of the property when I took a call from Det. Katt. His agitation was pretty obvious in the tone of his voice.

"What the hell are you guys doing going to the girls house?. We just went by there and she told us you had picked up more property." With each sentence his voice goes up another half-octave.

"We'll be right over to pick up the property to inventory with the stuff we got".

"No, not quite". I said with some finality in my voice. "We don't have it inventoried yet. If you'll give us a list of the stolen property you are looking for we'll check it against what we have as soon as we are finished".

"Our boss thinks it would be better to keep all the property together." Now his voice is settling down and you can almost hear the wheels turning in his head.

"You know Katt, I think your boss is right, so why don't you bring the stuff you have over here and we'll inventory it together?"

By this time Cork and Hankins had picked up on what's going on and had gathered around my desk with smiles of varying widths across their faces.

"No" Katt says, "that's not going to work. We have the most stuff and it would be easier to move your stuff".

"That's O.K. we'd be glad to come out and help you move it. But if you want to take a look at it in the meantime why don't you come by tomorrow afternoon and take a look at it. Oh, that's right, you're having your showing then. O.K. I'll talk with you about it when I bring my victims out tomorrow."

"O.K. Downey, we'll talk to our boss about it and see you tomorrow. So long."

"Adios" as I hung up. We were all sitting with wide smiles and a few chuckles then.

Hankins asked, "What do you think you'll face out there tomorrow?.

"Probably some open hostility but it may not show to much with our victims around. I don't think they'll be openly upset, at least 'til they get to see what we have. I've got to get hot and round up some of our more likely victims for the viewing. I think I'd better drive them so I can be sure they all get there about the same time and I can try to assure they get a reasonable look at the stuff."

"Yeah", Cork said, "See how many you can contact. You may need to take more than one car. If you do, I'll go with you."

"Good, maybe a show of force will have some effect. I don't want them going out there by themselves. I just don't know what they can expect. At least if I'm with them I can see what kind of a hustle they get."

From what Terrell had told me about Browns M.O. and his statements, I can sort through our files and pick out several possible victims.

Mrs. Hallstrom headed the list of people I called to arrange to pick up the next day and take them to Santa Monica. After contacting eight possible victims, only four could go at the time specified.

Three would ride with me and one would meet us there. We all agreed on a pick up time and they were advised to bring any receipts they may have or any further descriptions of their missing property.

With that settled it was time to sort through the property in the box and footlocker. I finished the inventory in about a hour. Two minks stoles, two mink trimmed sweaters, a movie camera, three 35mm cameras, an electric portable typewriter, several pieces of jewelry and an assortment of pieces of silverware. Some of the stuff I recognized as coming from some of our victims. Both of the furs still had the victims initials in the lining. They should be easy to trace.

I called Frank and read him the list. He immediately responded that one of the furs belonged to one of his victims and maybe a camera and some silver may be from the same victim. He'll be over in a little while with his property lists. In the meantime I would delay putting out a property teletype until we had completed tomorrows viewing.

I placed a call to Lt Terrell to fill him in on our progress to date. He told me Brown was very cooperative and would like to clear some cases for us if it would help him. Terrell and I agreed that he would ask Brown about his activities in Beverly Hills and West L.A. In return for his cooperation in finding any property and acknowledging his crimes, we would not file any further charges. Provided, he cooperated with Terrell in his case, and pled out his charges in Illinois. Terrell said he would get back to me after he had a chance to lay it out for Brown. In the meantime I would send copies of my crime reports fitting his M.O. to assist in refreshing Browns memory.

I was up to my hips trying to get crime reports together when Hankins told me he had just had a call from Wilshire Division that a fur store on Wilshire and Curson had been hit last night by the windowsmasher. A beat car had a brief chase with a Corvette about three blocks from the store about the time the alarm went off. The Corvette outran them in less than a half mile.

"I told Lt. Zimmer about your suspect and he said he would like to come over and talk to you about him today. In fact he's on his way over now. Have one of the clerks finish getting those reports together".

"I can't Captain. They aren't familiar with Browns M.O. or which cases I'm interested in. I'll get them together after the Lt. leaves. That is, if the day doesn't run out of hours."

"Well, you were looking for work when you came here. You can't say you're being shortchanged". He laughed as he headed back to his office.

Lt. Karl Zimmer arrived about fifteen minutes later and after introductions we went into the small office next to Hankin's office. I sat my pile of folders on the smasher on one corner of the table. Zimmer pulled a sheath of papers from his coat pocket and spread them on the table.

"We've had eight fur store window smashes and two in jewelry stores in the past six months. I understand Hollywood, Pasadena, San Marino and North Hollywood have all had several fur stores hit in the past few months." He said as he pointed to a group of case numbers written on the papers he has laid out.

"Yeah Lt., I know. I have a pretty complete list of the window smashes in the area. With the seven we've had here in town the list of fur stores hit is thirty one. I can only be sure of four jewelry stores done by the same guy. There've been more jewelry stores hit but most of the M.O.'s vary to much to tie them to our man."

"What makes you so sure your guy is doing these jobs?"

"Let me lay it out for you and see what you think about him."

I spent the next hour filling him in on all the circumstantial evidence I had gathered in the past few months. He was paying strict attention to what I'm telling him. He only interrupted twice with questions about matters I had inadvertently glossed over. He was obviously paying attention.

After going back over a few points, and a couple of minutes of cogitation he said "O.K. I'm convinced, what do we do to put him away? You've obviously thought about this a lot, what do you have in mind?"

"Well he hasn't got any pattern that I can work out. So that rules out surveillance. Until we can come up with something else, the only thing I can come up with is a stake out system."

" The one we tried didn't work out too well. One of our guys got off a shot at him but didn't even slow him down. Where he drops the cars, that's the only area where he has any consistency. That's the only place I know we can concentrate."

" We notify each City or Division where he's hit or is likely to hit and tell them to notify your Division immediately on the next hit. You have your troops alerted that when they get the word they set up a rolling stakeout in the apartment house area where most of the stolen cars have been dumped. Maybe we can spot him dumping one of the cars. I know it's going to take a hell of a lot of luck but it's the only thing I can come up with for now. I'm waiting for some kind of break to go at him some other way but I don't have it yet."

"Well that's it then, for now. I'll notify the other towns and set it up with our watch commanders. Like you say it'll take a lot of luck. Let me know what else you come up with and if we can give you a hand." We shook hands and he said his good-byes to Hankins on the way out the door. Hankins came into the room as I was gathering my files together.

"How'd he feel about your guy?"

"Oh, he's convinced we're working on the right guy but he knows we don't have anything to bust him on yet." I explained the mobile stakeout plan to him. "We both know it's a real longshot but what the hell else have we got at this point?"

It was 5:45 by the time I waited on the ramp for my ride home. By golly I may even beat my wife home today.

CHAPTER 18

That morning there was a note for me from Bob Bowers, the Night Watch Commander, asking me to call Chet Turner when I got in. I knew it was too early to call but I tried anyway. I was informed Chet would probably be in the office about 8:30 AM and to try then . Well, it was worth a shot. It wasn't like I wouldn't have something to do while I was waiting.

I'd just started going through the teletypes when people started coming in. Capt. Hankins was first, and reminded me that I was getting behind in my follow-up reports. Cork and Egger were next with Cork asking me if I'd heard anything on the Berle job yet. Egger asked jokingly if I'd have time to sweep the floor sometime that morning.

Moe and Britton and Valentine are long gone. I seem to be set for residential and commercial burglary, theft, shoplifting, pawnshop detail and anything associated. Yes, we have one 'real' pawnshop in town. Oh, we have several jewelry stores in town licensed to buy second hand merchandise outright but only one shop authorized to 'pawn' merchandise. It has a discreet second floor location in a multistory office building on Wilshire Blvd. with none of the outward signs of the traditional 'pawnshop'.

Each time a secondhand item is pawned or sold, a sale or pawn form must be submitted to the police department. All of these slips must be reviewed by detectives assigned to that detail. This city doesn't generate your run of the mill transactions. Loans of many thousands of dollars are made on a wide variety of collateral. Jewelry being the most prevalent of course.

By far the more interesting, is 'who' is selling or pawning whatever. After a while you start to get the feeling that you can predict the hard times in the entertainment industry. Pawning a ring for ten times my annual salary doesn't quite provoke me to excess sympathy. Then again, everything is relative.

I finally caught Chet in the office just after 8:30 AM.

"Hi Bob, how're they hanging?"

"To the right Chet, to the right. What's up?"

"We had a small timer in yesterday for shoplifting. He was trying hard to bargain his way out of a felony petty theft with a prior and he mentioned the Berle job. We pressed him pretty hard for what he had but he's in the county now if you want to go see him."

"No, I don't need to see him if you've talked to him. What did he have to say?"

"He dropped a couple of names on us that may be of interest to you. We felt we got all he had or we would have held him here for you."

"Whose names did he drop?"

"The first one was an `actress' named Barbara Lewis. She's supposed to be the gal Marshal was hanging out with on the Strip. Rumor also has it," he says, "she is connected with some members of organized crime. Some lesser members to be sure, but enough so she can rely on their attention if she needs it. He doesn't know just how she's involved except that she's around the joints with Marshal. The other name was Robert Dickey. According to our man Dickey may be a receiver and may have handled some of the Berle property."

"Who is this guy Dickey. Have you ever heard of him?"

"No, and we couldn't find a local record on him. He's supposed to be in his 40's and hangs around the `in' joints along the Strip. He's supposed to have a wife in her early twenties who likes to bar hop. That's about it Bob. We'll see if can ID these people a little better and let us know if you can put any of it together."

"I will Chet. I appreciate it. Did any of that property in Santa Monica look like anything from your area?"

"No, the teletype wasn't very descriptive but what there was didn't look like any of ours."

"Well, I'm on my way out there with some of my victims. I did see a jewelry box from one of my jobs and maybe we can ID something else."

"God Luck, Let us know if you can ID these other people. Let's go to lunch one of these days when you're in the area."

"O.K. I'll call you when I'm up there".

We said our good-byes and hung up. I went out to our ID section to try and find something on Barbara Lewis or Robert Dickey. Sam Bottleman, one of our most conscientious clerks, took what information I had and said he'd check on it and get back to me. Knowing Sam, if there was anything to be found in files in L.A. or locally, he'd find it.

By the time I got my notes into the Berle file it was time to pick up my victims and get to Santa Monica. From what I'd run into so far I didn't want to be late. Although I told the victims yesterday what time I would pick them up, I give Jack their phone numbers and ask him to call them and tell them I'm on my way. Just to be sure. Only one was not ready when I got there but she only took a few minutes off the clock. Luckily she was the last pickup and I had a little time to brief the other two about what to expect. I avoided telling them about my 'feelings' on the chance It just could be my misreading the whole situation.

We arrived just after one o'clock and went into the Detective Bureau. Katt came over to us and I introduced him to my victims. While this was going on I noticed a small group of people crowded around the doorway to the room where the merchandise was being displayed.

Katt asked us to wait a couple of minutes until the other group was done. I excused myself from the ladies and took Katt aside.

"Do you mean they are going to try to identify their property from the doorway?"

"Yeah, they can point out what they recognize and we'll bring it over to the doorway for a closer look".

"Look Katt, what the hell's going on? Do you want the property identified or not. You can't even see all the stuff from the doorway let alone identify it. My people are going to want to see the merchandise. They aren't the kind of people to be shuffled off into the corner some where."

"That's the way it's done here. We don't want too many people pawing over the stuff. it's too hard to keep track of."

"If that's your problem then let them in one at a time and walk around with them. They'll at least have a closer look. Just tell them to tell you which pieces look like theirs and you can pick them up one at a time for a closer look".

"I'll see if the Lt. will do it like that."

He left me and went into an office across the room. Another detective was now ushering the other people away from the doorway.

I began to escort my victims toward the doorway and Katt came out of the office and over to us.

"The Lt. says we can do it your way but we'll have to keep any property here if it's identified until we get the whole thing wrapped up. We'll need to get that property you recovered and combine it with ours to get a complete inventory".

"Yeah, well lets get this done first. I don't want these ladies standing around waiting while we discuss this. Just a minute, there's another one of my victims coming in the door. We might as well get them all together and do this one time."

I left him standing flatfooted while I went across the office and met Mrs. Hallstrom. After introductions all round for the ladies I turned to Katt and told him we were ready.

We explained the procedure to the ladies as we approached the doorway. Two of the ladies get a puzzled look on their faces and looked at each other. As the first one entered the room with Katt I started to follow. I was stopped abruptly by a second detective in the room. I waited beside the door as each victim viewed the property. Mrs. Hallstrom, of course, ID'd her jewelry box and a couple of small pieces of jewelry. One of them identified an expensive camera by a dent on the lens housing. All in all the viewing was not very productive.

When it's done I was standing in the doorway as Katt was coming out and asked him when the property will be released to the victims. He advised me to have their insurance companies contact him for release of the merchandise.

"What the hell are you talking about? What have their insurance companies got to do with them getting their property back?"

"Well if the insurance companies have already paid them for the property then the stuff should go back to them."

"That may be, but that's between them and their companies and certainly none of your or my business."

By now my boiling point had been reached. I was about to erupt when Mrs. Horne, one of my quieter victims, stepped in and said,

"Excuse me Detective Downey, don't get embroiled in any argument. I'll let our attorney handle the recovery of my property. And also find out if a subtle accusation of fraud has been made or implied. This whole business today has been a fiasco and I'd like to know why. That's why we pay an attorney and I'd like him to find out what's going on." Her voice had a finely honed, cutting edge to it. When she finished, you could feel the tension in the air.

"Thank you Mrs. Horne. That's it then Katt, I guess you'll be hearing from Mrs. Horne's attorney. Come ladies, Det. Katt will supply us with a list of property you have identified as soon as his inventory is done, if ever. If you don't mind, I have more property at my office I would like you to take a look at on our way back." There was an obvious smile in my voice.

"We haven't had a chance to see that stuff yet" Katt says with a some obvious indignation in his voice.

"Come by Monday afternoon. I'll have a showing for anything that hasn't been claimed by then".

As we are getting into our cars my three victims began to ask in varying ways "Just what went on in there?"

On the ride back I explained in more detail what I believed was happening while at the same time avoiding accusations and trying to let them draw their own conclusions. It was then they told me that they had the same general feeling they were being treated in a condescending manner and their questions and statements were largely ignored.

While I had not had time to properly display our property I took the ladies into the anteroom where the boxes were located and proceeded to lay the property out on the tables for their inspection.

Mrs. Horne immediately identified her mink stole and mink trimmed cashmere sweater. Each of the other ladies identified some item from the boxes as having been taken in their burglaries.

After tagging the identified property I advised them that the property would be released to them on Monday. I told them I would deliver it to their residences. I thanked them for their assistance and drove two of them home.

When I got back to the office I explained to Cork and Hankins what had happened and why I brought the ladies to the office to view the property before we were through checking it out. They both agreed it was the right move under the circumstances. I also filled them in on what Turner had told me.

I was at my wits end trying to decide what pile of paper to start working on when Sam came in and told me he'd found a minor record on a Robert Dickey in Burbank but nothing recent or with a mug shot. The address given then was obsolete and none of the directories listed anything recent. There were a couple Barbara Lewis' with prostitution arrests but our information was too vague to be sure if it was the right Barbara.

I filled Cork in over a cup of coffee. "I've talked to the Berles' a little while ago and they haven't heard from Marshal yet. Maybe we'd better get the word out on the street that we want to talk to him", he said as he finished his coffee and we left the drug store.

"I'm giving some thought to doing a little bar hopping and see if I can rattle any cages about him". I said as we crossed in front of the Crocker Bank.

We just had to look in through the windows as we passed. You just never know. As we waited to cross Canon Dr. I decided it was a good time to feel Cork out about one of my theories.

"Say B.L., have you noticed how many `peeper' and `prowler' calls we're getting on the morning watch.?" I ask.

"Yeah, they seem to come in spurts. Why ?"

"I was just wondering. I began to do some research on the number of calls and the days of the week. After going over six months of logs I began to get a pattern that disturbs me some."

"Let me guess. You found that the same Patrol Sergeant was working on most every night we got several calls."

"You knew ?"

"Well, not really. I just had a strong hunch. What do you think we can do about it ?"

"It would be damned hard to put a tail on him. If we did catch him in the `act', he could always claim he was checking on someone or something he had or had not seen. It'd be damned hard to prove."

"That's for sure. We've talked about this before. Oh yes, there are some others that have the same feeling. We just haven't figured out a way to nail him good. If you can figure out a new twist, let's talk with Hankins about it. Right now, we have enough on our plate."

We climbed the south stairs of City Hall and headed for the office. We had to get something moving on the Berle case.

I had thought I may be staying home that night but I guess not. Maybe if I bothered enough people something would shake loose. At least I was able to spend a couple of hours at home before making the rounds.

About 9:00 PM I headed out for the strip. I started with the Tailspin. I'd known one of the bartenders there since before I got out of the service. It didn't do me any good because he said he didn't know the people I was looking for. At least he knew I was still around. Next, the Nic Ric. I understood one of the owners, Leo Riccio, was quite familiar with some pretty unsavory people. I told the bartender, as he delivered my drink, that I would like to talk to Leo. In a few minutes a well dressed man came up to me and said "What can I do for the Police Department? I'm Leo". as he put out his hand.

"I've been told cops stick out like a sore thumb but we all like to think we're different. Obviously I'm not". I turned on the barstool to face him as he sat beside me.

"It was just a good guess. Besides, that bump under your arm didn't come with the suit. What's up."

I told him who and what I was looking for and why. He stared at the backbar for a while and called his bartender over to the corner for a short talk. He returned to his seat next to me.

"The Lewis gal comes in once in a while, usually with some hood type. Never had any trouble with her or her friends. My bartender thinks your man Dickey has been here a few times. He remembers because of the name on a credit card. He thought is was an unusual name. Had a young gal with him. Supposed to be his wife. Bill thinks they hang out at some joints farther out on the Strip. That's about all I can help you with".

"Well thanks a lot. I appreciate it. The sooner I can run them down and talk to them the less often I'll have to come in and make people nervous."

"You don't make me nervous".

"Probably not, but when I sat down here there were five other guys at the bar. Now there are two. Three quietly went out the door. Guilty conscience I guess". We both laughed as I paid for my drink and left.

Next stop the Saratoga, Whiskey A Go Go, the Melody Room and the Crescendo. Same routine at each stop, get the owner or manager, fill them in, they talk to the bartender or a couple of the waitresses, return, and say they don't know my people.

With the exception of the Melody Room. Bobby Adler, the owner, was very gracious and seemed to be pleased to meet me. He knew of Barbara Lewis but didn't know where she lived or who she ran with. He indicates he feels 'acting' is her second job. As I finished my drink and sat it down Bobby said, "I want you to meet someone", he took me by the arm and lead me to a tall man at the bar with his back to us.

"Bob, I'd like you to meet Clint Eastwood. You've probably

seem him in the series "Rawhide".

"As a matter of fact I have. I enjoy the show very much. It's nice to meet you."

"Likewise" he said as he slipped off the bar stool and stood up. This surprised me a little. At 6'2" I'm usually as tall as or taller than most people I run into. Not this time. He appeared to be about two inches taller. They certainly don't have to put him on any box to talk with his contemporaries in the business.

"Yeah Clint, Bob's a Detective with the Beverly Hills Police Department. If he accepts my invitation we may see a lot of him around here". Bobby said.

"Good" Clint says, "Bobby makes you feel at home and he doesn't water the drinks".

"Yeah, and we're putting in a piano bar and Ronnie Brown's coming over from the Saratoga in a couple of weeks".

"Now I know my wife and I will be back. We go to the Saratoga a lot to listen to him. Well gentlemen, I'll be on my way. I've got a couple more stops to make. It's been nice talking to you." I said as I headed for the door. Bobby walked to the doorway with me all the time repeating his invitation to come back.

As I pulled away from the curb I decided to add one more stop. I backtracked to Crescent Heights and Santa Monica and parked in the parking lot next to P.J.'s. It had opened not long before and had got them a quick reputation for being the place to go.

As I stepped down the few steps inside the doorway I saw a long bar on the left side of the rather narrow room. There was about six feet of aisleway along the right side of the room running the length of the bar. On the backbar was a small performing stage with a guitar player sitting on a stool. The room was pretty well packed and patrons were standing two and three deep behind the people on the bar stools. Four bartenders were working full tilt to pass out drinks and collect money.

It took me a few minutes to realize there was a larger room located at the rear of the place, with a juke box, tables and a dance floor. Getting through the crowd at the bar was going to be an adventure. Oh well, into the breach.

Working my way through the crowd proved to be full of thrills. These was no way to do it without close body contact. Very quickly you learned how to plan your route so that your required contact was not overly distasteful. There are a couple of startled looks when someones elbow or hand or other body part rubs, bumps or touches the area under my left arm and encounters the four inch barreled .38 Smith and Wesson hanging there. The questions flashed across their eyes about as quickly as they looked away pretending they didn't notice.

Once I'd made my way to the back room, I cornered a waitress, identified myself, and asked for the owner or manger. A few minutes later she returned with a well dressed man who obviously treated himself well. I introduced myself and asked for a few minutes of his time.

"How do you do Bob, my name is Paul Raffles, how can I help you?" He said as he guided me to a booth near the back of the room. We slid into the plush cushions as I laid out what I was looking for. He ordered us a round of drinks as I explained what I'm trying to do by hitting a lot of the more `in' places in town.

"You mean, that if you stir up enough crap for these people they will either get fingered by someone or be persuaded by some of the business people to give you a call. That way maybe you won't be coming around making people nervous. Have I about got it?" He said with a slight laugh in his voice.

"Yeah, something like that. Although I don't ever recall putting any pressure on anybody."

"Of course not. But the mere presence of plain cloths officers, repeatedly, at some places around town, not here of course, would tend to have a dampening effect on business".

"I hadn't thought of it quite like that but I guess it would have now that you mention it." "Never the less, I don't particularly

recall either of those people but let me chec with my people around here. They get to know our customers a lot quicker and better than I do." He raised his glass in a toasting gesture, as did I, and we both seemed to have come to an understanding. Of just what I wasn't sure, but he was definitely not the run of the mill gin joint operator found in Hollywood and environs. The whole place seemed to be a cut above the usual Hollywood hangout.

He waved over one of the three suit dressed men that seemed to float around the room and bar area. He introduced me and then asked the man to see if the other employees knew anything about the people I was interested in. The 'overseer' looked at me for a second and eased back into the bobbing heads and swirling bodies.

"We might as well have another drink, he'll be a while. How do you like our show out front. That's Trini Lopez. He really packs them in." He said with no small show of pride.

"I've heard of him but haven't had much of a chance to hear him. He sounds good, and he's certainly liked by this crowd."

"He sure is, I'm going to try to keep him around as long as I can. We're going to try for a recording session right here in a couple of weeks." He was obviously concerned with building a good business and from his conversation, a good reputation. "You know" he said, "all kidding aside, you and your friends are always welcome to drop in here. The type of people your presence would scare off would not be good business for this place anyway. Seriously, drop in anytime. And come through this door over here", pointing to a side door with and overseer standing by. "makes it easier than trying to push through from the bar".

The overseer named Jerry returned and sat down. He'd been gone about fifteen minutes.

"Nobody seems to know them by name. If you had a picture they might be able to help you. Three of our people aren't here tonight but I'll talk to them tomorrow and let you know."

"Thanks, I appreciate it. You might pass the word around about who's looking for them. They might get the urge to call me. Never can tell." As Jerry left, I finished my drink and said my good-byes to Paul. As I took out my money to pay for the drinks he waved my money away. I dropped a five on the table, "for the waitress", and went out the side door.

I was home in twenty minutes and damned glad to be. It had been a long day. As I came in the door Diana was watching T.V.

"Did you find what you were looking for?" she asked getting up and gave me a passing peck as she headed for the kitchen.

"Would you like a drink or a cup of coffee?"

"Coffee please. And no, not really. I got a few people a little irritated at my being there. And I met a couple of nice people. The guy that owns the Melody Room, Bobby Adler, and the guy who owns that new joint on Santa Monica, P.J.s. Adler introduced me to Clint Eastwood. You know, Rowdy Yates on Rawhide. And Bill Dana was at the Melody Room too. He was at a table with a couple of other people."

"Sounds like it was celebrity night" she said as she sat my coffee down beside me. "By the way, Mr. Campbell called tonight. He would like to talk with you tomorrow. He's going to the ranch this weekend and has a few things he wants you to know. How is that P.J.'s. I've read and heard a few things about it lately. Sounds like it's getting to be the `in' spot for the young crowd."

"It's pretty nice. Crowded as hell. Trini Lopez was playing on the small showstage on the backbar. He sounded pretty good. We'll have to stop in there some night."

When I called in for my ride the next morning Bert Sloane, the dispatcher, informed that my window smasher had hit again in the Wilshire Division.

Once I got into the office I got a more interesting story from Russ Peterson, the Watch Commander. It seemed that about 3:00 AM, McHuin had gotten into a short chase with a Corvette on Wilshire at Hamel. For the first block he was alongside the Corvette and got a good look at the driver. The 'Vette left him standing but he was sure it was Porterfield. About forty five minutes later Wilshire Division called and reported a fur store window smash about four blocks east of our town. A witness saw a Corvette leaving the scene.

I told Russ I wanted to see McHuin before he went home and I went into the office and called Wilshire Division and got Lt. Zimmer on the line.

"How'd it go" I asked. "Did we get the rolling stake out in place in time?"

"We only had one car to put on it and he didn't get your man. We did find something interesting though. Remember the Corvette one of your guys shot at a few weeks ago, well we found one with what appears to be shotgun pellet holes in it. The interesting part is, the engine was still hot. Not warm, but hot. Could be this guy has used the same car more than once. He may dump a car after a job then keep an eye on it. If it isn't recovered by the time he's ready to go again, he uses it again."

"That's very interesting. And maybe just a little dumb. How can he be sure it's not being staked out? Of course time is on his side. No Department can spare the manpower to stake out a car for too long. One thing holds true though, he still likes to drop his cars in the same area."

I went on to explain to him about McHuin getting into a short chase with a 'Vette driven by Porterfield shortly before their job.

"He's either got some balls to go ahead and pull a job right after he's chased, or he's getting too confident and thumbing his nose at us. I've got the stirrings of a plan in the back of my mind. I'll talk with our officer and see if it's workable and let you know later today."

"O.K. Bob. Let me know if we can help. This guy's getting to be a BIG pain in the ass."

"Right Karl, I'll be talking to you."

As the guys came into the office they were talking about last nights activity. I went into Hankins office where Cork was discussing it with Hankins.

"We've got to do something about getting this guy off the street somehow." Hankins said to me as he settled his huge body into what always appeared to be to small a chair.

"I know Captain. I'm going to talk to McHuin and if he's got what I need I think I have a plan." I also told them about the recovery of the hot hooded Corvette in the same area as the others. "Zimmer has taken a look at it and feels they are shotgun pellet holes. He's having it printed and'll let me know if they find anything'.

About that time McHuin came into the office and he and I headed for my desk.

"Hell Bob, I thought I had him for sure last night. I was sitting on Beckman Furs when he drove by. I was up on him on the drivers side before he spotted me. When I turned my lights on he turned toward me and took a quick look before he took off. And I mean took off. That `Vette was out of sight in about six blocks. He made three turns and I was left standing."

"Did you know that Wilshire had a job shortly after that?"

"Yeah, I talked to a patrol unit of theirs right after it happened. Someone saw the same colored Corvette. No plates, just like mine. He's getting gutsy."

"Or desperate. Maybe something's pushing him. I'll make a few calls today and see if I can find out what. I'll need a statement from you written out on a four page report. I'm going to see if I can get a warrant for reckless driving from Judge Alexander. Be sure you include your identification and all the traffic violations. Speed, turns, any weaving, what ever you saw that would indicate reckless driving. I've got to convince the judge we can prove it in court."

"What the hell good's a reckless driving warrant going to do? Even if you got one he'd be out on bail in an hour or two."

"Yeah, I know. But that's not the object. I've got something else in mind. Get me that report as soon as you can. I want to get this done today." He got up from my desk and went out the door to the front desk area. A short time later I had Carpenter on the phone.

"Is there anything going on in his case that would be pushing him? He was chased in our town at about three and probably pulled a window smash in Wilshire about 3:45." I went on to fill him in on the details of the night.

"I don't know of anything but I'll give a few calls and get back to you. If they find any prints on that car be sure they check them against him. I'll get back to you in a little while". We hung up and I went into the office with Cork and Hankins.

"Burglary/Auto is checking to see if they can find anything that might be pushing our man. I've talked with McHuin and I think I can get a reckless driving warrant on him."

"What the hell good is that going to do?" Hankins asked.

"I don't give a damn about the charge, I just want some legal reason to arrest him at the right time. I figure if I can arrest him while he's with his girlfriend, she may blurt out something or be wearing some of the merchandise. At least I'll be legal in searching the car he's driving. He's been driving his mothers car exclusively. Maybe he's careless and has left stuff in the trunk.

At the same time I arrest him I'd like to have somebody at his ex-wifes' place and talk to her. Maybe when she hears he's in custody, she doesn't have to be told why he's arrested, she'll give out with something we can use."

I let out a heavy sigh as I got up to leave the office, "Hell, I don't know what's going to happen. I just know we've been stymied too long and that whatever I do I want it to be legal. I don't want to blow it at this late date".

"Well Bob" Cork says, "It's a hell of a long shot but we don't have much to lose at this point. When do you want to do this?"

"I'll have to give that some thought. I want to pick the best opportunity but I don't want to wait long. I'll let you know."

I had time to do some work on my late follow-up reports while I was waiting for Kennys' report. It gave me a little time to try and map out a strategy.

When would be a good time to take him? He got three furs out of last nights job. How long does he hang on to them? Where does he store them? Who does he deal them to? It's strange, of all the furs and jewelry he's taken, none of it has shown up anywhere. He's either got one hell of a stash or he's got a good outlet.

Yeah, Monday will be as good a day as any if I can get the judge to sign the warrant.

Mourning told me that Carpenter is on the phone for me.

"Hey, what's happening?" I said as I sat down and started to play with my pencil.

"His appeal was denied last week and he's to be sentenced on the auto theft in three weeks". He said "That may be what's set him off. Maybe he's trying to build a nest egg before he goes in".

"That could be. What's he do to get at sentencing?"

"Probably two to five, certainly no more. It's his first felony. He probably wouldn't have had to do any time if so many cars hadn't been involved".

"Well, keep your fingers crossed. I'm going to try to scoop him up Monday morning with a chickenshit reckless driving warrant and see if I can shake anything out of the trees".

"Good luck Bob. Keep us advised and let us know if we can help any."

By the time I hung up Kenny was standing at my desk with his report. He was heading out the door as I began typing up the complaint and the warrant.

"Let me know when you're going after him, I'd like to go along"

"O.K. It'll probably be Monday morning, but I'm not positive yet. I'll let you know."

When I had the paperwork together I headed for Judge Alexanders' office on the ground floor of the building, after clearing with his clerk. There's a very small courtroom on the ground floor of the City Hall with a small office behind it. Not elaborate, but functional. The judge was outgoing and friendly but strictly a no nonsense guy.

I went over the entire case in about fifteen minutes and then made my pitch for a warrant after he read Kenny's report and my supporting complaint.

"O.K. Bob, all flim-flam aside, is this a legitimate reckless driving complaint or are you stretching it a bit just to get your warrant?"

"You read the report your honor. It's not been changed or amended."

"O.K. Raise your right hand." He takes my oath and then signs the complaint and the warrant. I thanked him and started out the door.

"I presume that if you make your burglary case you'll probably be dropping this complaint?"

"I'll be happy too, as a gesture of compassion, your honor".

"You're all heart, Downey."

On my way back to the office I stopped by the Clerks office to file the complaint and get the warrant certified. A few minutes later I was back at my desk wondering. What ifs', again.

I was so deep in paperwork I didn't hear the phone ring. Jack Egger took the call and from the 'yeahs', 'o.k.s' and 'uh huhs' I got the feeling that there was some cryptic message being delivered. He hung up with "we'll be right out".

Since we were the only ones in the office I presumed the 'we' meant he and I. We both get up and headed for the door.

Sgt. Peterson met us at the door.

"We've had a 459 silent from a house at 236 S.Bedford. The neighbor also saw a man leaving the premises and get into an older Pontiac with Calif. plates. He went south on Bedford and turned east on Olympic. We put out a radio call but haven't spotted him yet. He was carrying a small bag of some kind when he got into the car. Here's the name and address of who and where the car is registered.

I'll have the beat car check the area and round up any other witnesses. We'll let you know by radio what we find."

Russ had fed us this information as we were going down the stairs and out the door to our car. In the car we started to figure our next move. Here we are, in the car, heading we don't know where. Time to make a plan.

The name of the registered owner of the car is not known to us. Not unusual. The address where the car was registered was in the lower downtown L.A. area known to have many run down residential hotels. Might as well head there. Over the radio we requested a record or warrant check on the registered owners name.

We were told it was being done. Of course. Why wouldn't it be. We must have deluded ourselves into feeling we were the only ones who could think.

We had taken San Vicente to Pico and now were moving fast through light traffic toward downtown. On the way we were watching for the old Pontiac. We couldn't be that lucky. The radio broke our mind games with the information that our suspect had a record for business and residential burglary. He may also be on parole. They were still checking.

In a very short time we were parking in the side lot of an old six story residential hotel on the corner of 12th and Maple in downtown L.A. We had checked both parking lots for the suspects car. No luck. It was more than likely that the guy didn't even live here anymore, if he ever did.

Once on foot we checked the street in all directions to see if the car may have parked on the street. In the majority of cases, guys who live in places like this don't move far from the neighborhood even if they do move. They like familiar surroundings. If he was on parole, he probably wouldn't have gone to far. If we had no luck here we'd call his P.O.

We went into the hotel lobby and luckily only the desk clerk was there. He obviously had us made for cops the instant we walked in. He started to fidget, look around quickly, started to shuffle his feet and sway slightly from side to side. If I had to guess I would say this man was either an ex-con or he hung around them to much.

After a couple of questions we had a pleasant surprise. Our suspect still lived there in room 404. The clerk didn't think he was home right then but if we wanted to we could wait for him in his room. The hotel wouldn't mind. He took us to the fourth floor and let us in with a pass key. As he was about to leave, Jack pulled him aside and said,

"My friend, for your information, should our man show up in the parking lot or lobby and not make it up here to his room, we'll have to believe you tipped him off. That being the case, you'll have to go to jail for interfering with a police officer. Am I making an impression on you ?"

"Yeh, I know. I don't want nothing to do with this."

"That's fine. Now go back to your lobby and do the things you do. We'll see you on the way out.", Jack said as he closed the door.

We now had time to look around the room. It's bleak. You have to know anyone that would live in these surroundings needs help. It's a rather large room. A couch and tattered chair on one wall, a small kitchen table and two chairs in front of two windows and a single bed to the right of the doorway. A door at the far corner of the room lead to a cramped bathroom. A drape next to that door revealed a small two burner hot plate sitting on a small refrigerator, both next to a small sink. A small T.V. sits on a night table at the foot of the bed.

If this guy was our burglar, or any burglar for that matter, he was not very damned good at it.

From the windows you could see the rear parking lot of the hotel. While Jack did a quick shakedown of the place I kept watch on the parking lot. Jack finished, finding nothing, and joined me at the window. Jack decided the only place he hadn't looked was inside the T.V. set. When he looked at it he saw the screws in back were clean and freshly scarred.

In a few seconds he had the back open. He reached in and pulled out a small cigar box and brought it to the table. We opened it to find a few small pieces of inexpensive jewelry. We emptied the box and returned it to the T.V. and reinstalled the back. Should this guy hit the street for some crazy reason, imagine how he's going to feel when he opens the back of this set and finds the box empty. He's sure to figure some of his friends ripped him off. He won't get to see our arrest and evidence reports to know that the stuff has been seized as evidence. Maybe he'll get the feeling some of our victims do.

We'd only been back at the window a few minutes when we saw the Pontiac pull into the lot and park. Our man got out carrying a small canvas bag. He headed around the corner for the front of the building. A few minutes later there was a noise at the door like someone putting a key in the lock.

The door opened, and Jack took hold of his right shirt collar and I took the left and we propelled him into the room and onto the couch. He dropped the bag. When he quit bouncing we are on each side looking down on him.

"Mr. Stedman, you are under arrest for burglary. I'm Sgt. Downey and this is Sgt. Egger of the Beverly Hills Police Department. Please do us the courtesy of not feeding us a bunch of bullshit by trying to deny it. You were seen, your license number was written down, and I'll bet the loot is in that bag. Am I correct ?"

"Yeah, it's in there. How'd you guys get here so damned quick?"

"Better yet", Jack said, "What took you so damned long anyway? Where did you stop ?"

"I had to stop for gas, I almost ran out"

"Are you still on parole ?" Jack asked.

"Yeah, I've got a three year tail." Now he was starting to sound dejected. Like he'd just then realized what kind of trouble he was in.

"O.K. Stand up and let's get the hooks on and get out of here. Is all the stuff still in the bag ?" I opened the bag and looked inside just as he said, "Yeah, it's all there. I haven't had time to even look at it yet."

"I held the open bag toward him and said, "Here, take your last look. Make it a good one. You'll want to remember what it was that sent you back to the joint."

We locked the door and took him down the stairs and through the lobby. The desk clerk didn't even look up. After we got to the parking lot and searched the car we headed for the office. An hour later we had finished the arrest report and booked the evidence. We were back in the office just as everyone was preparing to leave.

We took some good natured ribbing about picking up a lame duck, and being handed a pigeon. How we might get spoiled working such soft touches.

-DOWN

“That’s O.K. guys. May it ever be thus. If you stuck around the office once in a while you too may get the easy ones. Come on Jack, let’s go treat ourselves to a beer to celebrate the successful conclusion of another intricate, mindboggling, investigation.”

CHAPTER 19

I had most of my follow up paper work arranged on my desk in order of priority and was just settling down for a few hours of drudgery when Lt. Pierce came into the office. He was Watch Commander for that day. He looked around for a second until I said, "Hi Lieutenant".

"Do you know that guy that does the Chipmunks thing on television ?" He asked with no pretext of cordially.

"Do you mean Ross Bagdasarian ?"

"Yeah that's the one. He just called and has been the victim of a burglary or theft in the last 24 hours sometime. I told him you would be up in a few minutes to talk with him". He started for the door.

"Are you sending the beat car to take the report? I'm only in today to catch up on some paper work. This is my day off."

"I know it's your day off but I don't want a patrolman to take the report, I want you. I told him I would have you up there in a few minutes. I'm not sure a patrol officer is prepared to take a burglary report."

"If they're not capable of taking a report then they should be trained. We can't be expected to take every criminal report that comes along."

"Maybe not, but you'll have to take this one. I've already told him you'd be there shortly". He turned and left the office. My protestations obviously fell on deaf ears. I was certainly not going to solve this situation by talking to him.

A few minutes later I had parked in front of the Bagdasarian house. It's located on the northeast corner of the intersection and had a brick wall about six feet tall running the length of the south property line on the street side. From the outside you could see the roof of a small building appearing to be a garage located near the rear property line of the house.

As I approached the front door it was opened by a solidly built man looking to be in his mid thirties. He extended his hand and said,

"Hi, I'm Ross Bagdasarian. Come on in. We can go out to the studio through the dining room."

I introduced myself and followed him out into the back yard. It was obvious now that what looked like a garage, wasn't. The garage was located next to the studio. There was a wooden gate opening onto the alley for access to the garage.

"We just finished the studio a short while ago and I've been doing a lot of my work in here." He opened the door and lead me inside. The inside was equipped with several large tape recorders along one wall with other electronic gear in various locations around the room. The center of the room was occupied by a beautiful, large, executive desk and leather chair. The desk top appeared in disarray and somewhat empty.

"There are several small tape recorders and radios missing but the things that I'm maddest about is my desk set. My family bought it for me when we opened this studio. It's maroon leather with gold embossing. It's the complete set including a waste basket. You know, with pencil cups, clip holders, the works. It's not the price of it but the fact it's a gift from my family. I wouldn't care about getting the other stuff back if I could get the desk set back".

We made a preliminary list of the missing property then looked for any signs of forced entry. We didn't expect to find any. He was right. He had said he seldom locked the door. As we were discussing the burglary he gave me a tour of the studio and explained some of the work he does there. We drifted far afield in our conversation, at times discussing some of his movie work, and his recent purchase of a winery in central California.

In about an hour, I'd wrapped up my preliminary investigation. I'd requested that he obtain any serial numbers available on any of the electronic gear and call me Monday or Tuesday. I left with the feeling that I'd met a very nice man, especially under the circumstances.

When I got back to the office Cork was at his desk on the telephone. I turned my report in for typing and I started my paperwork again. Cork finished his call and sat down at my desk. I filled him in on the Bagdasarian case and the fact that I couldn't understand why a Patrol Officer couldn't be sent to take a preliminary report. Not that I minded taking this one after I had gotten there.

"Well Bob, you did the right thing. You know you can't reason with Tom. He doesn't have any confidence in his Patrol Officers. You can't find any more devoted officer than he is but he has reservations about his troops."

"For crying out loud, if they need training in report writing we can give it to them. Do you know how much time we waste taking preliminary reports? Of course you do. Why wouldn't you?. Do you know of any reason why it's done this way?"

"No, except that they feel it will be a detective case anyway so why not let them take it to begin with."

"Well, the hell with it for now."

"Say Bob, are you and the wife doing anything special tonight?"

"Not that I know of. What did you have in mind?"

"Why don't we take the ladies out on the town tonight. Go catch a floor show and then a late dinner. There's a new comic named Lenny Bruce at the Cloister. We can catch him and go to the Plymouth House afterward for dinner."

"Sounds good. What time do you want me to pick you up?"

"About seven-thirty I guess. The show should start about eight."

"O.K. I'll see you then." We walked out to the ramp together and headed for home.

By eight fifteen we were being seated at the Cloister and waiting for our first round of drinks. Mayzelle, B.L., Diana and I. At 8:30 the lights dimmed and the show started. By the time our second order of drinks arrived, we were getting up to leave. We stuffed some bills in the waiters hand and headed for the door.

"If that guy talked like that on the street he'd be slammed in jail. I don't understand the Sheriff's Office." I said in disgust as we waited for our car.

"He's got a foul mouth for sure." Cork said. "I understood he was pretty rank but I didn't think you could get away with that in public."

"Hell, I don't even talk to some of the bums I arrest like that. There was more embarrassed laughter than for anything funny that was said. Well, I know where to tell people not to go."

A short time later we were enjoying a good show at the Moulin Rouge, then on to the Plymouth House on Sunset for dinner and some quiet time around the piano bar for an after dinner drink or two.

After dropping B.L. and Mayzie off, Diana and I were about home when we changed our minds and drove up Benedict to Mulholland. We found a good observation point and shut down the engine, turned the radio down low and leaned back to watch the lights of the city. It was one of those nights that had no limits on view. The piece and quiet began to soak in. The feeling of contentment permeated my body and the guarded thoughts started to drain out.

We talked about everything and nothing. Important things and inconsequential things. We tried to pick out landmarks.

The horizon in the east was getting lighter when we decided it was time to return to reality and began our slow descent homeward. By the time we parked in the driveway reality had started it's inevitable return. The last few hours had made for marvelous memories. They will be stored and dredged up when they are needed to drive out some unforeseen demons.

I went to talk to Mr. Campbell the next morning and helped him load his car for his trip as well as getting some instructions for the gardener.

My Monday morning plans were shot down with a big thud when I found a note in the detective bureau box telling me that

Milton Berle called and would be in the office at 9:00 AM to see us. So much for coming in early to get a head start. I told the Watch Commander to tell McHuin that our plans for the day are cancelled for now. We had planned to check several apartment houses in the area of where the stolen Corvettes were dropped to see if we could locate any connection with our suspect.

I was about through with the teletypes when B.L. came in. We went over to the drug store for coffee as I told him about the phone call and we turned our thoughts over in our minds, and out loud.

We got back to the Station at 8:45 AM and were going through the lobby when Policewoman Lyn Bertoglio signaled us to come to the desk.

"Milton Berle is waiting for you in the interview room".

"On time is good, early is better." I remarked to Cork.

"Yeah, and it could also indicate a need to get something off his mind". As we headed into the office we saw him talking with Capt. Hankins.

He rose and put out his hand as we approached.

"Hello, Mr. Berle, we understand you want to see us."

"Yes, I was just telling the Captain, Marshal called yesterday and told us he had something important to talk to us about. He came over a while later with a girl he introduced as Barbara Lewis. She told us she knew who had pulled the burglary and might be able to help get back our property but she wouldn't name the thief."

"How did she propose to get the stuff back?" asked Cork.

"She said only that she could maybe contact some of the people she knows and try to help us. She didn't want to tell us anymore until we could assure her that the case would be closed if we got our property back and there wouldn't be any charges filed against anyone. She told us Marshal had been living with her at her Thrasher St. apartment and that we could tell Marshal what we decided and he would let her know. She left and Marshal stayed around a while longer then left."

"What did you tell Marshal about getting the property back

or dropping the case ?"

"Nothing, we tried to ask him more questions but he evaded most of them. He seems to be completely under her influence."

Cork and I looked at each other for a few seconds and then Cork said, "You do realize, of course, that Marshal is probably the one who took the stuff from your house and turned it over to the girl, don't you ?"

Berle's eyes closed for just an instant, heaved a big sigh, and then he said,

"Yes, it seemed that way to us too. He finally admitted he had done it after we pressed him pretty hard. He admitted she had pressured him to steal the stuff and turned it over to her for disposal. He was very remorseful and wanted to do anything he could to get the property back.

My wife and I talked it over and what we're going to do is wait for our attorney to get back to town and have him bring Marshal in to your office to talk to you. He's still my nephew and if he's in trouble I'd like to help him if I can."

"That may be fine but you know that a lawyer is going to tell him not to say anything. If that happens we may not be able to recover any of the property or prosecute anyone."

"Well that's what we've decided to do. Our attorney should be back on Monday and we'll make arrangements then", he said as he rose to leave. His tone and actions had the air of dismissal and finality about them. As though he were saying "We've made our decision and that's all there is to it. There is no room for other opinion or action." He left without further comment.

"Well I guess we were told", I said as I took a deep breath.

"I guess he feels that's all there is to it, he's made up his mind and that's the way it's going to be." Cork said with a note of incredulity in his voice.

We walked back to our desks still trying to comprehend what had just happened and what we had done to make anyone believe that someone else was controlling the case.

Back at my desk I had a message from Lt. Terrell, in Illinois, to call him. Terrell told me Brown had admitted five of the ten cases I had sent him. One was Col. Parkers. He told me Brown had said the pipes had been at the girlfriends apartment with the other property. He also told me Brown had pled guilty to three burglaries in his town and was due to be sentenced next week. I told him we would release our hold whenever he advised he didn't need it anymore. He was sending me a copy of their final report for my records.

After I hung up I gathered up the property I had been able to recover from Santa Monica P.D. and from Sally Sheldon's house. I went to Col. Parkers house on Maple Dr. after making sure he would be at home.

Once inside I returned what merchandise we had recovered so far. There were a few items still missing but the pipes were the most important and stuck in my crop. I briefed him in full on the arrest and subsequent recovery from Santa Monica and the girlfriend.

The Colonel was very gracious and pleased to know the guy was in jail and that he had some of his property back, but he was still anxious to find the pipes. Leaving, I assured him I would continue to hunt for the pipes. He thanked me and wished me well.

On the way back to the office I kept thinking about the fact that I knew that I wasn't going to recover all the property on every case. Probably not very much on a lot of cases, but this one just didn't set right. I had the feeling I had missed a step somewhere. I had a good idea what had happened, considering the inscription on the brass plate on the box holding the pipes. If I don't find them they'll eventually show up in someones personal collection. I just couldn't figure out what skullduggery I could use to shake loose those pipes from whatever receptacle they had dropped into. Exasperating.

Back at the office Hankins called us in to discuss the threatening letter to Janet Leigh. He had talked to L.A.P.D. and the studio. No additional threats had been received and the P.D. had run out all the possible leads without any developments. The studio was going to maintain heightened security on the actress when she was at the studio.

A couple of weeks ago her studio had called telling us she had received a threatening letter at the studio making specific reference to her movie, Psycho. The letter had contained some pretty violent threats against Miss Leigh. I had been sent to her house on Summit Dr. to interview her and her husband, Tony Curtis.

When I got there I had been escorted to the master suite dressing room and seated by the housekeeper. A short time later Janet Leigh came into the room looking like she had just walked off the cover of a magazine. She had to have something special to look that good at this time of the morning.

A few seconds later two little girls came running into the room and wrapped themselves around Janet's leg. They all let out a laugh that sounded like it came from pure love and joy. Crisp and clear, like crystal.

She didn't have a copy of the letter but would have the studio send it, or a copy, to us. We discussed the precautions our Department would take and the things we would like her and her family to do to insure their security. During the conversation, her husband joined us for a short time then departed for his studio.

After advising her of our special watch procedure she showed me around the house. I made a few suggestions about door and window security, then asked for a tour of the grounds. We needed to have some familiarity with the grounds to pass on to the Patrol Officer in the event of a prowler call.

Our beat cars would keep a special watch on the house and set up periodic surveillance. I got a list of all their employees and their hours and vehicles. Until something else happened that was all we could do. I would pass the information along to the patrol division and requested special attention.

I requested they notify us of any unusual telephone calls or any incident that seemed out of the ordinary. She agreed to cooperate fully. The staff was told to write down any vehicle license numbers they felt were hanging around the area. Given all the personalities living in the area, that would be time consuming. The Movie Star maps sold on the edge of town didn't help the situation.

I took my leave, feeling that she was assured of our concern, and felt we were taking every precaution we could.

In the next couple of weeks our patrol units found nothing unusual and the studio found nothing else to cause further alarm. We would continue to maintain the special watch of course. I had written my latest follow-up report and placed the case in the suspense file.

We got back to discussing the Berle case and began to get more intransigent in our feeling that we were not going to lose control of the case. We didn't feel the progress of this or any case should depend on the convenience of any attorney.

We discussed this development and decided to confer with Bill Ritzi at the D.A.'s office. After a short discussion Bill agreed that the process of law enforcement would not be delayed for the convenience of any attorney. For the purposes of surrendering, most any attorney would suffice. We were to proceed on our best judgement.

We kicked around just what effort we would put in on locating Marshal. We wanted to give consideration to the Berle's position but we also wanted to leave no doubt that we would do what we got paid for. After our discussion, I notified Hollywood Divison and the West Hollywood Sheriff's Office that we were looking for Marshal in earnest.

By ten thirty the next morning Frank had been brought up to date on the Berle case and Harold Brown. Brown had admitted a couple of burglaries in Frank's area. Some of the property we recovered from Sally and in Santa Monica was from his area. He said he would contact Lt. Terrell and see if Brown would help clear up some of his caseload and locate more of his property.

While discussing some of the burglars and receivers of stolen property we knew or had good reason to believe are active, we kicked around the idea of picking out a couple we know are very active and tailing them for a couple of days. If we can gather enough cars at one time. The chances of catching them dirty is remote but it's better than we are doing now. Trying to do it with only one or two cars makes it more of a challenge. We agreed to give it some more thought in a couple of days.

Cork, Egger, Mourning, and I were conversing about crime in general when I answered the phone and heard a familiar voice on the other end.

"He's here right now watching T.V. The rest of the family is out. Are you going to come right up?" She said softly.

"You bet, we're on our way." I hung up and said to Cork, "Let's go, pay dirt. He's at their house right now." The latter was said as we were getting into the car. It didn't seem to take very long to get down the stairs and out the door.

Less that three minutes later we had parked on the street and walked quickly down the driveway to the front door. Just as we were about to ring the bell, the door opened and an arm pointed to the den. As we entered the den we saw Marshal seated in a large chair facing the television. As he looked at us he began to get up.

"Marshal Berle, you're under arrest for burglary, grand theft, and receiving stolen property." I said to him as Cork turned him with his back to us and applied the handcuffs.

"What's going on? I'm supposed to surrender with my attorney on Monday. My uncle has made the arrangements."

"Not quite the way it works. A thief goes to jail at our convenience, not his." We hustled him out the door and into the car. On the way to the office he told us his attorney was to work out a deal for him and he'd testify against Barbara.

He was quick to add that the entire idea was hers and she had put undue influence on him. He was told that was between the

D.A. and his attorney. As far as we were concerned this case was about over except for the missing property. He indicated that Barbara handled it and it was gone and couldn't be recovered.

After the booking Hankins told us he got a call from Milton Berle extremely upset that we had gone back on our 'deal'. He was advised there had been no deal, merely him telling us what he proposed to do. A deal requires concurrence on both sides.

Shortly after the booking, I was talking to Johnny Meyers, LASO Safe Burglary detail, about our next meeting, when I happened to mention to him that we had just booked Marshal. It seemed a damned shame that we had enjoyed so much negative publicity when the burglary happened that we didn't get a little favorable press now that it had been solved. We finished our conversation just as I remembered John's office was next to the press room at the Sheriff's office. Golly.

Within ten minutes the phones were all busy with media wanting to know who we had arrested on the Berle case. In another 30 minutes the lobby was full of T.V and newsreel cameras.

"What do you know about that? How do you suppose they found out about this?" Cork asked as we headed down the back stairs for home. "You don't suppose there's a leak somewhere do you?", I asked.

"Nah", we both said in unison.

CHAPTER 20

Walking into the office the next morning Hankins called me in to join him, Cork, and Capt. Smith. Piled on his desk were a bunch of phone messages from various news agencies wanting an update on the Berle case. Captain Smith said he'd have the desk start referring all the calls back to the Bureau.

"They tell me the phones have been ringing all night long" he said as he walked out the door rolling the everpresent toothpick from corner to corner in his mouth.

"When did they serve the writ?", Cork asked him.

"They got here about midnight I understand. The place was still loaded with news people when he got out." Captain Smith replied.

"Well there's not much more we can tell them until we go to preliminary hearing." Hankins said. "What do you guys propose to do now?"

Slowly rising from his chair Cork said "I guess it's time to concentrate on Barbara. All the rats will start scurrying for their holes now that the word is out that Marshal has been popped. Who knows, maybe someone will be anxious to get their name in the paper and help recover the property."

"In the meantime I guess we can get together the paperwork for a complaint against Marshal. Whatever happens, we'll have a hammer on him that we can always dismiss if we have to." I had started to pull the file together as Cork answered the phone.

When he hung up he headed for Hankins office and waved for me to follow. We were spending a hell of a lot of time in there lately.

"That was Bill Ritzi on the phone just now," Cork said, "he

wants us to come to his office in about an hour. He says Marshal and his attorney will be there shortly to try to work out some kind of deal. Bill wants us there for the meeting."

Hankins leaned back in his chair, not too sure which side of this coin he should come down on. "Work out whatever you can with Bill. If the Berles don't cooperate we won't have much of a case anyhow".

Now that's what you call shifting the decision making responsibility to someone else without causing a ripple on the water.

Capt. Smith was right. When he switched the media calls from the desk to the Bureau we became a bustling newsroom. Calls from local press and T.V as well as several from international news services. No matter how much you told them, they always wanted more. Even if there was no more. It was very much like they wanted you to make something up.

A small feeding frenzy had started and they didn't want to stop. Media people you never heard of were calling you by your first name. How did they know it?. Would you mind being quoted? Why not? You hadn't said anything. Being rude didn't deter them. Polite didn't help. We finally had to stop answering the phones and head out the door.

A half hour later we were discussing with Bill Ritzi the fact that without Marshal's testimony we didn't have a case against Barbara. We certainly had nothing we could pressure her with to help us get back the property. By the time Marshal and his attorney got there we were agreed that Marshal would be granted immunity if he made a statement about the entire case, helped us recover property and testified against any others involved. Bill, Cork, and I joined Mr. Rothman and Marshal in the conference room along with a stenographer. Mr. Rothman started to lay out the conditions for Marshall's cooperation when Bill interrupted with the statement,

"No, Mr. Rothman, let's get started on the right foot. Here are our terms, Mr. Berle makes a full and complete statement right now. He holds nothing back. He agrees to give his full assistance in recovery of any merchandise, and he agrees to testify against any other participants in this case.

In return he will be granted full immunity. It's a simple straight forward deal and is only on the table for the next five minutes. If you wish to take that time to talk it over with your client we will be happy to leave you alone."

I hadn't seen this side of Bill before. No nonsense, no ambiguity, and certainly nothing that could be misunderstood. If there was any question about how this was going to be handled there was no question then.

Bill started to rise from his chair and we followed, when Mr. Rothman broke the tension.

"That's perfectly agreeable. Marshal is ready to make his statement right now. I have advised him of his rights and he assures me he will cooperate fully."

"O.K." Bill says, "we'll start now. Lt. Cork and Sgt. Downey will ask whatever questions they want after the initial statement. Is that agreed?" Bill looked at us as he asked. We nodded our agreement.

The next thirty minutes was filled with a detailed statement by Marshal about his activities surrounding the theft and the disposal of the property. He stated that after he had removed the property from the house he had gone to Barbara's place and turned the stuff over to her. He felt sure that Al Loeb, Barbara's landlord and neighbor, knew about the theft and may have handled some of the jewelry.

He also indicated that another couple, Robert and Kay Dickey were at Loeb's house when Barbara showed the sable coat to them. He felt they may have bought the coat.

He went on to say that Barbara had handled the disposal of the property and told him she had gotten only $1200 for the lot. He felt she was lying to him but he was enamored with her and didn't challenge her. He stated that shortly after the discovery of the theft Barbara had gone to Vegas and was still there. He agreed to assist us in getting her to return to the L.A. area.

Based on his statements Bill drew up a search warrant for Al Loeb's residence and we made arrangements to serve it and find the Dickeys and interview them.

The search of Loebs house was fruitless but it seemed to shake him up pretty well. Loeb was very nervous and was going out of his way to be cooperative. Among other things he provided us with the address and phone number of the Dickeys.

Once back at the office we phoned the Dickeys and advised Robert Dickey it was time for him to come into our office and talk with us. He gave every indication he had been expecting something like this. Because it was already evening we told him to come in at 8:30 AM the next morning. That seemed to throw him off stride. He had obviously expected to be brought in right away. This delay didn't fit into his scenario. He had to be mentally revising his game plan and he now had an unexpected wrinkle in the program.

It never hurts to keep your adversary off balance and wondering, just how much do they know? Do they know anything? Why don't they want to talk to me now? Aren't they that interested in what I have to say? Are they just trying to make me nervous? How much can I tell them without telling them to much? . . . I won't tell them anything. . . . Maybe I'd better tell them something or they'll think I'm not trying to cooperate . . . The 'what ifs' are on the other foot.

After filing our reports and putting our notes together we got out of the office about midnight. As we were leaving the office Cork said, "Well Bob, with any luck we should be able to wrap this up tomorrow."

"Yeah. Getting Barbara and whatever property we can should do it. We'll have to get her back from Vegas somehow."

"Marshal said he could help us with that. If all goes well it'll all be over in a few days. Then maybe we can get back to some straight forward crime. These inside family things are always a pain in the ass." I bade him good night as I got into the patrol car for my short ride home.

By the time I opened the door to the apartment I started to

wilt like a wet dishrag. Diana was asleep in the recliner with a blanket over her and the television still on. She hardly opened an eye when I aimed her toward the bed and shut everything down. She was still in the same position she was in when she laid down last night as I came out of the shower and dressed. I woke her up as I left the house to catch my ride.

"How'd it go?" she asked with a big yawn and eyes half open.

"Not bad. It should be over this week. I'll call you when you get to work. My ride's coming up the driveway. See ya later", as I closed the door and headed down the stairs. It seemed like I had just come up these stairs a few minutes ago. I know I'm getting screwed up when the officer driving the car was the same one who brought me home the night before. Or that morning, or whenever.

Cork and I hit the door about the same time and at the top of the stairs, John Wright, the midnight dispatcher told us Robert Dickey had called and will be here at 8:30. We looked at each other, raised our eyebrows, and walked into the bureau wondering. Why would he call and tell us he would be here at 8:30 ? We already knew that. O.K., now what kind of game is he trying to play with us? Or is he smart enough to play games? From what we've heard he's no Einstein. Shifty and clever, and a little strange, but not that many wrinkles in his blueprints. Well it won't be long to find out. Just enough time to pile up the nights papers and go through some teletypes.

At 8:20 he walked through the door. The people who had described him to us were not far off. If anything could be said it was that he was a strange man. Not that you could quite put your finger on what made him that way, it was just his overall, general . . . him.

We introduced ourselves and motioned for him and Barbara Ezell, the policewoman assigned to the bureau, to follow us into the interview room. Barbara had been assigned to us for a while and beside taking shorthand she was good at not appearing to be there but never missing a word, a gesture, or a phrase. She was pleasant and competent. And could make herself virtually invisible in the room. She also had what it took to go out and mix it up on the street if need be.

Dickey started out with the number 6 routine.

"I think I know why you want with me and I'm very willing to cooperate all I can. I don't know how much help I can be though. Why don't you tell me what it is you're after and I'll tell you if I can help?" He's practiced those drooped eyelid, sleepy looks. There's so much pure innocence pouring from those eyes you could go into a diabetic shock. He's good.

Cork shocked us all with a sharp laugh. He never laughed. Suddenly he stopped. Leaning across the desk and right into Dickey's face he very quietly said,

"Look Dickey, you've just seen all the nice there is in us. We've heard all of the amusing sayings we're going to from you. You now have reached the point of no return. You start laying out all you know about this Berle job, naming names, times, locations, and anything else we may think interesting or this interview is terminated and you are in the slam."

"Based on what Marshall has told us, and what Loeb has said, it won't be too hard to get a complaint on you and your wife for accessory after the fact and receiving stolen property." Cork started to settle back into his seat as he finished with, " what's it going to be?" He'd done what he intended. Established an almost electric tension in the air, and Dickey felt it.

Dickey swallowed hard, very hard, and said, "Where do you want me to start?"

"From the time you first met Marshal, and where, right up 'til this morning. And we don't like asking a lot of damned questions so don't leave anything out."

Dickey lit a cigarette and settled back in his chair. He began about seven weeks ago with meeting Berle at P.J.s with Barbara and laid out pretty much in detail how he and his wife, Kay, had found out about the theft and how they had come into possession of the coat.

After a few questions about locations and times we began the process of recovering the coat.

"You know, of course, we weren't really sure this was the coat from Berle's place. It just was too good a buy to pass up." They just have to push their innocence on you. At least make one last try.

"Yeah, we know how hard it must have been to identify the coat, especially with Ruth Berle's name embroidered on the lining," I said shaking my head. "You have our permission to tell yourself we believe that crap, now let's get the stuff back. What else did you get from the job?"

"Nothing, that's it. We didn't even see anything else. I think Barbara must have dealt the jewelry to some of her mob connections." He shifts in his chair. "She has them you know. Here and in Vegas. If she gave the stuff to them you'll never see it again."

"O.K. For now let's just concentrate on getting back whatever we can from you." Cork said with some irritation in his voice.

"Just let me at the phone and I'll call Kay have her bring it over." He said as he was reaching for the phone.

"Dial nine for an outside line", Barbara told him.

In a few seconds he's 'honeying' and 'sweetieing' whoever he had on the other end of the line. And quickly his tone of voice changed and he was saying "What the hell did you do that for?" Shaking his head and saying, "but it's all right here, why the hell didn't you wait for my call?" He seemed to settle down a little and said, "Well, there's not a lot we can do about it now, we'll have to go from there. Where did you say you put it? O.K. I'll tell them. I'll be home before to long." He was not sure of that statement because he looked at us with a very quizzical look, and hung up.

"O.K., now what?" I asked.

"Well she was scared and instead of waiting for me to call she took the fur to a large mail box at Sunset and Laural and put it in the box. She had put it in a brown paper bag before she put it in. She was just scared and didn't want it around".

"Is there anything else that can screw this thing up?" I said to no one in particular. "I'll get hold of the Postal Inspectors and see how we can go about getting the box open, if some mailman hasn't already done it."

I was on the phone when Cork and Barbara came back into the office. "We cut him loose for now", he said to me as he slumped into his chair.

The Postal Inspector came back on the line and told me a postal driver had already found the fur in the mailbox and turned it in to the Hollywood Post Office. He said he had informed the Postmaster to release it to us whenever we got there. He added that they had found a wide variety of things in mail boxes but this was a first for him.

An hour later we were examining the coat in our office. Ruth Berle's name was still on the lining. So much for not knowing where the coat came from.

While I was gone, Cork said, Marshal called and said Barbara was due to come in on Westerns 2:15 PM flight from Vegas. She wanted Marshal to pick her up. He told Marshal we would see him at the airport.

"We can get a bite to eat at Roseati's on the way", he said as we headed out the door.

AT 2:00 PM we were sitting in the lounge area watching arrivals when Marshal approached. "If it's O.K. with you guys I'd like to talk to her for a minute before you pick her up".

After some thought we told him to go ahead but don't tell her we were there. We asked him to impress on her the desirability of helping get back the merchandise. He agreed and moved to the passenger waiting area. She was not hard to spot as she got off the plane and headed for the stairway.

Marshal approached her and they moved to an area where they could talk without being overheard. Their actions were quite animated for a short time, then she moved to the nearby phone and made a call. She talked for a minute or so and while she was talking Marshal looked at us and shrugged his shoulders.

When she hung up the phone she talked to him for a few

seconds and his head sagged as she started to walk toward the terminal, with Marshal following a couple of paces behind. There was not much doubt who ruled that roost.

As she approached the terminal, with Marshal still trailing, Cork moved up on one side of her and I on the other. I displayed my badge and credentials to her and quietly said, "I'm Sgt. Downey and this is Lt. Cork, we're from Beverly Hills P.D. Barbara, and you're under arrest for Burglary, Grand Theft, and Receiving Stolen Property. Do you have any other baggage on this flight? May I see your ticket envelope please?"

She seemed somewhat startled, first looking at me, then at Cork, then finally at Marshal who had managed to distance himself from us all.

"No, this bag's all I have" as she handed me her ticket. It did not indicate any checked baggage.

The ride back to the station was very quiet with a distinct air of hostility. She fumed even more as I searched her bag on the way. Back at the station Barbara Ezell met us at the elevator and took her on up to the jail floor for booking.

By the time we had finished the arrest report, an attorney and a bailbondsman had called and are enroute with a writ to get her out. She must have had some connections.

As we were leaving the building. Cork remarked, "Well, other than getting the complaint, that should just about do it for this one".

"Yeah", I said, "but there'll be some one else tomorrow".

"Yeah, it is ever thus." He said as he headed for the parking lot.

CHAPTER 21

"Hey Bob, how'd the prelim go on Berle?"

"O.K. Jack. She was held to answer. You missed the action though. She came to the hearing with one of her hood friends apparently to provide her `protection'. You know Buddy, the photog from the paper, he was trying to get a picture in the hallway and Mr. bodyguard started to manhandle him. As it happened Cork and I were on either side of him when he grabbed Buddy. He's now being booked for assault and little Barbara is all alone in court. This should pretty well wrap it up. Doesn't look like we'll get any more property back though."

Egger was at Valentine's old desk at the back of the room and my permanent desk was just in front of his. Pederson's was next and McCarthy and Mourning share the desk next to Cork.

The last few days had been time to catch your breath and clean up on paper work and court appearances. There was time then to return those 'not time sensitive' phone calls. If things didn't blow up in the next couple of days I would be able to make the Porterfield arrest and either close the books on the windowsmashes or start in another direction.

There was time to have lunch with Gravante, Unland and Jones from Intelligence and Gusty Regan and her partner from Intelligence. We'd had some serious talk, and thought, to picking out some burglar or receiver we knew was very active, just staking them out and tailing them until we caught them dirty. Pete Meaney had agreed to throw in some information from his sources to help us target someone.

Frank and I had broached the subject with L.A. Central Burglary and while not actually being laughed out of the room, we were told that it was a foolish idea and unworkable. They were too busy actually trying to put burglars in jail than spend wasted effort staking them out and following them. After all, you could never be sure when they were going to pull a job. You might have to sit on them for a couple of weeks and still not get them on a job.

We took our plan and ideas to more receptive ears. We got a tentative commitment for some manpower from Lt. Phillips of L.A. Intelligence. We also got a promise of some equipment such as cameras, portable radios, and car bugs for directional use. Now we had to pull together the loose ends of our plan.

While sitting over some hamburgers and coffee at the outdoor diner at LaCienega and Santa Monica, we had settled on our first target, Murray Fellman. Murray was known to all of us to be a very active receiver of stolen property, and a finger man for residential burglaries. Our only hitch was that he was also known to be an FBI informant. If we did work him it would have to be very close to the vest. We couldn't even hint to those FBI Agents we knew to be sympathetic to our plight that we were working one of theirs. They'd be duty bound to tell Murray's handler and he would probably cool him down or shut him down for a while. Not that they condoned his activities. But you don't get your informants from the pulpit.

That settled, all that remained was to find a time when we were all free enough to work on him. We separated with a plan to meet again the next week and bring together all the preliminary information we could gather on our target.

Back at the station, parked in the underground area of the garage, was a Rambler station wagon with the rear end loaded with upholstered chairs, a mirror, a small gold leafed table and gold leafed mirror.

When I got upstairs the Desk Sergeant called me over and informed me the day shift had arrested a man for stealing furniture from the lobby of apartment buildings. In the past month or so we had been plagued with a rash of thefts from the lobbies of apartment houses. Everything from wall hung shelves to small light fixtures. Mirrors, tables, large and small, shelves, even small rugs.

In any event this guy had gotten a flat tire in the driveway of the apartment and was changing the tire when a motor officer drove up and ultimately arrested him.

After looking over the car and property, I went to the jail to interview Mr. Clarence Dixon. Mr. Dixon was tall, thin, light complexioned black man with a very pleasant personality. He was a practical man who realized he had been caught cold and was quite willing to take the consequences. He was, however, not willing to go any further. As far as he was concerned he knew nothing about any other thefts. He had also forgotten where he lived.

Now, all that attitude does, is peek your curiosity.

It wasn't long into the conversation before I realized he just wasn't about to offer any more information. He was too pleasant to get upset at. Which left the only other thing to do, dig. Back at my desk, I poured over every slip of paper in his wallet or in his car. I checked L.A. records and found he had been arrested on other occasions for petty theft and burglary. None of the addresses found with any other arrests was valid now.

I figured I was dead in the water when I started going over the car again. On the doorpost was a sticker from a gas station where the car had been lubed a few days before. Could it be that easy ?

By the time Mourning and I got to the gas station it was just getting dark. A short talk with the attendant told us that Dixon was a regular customer, and he got us his address out of the records. A few minutes later we were parking in front of an apartment house on South Manhatten Place. The directory listed Mr. and Mrs. Clarence Dixon in apartment 4, on the ground floor.

It was full dark when we started knocking on the door of apartment 4. The light was on inside but we were getting no response.

Clarence hadn't made any phone calls so unless they had some code worked out, anyone inside should not know he's in jail.

We continued to knock, loudly, on the door. Neighbors were beginning to look out their windows and doors. Finally, there was some noise behind the door. The chain was being unhooked and the knob was starting to turn.

As the door opened a very sleepy looking young lady said "yes?", in a halfhearted way. As she opened the door further I could see why it took so long to open. Aside from the fact that she was probably asleep, she would have had trouble finding the door. From our vantage point, the entire apartment was stacked, floor to ceiling, with furniture, lamps, rugs, clothing, and apparently anything that had not been nailed down where ever it had previously been. We crowded closer to the doorway and introduced ourselves.

"Mrs. Dixon, we're from the Beverly Hills Police Department. I'm Detective Downey and this is Detective Mourning." showing her our badges. "Clarence has been arrested and from the appearance of this apartment, you're under arrest also, for suspicion of burglary, theft, and receiving stolen property".

With that said, I tried to enter the apartment. I had taken hold of her arm as she stepped back. The door had been opened about ten inches. That's all the further the door would open. We had to turn sideways to enter. Once inside we continued to be flabbergasted with the property stacked throughout the apartment. As Jack stayed with Mrs. Dixon, I toured the place. Every room was the same way. One small trail to the bed. Barely room enough in the bathroom to make it functional.

A few short questions revealed that she was aware of her husbands activities. She couldn't understand what he was going to do with the stuff. He hadn't sold or disposed of anything he had stolen. They both had jobs that paid the rent and food. She was exceedingly cooperative and clearly relieved that it was over. She said he had been active in Hollywood, West L.A., Beverly Hills, and West Hollywood. He had never offered any explanation for his actions.

When I called our office, I had to explain, twice, why I wanted a 12 Ton flatbed truck, our traffic station wagon, and another police unit to load the merchandise. And a policewoman to transport our prisoner. When I was sure the request was being handled, I called LAPD for a car to standby while we loaded. I also called Frank and asked him to contact our associates in the areas effected and request that they come to the station the next morning to ID their property.

It was pretty obvious we were not going to be able to store all that property and would need to return it to the owners as quickly as possible.

An LAPD unit arrived shortly and stood by while we began loading the property. Six officers spent two hours emptying the apartment. Mrs. Dixon took an active interest in identifying property that was and wasn't stolen. Very little was not stolen. Including dishes from a restaurant Clarence had relieved of some of it's inventory.

The process of loading took me to a corner of the room where I was startled to find a maroon leather desk set, complete with pencil cups, clip boxes and matching waste basket. Aside from the fact that Ross Bagdasarian would be a happy man, it put Mr. Dixon into another category. Residential burglary. We would have to broaden our horizons in looking for his victims.

It was right at ll:00 PM when we parked the loaded truck and our station wagon in the basement of the City Hall.

We unloaded our car into the small office next to Hankins office. Mrs. Dixon was taken to the booking desk. From a quick look at the property in the room it appeared we had recovered all the property Ross had reported stolen. I would be anxious to see the look on his face when he sees his desk set.

Jack and I went to the interrogation room where the policewoman, Esther Kielty, was waiting with Mrs. Dixon. I got Clarence out of his cell block and had obviously woke him up, but had not damaged his pleasant attitude.

He continued to make light small talk until he stepped into the interrogation room and saw his wife. He kneeled beside her chair, took her hands and began to weep and apologize at the same time. A few minutes later he settled back into a chair and resignedly asked, "what can I do or say that will keep her out of this?"

"We don't know if it can even be done. If so it'll have to with the D.A.'s approval. I can tell you a lot will depend on just what you say and do to clear these cases and get the property back to the owners. We can then make a recommendation to the D.A. He usually goes along with our requests but only if we assure him you have fully cooperated."

"O.K., I'll do whatever I can to cut her loose. Can she go home tonight ?"

"Not hardly. She's going to spend the night with us. We'll have to see how things go in the morning before we can make any commitment. We have clean facilities here and serve a good breakfast so it won't be too distasteful." I extended my hand to Clarence and he shook it as we all rose to leave the office. Esther put Mrs. Dixon into the women's cellblock as I returned Clarence to his cell.

By the time we got the arrest report done and filed it was hard onto 2:00 AM. The property inventory would have to wait til morning. Mourning headed for home and I took a Bureau car home for the night. The lights at home were still on when I drove up the driveway.

"I had to hear in person why you were on the radio so much tonight. From the sound of it you must have arrested someone and recovered a truck load of property." Diana said as I came in the door.

"Yeah, it's been quite a day." I accepted the drink she had made while I took off my clothes. I stretched out on the recliner and gave her a brief recap of the day. By the time I was done I couldn't find the energy to get out of the chair to go to bed. The last thing I remember was Diana covering me with a quilt and turning out the light.

At 6:00 AM she was shaking me awake.

"Come on honey, you wanted to go in a half hour early this morning. You could have stayed there a couple of more hours and not had to worry about getting up." she said, only half jokingly.

Driving out of the driveway at 6:45 there was a black and white parked at the gateway. Bill Hutchins was working on his paperwork while he waited for my call to be picked up.

"That's a fine How Dee Do," he said, "not satisfied being chauffeured to the office in the morning ?"

"Just trying to keep you on your toes. Didn't get to come home till pretty late so I brought a car home".

"Yeah, we had a look at some of that property. What the hell was he going to do with all that stuff."

"That's the real crazy part, he doesn't know himself. See ya Hutch."

At the office I got the paper work together for the complaint. I made arrangements for Jack to handle the phone calls from the other agencies while I went to interview Clarence again. I was particularly interested in the Bagdasarian burglary. If there was one, there are probably more.

He'd just finished breakfast when I got him out and we went into the interrogation room.

"Is my wife O.K.? Can I see her?" he asked even before we sat down. He was sitting on the edge of the chair and fidgeting excessively.

"What's the matter with you?. You're bouncing around like a drop of water on a hot skillet."

"I'm just anxious about my wife. I want to get her out of here. She's never been in trouble before".

"I'll get her in here in a few minutes. What I want to tell you is I'm going to go get the complaint this morning. I'll make arrangements for one of our guys to take you to the property and you can tell us where each item came from, as best you can remember. We know with all that stuff you won't remember it all but you'll have to give it your best try. One thing I really want to know about though is that maroon leather desk set. When and where did you get that."

"I got that about a week ago. Isn't it beautiful?. I was cruising around town and saw this back gate open into a big yard. I parked on the street next to the alley and went into the yard. There was a building there and the door was unlocked. When I went inside it looked like an office and a recording studio of some kind. I grabbed a couple of tape recorders, a radio and this desk set. I had to make two trips. I was going to go back a third time but I heard someone in the yard so I left."

"How much of that other stuff did you get from houses. I don't mean apartment house lobbies, I mean houses."

"I've never gone into a house. This wasn't a house, it was just a building on the back of the property."

"That building, Clarence, is not like an apartment house lobby. I'll have to get a reading from the D.A. on it. I'll bring your wife in for a few minutes then I have to head for the D.A.'s office."

I brought his wife in for about five minutes and they discussed her getting out maybe today. I assured them that I would discuss it with the D.A. if Clarence continued to cooperate. I put them back into their cells and went back downstairs.

Frank had done well. The phones had already started ringing when I got back into the office. I made arrangements with Hankins to have Clarence brought down to help ID stuff while I got the complaint. I called Ross and asked him to meet me at the office at l:00 PM to see if he could ID some property we had recovered. He was ready to come right away but I told him I wouldn't be back for a couple of hours. Frank and Little Andy were arriving just as I got into my car. I stopped briefly and filled them in. With the paperwork in order and no backup of people getting complaints, I was out of there in record time. Clarence would be arraigned this afternoon and a Public Defender would be assigned. DDA Chuck Weidman had agreed to dealing away Clarence's wife for his continued complete cooperation in returning the property. There wasn't much doubt he would, but you can never really be sure.

When I pulled back onto the parking ramp there were people coming out of the garage carrying a wide variety of small items of furniture. Back in the office the guys were taking the receipts and compiling them so we could make an inventory for the final report. Cork told me that Clarence had been very helpful in returning the property. The most asked question among police and victims alike was of course, "What the hell was he going to do with all this stuff?"

At 12:30 Ross came into the office with his usual smile on his face. I went to the door to meet him and ushered him into the ante room where his property was stored.

"Some of this stuff looks like it may belong to you I wonder if you could possibly identify it?" I asked him in a voice hardly covering my happiness at being able to return something that has so obviously meant so much to him. This was one of those times that made what you do seem so very worthwhile. It happens fairly often, but not often enough.

As his enthusiasm at the recovery subsided, introductions are made all round. The property was photographed for court purposes and was returned to him. His departing smile was a pleasure to behold.

After Clarence's arraignment we took him into the interrogation room with his wife.

"O.K. Clarence, this is the way it's going. You were charged with two counts of burglary and two counts of Grand Theft. Any other charges are held in abeyance until we see how this case goes. If everything goes as expected no additional charges will be filed. Your wife is being released this afternoon and I'll have someone drive her home. If there is nothing that comes up in the future that you or she should have told us, she will not be charged. Is that understood and agreeable with you two?"

"Yeah that's fine" they both said after looking at each other for a few seconds. "Can I talk to my wife for a minute in private?"

"Sure, but it will have to be in the visitors room, under observation." I told them as I led them to the small room next to the drunk tank, and opened the door. The room was about five feet by eight feet with a small metal table and two bench seats bolted to the floor. There were small observation windows located in two inside walls. If you didn't already know you were in jail, this room would sure tell you. In spades.

Fifteen minutes later, Clarence was back in his cell and she was on her way home. Now to try and reconcile all those reports and bring them together with the original report used to get the complaint. About half of the property had been returned and half of what was left had been identified so there wouldn't be too much of a storage problem. Photos of the victims with their property had been taken for future ID if necessary.

Frank called just as I was turning in the report for typing. We had a meeting set with Intelligence in an hour at the same curbside diner and, he'll pick me up on the way. I was waiting at the curb when he drove up after letting Hankins and Cork know where I'd be. A few minutes later we pulled into the curb next to the diner. Our arrival brought the gathering to eight.

Scouting reports revealed our surveillance target, Fellman, operated from a storefront on the south side of Fountain just two doors east of Vine. On the northwest corner of Vine and Fountain was a church with a two windowed office facing the intersection. Arrangements had been made with the minister to set up our movie and still cameras in this office. Fellman's shop was easily visible from there.

We would start operations on Tuesday morning in order to give us time to handle Monday morning problems. The time crunch had come. I needed to serve the windowsmash warrant in the next couple of days. We finished the meeting setting an 8:00 AM meeting time Tuesday, three blocks from our target.

I was rapidly running out of time to arrest my windowsmasher. Tomorrow morning had to be the time. I made plans for Pederson and Mourning to go to Porterfield's ex-wife's house, and stand by while Ken and I served the warrant. If we turned anything incriminating in the search of the car we would notify them by radio and they could then approach his ex- wife and attempt to get some information from her. Ken was asleep when I called and told him that "tomorrow is the day". The next hour was spent in "what ifs" with Capt. Hankins and Cork.

When we thought we'd covered all the bases I retreated to the kitchen of the jail, poured myself a cup of coffee, and sat down to contemplate all the angles, possibilities, twists and turns that could occur to make this operation go haywire. I finally came to the conclusion that now it's "hope for the best" time.

Al Grevelding, the jailer, came in just as I was finishing my coffee and leaving the kitchen.

"O.K. Bob, how many am I going to have in jail tomorrow when I come in?" He asked with a smile on his friendly, ageing face. "Every time you guys sit around with your planning faces on I end up with a bunch of people in jail".

"Well Al, this time I hope you're right." I cleaned my cup and got on the elevator as he locked the door behind me.

Yearly Inspection : Left to Right The Author, Officer Leon Snow,
the Mayor, Chief Clinton H. Anderson

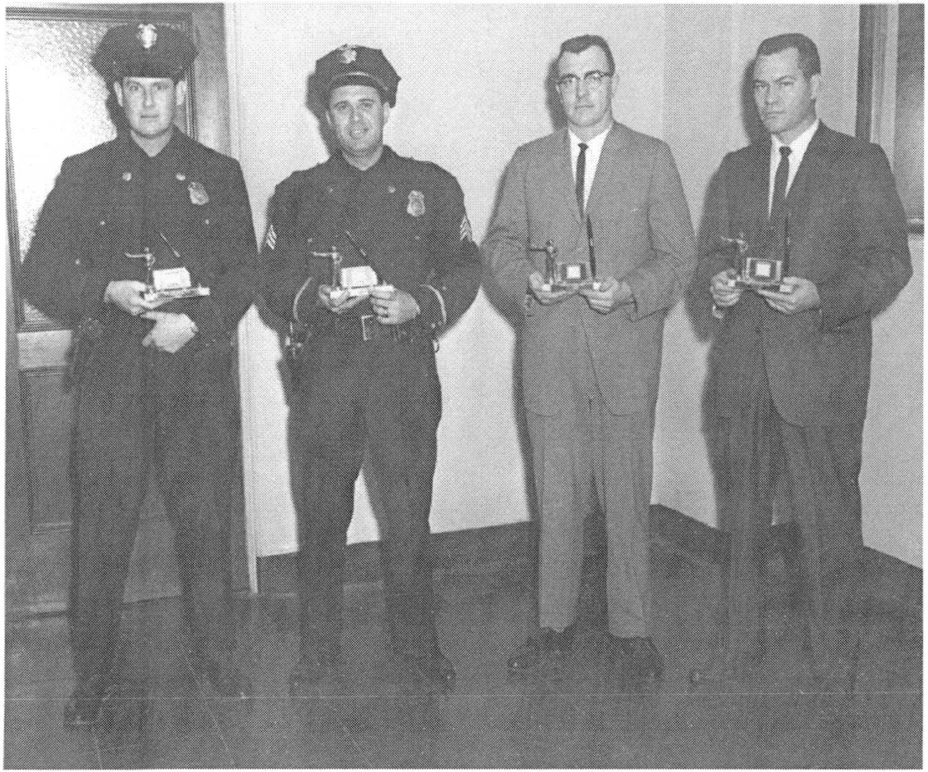

1962 Department Shooting Team. Left to Right
Off. J. Deegan, Sgt Polakov, The Author, Lt. B.L. Cork

1968 Buffalo, N.Y. Testifying in organized crime case
Lt-Rt-Author, Bob Estill, Jack Egger, Jack Mourning. Front Lt. B.L. Cork

PARENTS SHOT, SON HELD

Thursday, Feb. 18, 1965 8★ Los Angeles Herald-Examiner A-7

By WILLIAM E. GOLD
and HARRY TESSEL
Herald-Examiner Staff Writers

Bearded Gary Livingston, 22, who apparently resented his parents waking him at 1 p.m. today was under observation at County General Hospital after shooting his songwriter father, Jerry Livingston, in the arm, and his mother in the chest, Beverly Hills police reported.

He then barricaded himself in his second-story bedroom at 626 N. Rodeo Drive until officers flushed him out with tear gas. They found a 12-gauge shotgun, a 22-caliber revolver and a 22-caliber rifle in the youth's quarters.

With the suspect still in his pajamas, police booked him late yesterday on suspicion of assault with intent to commit murder, then took him to General Hospital.

The elder Livingston, 56, who wrote such hits as "Mairzy Doats" and "Talk of the Town," was treated at UCLA Medical Center for a 22-caliber bullet wound in the left arm and released.

His wife, Ruth, 54, today was reported in serious condition at the medical center.

Beverly Hills Chief of Police Clinton Anderson said the youth "claimed they (his parents) were bugging him."

"He said he had been treated by a psychiatrist," Anderson stated. "He's a nervous type fellow. His parents came to wake him at 1 p.m. and he resented it."

Anderson said both parents ran out of the house after being shot and that Mrs. Livingston fell beneath a backyard tree.

A neighbor of the Livingstons, Mrs. David Leavitt, of 625 N. Rodeo Road, told The Herald-Examiner:

"The first thing I heard was a siren that sounded like it stopped outside. I went out and saw rescue men and policemen leading Mr. Livingston from the side of the house.

"The street was full of police and plainclothesmen with their guns drawn. Spectators and house help were watching. Men were ducking behind cars.

"I heard policemen ask Gary's name. I don't know who gave it to them but then officers called to him, 'Come on down, Gary.'

"They brought tear gas bombs and threw several into the house through the front door.

"The police kept calling: 'Throw down the gun.' He threw it down."

Chief Anderson said the elder Livingston was the first to be wounded when he went into his son's bedroom, and that Mrs. Livingston then ran upstairs and was shot.

The chief said the youth flung down his rifle on officers' order to surrender, and then tossed out his revolver after tear gas was shot through his window.

The elder Livingston is a former president of the Song Writers Guild of America, and had been a pianist and dance band leader.

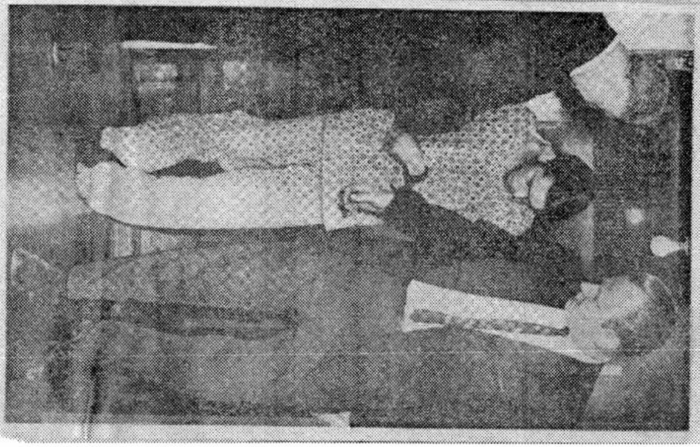

HELD IN SHOOTINGS—Gary Livingston, 21, barefooted and still in his pajamas, is led from police station by Beverly Hills detectives after he was arrested in the shooting of his parents at their home.
Times photo by George R. Fry Jr.

Barricade News Article - L/R Capt. John Hankins
Gary Livingston, Det. Tom McCarthy

The Author displays property recovered with
the arrest of two office burglars

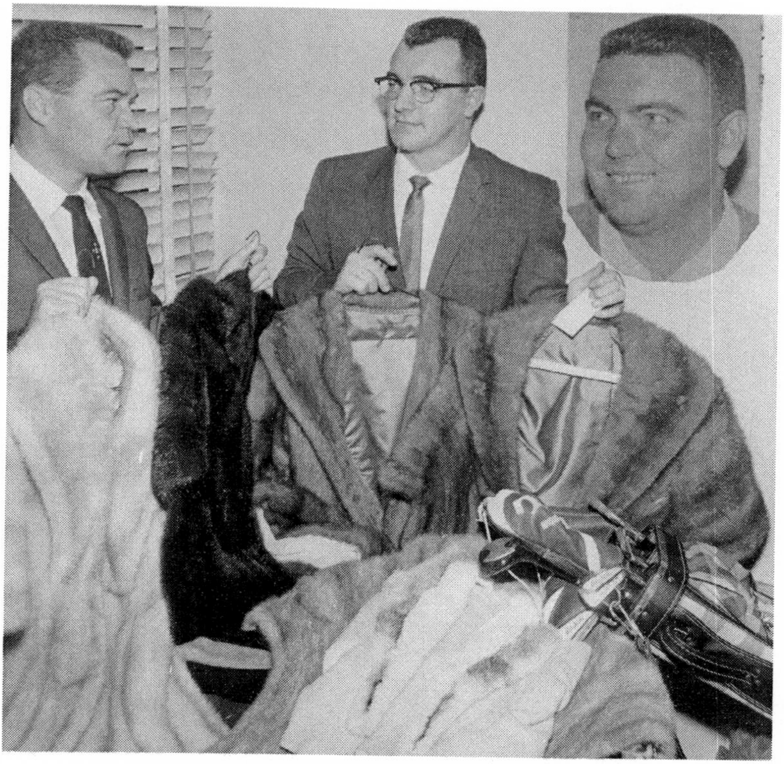

Lt. Cork and The Author display property recovered with the arrest of the Window Smash Burglar (inset)

LOS ANGELES EVENING AND SUNDAY
HERALD EXAMINER
CLASSIFIED ADVERTISING Richmond 8-4111 All Other Calls Richmond 8-1212 or Richmond 8-4141
LARGEST EVENING CIRCULATION IN AMERICA
VOL. XCIV Four Sections Section A 10 CENTS TUESDAY, DECEMBER 15, 1964 10 CENTS

—Herald-Examiner Photo

CARROLL BAKER IDENTIFIES STOLEN FURS, JEWELS
Beverly Hills Police Sgt. Bob Downey holds fur recovered from burglars

Trio Jailed in Cafe 'Tip-Off' Burglaries

By FRANK ELMQUIST
Herald-Examiner Staff Writer

Three accused burglars who allegedly used a swank restaurant's reservation list and telephone codes to prey on wealthy members of society and the film colony were arrested today by Beverly Hills police.

Actress Carroll Baker, who lost $11,800 to the nocturnal prowlers last Thursday night, was the ring's last victim, according to Beverly Hills Police Chief Clinton H. Anderson.

Taken into custody were Robert Klein, 21, of 350 S. Rexford Drive, Beverly Hills, assistant maitre d' at the swank eatery and accused fingerman in the operation; William DeSpain, 31, and John Tizzi, 27, both of 3651 Glenridge Drive, Sherman Oaks.

According to police Lt. B. L. Cork and Sgt. R. E. Downey, $5565 in cash, four revolvers and loot from Miss Baker's home were recovered.

The platinum-haired Miss Baker identified some of the loot taken from her home, including a $5000 Tourmaline Mink stole which she said had never been worn.

Total value of all property turned up was $35,000.

Furthermore, said the chief, detectives Cork and Downey discovered a "little black book" which listed the names, addresses and telephone numbers of 25 or 30 persons believed to be potential victims.

Anderson said the trio operated in this fashion:

A prominent movieland couple, or a society family would call for reservations at the restaurant which employed Klein. He would note the date and then alert his accused accomplices.

DeSpain and Tizzi would then, according to officers, go to the residence and burglarize it.

If—for some reason—the unwitting diners should cut their meal short and leave the restaurant, Klein would assertedly telephone the house, let the line ring twice and hang up.

DeSpain and Tizzi, detectives said, would flee the house immediately, taking what loot they could and leaving the rest behind.

The Author and Carroll Baker
identify her property

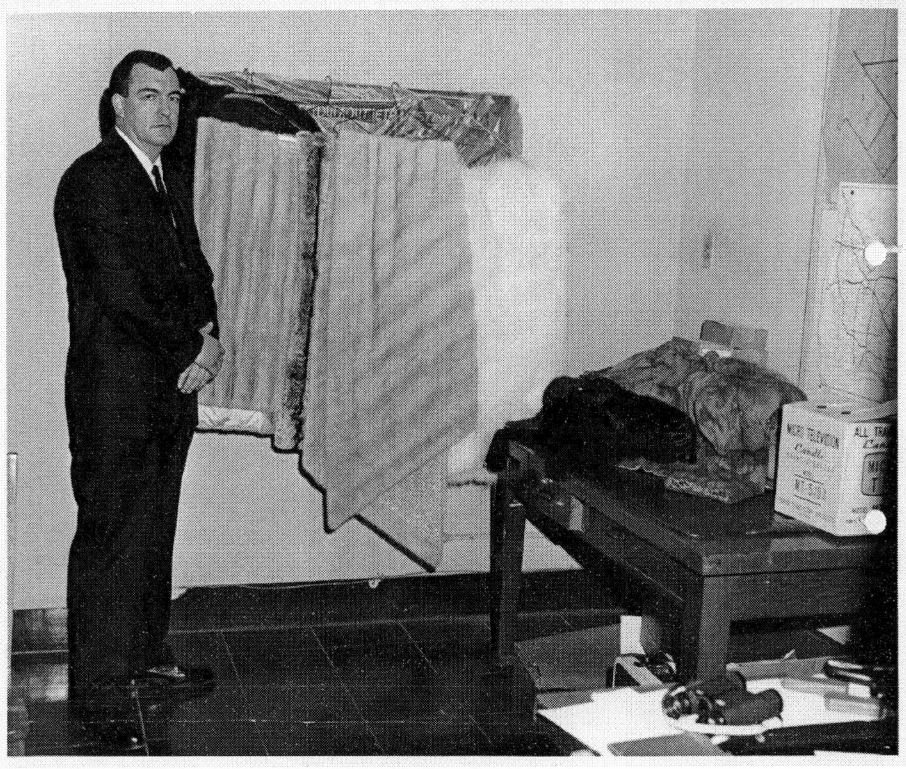

Loot recovered with arrest of the "Tip off Gang"

7 Held as Police Crack Half-Million Theft Ring

Lawyer, Suspected as Mastermind, Others Sought for Robberies in Exclusive Areas

A gang of thieves, believed masterminded by an attorney, has been broken up after it netted more than a half million dollars from robberies and burglaries in exclusive residential areas, police reported Saturday.

Police Chief Clinton Anderson of Beverly Hills said seven suspected members of the ring have been arrested. The attorney and three or four other suspected ring members were still being sought.

The gang, utilizing weird disguises and disfiguring their facial features with putty, operated in Beverly Hills, Bel-Air and Woodland Hills, the chief said.

During some of the robberies, Anderson said, the bandits coolly threatened their victims with death if they failed to co-operate. But in one instance they gave an ailing victim a vitally needed medicine.

Widow of Krupp

The arrests capped a four-week investigation by Beverly Hills and Los Angeles police, sheriff's deputies and the FBI.

Anderson said a quantity of weapons was found in the home of one of the suspects, Jeanette Chace, 24, of 4177 Arch Dr., North Hollywood. A shotgun was found at the home of a Burbank model who was acquainted with another of the suspects. She was not held.

One of the victims was Mrs. Vera Krupp, divorced wife of famed German industrialist Alfred Krupp.

Mrs. Krupp and her maid were terrorized by a gunman who invaded her home at 11005 Bellagio Rd., Bel-Air, Aug. 19 and robbed her of $60,000 in cash and jewelry.

"If you don't do what I tell you, I'll kill the maid and you," the gunman told Mrs. Krupp. "I've killed one policeman so it doesn't make any difference."

Other victims were Herbert Kronish, 55 a builder, and his wife, of 9439 Sunset Blvd., who lost $71,200 in valuables to three bandits two days before the Krupp robbery.

Supplied Pill

After he was bound with silk stockings, Kronish gasped he needed a nitroglycerin pill. One of the bandits got a pill from the medicine cabinet and put it in Kronish's mouth before he and the other bandits fled.

Rayford Camp, owner of the Camp Steak Co., Culver City, and his wife, Mimi, surprised two men burglarizing their home May 9.

The bandits fired two shots at the couple when they attempted to flee, then looted the residence at 5034 Serrania Ave. of $81,185.

Other Crimes

The gang also is suspected of 13 other crimes, including the $35,500 holdup of a Sunset Blvd. jewelry store.

In addition to Miss Chase, the arrested suspects were identified as Phillip Lee Tannehill, 35, of 8265 Sunset Blvd.; Edward R. Tarantino, 38, of 1920 N Argyle Ave.; Oscar B. Williams, 48, of 2026 Panamint Dr.; Gerald Felmann, 49, of 9626 Oakmore Rd.; John W. Hamlet, 37, of 134 W Pueblo St., Reno, and Frank Frilot, 43, of 1709½ Parnell St.

TOOLS OF CRIME—Beverly Hills Police Chief Clinton Anderson, left, and Sgt. R. E. Downey examine weapons and electronic equipment—including two-way radios—seized in crackdown on robbery gang.

Times photo

Chief Clinton H. Anderson and The Author display evidence recovered with the arrest of a residential robbery gang.

Det. Jack Mourning and The Author display
furs recovered from The Dutchess Fur Robbery

Property recovered with the arrest of Edmund Chuski

10—Nevada State Journal Wednesday, May 12, 1965

WHAT VACATION?

Beverly Hills Officer Nabs 'Hometown' Suspect at Tahoe

Journal Tahoe News Service

ZEPHYR COVE — A Beverly Hills, Calif., police sergeant on vacation more than 400 miles from home ended a 30-month search for a burglary suspect Monday at a Stateline casino.

Sgt. R. E. Downey of the Beverly Hills Police Department's Burglary Detail was on vacation here with his wife when he spotted Michael Blaustein, 37, of Beverly Hills crossing a parking lot at Harvey's Wagon Wheel resort hotel.

When Blaustein seated himself at a "21" table, Sgt. Downey alerted a club security officer, who called Douglas County sheriff's deputy Paul Delorey. The three officers closed in on Blaustein, who agreed to a talk at the hotel's security offices. That led to further discussions at the sheriff's substation here.

By early Tuesday, Blaustein had agreed to waive extradition on five counts of burglary. Total loot missing in the cases in which Blaustein is a suspect reportedly is more than $100,000.

The suspect identified himself as Jerry Brigandi and produced a California motor vehicle operator's license less than one year old. But "Brigandi" failed an impromptu test in the Italian language when he could not pronounce Sgt. Ralph Lovecchio's first name in the Italian version — Rafaeli.

A check on Brigandi's fingerprints and those of the burglary suspect, Blaustein, resulted in a decision by Lt. Charles Newton of the Ormsby County Sheriff's Office that the two men were one.

Blaustein was placed under arrest and held in lieu of $16,000 bail, the amount called for in warrants from Southern California.

Sgt. Downey, not at all upset by interruption of his vacation, reported Blaustein had been surprised at the scene of one of the Southern California burglaries, but eluded officers. Some $80,000 in loot assertedly was recovered at Blaustein's home afterward.

The two and one-half year search for Blaustein had led officers from the Los Angeles area to Nevada, northward into Canada, down to Connecticut, then into Mexico, across the Atlantic to Italy and back to Mexico, Sgt. Downey said.

Blaustein, a native of Czechoslovakia, became a citizen of the United States in 1951, police indicated.

An officer from Beverly Hills arrived Tuesday to return Blaustein to Southern California. Sgt. Downey and his wife have resumed their vacation.

Blaustein arrest news story

CHAPTER 22

Waiting. Again. The first thing a cop becomes an expert at is waiting. It starts with the entrance exam and continues through roll calls, stakeouts, surveillances, court appearances, promotions, and ultimately, retirement, if your stomach, nerves and heart hold out.

If you could shut off your mind while you were doing it, waiting that is, it probably wouldn't be so bad. Instead you have nothing but time to play "what if" games with yourself. What if your hunch on this one really is a hummer? Maybe the whole 11 months you have put in on this one is all based on one hell of a bunch of coincidences? Hell no, can't be. There are just too damned many coincidences.

Besides, I had the statements of his ex- girlfriend. So maybe they didn't actually put him in the fur store windows, they certainly support many of the other conclusions that have been established. The bank account deposits, the stolen and recovered Corvettes, his apartments. So what if the judge gave me the warrant relying on the fact that he trusts my judgement and I have established a good reputation in his court.

What if my suspect changed his pattern and didn't pick up his girlfriend that day. He usually drove her to work. What if he's driving someone else's car today. What if,,,, Oh hell, drop it. Play it out the way it's dealt and deal with the contingencies as they come up.

At least we were early enough, and God, what a beautiful morning it was. The start of one of those glorious Southern California days that was going to be just warm enough, just cool enough, and a slight breeze that would keep the smog down to tolerable levels. What a wonderful life. Getting paid to do a job you would pay them to let you do, for a city most people would kill to work for, at a time when God's in his heaven and all seems right with the world.

Sitting there on a wide, palm tree lined street, the early morning sun throwing long cool shadows on the well maintained lawns of the two and three story apartment houses that seemed to be becoming the trademark of residential areas surrounding Hollywood. The pastel colored stucco buildings that appeared to be the current fad colors for decorating, and that seem to attract the "will bes", the " wanna bes", and the "won't ever bes". The naive innocence of the recent arrivals. The core hardening cynicism of the hangers on that still reserve some minute glimmer of hope that today will be the day they are thrust onto the worldwide scene in some manner. It has ceased to matter exactly what manner. Just let it happen someway. Preferably today. Yes, we were early enough to watch them come out of their mostly impersonal cocoons a little hesitantly, to head off to their life sustaining endeavors. If you are an avowed people watcher, and every cop should learn to be, this was a very good time to practice the art. Pick one, size them up, see if you can predict a movement, an action, a car, the general make, the color. Right or wrong, you catalogue it. Pick another, repeat the process, all the time taking in everything that's happening on the street.

Observation, as our good uniform Captain was so fond of saying, pays dividends. You may snicker it off as a little trite the first time he says it to you but if you are mildly astute you soon come to realize it's a basic element of good police work. It's an element to be practiced and repeated until it becomes an instinctive habit.

The Captain may not have been every mans image of the ultimate policeman. But, you soon realized that somehow he had survived, and risen, and whatever attributes got him there were at least worthy of study. Whatever. He had persevered.

"He's late", I said.

"Huh"?

"I said he's late" Kenny shifted his weight on the car seat as he turned to look out the rear window.

“If she’s to get to work on time he should be here by now”. The fresh smell of the morning air had taken on a stale odor of scotch and cigarettes as he spoke. Ken was prone to get impatient on stake-outs but this was a little early even for him.

He’d been on the Department a couple of months longer than I had. He gave the impression of being eager and ambitious. Somewhere along the line though, he seemed to lose his concentration. He was a likable guy who always seemed, ‘rumpled’. He could put on a freshly cleaned and pressed uniform in the locker room, and by the time we got into the roll call room, he looked like he just got out of bed. I’d worked many nights with him and had coffee with him many times but still didn’t know very much about him. He just seemed to avoid personal conversations. It was his life. He could keep it to himself if he wanted.

“Well it’s Monday morning, maybe he overslept.”

I still didn’t understand all I knew about this guy. He’d been shacking with this gal for five months, she had a nice apartment, lived alone, and yet he seemed to spend every night at home with his parents. No matter what time he brought her home, even after he’d stayed for several hours, he still went to his folks house. He couldn’t be worried about her reputation, not and do the things he does.

“She had to have some idea what he does, she certainly can’t be stupid and hold down the job she does. Executive Assistant to the Director of a Savings and Loan is not your run of the mill employment.”

“Look Bob, why don’t we just go up to her door and brace her and wait for him inside her place? We might find out something while we’re waiting.”

“You know damn well why not. We need her with him at the car. The warrant is only for him, but we can search the car incidental to the arrest. If we find anything in the car it’s gravy. If not, maybe she will be shook up enough to let something slip or maybe he will want to be gallant and want to do something to cut her loose. You know as well as I do the warrant is only for reckless driving. If we don't get a break during this arrest we can kiss this whole operation down the tubes".

"His appeal on the L.A. car theft charge has been denied and he goes for sentencing next week. If we don't tag him now we've lost him for sure. Once he's in the joint he's not going to say anything. Right now he's cherry. He's never been away and he doesn't know what to expect. He's nervous, apprehensive. We need to get to him while this is still working on his head."

"Yeah Bob, I know, but this is a really slim shot. Sure, you know and I know he's good for those jobs but you got your warrant on my identifying him during that one chase. I only saw him for a second and the chase was only for two or three blocks. I still don't know how you got the judge to issue the warrant. I didn't see him with any furs and I didn't see him smash any window"

"Kenny, I told you before. I got the warrant on the basis of your statement of pursuing him in excess of 80 MPH in that Corvette for several blocks before you lost him. I only have a warrant for reckless driving, that's why I need a break."

"I've got Jack and Merv staked out at his ex-wife's place waiting for us to turn something here. If we get something they are going to bang on her door and see if she can or will answer any questions."

"I don't know if it's going to work out. I only know that I've been hung up on this thing for 11 months and done everything there is to do short of downright confrontation. My time is running out. If there was another way to do it I might give it some thought, but I doubt it. At some point you have to make a decision and go with your instincts. I'm going with mine."

"I know the Lieutenant told the Captain that he thought this was probably an exercise in futility. That falling on my face may be a learning experience for me. I can't believe my gut feeling is that wrong. You know as well as I do how much work has gone into this thing. Damn it, it's now or never."

"Hey Bob, don't heat up on me. I know what this one means to you. God only knows how much of your own time you have in.

Don't lose your cool now. If it happens, it happens. Just remember what first got you zeroed in on this guy. If that longshot led to this, anything can happen".

"Watch it. Isn't that a black Olds' convertible turning the corner down there, Looks like he's still driving Mama's car."

"Damn right. Maybe he's not too late after all", Kenny replied.

The two year old convertible eased to the curb a couple of spaces away from the walkway into the arched courtyard entryway of the apartment house. We watched as our man got out of the car, entered the courtyard and disappeared up the stairs to the right.

"Nice casual dresser huh?"

"Yeah, with the money he has to be making on those fur and jewelry jobs he can afford those hundred dollar slacks and fifty dollar shirts"

"Well he shouldn't be very long if she's to get to work on time. We'll wait till they start to get into the car before we brace them. He's not been known to carry a weapon and it didn't look like he had any place to hide one in those clothes, but be careful anyway".

"That didn't take long. Here they come. Let's go. You take the passenger side and I'll serve my warrant. Whatever happens from here on, the balloon is up". I said as I left the car.

CHAPTER 23

Neither Porterfield nor his girlfriend noticed us as we slid out of the car and crossed the street toward them. She was in her seat and Porterfield was about to close his door as I put my left hand on his arm.

"Andrew Porterfield, You're under arrest. I have a warrant here." I held up the warrant and my badge in my right hand as I told him,

"Keep your hands on the wheel." They were both looking at me when Kenny opened the passenger door and asked her to step out.

"Step out of the car Andy, and place your hands on the car."

As he complied he asked, "What's this for, what'd I do?"

"Come on Andy, don't tell me you haven't expected this for some time." I said in his ear as I patted him down and put the handcuffs on. I had spent so much of my time working on him and looking at his picture, I felt almost like I was arresting a personal friend. But when you think about it, I knew more about him than most people know about their friends. Charge accounts, checking accounts, phone calls, girl friends, doctors, dentists. Not too many friends have all that information.

"I don't know what you're talking about. Why are you arresting my girlfriend?" His voice was starting to show the signs of agitation and anger. His boyish, cherubic face was starting to redden.

"Did we say we were arresting her? We just don't want her getting in the way while we arrest you."

Ken had gotten her out of the car and was standing on the sidewalk with her. He had done a search on her handbag for weapons and was motioning that all was well.

As I brought Andy to the sidewalk. I went to talk to the lady.

"What's your name miss?"

"Lenora Karns, what's this all about? Why are you arresting Andy?" She was obviously confused, anxious, and attractive.

"We have a warrant. Has Andy given you any furs or jewelry since you've known him?"

"Furs, what do you mean? I never owned a fur. He's never given me any fur. What's this all about?"

"Well, if I'm wrong, I'll release you and apologize. Stand right here with Kenny while I search the car. Do you have any objections Andy?"

"No, why should I. What are you looking for?"

"Weapons, fruits of a crime, or evidence of a crime. Do you object?"

"No, I guess not. I don't have anything to hide. It's my mother's car."

"You do drive it a lot don't you. Keep in mind I've done a lot of background work on you."

"Yeah I drive it some, why would you be checking on me?"

"I'll explain it all to you when I finish searching the car." I pulled the keys from the ignition and opened the trunk.

The trunk was unusually clean except for a blue, navy type, draw stringed, laundry bag. The outside of the bag was heavily snagged all around the bottom and lower third. As I opened the drawstrings and looked into the bag I got that rush of adrenaline that stands all your nerves on end. I was ready to bust into a triumphant yell but I needed to rein myself in. I reached into the bag and carefully withdrew a small handfull of heavy paned, broken glass and showed it to Kenny. My next reach brought out a tire iron with glass fragments imbeded in the black paint. We both lit up with a mile wide smile. Paydirt. I hoped that big sigh of relief I had just let out was not heard by the whole block.

"Mr. Andrew Porterfield, you're under arrest for suspicion of burglary, grand theft, and receiving stolen property."

"I thought I was already under arrest."

"You were. But that was for reckless driving. Miss Karns may we go to your apartment, I would like to use your phone and we can talk a little?"

"Yes, I'd like to get off the street and find out what this is all about." She answered haltingly, obviously confused at the latest turn of events.

In the apartment I called the office and told Cork to radio Jack and Merv to make contact with the ex-wife. I also told him we had found enough to support our suspicions.

Lenora and I sat in the kitchen as I interviewed her about her background and relationship with Andy. She assured me that Andy had never given her any furs or seen any in his possession. She was under the impression he was working at a car dealership. Her openness and straightforward answers to my questions smacked of sincerity. She gave me permission to search the apartment for possible stolen goods.

As I made a search of the bedroom and bathroom, Ken was talking to Andy about his obsession with Corvettes. Their conversation was taking on the atmosphere of two old friends discussing their lifelong hobbies.

There was nothing more in the apartment that appeared to be stolen. Lenora and I returned to the kitchen just as the phone rang. She picked it up on the second ring, said "yes" a couple of times and handed the phone to me saying "it's for you".

I put the phone to my ear and said "Downey"

"Yeah, Cork here, BINGO!" He said with a broad smile bordering on a laugh in his voice.

"O.K. What'd they get?"

"When she answered the door, when she opened the screen door, on her ring finger, was that bow styled diamond ring from California Jewelsmiths. They arrested her and she took them into the house and to the closet where he's been stashing his furs. They got eight furs out of the closet. They're on their way back now. When will you be coming in?"

"We've about wrapped it up here. We'll be back in about half an hour."

"O.K. we'll expect you shortly. By the way, congratulations from all of us. It worked out well. See ya." As he hung up.

Taking Ken aside I told him what Cork had just said. It was pretty obvious he was as pleased as I was. We agreed to say nothing to Andy or Lenora about what had happened. The drive to the office seemed like it took a week. Hardly any conversation took place. We'd have to set the stage for just the right impact if we expected to get the full story and complete cooperation.

When we got to the ramp I sent Ken inside to tell our people not to mention the wife's arrest or the recovery. I took Andy and Lenora directly to the jail elevator on the ground floor and up to the booking floor without stopping at the main desk. Lyn Bertoglio came up with Ken to accomplish the booking. Once that was done and they were placed in their cells, I went back to the Bureau.

Sitting in the anteroom next to Hankins office was Andy's ex-wife Pat with a very frightened look on her face. On the table in front of her were a stack of mink coats and stoles as well as a diamond ring.

I talked briefly to Merv and Jack and then to Cork.

"She's pretty shook up. There's no doubt she knew he was stealing the stuff but she chose to ignore it. She's ready to lay out everything for you." Merv said. "How'd your search of the girls place go?" "Not bad" The real surprise came when I opened the trunk." I opened the paper bag I had brought in with me and showed them the laundry bag, glass and all.

Chuckles, laughs and grins flashed all round.

"Couldn't be much better than that." said Cork. "Well Bob, its' worked out so far, how do you want to go from here?"

"What I'd like to do now is take the furs and his wife upstairs to the interrogation room and have her seated in there with the furs on the table when I waltz him in. He doesn't know yet she's here. It'll be interesting to see his reaction and to hear hers."

"Sounds good, lets do it." Cork headed for the door with me and an armload of furs. Merv brought up the rear with Mrs. Andy.

Kenny said he'll be going home now because he has to be back at midnight for work. I thanked him profusely for his help and assured him his help was invaluable, which it was.

When we got the scene set, we asked Merv to bring Andy in as Pat is seated next to the desk where the furs are stacked. Cork was on one side of the desk and I was on the other. Lyn was standing to one side of the doorway. We could hear the cell doors clang as Andy was being brought in. This next few seconds ought to be very informative.

As Andy stepped into the open doorway his face went ashen as he saw Pat, and she let out and audible 'Oh'. He walked over to her and put his arm around her uttering words of comfort and condolence. He turned to me with a very decided note of resignation in his voice. His shoulders had drooped and he seemed to have gone limp inside.

"What's she doing here. She didn't have anything to do with all this."

"Sorry Andy, not true. She obviously has lots of guilty knowledge as well as storing and receiving the stolen property. Have a seat and let's talk about this." Merv closed the door as he left.

"I hope you fully comprehend just what your situation is now, Andy. With these furs, the jewelry, and the laundry bag we have about everything we'll ever need to prosecute you for several burglaries, at least. With her statements and the furs and ring, Pat is just as likely to go too. Lenora may be a different situation. I'm not sure yet. That'll take some thought. Do you follow what I'm saying?"

"Yeah, I know I'm had. I'll cooperate all the way. Is there anything I can do to take the heat off of the girls? I'll tell you about all the smashes and help you get back as much property as I can. I was due to go in for sentencing next week. What's going to happen on that?"

"I haven't given that any thought yet. Let's see how this goes for a couple of days before we try to get too complicated. Lyn, would you get Lenora and bring her in please?"

As Lyn left the room Cork and I started to sort the furs. A couple still had the labels in them. There appeared to be no other external marks or identification. We piled them on the table as Lyn returned with Lenora.

"Hi Lenora, please sit down. You do know Pat don't you?"

"Yes I do. We've met several times." From the tone of her voice and the look on all their faces it was apparent they are well acquainted with each other and maybe even friendly.

"What I'm trying to do with all of you together is explain just what we're after so there are no misunderstandings and nothing need be repeated. Later, if things don't work out, no one can say they were told something different than the others were told. O.K.?"

They nodded in agreement.

"Our primary interests are to clear up all the crimes involved, get back as much property as possible, and see that the perpetrator is punished. Andy says he wants to cooperate fully and he would like to get some consideration for you ladies. Is that right Andy?"

"Yeah." Straightening his back and shoulders slightly.

"O.K. We'll be talking to Andy for a while to see just how serious he is. In the meantime we'll have to put you ladies back in your cells. After we talk to Andy, I'll talk with the D.A. and see what we can do about you." Allowing enough time for that to sink in, I asked, "Is that understood?"

They nodded and said "yes". Lenora asked, "May I call my office to let them know I won't be in ?" as she was leaving the room.

"Sure, Lyn could you let her make a call please ?"

"I think we can handle that all right." As she led them out the door.

"Let's bundle up the evidence and go back down to the other office." Cork said, getting up from his chair. "We can get to the files easier and we have access to more phones if we need them."

Back in the small office next to Hankins, I had gotten my windowsmash files and tags for the evidence. We were ready to wail. The strain on Andy's face had eased. We started down the list of windowsmashes I had in my files. Beverly Hills, Pasadena, Wilshire Division, Hollywood, West. L.A., he cleared them all. Starting with the fur store where I had first stopped him and filed that FI card. That was job one. He didn't know it but the silent alarm on that store was out of order.

We hadn't found out about the burglary until daylight and one of our patrol cars saw the broken window. The alarm company took a lot of heat from the owner on that.

Part way through the conversation my mind started to drift. Thoughts flashed through my mind about the many hours and hours of drudgery that had gone into this case. The frequent self doubt when all the pieces didn't exactly fit. Trying to convince your contemporaries that you were on the right track.

When we had gone through the entire list of cases in my file, I called for a break. I felt the deep need for a few horn blowing phone calls. We put Andy in a holding cell and I sat at my desk and drew a very deep breath. With that breath came a warm feeling all over.

After a minute or two of mental case review, Hankins came into the office, glanced at me and said, "What's that sly grin on your face for ?"

"I don't really know, but the way I'm feeling right now it will stay there forever."

My first call was to Diana inviting her to dinner. Before I get the invitation fully out of my she said, "You got him didn't you ?" She always could read me like a book. "Yeah, honey, got him, good." We made plans to go to Whittinghills for some prime rib and mood music, then hung up.

Next, Karl Zimmer at Wilshire. I filled him in quickly and told him of the cases Andy had admitted in his area. He'll come over in a day or two to look at the evidence and talk to Andy. Next, Pasadena, etc, etc. Good feeling. One of the ancillary rewards of this profession.

As I put down the phone Cork was standing at my desk uttering something about lunch. The euphoric fog in my head started to clear when I began to notice that I was starved. That called for a steak sandwich at Paul's Steak House. A few minutes later we were toasting our good fortune and recounting the many places along the way that this case could have fallen apart. When we walked back into the office about an hour later my first message was from Carpenter at Burglary/Auto. He'd heard about the arrest and congratulated us. Call him when I get time. Yes, you are beginning to get the feeling you are starting to fit in.

A short time later we were again talking to Andy. He was helping identify the furs we had in custody and to recall names of people he had sold the property to. He said he never used a receiver and sold all the merchandise to individuals either directly or through friends. That would account for none of it ever showing up in the usual channels.

By about three o'clock we were convinced Andy was keeping his word about clearing cases and recovering property. We took a break as I called Bill Ritzi at the D.A.'s office. After some discussion of the case we agreed that we can release the women for the time being, and take a look at the overall case when we're through talking to Andy and the other agencies.

A short time later I was explaining to them that the ladies will be released for now and if everything goes as expected probably will not be prosecuted. This could change, however, if we uncover something that would significantly alter the circumstances. Things like, they were more deeply involved than they'd said so far, or that they had helped dispose of the property or have not told us where other property is located.

They acknowledged that they understood and were released. We recruited a uniformed officer to drive them home.

Back in the office we were busy writing down names and addresses as well as phone numbers Andy remembered of people he had sold furs and jewelry to. He had a pretty good memory but things started to falter when it came to people who had gotten property from Andy to sell to their friends. By this time the newspaper reporters and photographers were crawling all over the headquarters office. The rest of the day was used up in answering questions and the telephone. Andy was glad to get back to his cell away from the clamoring crowd.

The property lists and recovery procedures would have to wait till tomorrow. The arrest reports were done and turned in by 6:00 and we were on our way home.

Diana was waiting when my ride brought me up the driveway. She met me on the stairs and we headed for the valley as soon as I changed shirts. A half hour later we were in a booth and waiting for our drinks.

By the time we were through with our second round I had told her all the gory details of the day.

"It sounds like it went just as it should have."

"It sure did. It was like it had been scripted."

"Then you didn't really need to worry about all those so called `loose ends' you've been worried about."

"Maybe not, then again, maybe worrying about them helped figure out the problems and avoid them. I don't know which way it works, but I'm damned glad it did."

Our prime rib arrived and it was great as usual. It took a couple of bites for me to realize I could slow down and enjoy it. As we were finishing our dinner the piano start to play and we could see Bobby Troup seated there. This dictated a slow after dinner drink, or two, and cup of coffee.

Our ride back over the hill was quiet and comfortable. Shortly after getting into the house the telephone rang. What now ? I flopped into my chair and apprehensively picked up the receiver. I really didn't want to go in on a call tonight.

"Hello."

"Hello, Downey. Bert Sloane. If you were planning on coming in early tomorrow for your preliminary hearing on Clarence Dixon, don't".

"Why, has it been postponed ?"

"Yeah, permanently. It seems he was entertaining his cellmates in the day room area and was doing a dance for them when he keeled over with a heart attack and died."

"What? What the hell are you talking about? He's only 29 years old."

"I know. The doctor and medics say it's unusual but after talking to the other prisoners they feel sure it was a heart attack. They'll do the autopsy tomorrow. We thought you ought to know. Anyone you want us to call or notify. His wife's been told already."

"No, I'll take care of the rest in the morning. Thanks for calling." I hung up the phone and Diana was standing in the doorway just looking at me.

"You look like someone just hit you in the stomach."

"Sort of. Clarence Dixon died of an apparent heart attack in the day room of the jail tonight. Just keeled over while he was doing a dance for the other prisoners. Strange. He was a likable guy, a thief, but likeable. Nothing like a jolt to take the air out of your balloon."

"Yes. It kind of makes you think about everything evening out in the long haul, doesn't it ?"

We sat with two cups of coffee, closed our eyes and just listened to the stack of piano jazz she had put on the stereo.

After a night of fitful, disturbed sleep, I got to the office at 6:30 to read the report on Dixon and catch up on my teletypes. I was still mulling over yesterday's events when the rest of the crew came in.

Cork and I would be laying out the plans for recovering furs and jewelry today. We'd split up the names and phone numbers Andy had provided and began making contact. While the guys in the office tackled this, I'd be getting the complaint.

First, I had to call Ross and tell him what had happened to his case. He was really taken aback when I told him about Dixon's death. It began to sink in that the real world had crept into his previously orderly life and sometimes it's not nice. Before long he was asking how the wife was taking it. Somehow you would expect him to do that. I told him I'd call him as soon as I can to release the rest of his property. He thanked me and said he would be seeing me soon.

I returned Carpenter's call before heading for Santa Monica. He brought up a point that had been nestling in the back of my mind but I had forgotten until he mentioned it. Andy still had a lot of explaining to do about the Corvettes he used on these jobs. Carpenter said he and Hayes would like to talk to Andy whenever we figured it was convenient.

At the D.A.'s office we agreed on filing three counts of burglary and grand theft and hold the rest just in case. The girls would not be filed on yet. Again, just in case. Andy had made his phone calls but it hadn't been determined if he'd have the money for his own attorney.

Back at the office, after making arrangements for Andy's arraignment, the guys told me their quest for stolen goods was progressing slowly. No one wanted to admit they knowingly bought stolen goods.

"Well guys, you have to convince them that you know they wouldn't do it on purpose, that they'd just been duped. Then if that doesn't help, get Andy to talk to them on the phone. That might jar their law abiding spirit."

"You think he'd do it Bob ?"

"Why not? If I know him he'd think of it as the ultimate irony."

In the next couple of days we had gotten back 12 more furs and a couple more pieces of jewelry. We had a string of furriers coming to the office to identify their merchandise but surprisingly little was claimed. After talking to Andy again it became apparent what was happening. Some furriers were deliberately not identifying their furs.

Their insurance claims had been paid in an amount several hundred dollars more than the fur was actually worth and they were not about to admit they had overpriced their claim. No one wanted to face charges of fraud against their insurance company as well as having their policy cancelled. Luckily the cases we had filed were on burglaries where the labels were still in the furs when we recovered them and the jewelry was matched with photographs furnished by the victims.

After we talked with the insurance agents and adjusters, and the victims were assured they would not be asked to pay back any "erroneous" overpayments, we got several more identifications. Some of the "innocent" purchasers even got their furs back when the furrier `could not' identify them.

We cleared 31 fur store and four jewelry store window smashes. Andy's preliminary hearing was set for the next week and we finally had all the paperwork done and the evidence tagged and in the safe. Carpenter and Hayes waited and interviewed Andy at the county jail and he cleared some cases for them as long as he wasn't going to be charged with any more auto thefts.

All in all it was a pretty hectic, busy, frantic, and above all, rewarding four days. This was what you hoped for on any case you start. More often than not though you ended up frustrated, disappointed, and angry. Even when you locked up the suspect, there was still the victim. The one that doesn't get back that precious item that was a gift from a lost loved one, or that brought back so many wonderful memories when they looked at it. The deep disappointment in their eyes when they realize they're probably never going to get 'it' back, and that look takes you by the throat and squeezes.

This time though, you got a look at greed on both sides of the table. The 'victims' who overvalued their lost furs to collect more from the insurance companies, and the 'nice' people who bought stolen merchandise to save a few bucks. In a couple of cases Andy's count of the furs taken didn't tally with what the furrier said was stolen. Now just who are you going to believe?.

I dearly loved this job, but every day something happened to strip away just a little more of your naivete and trust. Hopefully, as the layers peel away they aren't being replaced by a harder and harder shell.

CHAPTER 24

At last. We had all finally cleared the time to concentrate on our first surveillance subject, Murray Fellman. The anxiety level had been high as we broke up our huddle and headed for our assigned locations.

Stone, from L.A. Intelligence, and I were inside the church office with a 35mm still camera with telephoto lens and an 8mm movie camera at 8:30 AM. Unland, Jones, Regan and Gravante were split up in three cars spotted around the intersection. Murray usually got to the store at about 9:00 AM.

For security reasons we had agreed to refer to Murray as the 'rabbit' on any radio traffic. We wouldn't call the street names, only refer to north, south, east and west. We knew, or at least we were pretty sure, we were dealing with an FBI informant and we weren't going to take any chances of a possible leak or of being monitored. The very last thing we wanted to do is create an embarrassing situation or hard feelings.

Our object was to photograph and identify people dealing with Murray, build a case against him for receiving stolen property, and arrest his suppliers for the various crimes they had committed. If we were lucky.

Stone handled the movie camera and I took the 35mm. Stone was a large, light hearted man. Between the two of us, the church office, which had seemed adequate before, had gotten a lot smaller. We had to move the desk and file cabinet to have enough room to move around. We had placed both of our chairs at one window facing Murray's store. The movie camera was on a tripod and the 35mm was resting on the window ledge. The window was raised about 6 inches. The venetian blind was lowered as far as we could afford to and still be able to see what was going on. We were ready for business.

We'd gotten so much negative input from our colleague's about that project, we were starting to get a little spooked. For the most part they felt we were wasting our time and manpower. Most of them just didn't feel it could be done. Well, we'd know in a few days.

Shortly before nine a man carrying two cases of cigarettes walked up to Murray's door. When he couldn't open it he sat the boxes down and leaned against the building to wait. He didn't wait long. Murray came around the corner and the two greeted each other like old friends. They stood in front of the store long enough for some good photos before taking the boxes into the store.

A short time later the visitor came out of the store and went to a car parked around the corner to the south. We got some movie footage of him getting into the car and driving away, including the license number.

While we were waiting for the registration of the car from DMV, Murray got another visitor. This one we all recognized as one of our more active residential burglars, Clark Roberts. He didn't appear to be carrying anything, but jewelry doesn't take up much room. While he was inside one of our cars located his vehicle about a block away. Now why would he park that far away ? It was decided that when he left two of our cars would tail him for a while and see where he went.

In a few minutes, Murray and he left the store carrying the two cases of cigarettes. They walked west to the combination drug store and lunch counter on the southwest corner. They entered, walked to the back of the store, and talked with what appeared to be the man in charge. A couple of seconds later the man picked up the cigarettes and put them behind the door into the pharmacy. He opened the cash register and handed some money to Murray and they all parted company, smiling.

As they got back on the street they walked past the store to the rear of Clark's Cadillac where they opened the trunk.

From our vantage point we could only see about half of the open trunk and were so interested in what was going on we almost forgot to take the pictures.

Through the telephoto lens of the 35mm, we could see Murray holding up a mink stole inside the trunk. He quickly put it back and they closed the trunk. They shook hands and Clark got into the Caddy and pulled away from the curb as Murray returned to the store. The guys tailed Roberts to the Nik Rik Bar where he parked in back and went in through the back door. They dropped the surveillance there and returned to our area.

By the time they got back Murray had another visitor carrying a small canvas gym bag. We photographed him entering and leaving about 15 minutes later with the bag folded under his arm. We watched him till he entered his car and drove away. Another license number to be checked.

The rest of the day convinced us that Murray needed a secretary to keep track of his business associates. Some carrying things, some not. We had seen both known and unknown criminals and thieves, and some middle weight members of organized crime enter and leave the premises during the day. It was pretty obvious Murray was very active in his chosen field of endeavor.

When he closed for the day we shut down our operation and met for a critique of the day. We all agreed that if what we had seen in one day was any indication we were going to be kept very busy for quite a while. We also agreed to brief only a select group of people on what we had seen and make sure the movies and photos are handled with discretion.

The daily film would be taken to the LAPD lab, where it would be developed and printed overnight and picked up by someone from our group the next morning. Because of some of the people we had photographed that day, it was understood that Frank would brief Chief of Detectives Thad Brown, personally, on our operation. Stone and I had drawn the assignment of keeping the surveillance notes because of our fixed post. We parted, looking forward to the next days revelations.

That night I briefed Hankins and Cork by phone on what went on. They agreed to have someone handle my cases for a few days so we could ride this out and see what developed.

We were all on site by 8:30 the next morning, after a quick cup of coffee and some last minute stake out revisions. This day was very much a repeat of yesterday with a long line of comings and goings by a wide variety of people. Most of them identified in one way or another as being connected to some criminal activity or another. Even the organized crime boys came by for a short visit.

Among the visitors is the guy from the first day with the cigarettes. This time he was carrying an armload of phonograph records. It took a little digging but we had identified him as John Rich, an ex-con on parole with a long record of burglary, theft, and narcotics. From the stuff he was bringing to Murray, he must be shoplifting. And, he must be pretty good at it.

By the end of the day, our list of suspects was getting quite long. At that rate we'd have to pick an opportune time to bust Murray and gather up some of his cohorts. Judging from what's gone in and come out of the store, there should be a fair amount of stolen property in there when we move.

We decided to give our operation at least two more days then play it by ear as to arresting Murray. We'd kept a trusted member of the D.A.s office briefed on our surveillance and he concurred with our plan.

By the forth day of our stake out, Roberts had come back and carried a large box into the store and came out later, empty handed. Rich had become a daily regular bringing cigarettes and/or phonograph records on each visit. On one visit he brought a large box with no markings, which got us all curious.

Several other arrivals brought other containers of property which we were unable to identify but none of them took anything with them when they left. Murray did, however, take four cases of cigarettes to the drug store on the corner and return without them. The state tax people would be very interested in that operation after we got our case together.

It was decided that we would stake out the store overnight to be sure the merchandise was not moved and make our move after the first transaction the next day. We might even get lucky and get two or three people in the place with their goods for sale. The arrest would take place in L.A. so we had decided West L.A. would handle Murray and the property recovered. We would decide who would handle any others when we saw how many other arrests are made at the time.

Like a Swiss watch, Rich showed up shortly after 9:00 AM this time with a carton of Chanel No. 5 perfume. We waited for someone else to arrive but as luck would have it that day, we only had Rich and Murray inside when we decided to move. We got to the front door just as Murray and Rich were about to leave, with Rich carrying the perfume.

"Gentlemen, you are under arrest for suspicion of receiving stolen property, grand theft and burglary". We all moved back inside, shook them down, and began a search of the store. The front office area was starkly bare. A desk with a telephone, a small metal file cabinet, and three wooden chairs. Through a doorway in the back wall was a large open room. Stacked against one wall were a half dozen or so assorted boxes. The file cabinet must be window dressing only, because it was empty.

Most of the boxes, when opened, contained what appeared to be shoplifted merchandise. We'd seen most of these boxes come in during the last two days. One box contained a couple of mink stoles. One of which looked very much like the one Roberts was showing Murray the other day. Another box contained some miscellaneous cameras, radios and many electric shavers.

Not much of a haul but enough to cause Murray some discomfort and maybe enough to get him to loosen up on some of his 'suppliers'. Some of the property that we saw came in over the last few days is not here. It had to have been removed during the nights we were not staked out on the place.

During the entire search Murray had been busy berating us for "not knowing what we were doing", and "not knowing who we were dealing with". He was assured we knew quite well but were going to do it anyway.

We decided Frank would take him to West L.A. with most of the loot and I would take Rich and the property we knew he had brought, with me and book him at Beverly Hills.

Enroute to the station Rich was already beginning to hurt. He was obviously due for a fix and we had interrupted his routine. Before we got to the station he was offering to name names and sources for the merchandise we had recovered. He told us that he was on parole and could help us with some of our burglary problems. It was hard to shut him up until we got to the station. After the booking he got even more intense. "What can I do for myself to get me a deal or get me out of here? You guys don't know what's going to happen to me if I have to stay here very long." He said while alternately sitting, standing and pacing from one side of the room to the other. "I just can't be locked up. I'll go nuts".

"Well John, you'll just have to begin thinking along the lines that you're not going to walk out of here today. If you need some help we can get the doctor to give you some medication but you're not going to get any narcotics while you're in here ". I could see the stark terror come over his face as I said it.

"Hey, I just can't stay here. You just don't understand."

The pleading in his voice was gut wrenching.

"Resign yourself to it John. You're staying with us. We'll have the doctor come over and see you but you're not going anywhere today unless it's to the hospital and I doubt that."

He was put in his cell and told to try to relax until the doctor got there. Dick Haas and I went back to the office to finish the booking report and make some phone calls.

Dick had recently been assigned to the Bureau from three-wheelers and was working burglary for the time being. Dick was a rather large man with a quick smile and a sort of relaxed attitude. Easy to talk to and comfortable to be around. Within the hour Dr. Laurion had arrived and examined John.

"I've given him a tranquilizer, and left some at the desk for him. He's a very heavy user and they won't help much but the bad pain should be over tonight. He'll hurt like hell tomorrow but he'll be able to stand it," he said as we walked him to his car. "Call me tomorrow if you need me."

"Thanks Doctor. We appreciate your help. Is he apt to hurt himself ? Should we consider sending him to a hospital ?"

"No, he'll survive all right. He'll hurt but it won't kill him. See you later." He said as he drove away.

"What do you think Bob, should we go and try to talk to him now ?"

"Let's just go up and see how he is. Let him know we're interested but let him relax in peace for now. We've plenty of time tomorrow?"

"Yeah, it isn't like we don't have something else to do."

As we entered the cell area John was pacing in the day room area. He saw us and started to ask when he can get out, when he can talk to us, how can he help himself ? "We're going to let you rest for now. Be thinking about what you know that we're going to want to know. Maybe we can work something out tomorrow. We're very interested in Murray. We're also interested in any burglary or robbery people that are very active right now. And we'll need details, not general information. We already have general info. See you tomorrow."

He was still asking questions as we left.

When I called Frank he told me Murray was not being very cooperative. He said all the merchandise we found was a legitimate purchase, including the furs. He's called a lawyer, and made another call we can only assume was to the FBI because five minutes later Frank got a call from an FBI agent inquiring about Murray. I told Frank I wanted to call Pete and tell him we'd popped Murray, as a good will gesture. He agreed. A few minutes later I had Pete on the phone.

"Pete, we wanted you to know we have busted Murray Fellman on receiving stolen property charges. I didn't tell you before we popped him because we didn't want to put you in the middle."

"What do you mean in the middle, Bob?", He asked.

"Maybe we've got the wrong info, but we understand he's a Bureau informant and we knew if you knew before hand you would be duty bound to inform his handler. Frank and I didn't want you to have to wrestle with that decision."

"I appreciate your concern but I don't know if he is one of ours or not. I'll just have to wait and see if anyone inquires. They know I'm fairly close to you guys so if they want to know anything about your operation they'll ask me to find out. What happened ?"

I filled him in on the operation and who was involved. I also let him know about the photographs and the movies in case he wanted to see them. That interested him greatly and he arranged to come to our office and review them when we had gotten all the material back from the photo lab. When we hung up I had the feeling that no bridges were blown.

Cork, Haas and I spent the next hour or so outlining just what we wanted from John the next day. The surveillance group had decided to stand down until Monday when we'd meet and brief everyone on what we'd learned.

On the way home I had that feeling of "what if" we were really on the right road for running down some of the parasites that give us and the citizens fits. Almost at the same time I got the feeling that we were shoveling sand against the tide. "What if' this was a fluke and the next surveillance just burned up time and man-power ?

Going into the office the next morning, Bob Bowers, the Watch Commander, stopped me at the desk and told me Rich had spent a very bad night. He had been given the rest of his medication but he had only slept a couple of hours. If you could call it sleep. I thanked Bob and went back into the office. I was the next to the last one in this morning. I looked at my watch, 7:20 AM, did I miss something special this morning ? When Pederson came in about 10 minutes later we all made an obvious move to look at our watches.

After going over the teletypes Cork and I went to the jail to see

John. When I brought him into the interrogation room he looked bad. As he sat down he looked like every nerve in his body was exposed. He squirmed and fidgeted, wiped his nose and rubbed his arms. We gave him a cigarette and lit it. He seemed to calm down just a little.

" Well John, what do you say ? Do you feel like talking with us or do you want to get some more rest? The Watch Commander tells us you had a very bad night so if you'd rather wait for a while we can wait." Cork said with just the right note of concern in his voice.

"Hell no, I want to get this over with. Whatever it takes to get out of here. Did you tell my Parole Officer about my arrest yet ?" His voice was loud, strained and crackling.

"No John, we decided we'd give you the benefit of the doubt for now and see what you had to say. It may not even be necessary to talk with your Parole Officer depending on what develops here. How's that sound to you ?" His eyes brightened a little when I told him that. You could read his thoughts now. He was deep into thinking there's a chance he can skate out of here and not get violated on his parole if he deals right. As the possibilities pass through his mind you could see him straighten up a little and start to concentrate.

"What do you want to know ?"

"Who's the most active residential burglar you know and how do you know it?" I asked as I open my notebook.

"There are several that attend my weekly meetings with the parole officer. Some of us go out and have a few drinks after the meetings and we get to talking." It seemed to start pouring out of his mouth.

"Wait a minute," Cork said, "aren't you guys supposed to stay away from each other and not drink while you're on parole ?"

"Yeah, but nobody pays any attention to that. Who have they got to check on us? If they violated all of us who drank or associated together the jails would be full. They can't afford to do that. They only use that crap when they're wanting to violate someone as an example when they can't find anything else to put them away. They also use it to help the cops put the pressure on someone."

"You seem to know the system pretty well."

"I should. I've been on parole three times. I've never been violated though. Always gone back for some other crime. Finished all my paroles without a problem."

"You mean you never committed a crime while on parole or you just never got caught ?" I asked.

"Naw, never got caught. When I was on parole I was more careful. When I was off parole I got sloppy."

"What about this time ? You're still on parole."

"Yeah, I screwed up. I let the drugs get to me this time. I never used like this before. Sure I chippied around with it before but never got really hung up like now."

"What's your habit costing you a day ?" Corks asked.

"About a hundred to a hundred and fifty a day. That's why I had to boost so heavy. I usually traded my stuff for the smack but when I couldn't connect right away I went to Murray. He was always good for cash on the spot. I'd leave his place and go score right away so I'd get straight for the day. Then when I started to come down I'd have to go boost some more for the rest of the days fix or for the start of the next day."

"What'd you tell your parole officer you were doing for a living ?"

"He thinks I'm swamping out a bar at night and cleaning the lobby of my rooming house for my room and board. he never has time to check on any of us. Usually has to take our word for it. Only when someone really screws up that he comes looking for you. If he has to do that there's no second chance."

"Lets get back to our original question. Who's working and where ?"

"I'm not really sure who is pulling any jobs right . . ."

"Whoa!!! Hold that bull shit right now. We don't have time to sit here and listen to you try to con us. If that's the way this is going to go we'll go downstairs and call your P.O. and turn you over to him today. How long a tail do you have?"

"Wait a minute guys. Let's start over again. I've got a four year tail I don't need to go back. With my habit I'll probably die in there."

"Let's not jerk each other around then. Let's get to the point and go from there." My voice must have an edge to it that John recognized had a strong note of finality to it.

"O.K. The busiest guy I can think of right now is Robert Johnson. He's in my group at the parole office. We all meet every Thursday night at 7:00 PM. We're through usually by eight and sometimes he doesn't go out with us. He jokingly says he's got an errand to run. He has said before that he capers then."

"What kind of jobs is he good for and where does he pull them?"

"From what he's said, it's residential and he works on the west side. West L.A., Santa Monica and Beverly Hills. He had some jewelry one time and it looked good. Said it was from Brentwood. I don't know who handles his goods for him, but I could try to find out." The last was said more in the form of a question than a statement. He was trying hard to figure some way to hit the streets.

"We'll let you know if we want you to dig up anything else on him. Where does he live and what kind of car does he drive ?"

"He's got a Dodge hardtop. It's beige or light tan, a two door. He lives in an apartment somewhere near Bonnie Brae and Burlington. He just told the P.O. last week that he had moved there. The P.O. will have the address."

"How often do you figure he capers ? Once a week doesn't seem like much for a high roller. Does he work anywhere ?"

"No, he says he's got a job at a lumber yard but it's owned by an ex-con and he covers for a lot of guys. Yeah, he has to go more than once a week. He's got a small habit too, and he always has plenty of dough. Burglary's the only job he's got and I guess he's pretty good at it. He does mostly jewelry. A fur once in a while but he prefers jewelry. Says it's easier to carry."

"Who does he deal it to ?" I asked him. He's really warmed up to the idea of talking. His eyes were starting to brighten up and he had a slight smile on his face. He was scoring with us and he wanted to keep it that way. He was figuring it just may be the way to work himself out of here.

"I don't know for sure. He's dealt some stuff to Murray but he's not his regular guy. I don't know who else he deals with, honest. I'd tell you if I knew."

"O.K., John who else is capering regularly ?" Cork handed him another cigarette. He'd been chain smoking and if this kept up both Cork and I would have to get more smokes.

"There's another guy that just got off parole. He was in our group. Named Sam Pasich. I don't know too much about him but I think he works a lot. Drives a Ford station wagon. I hear he uses a pair of channel lock pliers on the door knobs. Breaks the pot metal flange that slips into the slot on the inside of the knob. It's soft so it breaks easy. He does apartments a lot because they have the cheap locks with the key in the center of the knob."

"What's he take ?"

"Anything. He's even done some residential safe jobs. Takes a guy with him named Jack Reed sometimes. Reed's a big guy and is said to be able to pick up and carry a 300 pound safe. He doesn't use him all the time though. Sam's living with some gal whose old man is in the joint. He used to be one of Sam's pals."

"Who's he deal with ?"

"He dealt with Murray until a short time ago. Murray shorted him on a deal not to long ago and Sam got sore. I don't know where he's dealing his stuff now. Did you know Murray's house got hit a few weeks ago ? He was really mad. He thought Sam might have done it just for spite. He's not too happy with Sam. He's not sure but he thinks it was Sam."

"O.K. John, who else ?"

"The only other guy I can think of right now is a guy called Dutch Holland. I don't know his real first name. I only seen the guy a couple of times at a joint on 8th near Alverado. I went there with a guy I know who introduced me to Holland. From what my friend said Holland is a real high class burglar. He's supposed to work in a small gang. Three or four guys. They all set up the jobs but only one or two go at a time. They got some guy up in Hollywood that handles all their merchandise."

"What's his name ?"

"I don't know. I never heard it. He's just off Hollywood Blvd., somewhere near Sherry's. I know they meet him sometimes in Sherry's or in the parking lot. That's all I know about him." I did hear someone call him "The Hat". I don't know why. John paused like he was thinking deeply. We waited to see what else he would come up with or which direction he was going to go from there. We didn't want to slow him down.

"The only other thing I can think of right now is the joint on Figueroa that rents pass keys. You guys probably know about that though." He said offhandedly.

Cork and I had come to attention internally. No, we hadn't heard about that place but we damn sure wanted to, without him knowing it.

"Just what can you add to what we know ? We've heard rumors about the place but haven't had enough to bust it yet." I hoped we hadn't left him an opening to call our bluff.

"They keep the keys in a safe in the back room. If they know you, you can rent a pass key from them. It costs you a minimum of $50.00. Higher for certain areas. You got to pay up front. I've heard of some keys going for a couple of hundred. It costs you five hundred if you lose the key or get busted with it."

"How do they know what the key fits ?"

"They come in an envelope with the addresses on it. If a guy uses it and finds another place it fits he adds the address to the envelope. They're all for apartment houses so the key fits most apartments in the building. You can even buy a whole set of Schlage keys from someone in the place for about $2000.00 I hear. That only takes about 12 or 14 keys." He sounded like he was drifting.

"Is that the place on the corner or near the corner of eighth and Fig?"

"Nah, it's in the 2100 block. The `Past Time', you know the place."

"Oh yeah, I was thinking of that other place where we busted that guy, hell Cork, I can't even remember his name now. You know the one I mean."

"Yeah, I do, but I can't recall his name either. Been a while." We both knew we didn't know what the hell we were talking about but we did know why we were talking.

"John, who's dealing the keys out of there? Is it just one person or do all the bartenders do it? How do you set it up to get one? Do you have to call ahead or what?"

"No, they don't deal with just anyone. They're damn careful about it. Even if you've been a long time customer they won't deal unless they know you. Being on parole helps but you still have to be well known by someone who's done business with them before. They're not careless or stupid. They've been in business a long time."

We were all getting tired of talking and listening. I had taken rough notes but it was time to relax and clean up the notes. We told John we'd check out some of the stuff he'd been telling us and get back to him. He'd told us where he lifted the cigarettes and the perfume. It seemed he'd been making regular stops at a shipping warehouse and boosting whatever is on the dock when he went by.

He also told us that Murray sold all his cigarettes and maybe some other stuff to the drug store on the corner. The guy will take all the cigarettes Murray gets. We'd already figured that out. He said he didn't know who brought in the carton of electric shavers that were in the place.

"Well John, we're going to go down and check out some of this stuff you've been telling us. I hope you're not feeding us a line of crap. If it checks out, we'll see about getting you on the street. If you do get a pass it'll be tentative and depending on you keeping your mouth shut."

"Hell, how stupid do you think I am. Do you think I can tell anyone that I've told you what I have ? I'd be dead in a week."

"John we all know there are ways you could tip off your friends without you getting in the middle. If you really wanted to help yourself, there are ways you could stay on the street and still make a few bucks without breaking the law. You think about that and we'll talk about it later."

We went back to the Bureau after getting John a cup of coffee and putting him back in his cell. His nerves had calmed down a bit and he was not quite so jumpy.

Once back in the office we contacted Frank and made arrangements for a meeting with our surveillance group at 2:00 pm at the usual drive in. Frank said Murray had been writted out and wouldn't be back in court until the following week.

Cork filled Hankins in while I got approval from the D.A.s office to cut John loose when we were satisfied we had gotten all the information we could. We certainly had no victim that had reported any of the losses. We'd return what we had to the warehouse. They won't have missed it but will be glad to get it back. At least their insurance company would.

I spent the next couple of hours on the telephone checking John's information. It all seemed to come together. Toomey told me that they are working on information that Holland had just pulled a good sized burglary in the Hollywood Hills. They were trying to bed him down and bust him. I told them I'd talk to John again and see if he knew where Holland was.

A quick look at my watch and I saw I barely had time to pack up my notes and head out for the meeting.

CHAPTER 25

At two o'clock we had a different group at the meeting. The same people, but different attitudes. The smiles were easier, the laughs more spontaneous. The relaxation level had dropped about 10 points and judging by the comments being made, they were getting a lot of ribbing from their contemporaries. Things like 'time wasting', 'pie in the sky', 'do something productive'.

Apparently that four day operation had drawn some attention, even in high places. Frank said he'd been ordered to supply copies of all our reports to Thad Brown's office as soon as they were finished. Even the interim reports. The people from Intelligence had been told to make themselves available whenever necessary to continue the operation. Frank was also told we could have an extra car or two if we needed it.

All in all we seemed to have gotten off on the right foot. We needed to decide who would be next. Another quick one would be nice. It would sure help solidify the concept that it could be done.

After a few short soft drink toasts we settled down to selecting our next target. The information gleaned from John was laid out for discussion. We all had our own ideas of who we would like to see busted next, but most of that was based on personal feelings and not solid intelligence. We definitely needed another quick one.

For years I had heard arguments from certain groups, preaching the theory that if you give cops too much authority they would run wild. Prey on the innocent populace. That they would get out of control and run amok in the cities and counties.

But I always come back to the simple concept that if ten detectives or police officers compiled a list of crooks they know are active, prioritize their lists, concentrate on that list, one at a time, they wouldn't have time to 'terrorize' the innocent population. They'd be to busy putting crooks in jail.

With each arrest they would gather more information on active suspects. They would add more people to the list. They would constantly reshuffle the list to keep the most active on top, and pursue that one until he's put out of business.

The primary thing that would put a hitch in the cog of such and operation would eventually be the court system. As the cases stacked up, and the defense lawyers continued to seek delays, especially after learning of the operation, cases would be scheduled for the same day in different courts, and lawyers would start to 'confer' about getting same day appearances for their clients. Add that to the continuances they get from the judges in order to get paid before they plead their clients guilty you would have a terminal backlog.

It's very amusing sometimes to be in certain courts and watch the defense counsel do his number on the judge for a delay because he hasn't been paid yet. Of course if his client is still in custody he makes an eloquent and impassioned plea for 'reasonable' bail. After all he can't raise his lawyers fee while he sits in jail. It had gotten so blatant in some cases that the attorneys and judges had code words to let the judge know they hadn't been paid yet and need time.

One attorney used the phrase, "I have a conflict on that date you honor, I have an appearance with Mr. Green on that date". Green being the code word for money. It got so obvious that when that phrase was heard in court many lawyers and police officers in the court openly laughed. The code was changed more frequently thereafter.

Any way you shape it though, Police Officers have more to do than prey on the general population.

We had been sitting around for about an hour drinking coffee and sifting out ideas and plans of action. All agreed that we needed another quick success to really sell this operation. We settled on Robert Victor Johnson as our next target. One team was assigned to bed him down. Another to isolate his vehicle, another to contact his parole officer.

This contact has to be made carefully. You can never be sure just how much rapport the parolee has with his Parole Officer. You can be sure though that no P.O. wants to be made a fool of. If he's being used by the parolee he can get VERY upset. In this case our suspect is using the parole meeting nights as his excuse for being around fellow parolees and as a prelude to pull his jobs. The fact that the meeting nights are on Thursday helps too. Servants night out in many, many households. It would be interesting to find out how Thursday was selected for the meeting night.

We separated, agreeing to meet in two days and compile our information. The day after that would be Thursday and 'go' day if everything comes together.

Back at the office I filled Hankins and Cork in on the plans. It's understood I would be spending more time on this project for a while and maintaining the reports and records. Bill Payne and Bob Estill would be assigned to handle more of the burglary and theft investigations for the time being.

At about four PM Paul Stevens came into the Bureau. State Parole Office had shown that Paul is P.O. for Johnson and when I talked to him on the phone he agreed to stop by our office on his way home. He was about my age and size. By the look in his eyes you could see he had looked over our entire office in the few seconds he had been there. He hadn't missed anything. Introductions were made all round and I escorted him into the interview room.

In a few minutes I had outlined the surveillance operation and it's intent. And it's results so far, without names. He sat for a few seconds appearing to absorb what had been said. He then leaned forward in his chair and said,

"I presume I'm here for a reason, and I presume that reason is that you have targeted one of my parolees. Am I right so far?"

"As a matter of fact you are." I told him. "We really wanted to feel you out about how you would feel if one of your charges was on our list. It's sometimes hard to figure with different P.O.s, as you well know."

"Yeah, I know. Let me put it this way. If a guy deserves a break, I'll go out of my way to give it to him. By the same token if he's dirty I'll be the first to send him back. Does that answer your questions?"

"Yes and no. If we target one of your people how likely is he to learn about it. That's putting it pretty bluntly but we can't afford to take a chance and find out later we've been short-circuited by a well meaning social worker."

If that didn't piss him off he'd probably be O.K. to work with.

He smiled slightly and said, "I see, you want to know if I can be trusted not to tip off your operation. Well don't worry about it. You go ahead and do your job and if I can help you in any way just say so. If it's one of my people just give them a fair shake. That's all I ask. As you know part of their parole is to give up most of their rights so if you need me to go along on a search or something just say so. And, unless it's necessary, I don't even want to know who you're working on until you bust him or need my help. How does that suit you?" He'd made his point and didn't seem a bit upset. Then we knew.

"That suits us just fine. You can understand our reluctance to go too far without knowing who we're dealing with. We now would like your help. What can you help us with on Robert Victor Johnson? Anything you've got will help. We have it on pretty good authority he's capering at least once a week, usually on Thursday night, which we understand is his meeting night." I leaned back, lit a cigarette, and let that soak in.

"You're information is probably right. Our meetings only last about 45 minutes, I have two meetings on Tuesday and Thursday evenings. Johnson is a quiet one. He moved a couple of weeks ago." He pulled out his loose leaf notebook and began to thumb through the pages. "Yeah, here it is. That's his new address, his phone number and his car. He's supposed to be working at a lumber yard but that's probably a cover. His hands are too soft to be doing manual labor. That's supposed to be his work number there." pointing to a number at the bottom of the page.

"From what you know about him I have to assume that you got it from another of my parolees. Without telling me who it is, just tell me if it looks like I'll have to violate him." This guy seems pretty sharp, or was he just fishing?.

"I don't think you'll have to worry about that just now. I'll be sure to let you know if it changes though. Thanks very much for coming in Paul. I'll keep you up to date on anything we do." We both got up and shook hands as he headed for the door. "Keep in touch, you have my home number", he said on his way out.

Well that seemed to take care of that. Time to talk to John again and see if he can add anything to what he's already said. By now he should be hurting real bad. I can make him feel better by telling him we are going to put him on the street for now. The problem with that is, is he going to say anything to our new target, or anyone else. Probably not.

At least not if he's not doped up. High, he just might open his mouth without realizing what he's saying. That's one of those chances you live with when dealing with an informant, and a junkie. Especially this type of informant.

You can NEVER really trust them. NEVER really take their word for anything. Always figure they have more than one motive for telling you anything. And never, never, never get indebted to one.

John was about to come out of his skin when we got into the interrogation room. I'd poured him a cup of coffee and gave him a couple of aspirin. "What the hell's that for? Is that supposed to take the edge off?" He was almost shouting.

"No John, it's supposed to help get you over your hurting a little bit. But if you'd rather not have them, that's O.K. too." I reached to pick up the aspirin off the desk. Too slow. He had scooped them up and swallowed them with a mouthful of hot coffee before I had a chance to stop him even if I had wanted to.

"O.K. John. Here's the program. You can go along with it or not, as you please. But be advised if you don't go along with it I'll make every effort to file those shoplifting cases on you. With your record and parole tail you'll go back for a long time. What we're going to do is cut you loose today", his eyes lit up and he sat straight in his chair, "but I expect to get a phone call from you every day. Even if it's just to say hello. Under no circumstances are you to say anything to anyone about our conversation. You got that?"

"Sure I got it. Do you think I'm crazy?"

"I don't know what you are yet John. I'll know better after we've worked together a while. Also, for your own protection, I filed some cover papers in the court clerks office indicating you have been charged with shoplifting and are waiting trail. "

"Do I have to appear for trial?"

"No, I told you, they're just to cover your ass if Murray begins to wonder why you're not still in jail or one of your buddies starts to ask questions. You got that straight now?"

"We're going to do some work on your buddy, Johnson. If we pop him and make some decent recovery I may even be able to get the insurance company to come across with a few bucks for you. Is that O.K. with you?"

"Yeah, sure it is as long as only you and I know about it? No checks or anything, right?"

It was now beginning to seem like John had done this before. If he was a virgin at it he sure knew a lot about the angles.

"Right John. We'll give you a phony name so if they have to issue a check it won't be to your name."

"How can I cash it then. Do I get phony I.D.?"

"No John, I'll walk over to the bank with you and vouch for you. We're not about to hand out phony I.D. to anyone."

"O.K., O.K., don't get upset. I just wondered how it would

work. When can I go?" He was really antsy now. He could already feel that needle in his arm. God, what a way to live.

"We'll take you down and check you out now. Your P.O. has not been told about your arrest so you don't have to go and confess to him. The fewer people that know, the better. You got all your stuff from the cell?"

"Yeah, I'm ready. How'm I supposed to get to my place. I didn't get paid for the razors from Murray before you guys busted us and I only got about three bucks in property."

As we went down in the elevator I gave him twenty dollars to get him home. "Remember John, that's to get home and eat, not to shove into your arm. And I thought you said those razors weren't yours?"

"I know, besides, I couldn't get very high on $20.00". Yeah, I forgot, I did bring some razors to Murray"

"Remember, I get a phone call from you every day. I don't, and you're mine. If you remember anything else about Johnson I want a call right away. Got it? Those razors are your first and last lie to me, right?"

"Yeah, sure I got it."

A short time later he was going out the back door and heading for the bus stop on Santa Monica Blvd. I wasn't going to hold my breath 'til I got a call from him but this was where you find out if you've made another mistake. Right now you put him in the column of "uncertain". Dealing with thieves, bums, shady characters, and crooks of all types, you find yourself occasionally buying into their hard luck story and going out on a limb for them. Giving them a few bucks, helping them get a job, things like that. Not bending the rules, but leaning in their direction sometimes.

Then you usually find, more often than not, that they've stuck it in and broke it off for you. So much for your soft side. Once you get used to it, you chalk it up to experience and vow never, never, to do it again. Then, once in a very great while one of your 'projects' calls you, or comes by the office to tell you about their job. Or better yet, their boss calls to tell you how well their doing. Then your 'never again' becomes, well, maybe. But invariably they get less and less.

You try not to stop and dwell on it but once in a while, in an unguarded moment, you realize more and more of your naivete is being slowly peeled away and being replaced with hardened cynicism.

Then there are those you don't believe for a second. Your only purpose in doing anything for them is for quid pro quo. And then only if you get more than they do. You know going in it's strictly business. The only thing you have going for you is your reputation for keeping your word, so you make sure that remains in tact.

And then there are those who tell you things and deal with you for no obvious reason. Somehow or another you've struck a responsive chord. You don't have anything on them, they don't owe you anything, they're not really law breakers, merely in positions to hear or see things. And they come out of odd circumstances. Then what made them pick you as their release? You hope it's because they have respect for you but you don't know what in particular you've done to earn it.

You only know that you welcome it and hopefully won't do anything to ruin it. You don't ever pressure them. You try never to overuse them. Mostly you wait for their calls. Once in a while you stop by to pass the time of day, ask about a family member, or just say hello. You can't figure why it came about, but you nurse it, value it, and respect it.

Having gotten rid of John, I called Frank and filled him in on my visit with Paul Stevens. We're pretty comfortable with our plan and set noon Wednesday as our next meeting date, at the same place. After I filed my follow-up report of John's release and filled in Cork and Hankins, I caught my ride home.

Diana got home a short time later to find me dozing, loudly, in my recliner. After a very pleasant evening of food, talk and relaxation I turned on the eleven o'clock news as I got ready to fall into the arms of Morpheus. Sitting on the edge of the bed, half listening to the newscaster, I caught the words, "Beverly Hills" and "major burglary". Now, a lot of times Beverly Hills is mentioned, but the location is just outside the city and the media uses the name for news value. No such luck this time.

By this time I was back in the living room watching the newscaster describe the burglary of the residence of Carroll Baker, and gave her address. They also had live pictures of her holding a $30,000 necklace that the thieves had overlooked.

Her husband, producer Jack Garfein, narrated to the camera that the family and staff had gone out for dinner and when they returned they found the house ransacked. Mrs. Garfein added that the necklace she was holding had been laying on a shelf in the same closet where the other jewelry and furs had been taken. "They just must have been in too big a hurry and didn't see it", she said.

By this time I was holding my head and saying "Oh God", "Oh God" as Diana sat down beside me.

"Is it going to be one of yours?" she asked.

"Oh Yeah. And she just invited every burglar in the country to come back and try for that damned necklace. Great".

The ringing telephone interrupted my beginning tirade.

"Hello, yeah Fred, I'm watching it now. What'd they do call the press before they called us?"

I listened as Lt. Colford filled me in on the information. When he was done I asked a few questions about alarms, point of entry, and if I needed to come in tonight. He told me no, The night detective had made the preliminary report and he's told the Garfeins that I would be up to see them at 8:30 AM the next morning. I thanked him, hung up, and slouched back into the recliner.

The night passed fast. I was back in the office at 6:30AM and reading the reports. As the Identification Bureau people came in I got them to show me what physical evidence we had, if any. None. Entry was apparently made through french patio doors using a screwdriver as a pry bar. There was no burglar alarm on the house, and there was not much ransacking. No apparent fingerprints. By the time I digested the reports and the activity log the rest of the Detectives were in. Dick Haas and I would make the followup at 8:30. Any more media contact will be handled by the Chief.

The Chief had an unpublished policy and philosophy that the media didn't need to know any more than we wanted them to know. He was also a firm believer in the philosophy that a 3 inch headline, "Burglar shot in house", was the best crime deterrent. It was an established fact that burglaries went down dramatically in the weeks after such a headline.

Haas and I pulled up in front of the house at 8:25. I had a full head of steam already. The phones had been ringing off the hook wanting information on the "Investigation".

What Investigation? We didn't even have a list of what's missing yet.

The maid let us in and ushered us into the living room. She'd set out a pot of coffee and several cups in anticipation of our arrival. Jack Garfein came in right away and told us his wife would be in shortly. He offered us a seat and poured us a cup of coffee without asking if we wanted one. We asked him to show us the point of entry and where the merchandise had been. As we were leaving the living room Mrs. Garfein came into the room.

The Good Lord hadn't slighted her when it came to beauty, and, as I was to find out later, charm.

After a brief tour of the house we proceeded to the dressing area of the master bedroom on the second floor. She explained that her jewelry had been haphazardly distributed on several of the shelves along one wall of the dressing room. The missing jewelry had all been on one shelf.

The necklace had been on the next shelf down, partially covered by a scarf. Apparently the thief hadn't bothered to look any further.

The missing furs had been in plain view at the other end of the closet and dressing area. One fur was particularly unique. It was an extra long, rectangular, white fox, lined with bugle beads in an open mesh design. It had been made for a movie she had just done, “Harlow”, and she gave me a publicity photo of her wearing it. It would not be hard to identify.

Once back in the living room we accepted the coffee and began to discuss the circumstances surrounding the burglary.

They told us they had gone to the Luau Restaurant on Rodeo Drive for dinner and had taken the children and the maid with them. Taking the children and maid along was not something they usually did and had done so on the spur of the moment. No one had known of their prior plans and they had made reservations barely a couple of hours before they left. They had told the restaurant that it was a celebration for one of the children so they could prepare a small cake. They arrived at about 7:45 PM and returned home at about 9:45.

“We went over all this last night with the officers. Why are we going over it again?” he asked, moving to pour more coffee.

“We often find that the victims remember things they had forgotten the night before. After the initial shock of such an event it’s not unusual for the victim to overlook some apparently insignificant detail. The next day often offers the opportunity to think more slowly and clearly. Approximately what value do you place on the missing property? It doesn’t have to be accurate, and it’s only a preliminary figure. Your insurance company will want you to be more specific.”

“It looks like it will be between 10 and 15 thousand dollars” he says.

“But actually,” she said, the ‘Baby Doll’ bracelet has a great sentimental value. It was given to me as a momento after I did the movie ‘Baby Doll”.

“Yes, I remember reading about that. It was a charm bracelet wasn’t it?” I asked.

“Yes it was. There is a description of it and the charms on that property list I gave you.”

“O.K. I guess that will be all for now.” We got up and headed for the door. “I hope your neighbors won’t be to hard on you or give you to much trouble. Let us know if they do.”

"What are you talking about?" they asked almost in unison.

"Well, after all that publicity, and giving out your address and all, it wouldn't surprise me if most of the burglars and stickup men in town don't give some thought to coming back and trying for that necklace. If not that, they may take a chance on some of your neighbors. Knowing they missed that necklace is a blow to their pride."

"If I were you I'd put my valuables in a safe deposit box real soon, or barring that I'd get a good strong safe. It's not unusual for burglars to be drawn to certain areas by publicity. They figure there has to be more than one celebrity living in the area. We'll be in touch as soon as we learn anything. Good Bye."

On our way back to the station Dick said, "you just had to get that shot in didn't you?"

"What are you talking about?" I asked in my most innocent tone of voice.

"You know damn well what I'm talking about. You didn't want to raise hell about all the publicity but you wanted them to know it wasn't appreciated and could cause problems."

"Now would I do something like that? I'm deeply wounded that you could think I would be so sneaky." I put on my best wounded face as we pulled into the parking lot.

By noon the teletype describing the property had been sent and the followup report had been written. Then came the task of calling the different contacts in other departments and filling them in on the details. First, Frank, then Pete. Toomey and Turner in Hollywood Division, and the West Hollywood Sheriff's Department. Lt. Johnny Meyers at the LASO safe burglary detail too.

As I talked to each one I specifically asked them to recall, or check with their victims, if any of them had been to the Luau Restaurant on the night of their burglary or shortly before their burglary. I filled in Lt. Phillips at Intelligence too. They gathered a lot of information in that office. All the bases have been covered. Now to cull my own file for the same information and wait for the pot to boil.

It didn't take to long to reach the boil. Within a couple of hours I'd gotten calls back from Frank and Turner. They both had victims that either were at the Luau when they were hit, or had been there a few days before becoming victims. Now comes the problem of isolating who at the restaurant may be tipping off the burglars. It's pretty obvious somebody was. We've got to quietly acquire all the background information we can about the employees and begin weeding them out without alerting them to what we're doing.

After some consideration we decided that the owner of the Luau, Stephen Crane, would be the best source of the information we would need. He could gather the information as an 'administration' procedure without drawing much attention.

We ran into the age old brick wall when we found he was out of town until next Wednesday. That plan went on hold for a few days while we tried to put the case together in other ways.

CHAPTER 26

That damned telephone again. It was eleven o'clock and we had just gotten into bed. What now? Diana was sitting up as I went into the living room to answer it.

"Hello."

"Hey Bob, Howard, do you know a Sam Pasich ?"

"Sure Howard, I just put his picture and description on the bulletin board day before yesterday. Why?"

"I sure didn't see it. Where did you put it?"

"Right in the center of the board. He's a very active burglar. I had his brown Ford station wagon license number with his picture. He's an apartment burglar and sometimes uses channel lock pliers for entry. Why?"

"Damn it. I knew it. I just had a feeling this guy wasn't right. We stopped him on North Clark Drive loading a Ford station wagon with a T.V and other stuff. He said he was moving from his apartment. He had a good story and sounded convincing. He had a guy with him named Jack David Reed. A big sucker. They were both very cool. Damn it. When did you last see that picture on the board ?"

"The day I put it up. Why the hell would anyone take it off ?"

"I don't know, but it sure isn't there now. This is my first day back and I checked all the new information on the board before roll call. And I just checked it again when I came in now. Not there. Someone is making their own mug shot file."

"That's a stupid thing to do. That could get someone killed."

"Anyway, We just took a report of an apartment burglary on North Clark. A big T.V and other stuff was taken. It's the same stuff that Pasich and Reed were loading in the station wagon. I have two F.I. cards we filled out on them. I don't know if the addresses will be any good. Are you coming in ?"

"I guess so. Who's the night detective tonight?"

"Jim Thomas."

"O.K., tell him to wait for me. I'll only be a few minutes. Send a car up to get me."

"I'll come up. I can fill you in on the ride back."

"O.K., I'll only be a few minutes."

I was pulling on my jacket as Howard drove up the driveway. Diana wasn't too thrilled about my leaving at that time of night. "Another no sleep night, Huh?" she said.

"I guess so. I don't know if I'll be back before morning or not."

"I do, I can tell by the way it's starting it'll be another all nighter. You're never going to get any sleep."

"Vacation's coming up pretty soon. Maybe I'll take the first three days and sleep."

"Ha, a likely story. Be careful."

"O.K., I'll call you when I get a chance."

I closed the door and headed down the stairs. Howard was filling out some paperwork when I got into the car. On our way to the station he gave me the two F.I. cards and continued to berate himself for not busting the two guys when he had them. Knowing the kind of cop Howard was I knew this would grate on him for quite a while. A man that conscientious about his job does not leave himself much leeway.

We discussed the idea of someone removing mug shots and information from the bulletin board. When we got to the office we went into the Bureau and I showed him the duplicate of the notice that I had put on the board. He was irate. I knew that the only way he'd feel any better is if we could arrest Pasich before he can get rid of the merchandise.

There was no doubt that he'd know he'd been fingered for this job so he'd be getting rid of the merchandise quickly.

Jim Thomas was the night detective and was waiting quietly for us to get done talking. Jim had been in the Bureau for only a few weeks from the Traffic Division. He hadn't gotten much Bureau experience but seemed eager to learn and help. He'd had a good reputation following him from Traffic but the Bureau was a whole different ball game. We got into the car and headed for the address on the F.I. card. It was the same address I had listed on the bulletin board. That seemed strange. People like Sam Pasich never stayed in one place too long. Well, we'd see what we find. Jim seemed fidgety and sort of nervous. Pre- arrest jitters I guess. He hadn't had too long to become comfortable in his new position, although he'd been a cop long enough to have gotten some whiskers and be settled down.

We found the address just west of downtown L.A. It's an older section of town and full of residential hotels and small apartment buildings. They are all sort of run down but somehow gave the feeling of having been stately and attractive at one time. The one we were interested in was a residential hotel. Desk clerk and all.

Much to our surprise, Sam Pasich and his 'wife' and kids were still living here. And were in their room. He had seen them come in about two hours ago. We advised him in somewhat forceful terms that we would not be happy if he should happen to let them know we were there. He got our point. I used the phone to call for backup from L.A.P.D. and while we waited we located Sam's station wagon in the alley behind the hotel. Empty. So much for finding the property easily.

A few minutes later a black and white pulled up to the hotel and two uniformed officers got out. We introduced ourselves and filled them in on our suspect and what we proposed to do. They looked at each other, and with no wasted motion, they are on their way into the building. On the second floor landing we gave them the room number and they took up positions at each end of the hallway.

Jim and I approached the door, standing on each side of it. I quietly slipped the key we got from the desk clerk into the lock and turned it. It turned quietly but as I tried to push the door open, it stopped after an inch or so. Something was against the other side of the door.

No time for finesse then. I stepped back and gave the door a resounding kick. The door opened about a foot and started to close. As it was coming back to close again, I hit it with my right shoulder. As I did that I heard a shot, and thought I felt a tug at my right sleeve. I was committed to the door but had a strange feeling the shot came from behind me. As I got through the doorway I saw that a chair had been placed against the door to keep it closed. I flipped on the light switch as I passed the bathroom door and headed into the bedroom, with Jim behind me.

Sitting upright in bed was Sam Pasich and his 'wife'. The two kids were in a small bed at the end of the room. Sam and the girl put their hands in the air without being told. The kids hardly stirred. Thank God. They really didn't need to witness this. The uniformed officers followed us into the room. When Sam was handcuffed and the room secured, one of the uniformed officers motioned for me to come into the hallway.

"Are you all right ?" he asked.

"Sure, I guess so, why? "

He pointed to a hole in the door, from the outside in, and said, "It looked like your partner may have winged you on the way in." He then reached up and put his finger through the in and out hole in my right jacket sleeve. It took about three seconds for it to sink in. Then my mouth got very dry and my knees started to shake. I must have gotten pretty pale too because he took hold of my arm.

"I've got to notify the sergeant about shots fired. He'll probably want to send a shooting team out. You might want to talk to your partner before they get here. We'll watch your prisoners." He moved past me back into the room.

I waved for Jim to come into the hall.

"What the hell happened ?"

His face was ghostly white. "I don't know. My gun went off as I hit the door. I thought Sam was reaching for the bedside table."

"Dammit Jim, you didn't hit the door, I did. Did you have your finger on the trigger?"

"I guess so, I don't know what happened."

"O.K., O.K., It was an accidental discharge. Just tell that to the shooting team that shows up." I told him as I walked back into the room putting my finger through the holes in my jacket.

An hour later we were headed back to the station with Sam in custody. Because of the kids we had decided to leave 'Dotty' at the hotel with them.

The shooting team made short work of their investigation and closed it as accidental. We had searched the room and the car and found no evidence of any value to our case. Sam naturally declined to cooperate. He knew he was had and was going back to prison. He was still on parole, contrary to our previous information.

While Jim was booking Sam into the jail, I was starting on the arrest report. About half way through it, the door from the outer office opened and closed. Just when I thought Jim would be coming into the office, that distinctive voice said, "What happened ?" There was no doubt who had come into the room. It's close to four in the morning and he's here already. The Chief.

I started to tell him about the burglary and the arrest when he stopped me with, "I mean the shooting. The L.A. Division Commander called to notify us. What Happened ?"

"I don't really know Chief. I had my back to him as I hit the door. I heard the shot but was to busy to worry about it at the time. Later I asked him what happened and he said it was an accident. He was real shook up when he saw the hole in my jacket. That's all I know about it."

"All right. Is that the arrest report ?"

"Yes Sir, I'll have it done in a few minutes."

"All right, I'll want a report on the shot fired too."

"O.K. Chief," I said to his back as he left the office.

A few minutes later Jim came into the office and asked if the Chief had been in. I told him yes.

"Did he say anything about the arrest ?"

"Yeah. And he asked about the shot. L.A. had notified him. He wants an incident report on it."

"What'll we say ?"

"The truth. That's the only thing we can say."

Jim started to get nervous again. He sat down and looked out the window. At quarter to five in the morning there's not a hell of a lot to see outside.

"Jim, you make your report about what happened and I'll make mine. It was an accident and that's all we can say."

"Yeah, I guess so. Damn. Do you think it will affect my staying in the Bureau ?"

"I honestly don't know. You never can tell about the Chief. Go ahead and start your report while I finish the arrest report."

I continued typing the report as I glanced over at my jacket hanging on the back of the chair. My knees started to shake again and my stomach rolled over a couple of times. I stopped pounding on the typewriter. I'd have to leave the jacket at the office. Diana would have a fit if she saw the sleeve. She'll have to be told about the shot because that's something that won't stay a secret. She doesn't have to know how close it came.

By the time all our reports were finished the day shift was coming in. As Capt. Hankins was coming up the stairs the Watch Commander directed him to the Chief's office. It's obvious our little 'incident' is going to get further discussion.

A short while later, Cork, Egger, Mourning and Estill have come in. By the way they look at Jim and I as they come in it's pretty obvious they had been told 'something'. How much of it was true was hard to tell. Jim was sitting at the end of the room attempting to make small talk. Cork turned around heading for the door, motioning for me to follow. As we got to the top of the stairway going to the roll call room Hankins spotted us and called us back.

We went into his office with Jim watching us from the other room as Hankins closed the door.

"O.K., exactly what happened ?" he asked.

"Everything, and I mean everything, is in my report. I had my back to Jim as we went through the door. I heard the shot and didn't know where it came from until the L.A. man told me who had fired. He pointed out the hole in my jacket.

I asked Jim about it and he said it went off accidently. I told him to keep his finger off the trigger next time. I do know I started shaking after I saw my jacket. That's it."

"What's Thomas say ?"

"I told you. He said he probably had his finger on the trigger and it went off accidently. Nothing else."

"O.K., send Thomas in."

"John is it O.K. for Downey and I to go get some coffee? We'll be back in twenty or thirty minutes."

"Yeah go ahead but don't be gone long."

"Right", Cork said as we headed out the door. I waved for Thomas to go into Hankins office as we left.

There wasn't much said as Cork and I walked to the drug store at Canon and So. Santa Monica.

By the time we had our coffee served my knees started to shake again. Not as bad as before, but still noticeable.

"Shook you up pretty good, Huh ?"

"Yeah, thank God I didn't know where the slug went while I was still in the doorway. You know how it goes. You have your mind channeled on what you have to do and you don't need any distractions. He tried at first to tell me he had seen Sam go for the nightstand like he was going for a gun. Hell he couldn't see into the room. He was behind me and even I couldn't see into the room from where I was."

"Well, it tells us something important though. Who you don't want behind you, or even with you when you go through a door. We've got to be grateful that this lesson was so cheap. It could have been worse."

"Just remember that when you partner me up with someone from now on." I finished my coffee and motioned for a refill.

"I'll do that. Now what about Sam. Do you want to talk to him or do you want to go home and get some rest ?"

"No, I'll stay and talk to him with you. We still have Jack

Reed to get yet. Maybe Sam can help us with that."

"I'm not going to hold my breath. Is Reed still on parole ?"

"Yeah. It shouldn't be to hard to locate him. Let's go and see Sam. Sam's still on parole too."

When we got back to the office Sam's girlfriend was waiting for us. We had a few words with her then had her wait until we had a conversation with Sam.

I introduced Cork to Sam as we were seating ourselves in the interrogation room. We had stopped by the jail kitchen and picked up three cups of coffee. Sam was a personable guy. He was pleasant and smiling. His attitude was one of resignation though. He knew he was going back to prison and had accepted that fact. Now it was up to him to try to work out the best deal he could for himself.

We told him 'Dotty' was waiting to see him after we got done talking.

In a few minutes we were dancing around feeling each other out. A little jab here, a little faint there. Sam was trying to figure out just how much he had to tell us to get some kind of break. He knew he was nailed for the apartment job the night before, but he also had his parole tail to worry about. The only deal we could make, with the D.A.'s approval, was for his sentence to run currently with his parole violation. In return, he would name all his burglaries in our area and West L.A., and try to get back as much property as possible. That was it as far as we were concerned, providing West L.A. agreed. We left him to chew on that while he visited with 'Dotty'.

Once back in the office I called Frank Gravante in West L.A. to fill him in on our arrest and possible 'deal'. He said he would confer with his powers that be and get back to me. A half hour later he called back with a yes answer. Considering we had no additional evidence against Sam, we were getting a pretty good deal. The judge would probably have sentenced him to serve his new time concurrently with his parole violation anyway. This way we'd get some property back and some cases cleared. The next thing was to find and arrest Jack Reed.

When we got back to Sam he had made up his mind to accept our proposition. He had told 'Dotty' to call me the next morning and set up a time for her to bring in his stash of stolen property. I had agreed that we would not arrest her for receiving stolen property, as long as she cooperated. Besides, she knew where the property was. We didn't.

We got around to Jack Reed. Sam said he thought we'd have a hard time finding him because he knew he would be 'hot' for this job and had decided to take off last night. He gave us the same address we had on the F.I. card that Howard had filled out. We put Sam away and started out to look for Reed.

We could have saved the trip. He had only a small room in a flea bag hotel near where Sam was living. He had cleared out about midnight the night before. No one around there could 'offer' any help with where he might have gone.

The only thing left to do now was notify his parole officer and file a burglary complaint against him. Chances were he wouldn't contact his parole officer either. Oh well, a bird in the hand.

The next morning I stopped by West L.A. after I had gone to Santa Monica to get my complaints against Pasich and Reed. Frank and I settled on a time for him to come to our office and we would talk with Sam and start clearing cases. The D.A.'s office had agreed to our 'deal' with Sam.

By the time I got back to the office I had a message from Dotty. I returned her call and we agreed that she would come to our office at 1:00 PM, with the loot.

Shortly after Cork and I returned from lunch Dotty came into the office. She told me she had four boxes in her car and wanted to know where to park so we could unload them. She backed the car into the parking ramp by the back door and carried the boxes up to the Detective Bureau office. Once she had taken her car to the parking lot she came back to the office and I started to open the boxes. They were packed full of a wide variety of merchandise. Cameras, radios, furs, a hand gun or two and some costume jewelry. While I was emptying the boxes I became aware that toward the center of each box the merchandise was ice cold. Like it had just come out of a refrigerator. I didn't indicate to her that I had noticed this as I made small talk about why there was no good jewelry among the items. She said I would have to talk to Sam about that. I made a mental note about the refrigerator for later use.

A short time later I brought Sam from the jail so he could look at the property and fill me in on where it had come from. He didn't seem to be in the cooperative mood he had been in before. It took a lot of small talk and some convincing before he started to come around again. About this time Frank Gravante arrived from West L.A. and I introduced him to Sam and Dotty. We spent the next 30 minutes discussing our deal to only file one charge against Sam in addition to his parole violation.

When he was certain we meant to keep our word he began to identify the property and where it had come from. When we got to an 8MM movie camera, Sam and Dotty both smiled and joked about it. He finally let us in on the joke.

It seemed that Murray Fellman had been handling most of Sam's 'hot' merchandise and was being fairly honest about it. However on one occasion he really stuck it to Sam on some very expensive jewelry. Sam called him on it but Murray told him to get lost. Sam started to deal elsewhere. He had a long memory however. A few weeks later it seemed Murray's house in the valley got burglarized and a large amount of property was taken, including that camera. Murray knew damned well that Sam had done it but what could he say. It seemed most of the property Sam got away with had been stolen property before Murray had gotten it. Who was he going to complain to? Sam kept the camera as a momento.

Frank and I put Sam back in his cell while we started to put the merchandise with the reports. When we had finished we had identified six additional burglaries and three possibles, I also filled Frank in on the 'cold' merchandise. We'd have to start paying more attention to cold storage lockers near the residence areas of our thieves.

Now came the drawn out procedure of having the victims come into the office and identify their property. You can get very disillusioned during this process. When the burglary happens you can really field a lot of irate comments and veiled innuendos from the victims about your ability and effectiveness. Then when you've had some success and recovered some loot, you find that in some cases your victims have been reimbursed by the insurance companies and they have no desire to identify their property. Somehow they had been paid two or three times what the property had been worth and now they didn't want to admit they had scammed the insurance company. Certainly not all victims were like that but those that were gave you a very bad taste in your mouth.

You'd end up going back to the insurance company and explaining that your burglar identified the victim but the victim was 'reluctant' to identify the property. In most cases the insurance company let the false claim stand unless it was an exorbitant amount. "Don't want to insult the client, you know." The insurance company would end up getting the property back and would sell it to try to recoup their losses. A hell of a way to run a railroad.

Sam's parole officer violated him and he was also sentenced by the judge to State prison. Sam was on his way back to prison. Little did we know that we would be picking Sam up again in just a few short weeks.

A few weeks after Sam Pasich was sentenced to State Prison, Frank Gravante called me to let me know that he had just found out that Sam was already on the street. It seemed Sam's attorney, Harry Weiss, had found a loophole in the way the judge had worded his sentence. Interpreted literally, Sam's new sentence was only to last as long as his parole violation would have lasted. Which in effect meant that Sam only had a few months to serve. His parole only had a few months to run so when it was over, according to his attorney, so was his new sentence.

By the time we heard about it Sam had been released from San Quentin and was back among us. Gravante and I went to the D.A.s' office to see what could be done. From there we went to the judge, with one of the Deputy D.A's. The judge, once the situation was explained to him, was irate. He was not happy with the fact that an attorney had taken advantage of a slight wording mistake. So what else is new ? The judge issued an immediate bench warrant for Sam's arrest.

Once back at the office Frank and I began the arduous task of trying to locate Sam. Since he had been released from parole it was no longer easy to get his address from his parole officer. As luck would have it, or good investigative technique, I had managed to make notes of Dottie's kids school. Actually I hadn't thrown away my notes from our prior conversations and found them in the file folder.

A fast check of their old school showed a transfer to a school in West Covina. A few minutes later I had an address in West Covina. Early tomorrow I'd have to make a trip out there. Frank had court the next morning so I'd have to make the trip alone.

By nine A.M. the next morning I was staked out on the house. I didn't know if Sam and Dottie were still together. After all her husband may have gotten out of the joint in the meantime. He and Sam had been buddies during Sam's previous tour in the bucket and Sam had agreed to take care of her for him. Good buddies.

As I slid down a little further in my seat and tried to keep my eyes from closing, the music on the car radio was interrupted for a "Special Bulletin" .. "President Kennedy has just been shot in a motorcade in Dallas, Texas. Stay tuned for further information." No problem keeping my eyes open then. What the hell happened. Had I actually heard what I thought I heard ? I spun the dial on the radio trying to get more information. I ran into the same announcement on two other stations. Back to the original station.

"The president is being taken to Parkland Hospital. His wounds appear critical." I still couldn't believe what I was hearing.

I started the car and headed for a more populated area. I don't know why. What was I going to find there? What would they know that I didn't? Maybe I just needed someone else to verify what I'd heard. I pulled into a gas station that had three people in the office standing near a radio. I stepped out of the car and to the doorway.

"Did I just hear right ? The president's been shot ?"

They all looked at me and shook their heads, yes. Now what was I going to do ? My hearing had been validated, now what ? I got back in the car and headed back to the stakeout.

I sat there for a couple of hours longer. Hanging onto every word coming over the radio. The desperate measures to save his life. The futility. The announcement of his death. My God what's happening. The information was all a jumble. Everyone was expressing some theory or another. No one knew for sure. More questions, few answers.

In the middle of this maelstrom of reports and supposition a car drove in the driveway of the house I was watching. Sam stepped out of the drivers side while Dottie and the kids got out the other side. I pulled into the driveway as they closed their doors.

THEN it dawned on me. What the hell was I doing there by myself? Sam's looking at going back to jail for a long time and just may not want to go back willingly. That could get ugly in a hurry. As I stepped out of the car I waved for Sam to come to my car. He waved back and with a smile on his face walked back to the car.

"Sam, I've got some bad news for you."

"What's that ?"

"The judge has issued a bench warrant for your arrest. It seems he didn't appreciate the fast one that Harry pulled on your sentencing."

"What fast one ?" he asked, with a knowing, ever so slight smile on his face.

I got the feeling he had been waiting for something like this. No argument. No hesitation. Just resignation on his face.

"Let me unload the car and get some things to take along".

Dottie had been listening and turned to head for the house. I guess when you are in their business you expect a few bumps along the road. Some bump.

A few goodbyes and a few minutes discussing "the shooting", and we were on our way back to Beverly Hills. A lot easier than I had started to think. A little courtesy and respect goes a long way.

On the way back to the office Sam took special pains to assure me that since he'd been out he hadn't been pulling jobs on the west side. Not in Beverly Hills or West L.A. That was reassuring, if you could believe him. After all, he's still a burglar. He'd have to get the benefit of the doubt though. At least until it was proved otherwise.

After a short booking process we were seated in the interrogation room listening to the radio about the assassination. It was still hard to believe. By now though there was a suspect in custody. Lee Harvey Oswald. He had shot a policeman during his capture. At least they got him alive. Now maybe we'll find out what's behind it all.

After Sam and I shot the breeze for a while I asked him about Jack Reed. He told me he'd heard Jack was in the San Francisco Bay area but he didn't know exactly where. I don't know why but I believed him. A little while later Sam went back to his cell and I got back to the office. When I got off the elevator from the jail you could cut the 'quiet' in the business office with a knife. The whole building seemed eerily quiet. The guys in the Detective Bureau were talking quietly and listening to the radio at the same time.

Things outside seemed to have slowed to a crawl. Few cars and almost no one on the street. No noise. The impatient horns not blowing, the engines not being reved up. It was all just eerie. Slowly, very slowly, the activity started to pick up. Not much, but a little. Now a phone rang every once in a while. Conversation started up again but still muted. No one was going to return to 'normal' very soon.

I happened to be talking to Sam later when word was announced that Oswald had been shot while being transferred from one jail to another. What the hell was going on in the world ? Sam wanted to go back to his cell and I went home. The next day he went before the judge again. This time his attorney is beside him when he is sentenced to "the term prescribed by law". There's not much conversation between them. We said a quick `Adios' and Sam is gone again.

A few weeks later Frank called to tell me the same victim Sam and Reed had hit before had been hit again. We decided we'd better go talk to Sam again. This time he was in the men's facility at Lompoc. This trip would take a couple of days. We got to San Luis Obispo the next day. At the prison we met with Sam in a nicely equipped interrogation room. It didn't hurt to take along a carton of cigarettes to break the ice. Sam was certainly not a happy camper. Who would be?

"Sam, the Harris penthouse got hit again. Do you think it's possible that Reed could have gone back ?" Frank asked.

"It's possible, but not by himself. He didn't like that place the first time. Was the dog still there?" he asked.

"No, the dog had been put into a kennel, why?"

"Hell that whole thing was a fiasco the first time. You might tell people to tell their answering services not to be so accommodating. I stiffed a call in to the apartment to see if anyone answered and got the answering service. I asked if they were home and was told they wouldn't be home 'til Saturday but if I wanted to get in touch with them they were staying at the Riviera Hotel in Las Vegas. I thanked her and said goodbye before I busted out laughing." The whole story brought another smile to his face.

"The surprise came when I got into the place. Jack had boosted me onto the roof. There was a skylight just inside the front door. I pried it open and dropped to the floor. I was still down on my knees when the biggest damned German Shepherd I had ever seen was standing there staring me in the face. You talk about your life flashing in front of you. I put my hand out to hold him off as I started to reach for the door and the damned thing started licking my hand. I like friendly dogs." He leaned back in his chair with a very self-satisfied look on his face.

"We couldn't keep the dog out of our way while we prowled the place. Jack was not happy about the dog being around. I don't think he would have gone back there by himself. Isn't he still up in San Jose ?"

"We don't know. We haven't heard anything about him. Who would he take any good jewelry to ?" I asked. Sam had never told us who handled his `good' stuff and I hoped to slip this one in on him. Didn't work. He was still on his toes.

"Come on guys. I have to keep some things to myself. I may need them if I ever get out of here. Beside that I can always depend on them for a couple of cartons of cigarettes if things get tough in here." he answered with a chuckle.

This visit had come to an end. A few minutes of small talk and we were on our way. I hadn't noticed it before, but I was sure glad when that last gate closed behind me. I don't know how you could ever feel comfortable in that place or any other like it.

We were on our way back to L.A. the next morning. We didn't get a hell of a lot out of that trip. Except that bit about the answering service. The victim might like to know about that.

A few weeks later the phone rang and Frank said "Are you ready to go again ?"

"Where ?" I ask.

"San Jose. I just got a call that Jack Reed is in the County jail up there for armed robbery. It seems he walked into a jewelry store and when the owner didn't cooperate Jack pistol whipped him something fierce. Blinded him in one eye they say. You still have a warrant for him don't you?"

"Yeah, when do you want to go. I'll send an abstract of our warrant up there to place a hold on him."

"I can start early in the morning, how about you ?"

"Hang on a second and I'll find out." I covered the mouthpiece of the phone when I called out to Capt. Hankins,

"Hey Captain, Reeds in jail in San Jose and Frank wants me to go with him tomorrow. How about it ?" No answer. I should never spring surprises on him. He's just not ready for snap decisions.

A few seconds later he came slowly walking into the room. He saw that I was still on the phone and started to ask questions. I held up my hand to wait then I told Frank I'd call him back in a few minutes.

After the obligatory meaningless questions the Captain 'supposes' it'll be all right to go. Hell, I knew that before I asked him. I just hadn't given him time to act 'administrative'. I really don't know what difference it made, we'd always had to travel on our own money anyway. Sometimes though we got to do it on company time. If everybody was in a good mood. This was going to be one of those times.

Frank and I were in San Jose by late afternoon the next day. We contacted the County jail and made arrangements to interview Jack Reed the next day. When we got checked into the jail I noticed one of the jailers looking at me rather curiously. He seemed familiar to me also. As we approached each other it dawned on both of us at the same time. We had been assigned to the same investigative unit at Edwards Air Force Base several years before.

"Duffey" I said as I pushed out my hand.

"Cranston" he says as he took hold and shook it.

'Duffey' his nickname from the show "Duffie's Tavern" and 'Cranston' my nickname from "The Shadow". Neither of us knows why we got hung with those particular names but we did. His real name was Keith Burton and we had worked together a couple of years in the Air Force. In the U.S. and Korea. He had paid me a visit at my house a couple of years ago but my wife wouldn't wake me up because I had just gone three days without sleep and she was guarding me like a grizzly bear guards her cubs. It was good to see him again.

We spent a few minutes catching up before he led us to the interview room with Reed. Frank started to break the ice.

"Jack, I'm Sgt. Gravante from L.A. and this is Sgt. Downey from Beverly Hills. We'd like to see if we can talk to each other and get a few loose ends straightened out."

"Yeah, I heard you were coming. Before I say anything I want to know what you can do for me." This was already not starting out good.

Frank started again.

"Well Jack, what we can do `TO' you is slap at least two additional charges of burglary and grand theft to the ones you now have pending if you want to start out hard assed about this. We've driven a long way and we're tired. If this is going to be your attitude we can get out of here and just leave our holds in place until you get out. IF you ever do."

"My turn, Jack." I said. "You're going to go to the joint behind this robbery and assault charge. What do you think your chances will ever be for parole if you have two warrants hanging over your head. Pretty damned poor I'd say. Now if we were to withdraw those warrants you could possibly see the light of day again sometime. Then again you never know."

It went back and forth like that for a few more minutes. It usually does. Everybody jockeying for position. The best part of this is that we had the position, and he needed some.

"O.K., O.K., what's it all about. But first I want you guys to know that I haven't done anything down there since I left after that thing with Sam in Beverly Hills. Hell, I knew you had a warrant for me. I wasn't about to go back down there."

"Jack", Frank started, "do you remember the Harris penthouse on Wilshire. The one where Sam went in through the skylight and had the dog in the house ?"

"Yeah, scared the shit out of Sam. The dog damned near licked us to death. He was lonely. What about it ?"

"The place was hit again a couple of weeks ago. Pretty much the same M.O. Since you say you haven't been back there then maybe you can help us with who might have pulled the job. Someone you may have talked too about it. We've already talked to Sam at Lompoc and he didn't recall telling anyone."

"Did you see Sam ? How is he? How long is he going to do this time ? Harry did all right for him when he got out the last time. To bad it didn't stick."

He leaned back with a smile on his face. Anytime they can put a fast one over on the law is a good day for them.

"I can't think of anyone in particular I told about the place. I shot the shit with several guys about that job. We had a few laughs but I can't think of anyone who would have gone back there. Most everybody I've talked to is still in jail I think. Nah, I can't help you. What about my beef. I would help you if I could. Are you going to leave those holds on me?"

"Here's what we'll do Jack. We'll leave those holds in place until you're finished with this case. We wouldn't want you to be able to bail out and disappear on us. The local P.D. wants you to stay put until your trial is over. Those holds will do that. When your trial is over you write to us and we'll take care of those holds. At least they wont be hanging over your head if you ever come up for parole. How's that ?"

"I guess that's O.K. Give me your cards so I can write to you. I couldn't make bail anyhow. It's to high."

"Yeah, but that could change." says Frank. "It'll be more certain that we will know where to find you this way."

As we stood up to leave the jailer opened the door and ushered Jack back to his cell. We hadn't gotten a lot out of this trip. After a cup of coffee in the jail with Duffey, we were on our way back to L.A., with Frank's new Harris case still at a standstill. He at least had an admission from Jack that he was with Sam on the first job. Not much but something.

It was a long, boring, drive home.

CHAPTER 27

Our noon meeting that day got off to a late start. Unland and Jones had to go to court that morning and would be a little late.

Jack Mourning had come with me and would work the surveillance with me if we decided this was the night to go. Frank had verified the address and utilities. Regan had verified the vehicle and had even staked it out a couple of times, where it was usually parked, and how our man usually dressed.

We were finished with our coffee and sandwiches when Jones and Unland joined us. They'd done the background on Johnson and hadn't found any local relatives or close connections he could run to if we scared him off or lost him in a chase.

So, It was decided. tonight was the night. We met two blocks west of Johnson's at six- thirty and spread out from there. I had to go to L.A.'s electronics shop and borrow another big battery walkie talkie in order to work with them on the radio.

For surveillance purposes I was using one of West L.A.'s call signs, 8-W-5. I'd done my best to 'cool down' my plain four door detective unit. I had put 'moon' hub caps on it and false white sidewalls. And ham radio call sign numbers in the rear window.

I even installed a 'good time' radio and antenna, and bought an undercover antenna for my police radio. Herb Twitchell, our radio technician had installed it for me. We all knew our cars stood out like a sore thumb but if they were to be cooled down, it had to be done with your own money. There was just no money available for the frills.

When we got back to the office there was time for a few phone calls before we headed for the rendezvous. One of the calls, was to Diana, telling her I'd be late, again. As we left the office the dispatcher handed me a message. John Rich had called and will call tomorrow. What do you know ?

It got dark pretty early that time of year so we had to be careful where we set up so we could be sure we saw his car when he left. He drove a Dodge 2 door sedan with bulls eye tail lights high on the fender fins. We jointly discussed the desirability of having some distinctive marking or indicator on the rear of the vehicle because all the tail lights of the other vehicles blend together at night. He would sure be easier to follow.

During our discussions, Jack and Deke decided to take a walk and case the area before we had to get underway. As the rest of us were continuing our conversation we heard a distinctive sound of glass breaking in the direction of our suspects car. Shortly, Jack and Deke returned to our location and we moved to assume our positions.

"What happened down there?" I asked Jack as we were turning around and parking.

"Down where?" he said.

"We heard what sounded like glass breaking in the area of Johnson's car while you guys were gone."

"Yeah, we heard it too. Thought it might be one of you dropping your watch or something. Actually, it sounded like a tail light lens being popped. Couldn't be sure though."

"Whatever it was, wasn't any to soon. There's our man getting into his car. 8W5 to concerned units, he's in the car and will be heading north." As he pulled from the curb with his lights on, it appeared his left rear tail light lens had been broken somehow and was showing a bright white light. "8W5 to concerned units, our subjects left tail light seems to be broken and giving off a bright white light."

"Yeah, tell me that justice and luck aren't on our side" came over the air from one of the units.

The first part of the tail was easy. We knew where he was going and he did it. He turned north on Western Ave. and went directly to the Parole Office. When he was out of the car the rest of us took up positions to await his return.

We didn't have to wait too long. Forty minutes later he was getting back into the car. He made a quick "U" turn and went north to Sunset and turned west. If I didn't know better I'd think he was trying to shake a tail with the "U" turn. When he got to Laurel Canyon he turned north and headed into the hills.

Now it started to get tough. With all the side streets, narrow streets, and dead end streets, it was hard as hell to maintain a surveillance. When he turned west off Laurel we had to stay way back. For the next thirty minutes we played cat and mouse, spotting him, then losing him for a short time. The only thing we were sure of was that he had not been out of our sight long enough to have pulled a job. Now he was heading back to Laurel Canyon and south to Sunset where he turned west again.

We crossed Doheny and were about to enter Beverly Hills. My adrenaline gave me a quick jolt.

"Jesus Jack, you don't think we might be lucky enough to get him pulling a job in town do you?" I asked with just a little wishful anticipation in my voice.

Jack picked up the Beverly Hills mike and notified our desk and Beverly Hills units we had just entered town on a 4 car surveillance, west on Sunset, and asked the black and whites to drop out of sight for a while. The desk responded and acknowledged. The north end units also responded.

We proceeded west on Sunset, past the Beverly Hills Hotel, to Roxbury where he turned north. He slowed down now and seemed to be looking around from what the closest car could tell. He turned East on Lexington and pulled to the curb and parked, just east of Beverly Drive. The other units scurried for hiding places as Jack and I parked under the trees a quarter block west of Beverly.

He got out of the car and leisurely walked back to Beverly and turned south. I was out of the car and quickly walking toward Beverly, sticking close to the shrubbery. As I neared the corner I saw him walking slowly south toward Sunset.

The streets were well lighted in the area so it was pretty easy to see someone walking on the sidewalk. My problem was, if I could see him, he could see me. I decided to stay close to the house line and in the shrubbery as much as possible. We kept this up 'til he was almost to Sunset and he decided to cross to my side of the street and head north.

Oh great, where do I go now? If he keeps coming before I can find another place, he'll step on my foot, or something else meaningful. I found a large bush and laid down beside the bush and the hedge. He continued his slow pace north, giving every house some very close scrutiny. He passed within five feet of my prostrate body. The next house past my position he stopped, looked at the house, and took two or three steps toward the front door.

Oh golly, gee whiz, shucks, it just couldn't be this easy could it? If he got in I'd just have to wait here for him to come out. If he went out some other way, the guys would just have to get him at the car. But how are they supposed to know that he's gone in? I don't have a radio, and they aren't behind me anywhere so they can see what's going on. Hell, I'll worry about that when it happens. More 'what ifs'.

While my brain had been spinning all those possibilities around, he'd changed his mind for some reason and went back to the sidewalk and continued north, then crossed the street to his car. Back in the car and on the go again he headed farther west on Sunset into West L.A. He cruised the streets in Holmby Hills for a while, stopping several times to park at the curb and just look. It was getting late and the traffic was starting to thin out. Soon it would be very hard for us to blend in with other traffic.

The frustration was starting to tell on the other 'tailers' too. The 'tailee' was just not playing according to the script we all had sketched out in our minds.

He headed back to Sunset and turned east. He seemed to be driving with a purpose now. Jack radioed our office that we were headed out of town. The Watch commander radioed back that they have just gotten a silent 459 alarm from a house on Whittier Drive and could that be our man. We answered no and kept going.

He stayed on Sunset to Western then south. Appearing to be

heading for home, one of our units picked up speed and took some side streets to beat him there. We wanted someone in position to see just what he did when he got home. We had guessed wrong. He parked in a parking lot next to a small bar about three blocks from his apartment and went in.

We gathered a couple of blocks away to discuss the events and leave one car watching the bar. In about 10 minutes, he came out of the bar, got into his car and went home. That last move caught us flatfooted. We were still scrambling to get to our cars and get on the road when he pulled into the curb in front of his place. He was more than likely not going to go back out to caper tonight but we would hang around for an hour to see. About eleven- thirty we all decided to head for the home.

Near misses don't count. Everybody was expressing varying degrees of disappointment as we separated. It had been a long day. And a shorter night and morning. I no sooner got in the door and the telephone rang. Diana answered it and handed it to me. Fred Colford again.

"God Fred, I'm getting to where I dread to hear from you. What now?"

"Well we just took another burglary report in the north end from a Herb Soloman, on Shadow Hill Way. Across the street from Mel Torme and a few doors from Tony Martin. I just thought you should know now because it may tie into the Baker case. Same kind of entry, same time element and same kind of stuff taken, in a cluster of celebrities," he quickly narrated.

"Do we know where they were when it happened?"

"Not really, except Tom said they mentioned they had been out to dinner somewhere. Sorry I tore up your evening but I thought you might want to know with that surveillance you had going tonight. Any chance your guy might have pulled this one ?"

"No dammit. For once our guy has a very good alibi, four

police cars tailing him. It couldn't be that easy. Did you set a time for me to do the follow-up?"

"Yeah, nine AM. Figured you might want to oversleep a little in the morning. Ha! See you later. Pleasant dreams."

"You've got a sadistic sense of humor". As I hung up.

"Another one" Diana asked as she handed me a tall vodka and tonic.

"Yeah, and only about three blocks from here. Same kind of entry as the Baker case and the people were having dinner somewhere. It'll be interesting to find out where, tomorrow".

My third draw on the drink emptied the glass. I was sitting undressed on the bed when she handed me another, short this time. It wasn't finished before I was asleep.

Pulling into the Soloman's driveway the next morning, I couldn't help noticing that the house sat high up from the street at the end of a fairly steep driveway. Bob Estill was with me and I remarked, "No one could case this place from the street. You can't see the garage, the end of the driveway, any windows or the doorway. Someone had to have prior information on this one."

"Yeah, it sure looks that way." Bob said. He'd been in the bureau a couple of months from patrol division. He was somewhat slight of build, a good dresser, and a bass voice that made you look for the rest of the quartet. His wife was a police officer with LAPD Intelligence.

As we pulled up to the garage Mr. Soloman was coming out the door to meet us. He was obviously very anxious to talk to us. We introduced ourselves and he lead us around to the patio door and pointed out what appeared to be screwdriver pry marks. We then went into the house through the patio door and into the master bedroom.

He continued his narration of his theory about the perpetrators actions and why they did things the way they did. When we finally got into the den he wound down a bit and stopped talking long enough to take a deep breath. His scenario seemed to fit the circumstances pretty well.

Now it was our turn.

"I understand you were out to dinner last night when this happened. Where did you go for dinner?"

"Why, we went to the Luau. We go there quite often. Why?"

"Just routine questions. We have to cover all bases. When did you make reservations?"

"About six-thirty. I didn't think we'd get in because we called so late but the Assistant Maitre D' is the son of a good friend of mine and he put us on the cancellation list. We had to wait for a few minutes when we got there but when he got the first cancellation, we got the table."

"Does he know where you live?"

"Sure, I told you his Dad is a good friend of ours. He's been to our home often. Surely you can't suspect him?"

"We're not suspecting anyone yet. Just asking questions. Sometimes these questions are uncomfortable but they need to be asked and answered so we have a starting point." Estill chimed in.

"What seems to be upsetting you Mr. Soloman? I mean besides the burglary. You seem to be talking to us but thinking about something else. Is there something else we should know about?"

"Yeah, but it's not what you would think. I'm just totally pissed off at my wife."

Bob and I looked at each other in a joint, silent, sigh of relief. At least we were not going to be treated to a tirade about lack of protection or something like that.

"A couple of weeks ago" he went on, "I told her to get $12,000 out of the bank for a trip to Europe we were planning. After she got it, we changed our plans. I put the money in our safe for her to take back to the bank when she went downtown again. She told me she had forgotten to take it back on several occasions until I finally got quite upset. The other day she told me she had taken it back. Last night, after we got home and found out about the burglary, she admitted she hadn't taken it back. I went to the safe right away, it hadn't been locked, and of course the money was gone." He drew a huge breath and as he let it out his shoulders seem to sag several inches.

Just being able to tell somebody how he felt seemed to have lessened his load. He took us into the living room and introduced us to his wife. She is very courteous but seemed somehow subdued. She was not a happy housewife.

She handed us a list of stolen items saying "That's all I can think of right now."

"Did you put the $12,000 on there ?" Herb grumbles in a low growl. It's pretty obvious his growl is far worse than his bite and that they'll be back on good terms very shortly. It's just time to display the `ruler of the roost' syndrome for a while.

"How about the servants, did they know you were going out?"

"No, yesterday was their day off. They weren't around when we decided to go out."

"How about deliveries, were you expecting anything yesterday, especially in the evening? Did you order anything from one of the department stores and possibly tell them not to deliver it after a certain hour? Anything like that?"

"No, nothing."

"It's pretty obvious someone had to know you were gone. They can't case the house from the street, your phone is unlisted, were there any newspapers or periodicals in your mailbox or driveway when you left yesterday?"

"No, the gardener had cleaned everything before he left."

"What time did he leave? Did he have any way of knowing you were going to be gone?"

When we got several more 'no' answers to our other questions we went over the stolen property list before leaving. The loss amounted to about $10,000 in jewelry and furs in addition to the money from the safe. I thought I'd take the heat off one or the other of them by NOT asking why the safe had not been locked. One of my more magnanimous gestures.

"By the way, what is the name of the Maitre D' you called at the Luau?" I tried to make the question sound like an afterthought. I didn't want him doing any personal investigating just in case this guy was our man.

"His name if Bobby Klein, but he couldn't have anything to do with it. His father and I have been friends for years."

"Well it would be just as well if you didn't mention anything to him about this at least until we have time to check out several things."

"Of course, whatever you say. We've notified our insurance company this morning. The cash, naturally, is only partially covered."

"Even if we nail these guys, getting cash back is pretty near impossible. I wouldn't expect too much." I was trying to prepare him for the worst. Cash is usually the first thing that is gone for good.

"I figured as much" he said as we were getting into our car.

On our way out the driveway I was about to bust a gut.

"It looks like our employee suspect list at the Luau has been narrowed down to one rather rapidly. We'd better be very cautious though just in case it's someone that works with this guy." I could feel the blood pumping, the nerves starting to jump, and the mind racing a thousand miles an hour. The adrenaline had started again and now it was time to be even more cautious. No mistakes. No false moves.

Back in the office I called Frank and passed on what we'd found out about Klein and told him I'd call him as soon as we checked it out further. He said he'd found another victim who had been dining at the Luau.

Cork, Hankins and I sat down and discussed just how we were going to get the information needed from the Luau without stirring them up. No consensus was reached. We separated for the time being to give the problem some thought.

John Rich called about 12:30 and said he was at the drug store coffee shop and wanted to talk to me. I could already feel the bite on my wallet. I couldn't blame anyone but myself. I started it, I guess I'd just have to deal with it. I told Cork where I was going and a few minutes later I slid onto a stool next to John. Cork came into the shop shortly and sat at the other end of the counter. Even in the middle of the day, in public, it was still best to have cover.

"John, what are you doing in town? Not practicing your trade I hope. That would NOT be wise."

I wanted to start off this association with some ground rules. If he got the habit of coming to town he may just get the feeling he could get a pass if he decided to do a little business before leaving town. In most cases though, we'd get a call a few seconds after he entered a store. His demeanor and appearance would not render him unnoticeable in Beverly Hills.

"Hey, I got a ride out this way so I thought I'd come out and tell you."

"Tell me what?"

"He's probably going to caper tonight." he said in a very soft, conspiratorial voice. Looking around like he was trying to avoid a swarm of wasps aiming for his head. If you had a movie of his actions you could use it for training rookies about looking suspicious. If he acted like that all the time I didn't see how he ever got away with some of the stuff he pulled. Maybe that was why he'd been in jail so much.

"Just how the hell do you know that? Have you been pumping him? That's all we need is for you to try to play `undercover' and make him suspicious."

"Nah, Nah, we were having a few beers last night and he was talking about how he was running short of cash. He said that tonight would be a good night on the west side because of the UCLA game. He said a lot of the UCLA types live in Brentwood and Westwood and would be at the game."

He'd finished one cup of coffee and ordered another. He looked at me with those empty, questioning eyes, that are obviously asking if it's O.K. for him to order food and would I pick up the tab.

I fed him a small smile and nod and he quickly ordered a sandwich and another coffee. "Do you think there could be anything in this one for me?" he said. Now quietly again, "I'm hurting bad. Murray is playing it close to the vest trying to figure out who set him up so I can't get rid of anything right now. I'm running real short."

"When did you see Johnson last night?"

"He stopped at that bar on Melrose about 11:00 last night for a few minutes. He went home and came back about midnight. We sat there at the bar until they closed. When we left his car wasn't around so he must have walked. It's only three or four blocks from his pad. Why?"

"Just curious. How'd you get home last night?"

"I caught a ride with the bartender and stopped at a joint I thought I could score in but I didn't have enough bread. I'm really hurting today. Do you think you could help me out?"

"I already got that idea when you called from in town. If this one goes down all right I'll try and get you something from the insurance company. It'll probably be a couple of days though, can you hold out that long?" I was ready to give him something to hold him over but I didn't want him getting the idea that he could stop by anytime and tap the Downey till.

With our Department, as with most, what money you operated informants with came out of your pocket. Sometimes you could get them some recovery money from an insurance adjuster or agent if your arrest recovered property for the agents insurance company. And the suspect was being prosecuted.

You had to be damned careful with that too. It was not unheard of for an informant to set up some burglar they knew to pull a job. They would then have a cooperating cop arrest the burglar and recover the loot, then split the recovery fee. Or have the informant act as the receiver, turn the loot over to the right cop and insurance agent, and again split the fee with the burglar and the cop. These "buy backs" were pretty notorious for a while and caused a lot of heartburn for some "well thought of" detectives.

It was not too unusual for the insurance adjusters to get a piece of the action. As a result, you practiced being extra careful of any situation that could be misinterpreted as a "buy back".

When the story broke, the insurance companies of course, were furious. Some of the adjusters and agents were screaming foul. Some weren't saying much of anything. Other than, 'make this thing go away'. And some police departments and detectives were asking and answering a lot of hard questions.

In most cases when the burglar was arrested and prosecuted there wasn't much question of a "buy back". Except that a couple of times it was later learned that an informant had actually set up the burglary and got someone to pull it. Then he `sold' the information to a detective who made the arrest and recovery. The officer and the burglar were both `patsies' in that case. Even though the officer was clean, it just smelled bad.

Dealing with informants, paid or otherwise, and insurance agents and adjusters, called for extreme "CYA" caution. Everything out in the open, with a paper trail. If any party wasn't willing, forget it.

At one time, accepting rewards from insurances companies for recovery of stolen merchandise was a common and accepted, if not published, policy. Some officers did pretty well, financially, with this policy. Then, of course, as in most well intentioned things, someone had to figure out a way to milk the cow a little harder, and oftener.

Even our ramrod straight Chief got caught up in the turmoil. It seemed he had accepted some rewards on certain cases in the past. When this came to light some individuals attempted to use this information in an effort to dethrone the Chief.

They went so far as to have him investigated for failing to report the rewards as income on his tax returns. Their efforts were for naught when it was revealed that he had reported the income on his tax returns. Nobody could call that man stupid. Besides helping his squeaky clean reputation, it left large amounts of egg on his accusers face.

The longer you worked for that man, and watched him, the more complex you found he was. He had some strange and unorthodox ways of handling people but he usually got the results he wanted. His methods created many hard feelings but it never seemed to bother him. I once heard his method of management described as "always keep everybody off balance, that way they can't gang up on you".

"O.K. John, is that all? Do you know what time he's going out?. You didn't by any chance make arrangements to go with him did you?"

"Hell no. Besides, you told me not to get too close to him. Burglary's not my racket. Man, you could get killed doing that".

"What time's he going out?"

"The usual I guess, evening. I don't know exactly what time. Whenever he talks about working it was always night."

"O.K. John. Here's $25.00, to hold you over. That's all I got on me right now. Keep in touch."

"Hey, why don't you give me your home phone number so I can get ahold of you over the weekend or at night if something hot comes up."

"That's all right. You can call the department and they will get a message to me if it's important."

"What's the matter, don't you trust me yet?" He put on a very thinly disguised `hurt' attitude.

"Sure I do. I just don't want to be answering the phone in the middle of the night because you run out of dope money and decide to burn one of your friends to get yourself well. I'm not in business to keep you in drug money."

"Hell, man. I wouldn't do that. It's just that things, well, come up quick some times", in a defeated tone of voice.

"Well, let's try it this way for a while and see how it works out. Give me a call Monday and if this works out I should know if I can get you anything from the insurance company. O.K.?"

As I got up to leave I grabbed his check and left a tip. He joined me at the cash register and walked outside with me. Cork walked out and joined us a few seconds later.

Seeing Cork he said, "you didn't trust me after all did you?"

"Sure I do John, I just don't like having my back exposed. Who knows, somebody might be after you and get me instead."

"Hey, don't talk like that. These people don't fool around.

Especially Murray. He knows lots of people. There's no chance they're going to find out I'm talking to you is there?"

"Not from me. Just don't fool around and get loaded and start talking to much or your friends will figure it out for themselves." Cork and I crossed the street and John headed for Santa Monica Blvd. and the bus. He was still ducking his head and looking around waiting for someone to tap him on the shoulder. It beats me how he ever got away with being a thief.

As we started across the street, Cork asked, "What'd he have?"

"He thinks Johnson will caper tonight. He had a few beers with him last night after our tail ended. Johnson mentioned tonight would be a good night because of the UCLA game".

"He could be right. What are you going to do?"

"I'll get ahold of Frank and see if we can get the crew together for tonight and set up on him. It's useless if we don't get at least three cars. We'll see," as we were entering the City Hall.

A few minutes later I was talking to Frank and telling him of my meeting with John.

"What are you two, joined at the hip?" he chided. "He gets much friendlier he'll be on your income tax as a dependent. Do you think he's being straight?"

"Who the hell knows Frank. You pays your money and you take your chances. I know he thinks he can score big from an insurance company if the information is good. I don't think he wants to screw that up."

"O.K. Bob, I'll get back to you as soon as I can. Anything else on your Maitre D' yet?"

"Not yet, I'm still working on getting the info we need without heating him up. He's not listed in the phone book so I'm having the phone company see if they can find a listing.

"O.K. see you later."

After checking the work schedule for the four to twelve shift that night I went to Hankins office where Cork was already talking with him.

"What'd you guys decide?" Hankins asked.

"Frank's working on getting the team together now. He'll call me as soon as he finds out. We'll need at least three cars but we'd rather have four obviously. If we do have a go for tonight I'd like to take one of the policewomen with me. It's a lot easier to stay cool if there's a woman in the car, besides, she can handle the radio while I drive."

Hankins looked like I've just hit him in the stomach. His eyes are saying, WHAT, take a policewoman, the Chief won't like that. It may be dangerous. What if she gets hurt? All these questions and many more were flashing across his mind and face. He was trying hard to figure out a logical reason to say no, but logical is the operative word. John Hankins was not strong on hard decisions, fast, or any other way.

The few Policewomen we had, had been used more as clerk-typists and matrons than police officers although they had been getting police officer pay. Finally he said "Who would you take?"

"Well, Esther Kielty and Betty Miller are both on tonight. Esther has been on longer so I'd like her to go. It's hard to drive and operate the radio at the same time. Especially that walkie talkie I've borrowed. It sets on the floor of the passenger side and I have to keep reaching across the seat to get the mike when I need it. It's just so damned inconvenient".

My voice had picked up my impatience and has gotten more strident. I was trying in my mind to find any justification for refusal. I needn't have bothered. Hankins said he would talk it over with the Chief and let me know. A few minutes later he was heading for the Chief's office.

By two o'clock Frank had called and told me that with my car and his we had four for the tail. Hankins told me I could take Kielty if she was willing to go, but I had to ask her if she volunteered. I began to wonder when was the last time I was given the option of volunteering for an assignment.

Knowing Kielty, she'd jump at the chance. Anything to get out of the office. She'd be insulted when she found out she was given the option of the assignment. She was not the kind to duck any assignment. Anyway, I'd ask her when she got in. Gotta play by the rules.

By four o'clock, Esther had 'volunteered' and been filled in on the procedure. She'd be ready for me to pick her up at five thirty to get to our meeting place by six.

I called Diana and told her I'd be home and gone before she got there and to keep her monitor on that night.

CHAPTER 28

At six o'clock all four cars were gathered at the back of the parking lot of the coffee shop at Vine and Melrose. I introduced Esther around and then filled them in on what John had said. I took some good natured razzing about taking John to raise and other uncomplimentary things. All in fun. They knew well the pitfalls of dealing with informants. After the coffee and the obligatory visits to the bathroom we were on our way again.

We were panicked when we arrived at the house. His car was not around anywhere. Now what? As we were discussing our next move on the radio, he obligingly pulled up, parked, and went into his apartment. Shortly after seven he came out of the house and got into the car. The blood pressure rose about 15 points when I realized, and radioed the others, that he was wearing dark trousers and shirt, and a dark stocking cap.

Our five car parade wandered through several streets but always westerly, then northwesterly. We breezed through Beverly Hills on Wilshire then turned north on Beverly Glen. Two blocks north of Wilshire he turned west again and definitely slowed down. It was close onto eight o'clock and he had begun his search. The way he was studying the houses he hardly noticed the cars that were passing. The possibility of someone tailing him was apparently very remote the way he was acting. And with that tail light, we could stay back further.

Having Esther was a godsend with all the "U" turns that had to be made and the brief driveway parking that took place. She was doing a great job handling the radio and at the same time giving the appearance of a romantic couple just out for a drive.

Not that Johnson would have noticed. He had his mind made up. And a target in sight.

He'd parked close to the corner, gotten out and was walking back down the street. We all parked in any available space or driveway, and Frank and I got out to try to take up a foot surveillance. In less than half a block Johnson stopped for a second, took a quick look around and then walked up a driveway toward the rear of a house. The house was dark. Frank walked past the front and joined me a half block up the street.

"The number is 729. The driveway rises sharply from the street toward a fenced yard in back and a closed garage. We'll just have to wait 'til he comes out. I guess it'll depend on how long he's in there whether we take him or not."

"O.K. I'll go walk past in the other direction and go back to my car and wait. Jones and Unland have a good eyeball on the car and my car is only a half block away. We can't miss him when he comes back to the car."

With that I began my walk back in the opposite direction Frank had taken. It would've been a nice time to have a dog on a leash for a few minutes. As I got nearly in front of the house I saw a small light briefly appear on the second floor. Unless my eyes had forsaken me, he was in, and rummaging around.

I got back to the car quickly and radioed the other units what I'd seen. We agreed he'd been out of sight long enough to be burglarizing the house. When he returned to the car and started to drive off, we'd make the arrest.

Now came the wait. . . . And the time to play 'What If' again. The time had slowed down to a crawl. It was what seemed like an hour later that one of the units announced he was headed back to the car.

If he came our way, we'd pull out in front of him so he had to stop. Another unit would close in behind and one unit would pull alongside. Esther will take the passenger side and I'd take the driver's side. We were still working out logistics when his car pulled from the curb.

Now everything was moving like greased lightning. As he got close to our position I pulled from the curb into his path. I could see one of our cars directly behind him and another pulling out as if to pass. When I was squarely in front of him I stopped. With no wasted motion or time, Esther was out of the car with her badge in one hand and her gun in the other announcing, "Police Officer, turn off your engine". As I brought my gun to bear, Frank was opening the drivers door with his gun pointed at Johnson's head. Jones reached in, took Johnson by the collar and was assisting him from the car. With three guns pointed at his head, he was placed across the hood of his car and Frank began shaking him down. He removed a rolled up handkerchief from Johnson's right front pants pocket and a balled up kleenex from his left front pocket. No weapons were found, but then we didn't expect to find any.

Then, the pace slowed a little. The initial spurt of adrenaline had subsided and the 'self protection' mode had been satisfied. It was time to take a look at the 'evidence'. Frank started to unwrap both the handkerchief and kleenex. Each was found to contain several articles of jewelry. With that Frank announced, "Robert Johnson, you're under arrest for burglary, grand theft, and receiving stolen property. I might as well add parole violation too", as he applied the handcuffs.

We were all standing around with large smiles on our faces. We could hear the noise and shouts from the game at UCLA and had drawn little attention from the neighborhood.

Funny. During the whole time we were sitting there just waiting, I hadn't heard any noise from the stadium. Was there some? Was everything else shut out? I'd have to remember to ask the others if they heard anything.

Johnson said nothing during the entire incident, but he had a look of resignation on his face. He was placed in the back of Franks car and we decided to drive his car to the West L.A. station rather than wait for a tow truck. It needed to be thoroughly searched anyway, preferably in the daylight. On the way to West L.A. Esther and I were busily recapping the entire operation. It's a light, giddy, happy time. Smooth, effective, and with no one hurt.

At the station, while he was being booked, we were all in the coffee room reliving the evening. The feeling that comes with such a successful operation is almost indescribable.

A plethora of emotions run rampant. Outwardly you tried not to overreact. Just routine police work. Expected. Inside you were dancing. 'They' said you couldn't pull it off. Wastes too much time. Uses too much manpower. We all knew what we were thinking without the necessity for words. It just felt good.

The faultfinders would be quieter now. The negative comments would lessen. Add to that the fact that when they're caught like that there isn't much time wasted in court. All in all, it was a good night.

A patrol unit had been dispatched to the house to notify the resident that their property had been recovered. He returned with the information for the report as well as the information that our burglar was a true second story man. It seemed that he went into the pool area of the yard and found a ladder which he used to climb onto the porch roof. He entered an open second floor window after he removed the screen. The old timers used to refer to 'second story men' but you don't often run into them anymore. Whatever's handy I guess.

Johnson was locked away 'til morning and it was time to go home. We all went to the parking lot and headed for our cars, reluctantly. You don't want it to end. You want to milk that feeling. It doesn't come often enough. But you know you have to go home eventually. So you do.

Back at the office we filed our in-absentia arrest report and filled in the Watch Commander on the outcome of our surveillance. It was starting to wear off now. Time to go on home.

Diana was waiting up and while she fixed me a drink I get to relive the whole thing over again.

"I heard you moving along Wilshire, then going around in West L.A. but all of a sudden the chatter stopped. About a half hour later it all started again and I could tell from your voices you had gotten him", she said. "Who was the female in your car?"

"Esther Kielty, she did a good job. She was out of the car and covering him before I could get out of the car. I know that's one of the first things I'll be asked, "How'd she do?" I don't know what they'll be expecting to hear. As far as I am concerned, she's welcome to come along anytime."

I had finished my second drink and the euphoria had subsided to an internal, slow, cat-like purr. I must have fallen to sleep with a slight grin on my face.

By nine AM I was back in Frank's office waiting for Paul Stevens, Johnson's P.O. to arrive. I had stopped by the office to pick up a car, and filled Hankins and Cork in on the arrest.

Frank, Johnson, Andy and I were sitting in the W.L.A. Lieutenants office. Mostly small talk. Time killers.

Frank told me earlier that the car had been searched and nothing unusual was found. The search of his apartment will wait 'til he's had a chance to talk with his P.O. Being on parole, no permission from him is necessary to search his apartment but we'd like to get it just to cover all the bases.

Stevens arrived and after the 'howdys' were made all round we settled into the chairs and began our talk with Johnson. Stevens got a quick rundown on the previous night and then turned to Johnson. "Well, you've stepped in it this time Bob. What have you got to say?"

"What can I say, they caught me dirty, I know I'm going back, what can I do to help myself? I'm not going to give anybody up. I'll still have to live in the population when I go back in so I don't need a snitch jacket This banter and sparring went on for another half hour before the we started getting down to the meat of the situation. How many jobs had he pulled and where, and can we get back any of the merchandise?. Pretty straightforward and simple. What will he give us, what inducements can we offer him. He knew he was going back inside, it remained to be seen for how long.

How many new cases would be filed against him? He also knew we only have one good case for now and may not find anymore unless he told us about them. He'd already said he wasn't going to give anyone else up so that meant we probably wouldn't find out where the property went. Unless he figured the receiver had burned him. We couldn't use that bluff, it was to easy to call us on it.

And still the jockeying for position went on. He was no dummy, so empty threats wouldn't get us anywhere. Might even turn him off if he thought we were trying to make a fool of him. Crook or not, he's got his pride too. Maybe misplaced or undeserved, but it's still there.

After a couple of hours of idle chatter, empty bargaining, what ifs and so forths, he agreed, with the urging of his P.O. to clear cases for us but refused to name any other names. Provided of course we file no more than three counts against him. Considering we only had one solid case against him and the other two would be based only on his confession, it was not a bad deal. We all accepted. Frank and I agreed that because he was caught in W.L.A. he'd file two cases and I'd file one. We were just getting down to specific cases when I got a call from Don Barnes, our Watch Commander.

"Yeah Don, what's up? This is my day off again as if that has ever meant anything."

"I know, but this sounded urgent. That guy Soloman that had the burglary the other night just called. He wants to get in touch with you bad. He says it's very important and wants you to call him right away. Have you got his number?"

"I've got it. I'll give him a call right now. How long ago did he call?"

"Just a few minutes ago. I told him we'd get in touch with you right away. Good luck."

Oh Yeah, good luck. I just hoped he hadn't been doing any detective work on his own. I went into the bull pen and placed my call.

"Mr. Soloman, Sgt. Downey, you wanted to talk to me?"

"I sure do, can you come to the house right away? There's something here you need to know right away."

Boy, that guy was really agitated. It can't hurt for me to leave here. Frank would look out for my interests with Johnson. Over the weeks and months that we'd worked together Frank and I had learned that we could depend on each other. Not like family, but stronger. We had gone through a dozen or more situations together where unquestioning, implicit, trust was essential. Nothing needed to be said. It is just a natural act.

Cork and I had developed the same rapport in the past couple of years. It was instinctive. You can work with some men for years and never develop that special trust and feeling.

"O.K. Mr. Soloman, I'm leaving West.L.A. now and will be at your place within twenty minutes, is that O.K.?" Hell, it would've had to be O.K. I couldn't get there any faster anyhow.

"Yeah, I'll be waiting."

I called Frank out of the office and told him what'd happened. I said my good-byes to the others and headed for Soloman's. In twenty three minutes I was there. He was coming out the door as I pulled into the driveway. He looked exited and very conspiratorial. He took me by the arm and lead me away from the house to a low wall next to the driveway where we sat down. I hadn't realized what a great view he had from here. Overlooked a large part of Coldwater Canyon.

"That dirty bastard. I can't believe he'd do something like that. I've known his father for fifteen years or more." He was very unhappy and agitated. His voice was growling.

I was getting the picture. Oh God, I hope he hadn't braced the kid. "What are you talking about. You didn't talk to Klein did you?"

"Of course not. you told me not to. But this is even better. You probably won't need to talk to him now."

"Why not. What happened? Slow down and start at the beginning. And don't skip anything."

"Well, when we talked to you yesterday I hadn't even thought about it. I didn't remember it until I opened my desk drawer today."

"What is `it?' Mr. Soloman."

"Let me explain first. I've had some business problems lately. Not problems really, just some strange things happening, weird phone calls and such. As a precaution I had a recorder hooked up to my phone just in case I needed to record a call. It's not an answering machine, it needs to be turned on and off. It records anything coming in or going out if it's on.

Anyway, the other night when we went out to dinner, I had turned it on before we left. I didn't give it another thought until I opened the drawer today. It's my private business phone so I hadn't used it since then." He paused to take several breaths.

"I noticed there had been some tape used so I played it back. I couldn't believe my ears. That little bastard. He set me up. It's right there on the tape."

"Who's right there on the tape? Where's the tape? Maybe if we listen to it I'll know who you're talking about."

"Yeah, that's right, lets play the tape. Let's go into my office". As he said that, he headed for the house under a full head of steam with me following. I nodded hello to his wife as we passed her in the hall and she fell in behind us.

Seated behind his desk he proceeded to unlock the lower left drawer and pull it out. Inside was a small, voice activated tape recorder. He ran the tape back a few seconds then pressed "play".

The first thing you heard was the clicking of the dialing. A short time later, the ringing at the other end. Two rings and there's an answer. "Luau, this is Bobby, can I help you?"

"Yeh, Bobby, we're in, let us know if they leave. You know the signal."

"O.K. they just got here so they should be here a while. I'll call if they leave."

"Good" click, and then a dial tone for a couple of seconds, and then the machine turned off.

I sat there in stunned silence for a few seconds. My God, that just took all the leg work out of detecting that crime. Just what were the odds on something like that happening?

"Well, what do you think?" Soloman asked.

"I think they just put themselves in prison. We've got to save that tape just in case they won't talk after we nail them. Hearing their own voices on that tape would take the wind out of their sails."

"Oh, you can't use the tape. I just wanted you to hear it. I don't want anyone to know I have a tape machine. Besides, there are things on that tape I don't want anyone else to hear." He sounded quite adamant and his jaw was tightly clenched. It seemed he had made up his mind. No sense pushing him too hard.

"Well Mr. Soloman, just guarantee me you won't destroy the tape until we have this case resolved. Keep it in your safe deposit box. When we get Klein in custody I may want you to sit in the room while I talk to him if he decides not to cooperate right away. It depends on his attitude. How about it?" It's pretty obvious he didn't want anyone to know he had been recording his calls. He was even wondering about the advisability of telling me.

"I think I know what's on your mind Mr. Soloman. The best I can tell you is you trusted me enough to let me hear the tape, you'll have to trust me enough to keep your confidence. Do we have a deal?"

I didn't know what else to tell him. I couldn't force him to give me the tape, or even play it for someone else. He could deny there ever was a tape if he wanted to. We'd just have to see how it went. Beside that, we probably couldn't use the tape in court anyhow.

"We have a deal. I must have your assurance that it will remain confidential."

"Of course. If I can get Bobby to confess there should be no need for us to even think about it again. Now I have to get busy. Will you be around home the rest of the day?"

"Certainly, if there is anything you need me to do just call me here. Good luck."

"I've just had my share of luck, thank you." On my way back down Shadow Hill to Coldwater to Rexford and the station, I hoped I hadn't missed any stops or red lights because I don't remember any of them. The whole ride I was thinking about what came next. Which step comes first, then what. What if he does this, then what will I do. What's the best way to get his address and phone number? What if he wasn't home now. What if I waited for him to come to work tonight. No I couldn't wait that long. It was early afternoon, I'd have to work out something to get him before this evening. The longer it goes, the less chance there was of getting the property back. What if . . . .

Once back at the office I phoned Cork, filled him in without telling him about the recorder and asked him to come in. While I'm waiting I filled in Mourning and Estill to get their thoughts on how to get Kleins address without anyone at the restaurant tipping him off. Jack said he was very friendly with one of the day waiters and thought he could get it from him without heating the situation up. When Cork got in we decided to have Jack give it a try.

While Jack was gone we went over the whole Soloman case again, as well as the Baker case which we know now must be connected. I took Cork aside and filled him in on the recorder aspects and the fact that I'd given my word to Soloman. Cork agreed that we wouldn't break Soloman's confidence.

When Jack returned he had Kleins address on South Rexford Drive as well as his phone number and the make and color of his car. He was sure his source was reliable. We took off in two cars for Kleins apartment. As we approached his apartment we saw Klein's Black Buick parked in the driveway.

Cork and I took the front door as Jack and Estill covered the side entrance. Klein answered our knock and we advised him he was under arrest for burglary as we took hold of his arms and stepped back into his apartment. He was sputtering and asking questions at a mile a minute while Mourning and Estill followed us in.

Klein was about 25 years old, slim, well dressed and groomed. The apartment was in a newer building and attractively furnished. Nothing cheap or tawdry about it. Not in an inexpensive neighborhood either. He was not living here on what he made at the restaurant.

While we were getting some preliminary information the others were shaking down the apartment. Looking for anything that would or could be evidence. We told Klein why we were there and asked him to cooperate now without causing too much heartburn. He said of course he didn't know what we were talking about.

Before leaving the apartment we gathered up a couple of notebooks, address books, and telephone bills. Funny what some people put in phone books and address books. We gave the car a quick toss on the way and picked up one more phone book.

In the office on a quiet Saturday afternoon, we started to question Klein. For a guy without a record he started out being a hardcase. He was only 23 but he was trying to act like a 40 year old ex-con. Watched too many Jimmy Cagney movies. After a while his attitude softened but he said nothing yet.

I called Mr. Soloman and asked him to come to the office. When he got there Cork and I met him in the lobby and filled him in on our approach so far. He agreed to follow our lead in the interrogation. With that we went back into the office.

Klein saw Soloman and seemed to stiffen up a little. For the next hour we, and Soloman, give him a full dose about the betrayal of a friend, the breaking of a trust. The misplaced trust of his employers. The disappointment of his parents. The heartbreak caused the victims. The loss of keepsakes and heirlooms. The looks from his friends and associates when they find out.

Soloman had asked him in several different ways why he would do such a thing to him? What was he supposed to say to his father when he saw him?

Klein was no tower of strength. Getting through to him without Soloman would just have taken a little longer. Mr. Soloman's presence and input added just the right touch of pressure to speed things up.

We then laid out what we knew of the operation for him, step by step. How he got the reservations, tipped off his friends, got a call from them when they were in, and how he would call them back if the victim left the restaurant early. At that point we stopped for a few minutes and let him stew. We walked out into the hall, still in Kleins sight, and discussed quietly how we thought it was going.

Almost immediately Klein called us back into the office.

"I'm sorry Herb," he said, "I just didn't think about all those things. I'll try to help get your stuff back but I really don't know where it is. I never see any of the stuff".

With that the dam was broken. He was admitting that our 'theory' was correct. Hell, we knew that. As usual, he was trying to put the best light on his part in the operation. He allegedly didn't know exactly who his partners were or where they lived. Sure. With a couple other tales it was time to pull his chain.

"Bobby, there is just no way you're going to walk away from this without taking your share of the blame. Right now is where we find out just how sincere you are in helping clean up this mess that you helped to create. For one thing, if you don't really know who or where these guys are, how do you know where to call them to set up the job or get your cut." I stopped to take a breath and Cork took over.

"When we talk to the District Attorney is when we lay out for him just who and how much anyone has cooperated during this investigation. Your name can be on the plus side or the minus side, and right now is the time for you to decide. No more bull shit, which way is it going to be? . . . Now." Cork was looking him right in the eye about a foot away . . . Cork stared, Klein blinked.

"All right, give me my address book. I have their address and phone number in there. They live in a house in Sherman Oaks."

"What are their names and about how old are they?" I asked him as I went through the books for the right one. He reached for one out of the pile and opened it. He thumbed through a few pages and stopped. Pointing to an address and phone number he said "this is where they live. That's their phone number."

"What are their names?" My voice sounded a little more irritated, even to me.

"One is John Pizzi, the other is Bill DeSpain. They're both about thirty. One of them is from Pennsylvania. Claims to be connected with the Mafia back there. He says that's where he gets rid of the stuff. He acts pretty mean."

"Do they carry any guns?"

"I know they have some but I don't know if they carry any. I've never seen them carry any."

"How do you know they have them then?"

"I've seen them at the house."

"What kind of guns? Hand guns or long guns, rifles or shotguns? Where do they keep them in the house?"

"A couple of handguns, revolvers I think. I only saw them in one bedroom."

"Which bedroom. Here, draw a diagram of the house and who sleeps where, as best you can remember. Cork, I'm going to give Frank a call. He'll want to be in on this. He has at least a couple of cases he can clear."

"O.K. See if Estill and Mourning want to go along. It'll take at least four of us. I'll get the rest of the layout. It'll be dark before we get there."

"Frank, what are you doing at home? I called the office and they told me you had chickened out." He grumbled something about having to sleep sometime. "We have been talking to Mr. Robert Klein and he has seen the error of his miscreant ways and has decided to tell us where his associates are holed up. Cork, Mourning, Estill and I are about to venture out to Sherman Oaks and pay them a visit and thought you would be interested in joining us. Would you?"

"Wait for me, I'm leaving right now." I could hear Ruthy in the background saying something about forgetting where his home was as he hung up his phone. Thirty minutes later he was at our office being brought up to date.

There goes the adrenaline again. Starting to pump. Picking up slowly and you know it will build until you kick the door and see what's on the other side.

CHAPTER 29

We were on our way over the hill to Sherman Oaks. It was just dark enough to cover our approach to the house on foot. Depending, of course, on exactly where it was located, and the surrounding houses. Estill and Mourning in one car, and Cork, Frank, and I in the other. We had gotten the exact address from the phone company, and even with a map we had a hell-of-a-time finding Glen Ridge Dr.

It turned out to be one of those tiny lanes just south of Ventura Blvd., tucked just under the edge of the foothills. When they draw the maps of such areas the streets are so short and small I think they just squiggle the lines into the general area.

The street was short and narrow with no chance of parking our cars very close to the house. The house itself was a typical one story, L-shaped, ranch style on the north side of the street. The front door was on the uphill, or street side of the house and all the main living area overlooking the valley.

To the right of the sidewalk leading to the front door was a two car garage, and the windows of what probably was a bedroom. To the left of the sidewalk was a stone walkway going around the left end of the house and to the north side.

We had scoped out the house and met near the cars to make the final decision on how to enter. Frank, Mourning and I would take the front door, and Cork and Estill would circle the house and come in from the north side. We reminded each other that they were known to have handguns in the house. We didn't need to be told to be careful. I had gotten my shotgun out of the trunk of my car and we started. The north side team was not to make entry until they heard our team enter.

As we approached the doorway we saw Cork and Estill disappear from view around the side of the house.

When we neared the door we heard the conversation of at least three males coming from the bedroom next to the walkway. We listened long enough to determine that they were talking about cleaning and packaging what sounded like a fairly large supply of marijuana. So then we knew we had at least three people just to the right of the doorway, the rest of the house was a mystery.

We took up positions at each side of the door as Mourning prepared to kick the door. As he raised his foot, Frank reached over and turned the knob. The door eased open a few inches, unlocked. NOTE, To Memory. Always try the knob first.

We charged into the hallway looking in all directions at the same time and shouting "Police" "Don't Move" It was so loud I almost scared myself. Jack took off to his left toward what appeared to be a living room and kitchen.

Frank and I turned right and headed for the first doorway on our right, which had to be where the voices were coming from.

As we stepped into the doorway we saw two men sitting on the floor, next to a bed, with a pile of marijuana in front of them. A third subject was rising from the floor and seemed to be reaching for a handgun laying on the bed. He hadn't quite reached it when I pushed the safety off of my shotgun and Frank cocked his revolver. The accompanying sounds of those two simultaneous actions caused a deafening silence and froze the man in mid reach. At about the same time loud voices were coming from what seemed to be the kitchen area.

As Frank was handcuffing our suspects Cork came to the doorway and said,

"We've got another one in the kitchen. Seems to be all of them. My, my, what do we have on the floor. It seems we have interrupted a packaging operation with the ultimate goal of distributing devil weed to our innocent citizens".

Our arrestees didn't see the humor in the situation.

We had to borrow Cork's cuffs to use on our third suspect.

They were all herded into the living room where we told them that they were all under arrest for burglary, grand theft, receiving stolen property, and possession of marijuana. While Mourning and Estill collected their I.D., Frank called the Valley Division to send someone to stand by with our prisoners while we searched the house, cars, and garage.

In a few minutes a black and white arrived and the rest of us started our search. One subject in particular seemed to be acting very tough and hostile. It figured. He was Pizzi, the one who claimed to be mob connected.

During the search of the house he continually voiced his opinion of police officers and their ancestry. We had succeeded in collaring Pizzi and DeSpain, the other two were bonuses, and unknowns in our equation. We'd take them all in and sort them out at the station. The marijuana was enough to hold them all. It seemed to be about 5 or 10 pounds.

While the house was being searched, Frank and I were questioning each of our suspects separately in one of the bedrooms. No one was in a mood to tell all but it was obvious the two new players in the game were shook up. They would be worthy of further scrutiny when we had time. DeSpain had been down the road before and he was not about to play the game just yet.

Pizzi, on the other hand was quite a different case. He wouldn't shut up. Of course nothing he said could be repeated in polite society. The longer we talked and tried to quiet him down the more abusive he got. Judging from his bravado and bragging, he was very impressed with himself and his connections.

Frank and I had decided to call it a day, especially with Pizzi, and started to get up and leave the room. Pizzi had been seated on the end of a double bed. As I crossed in front of him he lunged at me and tried to head butt me while pushing me toward the wall. He must have taken umbrage at something I said. His handcuffs kept him from making a good attempt.

As it happened I was in just the right stance to bring my right arm around in a backhanded swing. With my fist doubled up, I caught the lower rim of his right jaw across the heal of my hand with a swing that had my full 190 pounds behind it. His feet seemed to lift off the floor and he did a low loop over the end of the bed and landed pretty heavily on the bare hardwood floor.

Frank immediately stepped over him, prepared to restrain him, and, of course, see if he was injured. Frank stared at him for a second or two, then slowly turned his head looking at me. He had a slight grin on his face.

"He's not hurt, but his eyes won't focus for a while. Maybe it'll be that long before his mouth focuses too."

"You know Frank, something like this really shakes my philosophy about questioning people. I've always tried to approach each interview with the attitude that you start out nice. Treat everyone with respect. There's always time to get nasty. But if you start out nasty, where have you got to go ?

Then you run into some asshole like this. He leaves you no where to go but nasty. It just ain't right to take advantage of a man's good nature."

"Yeah, Bob. It's hell isn't it ?"

We picked him up and took him into the living room with the rest of our group. While Frank talked to the Valley Division uniform guys, Cork and I continued our search. It wasn't proving very fruitful.

In the bedroom we had been using for an interrogation room, we found a homemade corner writing desk. It just didn't seem to fit. There were plenty of other places in the house to write. There were a few odds and ends of correspondence on top, but no writing instruments. Both of us grew more and more curious. We found with a slight effort, the desk became detached from the wall. It was held by two small screws. As we pulled it further from the wall an envelope fell to the floor from behind the desk. We looked at each other with that "ah ha" look in our eyes.

As I picked up and opened the unsealed envelope I saw a large sheath of $100.00 bills. How about that. Things were starting to look up. We sat on the bed to count it and came up with a rather strange total. $5555.00. Now how would you ever account for that sum? We called Frank in and showed him the money and the hiding area. We all went back to other areas of the house that may have similar additions. Nothing.

After another brief turn about the house in the off chance we overlooked something, we locked it up and left with our prisoners.

It was a joyous ride back over the hill. With the exception of Pizzi's mouth beginning to prattle again.

The good glow was starting again, inside. Things were coming together well. We had our finger man copping out. We had our two burglars in custody, not saying anything yet. We had some currency back and now we needed to recover all the property we could.

That was the only bump on the smooth road to state prison. Nothing but the money had been found in the house so there had to be a stash point somewhere. It's too soon to have gotten rid of all the Baker and Soloman stuff.

Not to mention the property from the other jobs that Klein had mentioned. No, there had to be a stash somewhere. But you could still enjoy a little of the good feeling.

It was a little after midnight when we got everyone booked in and bedded down. We had our obligatory bull session for a few minutes and separated and headed for home. Cork and I would talk to our two bonus players first thing in the morning. We had assured them that we would see them the next day as we locked them in separate cells. No sense in giving them the chance to cook up some outrageous story overnight. It was late but I called Herb Soloman anyway. I told him what we had so far and told him I would talk to him tomorrow.

Diana was asleep in my recliner and the scanner was still on when I got home. She woke up long enough to say Hi, and tell me I had the look of the Cheshire cat on my face. I didn't bother to tell her I would be going back to the office in a few hours. She'd know soon enough. Sometime during the night she woke up long enough to come to bed.

It seemed like the alarm went off before I got to sleep. By the time I stumbled through shaving, showering, and dressing, I had made enough noise to wake Diana and find her drinking a cup of coffee when I came out of the bathroom.

"I presume from the way you're dressed and the hour of the day that we're not going to spend a quiet Sunday at home". Her voice seemed a little sleepy but still had a slight edge to it.

"Nope. Got to finish this up while it's still hot. Got a couple of players in jail that we haven't sorted out yet and still have a lot of property outstanding. Don't know how long it will take. Would you pour me a cup of that coffee please?"

"It's already poured. Please take time enough to sit down and drink it before you call for your ride. I don't want to nag but you've got to get some rest some time. You guys have been going for days on end. Is everyone looking as haggard as you are?"

"Yeah, I guess so. But it's a good kind of haggard. You feel like you've accomplished something. When you can tell a victim their case is solved and the thief is in jail, it's just a good feeling. Even better when you can hand them back some of the property that had been stolen. We've still got a lot of property out on this one and we need to push the ones we have in jail now, before the word gets around they're in jail."

"I know," she says, "just slow down long enough to finish the coffee. Should I plan anything for dinner tonight?"

"I can't really say. Don't plan anything and if everything goes well we'll go out to dinner. For a change. O.K.?"

"Sounds fine. If it happens. Good luck." As I headed out the door.

As my ride pulled onto the ramp, the Chief was getting out of his car and walking toward the office.

"G'Morning Chief."

"M..ing. Put a bunch of people in jail last night. What's that all about."

"It looks like we've cleared up the Soloman and Garfein case. And possibly a few more. We've got the finger man, and now the burglars. We should wrap up in a couple of days."

By the time I'd said all that we were at the top of the stairs and he was heading for his office. End of conversation. A few minutes later Cork's ride dropped him off and we headed upstairs for the interrogation room.

We decided to talk to Alan Palmer first, since he was the renter of the house and Pizzi and the others were supposedly renting space from him.

"We're going to lay this out for you right from the beginning", I told him, "Here's what we've got." I proceeded to fill him in on Kleins part of the scheme and what Klein had told us so far. We outlined DeSpain and Pizzi's part of the plan and how we located them.

"Now, here is your situation as of now. We raid your house, arrest two burglars, recover several thousand dollars of loot, not to mention about 8 pounds of marijuana being packaged for distribution. You have rented the house and there is no doubt you knew about the marijuana.

About the burglaries, we don't know yet. But if you expect any consideration from us, now, and only now, is your chance to lay out your part of this action. Do you understand? We have four people to talk to today and I can guarantee you one of them will want to tell it all. Now, what's it to be."

"Jesus, you guys don't think I had anything to do with any burglaries do you?" He whined. "Sure, I knew about the grass but that's all."

I moved my chair a little closer to him and said "You know, I once brought in a life long burglar who was the last of a group we had been arresting for about a week. When we started to talk to him, the first thing out of his mouth was,

"Look guys, what do you want to know, I know the last fink doesn't stand a chance except to tell it all so lets go."

"You've got the first chance, and if you tell it all you have the best chance of getting the most consideration."

He thought hard for a few seconds, then,

"O.K. I didn't know exactly what they were doing but I guessed it had to be something crooked. I've only known them a few weeks. We met at Sneaky Petes on the strip. They were looking for someplace to live and we got to talking and finally they moved in."

"Who is `they'," I asked. "Remember we have four people in jail."

"Pizzi and DeSpain. Ed had known DeSpain before but they were not long time friends. Ed moved in a little later. He works at a clothing store in the valley. He runs around with them once in a while but they're not tight or anything."

"In the last few weeks have you noticed them bring anything unusual into the house."

"No, they've never brought anything into the house except their clothes and a T.V. or something. What kind of stuff?"

"Anything."

"Not that I noticed. I'm usually at work in the evening so I don't see much of them. I work at Smokeys restaurant in the valley. I had Saturday off this week."

"What about the dope. You couldn't help but know it was there, it smelled up the whole house."

"Yeah, I knew they were cleaning and packing it. I don't know which one got it. I know Ed didn't know about it before the others brought it home because he was very surprised when he came home and smelled it. He'd only been in the room a few minutes before you guys came in."

We continued to piece together his involvement for the next half hour. He seemed to be telling it straight. He was very anxious for us to accept him at face value. He had no criminal history or arrests and had been renting the house for over a year. He had lost two other roommates about three months ago and needed help with the rent. He'd been employed at the same place for two years. He did hang out with some rounders at some questionable places. That's not a crime though. Just stupid.

We put him back in his cell when we felt we had gotten most of what we needed.

Ed Stoner was a different story. He had a minor record for

theft and drunkenness. He also knew he was in a very tight spot. He admitted knowing that Pizzi and DeSpain were up to no good but he didn't really know what. When he came home from work on Saturday he smelled marijuana and went into the bedroom to have a look. He had never seen that much grass at one time and stayed to watch Pizzi and DeSpain clean and package the stuff. They mentioned something about having a distributor for it.

We started pressing him for a possible location that could be used to stash stolen property. Alan had no idea where they might have stored their loot. We talked with Ed for about an hour before he remembered Pizzi having mentioned taking a girl to an apartment in Hollywood one time. He didn't know why but he got the feeling that Pizzi rented the apartment. He thought that was strange because Pizzi was renting from Alan. He'd forgotten about it and hadn't said anything to anyone. We were just getting ready to put him back in his cell when the phone rang and I answered "hello."

On the other end came "Well, is it going all right?"

God forbid you didn't recognize the voice. His questions were short and to the point. I looked over at Cork who was going out the door with Ed, and mouthed the words "the Chief". Cork got a quizzical look on his face, and stood there.

"About usual" I said. "We're getting a little from each one. I think it'll work out O.K.".

"Fine, keep me advised." click. The end. Strange man. I didn't want to even consider the ramifications of not keeping him advised.

DeSpain proved to be more of a challenge. He knew he'd been had and wanted to dance around to see if he could work a deal for himself without giving us anything we didn't already have. The fencing, dancing, dodging and denials went for about an hour before we started to understand each other.

No deals on anything until we got back the property and clean up the paperwork on all the burglaries they pulled. He barely admitted the Soloman and Garfein jobs only because we had told him we had Klein in jail. He'd figured Klein had told us about those but he didn't know how many more.

We switched from the number of burglaries to where the merchandise was stored.

He began to get more serious. Cork and I got the feeling that there was something about the loot that bothered him. We decided to keep working on this facet of the problem.

Finally he let it out that he'd always been a little uncomfortable about the way the loot was handled.

He started telling us that Pizzi had insisted from the beginning that he, Pizzi, handle all the merchandise. He made a point of saying his connections back in Pittsburgh would take care of them and the property. Pizzi inferred he was still connected to the mob and they were backing him on this operation. DeSpain said he didn't know whether to believe him or not but as long as he got a fair shake he didn't care.

"If that's the case, why are you feeling funny about it now?" I asked him.

"The last couple of payments just didn't seem right. I never called him on it but I was starting to think I was being shortchanged."

"Do you know who he sent the stuff to?" Cork asked, leaning forward and lighting another cigarette.

"No, just back east, Pittsburgh I think."

"Did you ever go with him when he shipped the stuff? How'd he ship it, parcel post, railway express, how?"

"Parcel Post I guess. He took a couple of boxes into the Post Office but he didn't want me to go in with him. He always played it close to the vest when it came to handling the stuff."

"How about that apartment of his. Do you know where that is?"

"I don't know the exact address but I could point out the building if I was on the right street. It's on Serrano just south of Melrose. On the east side of the street."

"O.K. Do you want to go for a ride? But before we leave,

understand this, if you're bullshiting us or trying to fool with us just to get out of jail for a while, we are going to be very upset. Understand?"

"Sure. Why would I do that. After I've told you all this why would I screw up now?"

He's starting to appeal now. He too wanted to know if this apartment had been where the loot had been going.

"You get me to the right street and I'll point out the building. I've never been in the apartment but I've been to the front of it."

"Let's go", Cork said and we were on our way to the elevator.

Shortly before noon we were slowly cruising south on Serrano and DeSpain kept saying "no". Into the second block we're about to stop and have a heart to heart with him when he pointed to a building and said, "that's it, that's the one".

"I thought you said the first block" as I parked and got out of the car. "Do you know which apartment it is?"

"No, I just saw him go in the first stairway and come out that stairway."

As Cork sat with him I walked over to the building and read the mailbox nameplates. All the boxes had full names on them except Number 7.

It had the initials J.P . . . Bingo!

I located #7 on the second floor to the right of the stairway. I went and motioned for Cork to get out so we could talk. From the looks of the building, and the neighborhood, we didn't feel it was safe to go contacting the manager or any tenant. That neighborhood, and many of it's tenants, was "questionable".

We decided to take DeSpain back to jail and return here after doing a little background on the building and it's tenants. We were back at the station within a half hour with DeSpain complaining all the way. He really wanted to see inside that apartment. So did we.

We tried to contact the Pacific Gas and Electric, the telephone company and the water company but ran into the problem of the weekend. If it wasn't an emergency they couldn't help us 'til the next day.

We grabbed a bite to eat and returned to the building to stake it out for a while and see what happened.

After sitting across the street for about an hour we took a closer look. The parking space assigned to that apartment was empty. We were going up the stairs when an older man approached and asked if he could help us. He said he was the manager and from the tone of his voice he was suspicious of us. We took him into the alcove of the stairway and identified ourselves. At the same time I pulled out the mug shot of Pizzi that McIntire had just finished before we left.

The manager identified him as the renter of #7. We asked if there was anyone in the apartment now and he said he wasn't sure. He said once in a while a girl stayed there overnight. He added that he didn't see Pizzi very often.

We went up the stairs very quietly and listened at the door. We were about to go back down the stairway when the sound of something falling to the floor came from the apartment. The manager said "I didn't think there was anyone in there ".

We began knocking on the door vigorously. After a few seconds passed, the manager pulled out his keys and unlocked the door.

Cork and I drew our guns as we entered and suddenly the manager decided that inside was not the place for him. Cork and I fanned out to quickly scan the apartment for occupants. That done, we took a fast assessment of the place. Almost empty. Small formica dining table and two chairs, one arm chair in the living room and a rumpled double bed in the bedroom. The bathroom had one towel and one washcloth. No cooking utensils or dishes in the kitchen.

Once the initial entry was made and the apartment found empty, the manager came in. He seemed aghast at the lack of the usual things in the apartment. We asked him to get the records to determine just when the apartment had been rented and how the rent was being paid. He left muttering to himself.

Back inside we took a closer look around.

In the bedroom was a double sliding door closet along one wall. We stood to one side as we cautiously slid open one door.

Eureka . . . . Wide open smiles were plastered on both our faces as we slid the door wide open.

Stacked neatly inside the closet were five large cardboard cartons. On the closet shelf was a supply of package tape, scissors, and mailing labels. Cork and I looked at each other and while holding our breath we picked the carton on top and lifted it onto the bed. We were relieved to find the carton fairly heavy and the top not sealed.

We each took a flap on the top and opened it. We were greeted with a view of a white fox fur with bugle beaded lining. We couldn't tell the length of it but from what we saw it could only belong to one person. Emptying the box on the bed could only have looked like two kids unwrapping Christmas presents. Item after item coming out of the box fit the description of property stolen in the Garfein burglary as well as the Soloman burglary.

As we opened and examined the other boxes we found numerous furs and items of jewelry we recognized as stolen from several Beverly Hills victims. There were many other items we did not recognize. No doubt from burglaries not in our city.

The manager returned to tell us the place had been rented by Pizzi 4 months before and the rent was paid by cash each month. Last month by mail. We took him into the bedroom where he saw all of the merchandise on the bed. Silver dollars couldn't have covered his eyeballs. As he was trying to get his breath, we told him were taking the boxes with us and if anyone asked him about the apartment he was to try to get their names and refer them to us. He was nodding yes to our instructions as we herded him down the stairs.

We brought the car to the bottom of the stairway and began loading the boxes into the car. We did another check of the place looking for addresses or phone books but found nothing. We were hoping to find a Pennsylvania address somewhere among the address labels. No such luck. We locked up the place and left. We didn't want to leave the car sit out there with all that stuff in it for very long.

The ride back to the station was a very leisurely one. The conversation was quiet and comfortable. We both sat there with a warm fuzzy feeling inside. Neither one of us knew how much property we had recovered but we knew it was substantial and would clear a lot of cases. Another one of those times when all's right with the world.

When we got to the station we drove directly into the underground garage for unloading. We didn't want the world to know yet what we had found. To many loose strings and details to be wrapped up. By the time we locked all the boxes in the vault it was close to six o'clock. We decided to pack it in for the day and get an early start tomorrow. On our way out we told the Watch Commander to say nothing to anyone yet. We had many things yet to do before we let the word out.

My ride home was glorious. It was hard not to crow to the driver, but I managed. Once inside the apartment though, the crowing began.

"I thought you had a cat eating canary look on your face last night. By the looks of you today, he must have eaten a whole flock of birds. I'm guessing it turned out all right?"

"That qualifies as a major understatement. It turned out only one or two steps off of perfect."

While we were both dressing for our dinner date I filled her in on the days events. She had to stop me a few times to make sense of what I was saying.

By the time we got to Whittinghills my battery had run down and I was just breathing deeply, relaxing, enjoying good company, and good food. Life wasn't bad.

Those hours, days and weeks of frustration are not all wiped out. They certainly have some of the sting taken out of them when you have a couple of days like those had been. Gives you an almost fresh new outlook and desire to stay joined in the battle.

The feelings you had when you first came on the Department are back again. Oh, they never have gone very far, but just haven't been as prominent. You just hope they would not drift so far into your memory. Or that something would happen that would bring them to the surface more often.

Be thankful for what you've got, Downey.

CHAPTER 30

By seven AM we were sorting, itemizing, and tagging property in the jail floor interrogation room. The Chief had already been in to view the property and had agreed not to release anything to the press until we got a better handle on what we had. We were done sorting and tagging by nine AM and had identified four more Beverly Hills cases in addition to Soloman and Garfein.

I called Frank and invited him over as soon as he could make it and bring his property file. I didn't tell him why, but he knew we had come up with something.

We locked up the merchandise and went downstairs to pull some of the paper work together. We started to look over the papers we brought in from the valley house.

Most of the notebooks or phone books seemed just that. Nothing out of the ordinary. But one proved very interesting.

It contained many entries that were obviously in code. Each entry appeared to be a name, followed by a four, or five number entry. This was followed by a group of letters. These were followed by six or seven three sided boxes, or square 'U's, with the open end facing different directions. None of the `name' entries made any sense, They did not resemble any recognizable names.

We really started to get frustrated trying to work out the code. We finally pulled DeSpain out of his cell and presented him with the puzzle. He told us that Pizzi had set up the code and he didn't know what the formula was. He said Pizzi handled the book but he knew that he used that book to enter the names and phone numbers of possible targets. He did recall Pizzi mentioning that it was so easy it was like playing Tic Tac Toe. With that bit of wisdom we returned to our puzzle.

When Frank arrived we took him to the interrogation room and opened the door. A very large smile came over his face. We spent the next half hour identifying and sorting merchandise stolen from W.L.A. victims.

At least three of his cases were positively identified and two were possibles. We told him we would probably make the release tomorrow, after we solved our puzzle and talked to our suspects again. I showed him our puzzle book and sought his expertise. Hah. He shook his head a few times and started out the door with the comment, "better you than me. It looks like a hookers trick book". With that, he was gone. Thinking about it, it did look a lot like a trick book, but more complicated. After a brief discussion we decided, why not? Call up a couple of hookers we have dealt with and see what their formulas are for keeping the names and numbers of their clients in their books.

They gave us three or four formulas that the girls used. We sat back down and started trying different variations.

After our fourth try we came up with the letter solution. Just add two to the letters that were listed. Clear as glass. The names started to jump off the paper at us. We left the numbers alone for now and worked on the second set of letters. Subtract two from the letters listed. They became street names. So far so good. The four or five numbers before the street names were the actual street address numbers.

Now came the hard part. The open ended boxes obviously represented telephone numbers but how? About fifteen minutes of frustration led to embarrassment.

It was so obvious it was simple. We began to question each others intelligence it was so simple. Especially with the clue provided by DeSpain.

Tic Tac Toe.

We drew a Tic Tac Toe figure and started in the upper left hand corner with the number One. Two next to that and three on the end and so forth to nine at the end. Zero was represented as a blank space. With that formula we returned to the book and filled in all the phone numbers. The Garfeins and the Solomans were listed, with their private phone numbers.

We felt we had all the pieces we needed to talk with our suspects again, and this time we'd start with Pizzi.

We showed him the property before any questions were asked. Then we went into the visitors room and sat down.

"It's all over John. We have the property, your stash pad, and the formula for the intended victims in the address book. Some of them have already been victims. It won't be hard to match up your writing with that in the book.

Your prints will be all over the shipping boxes. Bobby has already spilled his guts as you know. Given all that, just what have you got to say ?"

I left it at that as I leaned back against the wall. Cork had sat on the bolted down stool closest to the door and now he leaned back against the wall.

"What the hell can I say. You have it all. You don't need me to tell you anything." He's still got that belligerent, smart mouthed attitude. If you were ever driven by temptation to pop someone in the chops, this could be the time. But, he was right. You do have it all, or at least enough to put him away for a goodly amount of time, so why screw everything up just for a little personal satisfaction?

"O.K. Just one more question. What happened to the $12,000 out of the Soloman safe. We found a little over five grand of it, what happened to the rest? I bet you thought you died and went to heaven when you found that bundle in the open safe."

"What the hell are you talking about. There was no twelve grand in there. There was barely five grand. You know how much there was. You found it behind the desk. We hadn't had time to get together and split it yet. What the hell are you guys trying to pull? Oh, I get it. Soloman's trying to get to the insurance company for twelve grand when we took only five. And they call us crooks. Shit. No way. I'll tell you everything we got at Soloman's place and there wasn't any twelve thousand."

"O.K. we'll take your word for it for now. And we will check on it. Now what I'm really interested in is the stuff from Carroll Baker's house. We found everything but the "Baby Doll" charm bracelet. The one she got for doing the movie "Baby Doll". I'd really like to get that back. It has a lot of sentimental value for her."

He started shaking his head. "Huh uh." He said. "Everything we got from her place was in those boxes. I read in the paper about the bracelet but we didn't get it. I really got pissed off when it showed on television that big necklace that we missed. It was like she was laughing in our face. I almost went back after it the next night. Who would have expected us to come back the next night. No, no bracelet, and no twelve grand. I think that's all I want to say right now. How much are you going to file on us."

"That depends on the D.A. and how cooperative you are from now on. West L.A. will want to talk to you and they have several cases. We can't control what they do but we do have a good relationship with them and can talk to them depending on your attitude.

One thing I would like to know is where do you send that property in Pittsburgh. I'm from a small town just 18 miles from Pittsburgh and it would be interesting to know." I didn't have a prayer of him telling me where he sent the stuff but I thought I'd give it a try.

"No, No. No way. I give you that and I'm a dead man. Those people are mean. Forget it."

"I didn't think so. But, I do want you to know I don't believe a damned word about your connections with "The Mob". I grew up in that area and I know that they wouldn't have anything to do with a small timer like you. It's O.K. with me if you want to impress your friends with that crap about being "connected", but don't waste the effort on me.

You've got some small timer relative back there who's laying off this stuff for you and probably getting burned for his trouble. He may be dealing it to some mobster, but not because he's connected, but because that's his only option. If he tried to deal with someone else they'd probably cut off his fingers. Now that you're popped they won't even know your buddy. That could be very healthy for him. Either way, you're done."

We put him back in his cell and headed for the elevator. While we were waiting Cork looked at me and said, "Jesus, I didn't know you had any sermons in you. You sounded like you had so much self righteous indignation I was ready to confess and convert ."

We were both laughing when we opened the elevator door on the business office floor and most of the people in the office looked at us like we were weird.

We went in and brought Hankins up to date and laid out our plan to make the news release the next morning, after we had time to complete our reports and display the property. Hankins said he would fill in the Chief and let us know.

When Hankins came back from the Chief's office we were up to our armpits in paper work. The Chief wanted to see the code book so Hankins took it back in to him. A few minutes later he came back with a broad smile on his face. The Chief must have been pleased. We never found out. He never did understand how the code worked. Hell, neither did we for a while.

By four o'clock the paperwork was ready to be filed for the complaints. That was the next days work. Right now we were all are sitting around just basking in the warm feelings that are coming tomorrow. Just before five I called the Garfeins'.

"Garfein residence".

"This is Sgt. Downey at the Police Department, may I speak to Mr. Garfein please."

"Just a moment please."

"Jack Garfein, how are you sergeant? Is there any news?"

"Mr. Garfein, remember all that publicity we had when your burglary happened? Well, we could use a little of it now."

"I take it you've caught the thieves?"

"Yes, as a matter of fact we have. What I'd like to do is for you to bring your wife down to the station tomorrow morning, about

10 AM if that's O.K., and identify what property we've recovered. We would appreciate very much your not telling any one about this until tomorrow morning. We don't want to be answering the phones all night and we still have a lot of wrap up work to do." We didn't, but I wanted his cooperation and I didn't want him to break it too soon. "Can I depend on you for that?"

"Of course. You say 10:00 O'clock tomorrow. Fine. And by the way, congratulations. We'll see you in the morning. Good bye." He hung up and so did I, with a very broad smile on my face.

"From the look on your face I presume it's all set." Hankins said. He'd been sitting next to Cork waiting for the call.

"Yep, 10:00 o'clock tomorrow morning. We'll see just how much coverage the arrest gets compared to the crime. We took our lumps then, maybe we'll recover some now."

We all went out the door as Hankins headed for the Chief's office to tell him.

That evening at home was one for the memory book. The recovery was going to be well over a hundred thousand dollars and at least 10 major cases cleared. There were quite a few residential and commercial burglaries still open on the books but we had taken a major chunk out of the high profile ones.

Each case, be it high value or not, is high profile for at least one person, the victim. Their case is very important to them. It just wouldn't do for any Police Officer to forget that. It's hard sometimes, with the press of cases, to make the victim realize that each case is also important to you. Something as simple as a phone call to let them know they're case is not forgotten can give them great piece of mind. And it doesn't hurt you a bit.

Diana and I had eaten well, talked long, and finally sacked out, dead tired but strangely refreshed. We had watched the news just before retiring. Nothing about the arrest or recovery. There is nothing like dealing with an honorable man.

By nine o'clock the next morning we had moved the recovered property into the room next to Hankins office. The phones started ringing at about 8:45 and kept it up. Cork and the Chief were handling most of the calls.

Yes, Miss Baker would be in at 10:00 AM.

Yes, photos of the property could be taken after any identification.

Yes, we had five people in custody. The whole operation would be laid out at about 10:00 AM. Local news, national news, international news. Mr. Garfein had done his job well. By nine-thirty we had to have crowd control in the business office because of all the T.V. and news cameras, as well as newspaper and magazine reporters.

Shortly before 10:00 the Chief had a large group into his office where he read a prepared statement about the gangs operation. He didn't name the restaurant but that wouldn't stay secret very long. One of the victims would surely let the name out. Not that there had been any agreement not to reveal the name. Just a courtesy to our local businessmen.

At precisely 10:00 o'clock Carroll Baker Garfein and Mr. Jack Garfein came through the front door and the cameras started flashing.

She was well prepared for the occasion. Strikingly beautiful would not be an overstatement. Only a few ladies in Hollywood could be grouped into her category. Gail Russell, Janet Leigh, Maureen O'Hara, and a couple of others. Many of the media were still in the Chief's office and were caught flatfooted.

I met the Garfeins in the business office and escorted them into the Detective Bureau and the property room. We had a uniformed officer keep the media out until they had a chance to view the property. She immediately identified all the items we had presumed were hers from her descriptions. After a few minutes conversation about the burglars and their operation I asked her to pose with her property for the media. She graciously complied. She even repeated our advice on national T.V to put the valuables in a safe deposit box, as she had done and was continuing to do.

On his way out the door Jack Garfein gave me a "was that O.K. look ?" It certainly was.

After the Garfein's departure the next couple of hours was spent filling in the media on the exact operation of the "Phone Tip Off Gang" as the media had dubbed them.

The next few days was a flurry of activity that ran from one to another seemingly without interruption and each accompanied with it's own level of emotion and satisfaction.

Our three suspects had been charged and arraigned. The other two had been released.

We had identified and cleared 7 of our own cases and five of West Los Angeles.

We had recovered and returned some merchandise from all of them. Not all of it, but some. The missing $7000.00 differential in the cash in the Soloman case was probably something they would have to work out between them. There just wasn't anything for the thieves to gain by lying to us at this point.

Later I was to find out from an unimpeachable source that the lady of the house had been using sums from the safe for "incidentals".

The code book had a list of an additional 38 intended victims. The media had aired or printed something about the case for several days after the arrests.

We had conducted telephone interviews with news media from England, Mexico and France. A friend even sent us a front page photo about the case from Madrid, Spain.

We also got those calls from other victims wanting to know why we had not solved their cases yet. We didn't have a good answer for them. At least not yet. But they had every right to ask. Who knows just what it will take to bag another group like this and give you that great feeling again.

These are the times that let you know exactly why you were in the law enforcement profession. That you're doing something for somebody that they can't do for themselves, and they appreciate it.

Most of the routine procedures were behind us. We were settling back into the ongoing business of frustration and disappointment. Chasing shadows and assuring victims that you'll do your best to get their case solved and their property back. The warm glow of the previous weeks had pretty well worn off.

Frank and I, and the rest of our surveillance group were anxious to start another adventure. We had a meeting set up in a couple of days. The parasites were still feeding off the general public.

For some reason we had all been living almost normal lives for several days. No emergency calls, no all night stake outs, no court on days off. Home most nights about six. It was beginning to feel strange.

About eleven PM the phone rang. Louder than usual it seemed.

"Hello", I said, half heartedly.

"Bob, Cork, meet me at the office as soon as you can. We've had an officer shoot a burglar in Trousdale, I've sent a car to pick you up. I'll meet you at the office."

He'd hung up before I could answer. I had put my feet on the floor before our conversation had finished. My ride was coming up the driveway as I finished putting on my clothes and went out the door with untied shoes and my gunbelt and handcuffs in my hands.

Gil White, the driver of my ride, filled me in with as much as he knew on our way to the office.

Jack Thorpe, working car 8, had come across a station wagon backed up to the front door of a house under construction in the Trousdale Estates. We'd had a hell of a lot of thefts from construction sites in the Trousdale area. Jack spotted the burglar running away and when he wouldn't stop Jack fired three shots. Gil seems to think the suspect is dead.

Cork and I arrived at the ramp at the same time. He told me Hankins was on his way in. After a quick stop at the desk, we headed for Trousdale and the shooting site.

The scene was secure and there were several police cars around. As we approached we noticed a woman seated in the back of one of the cars with an officer standing by.

Officer Jack Thorpe was leaning against the hood of the station wagon in the driveway and talking with the Watch Commander, Fred Colford, and the night Detective, Jack Egger.

Thorpe was a tall, lean, good looking young officer. He's enthusiastic and eager, with a quick smile and pleasant personality. In the few contacts I'd had with him he'd been level headed and cooperative. He'd earned a reputation as a good cop. His supervisors thought highly of him.

Right now he didn't look like he felt too well. Having to shoot someone affects no two people the same. God protect me from those that are not affected.

Cork stopped to talk to Jack and Colford while I went on to the pool area of the house where the activity was taking place.

The Fire Department ambulance crew had placed the covered body on a stretcher and was preparing to take it out front. From the several officers on scene I learned that when they arrived in response to Jack's call, they were unable to find the burglar immediately. After a short search they found his body laying right up next to the house.

When I returned to the front of the house, Thorpe had left with the Watch Commander and gone to Police Headquarters. Cork, Egger, and I met near the front door of the house. Just inside the front door sat a dishwasher. Apparently the burglars' target.

Cork then dropped the bombshell.

"You know who that was under the sheet?" he asked sort of incredulously.

"No, am I supposed to?"

"Your friend and mine, Robert Dickey. That gal in the car was his wife, Kay."

My jaw must have hung there for a while because he continued,

"Dickey had a floor polisher in his arms and threw it at Thorpe and ran when Thorpe challenged him. Thorpe fired three times and hit him each time. Apparently he was just at the corner of the house when he got hit and Jack didn't see him fall. He called for assistance and when help arrived they searched the area and found the body up against the house. They found her hiding in a closet inside the house. So much for notification."

"I knew this guy was a real flake but I never came close to thinking he had balls enough to be a burglar. And to take his wife along. Whoa. Has she made any statement yet?"

"Nothing," Egger says.

"Well, let's rap it up here and go talk to her", Cork said as we made one more tour around the place to see if there was anything we had missed. We'd have to come back in the daylight for a more detailed search but we could secure the scene here for the night.

After a couple of hours of non-productive conversation with Kay, and a couple of hours of report writing and talking with the coroner, it was early morning and time to make the trip to the Dickey house. We left Kay mulling over the fact that she very well could face a homicide charge. That got her attention.

She wasn't aware that she could be charged with her husbands death, as well as burglary. A death resulting during the commission of a crime could be charged against the others involved, regardless of who did the killing. She was in deep thought when we left.

Egger had gone home and Cork was going to stay at the office to handle the press and shepherd the paperwork. I had called Frank at home and he was on his way to our office to go to the Dickeys' with me.

When Frank arrived we headed for Curson Terrace in Hollywood.

We met two Hollywood detectives and a uniform car at the bottom of the hill to the Dickey house. As we wound our way up the hill we soon found that the view from the house was going to be outstanding. It had to be. There were no houses up here that didn't have a magnificent view.

When we rounded one corner of this narrow road we came to an iron gated drive at 7661. We drove in the open gate.

Once in the parking area of the residence you got the definite impression that this was not your usual home. In all areas of the large yard was a wide variety of construction equipment. At one end of the rear yard was a fairly large swimming pool. At least it was supposed to be a pool. It really looked more like a rectangular putting green. The algae had been allowed to grow and was so thick that only heavier objects would sink through the surface.

As we used Kay's key to gain entry to the house we asked the uniformed officers to check the equipment in the yard area to see if any of it was stolen.

The inside of the residence was about what we had expected. Appliances, tools, building equipment, furnishings, paintings and a myriad of other items located throughout the place.

As we worked our way through the place, the uniformed officers advised us that the dump truck, skip loader, and mobile generator in the yard were all on the stolen property file. While they arranged to impound those items we called for a stake bed truck to haul in the rest of the property.

While going through the utility area we found a large rheostat mounted near the electrical panel in the garage area. A closer inspection showed it had been taken from a house under construction in Beverly hills. The house was being built by a movie producer and the rheostat was to be used to dim the lights in the private theater in his home. The rheostat had been intended originally for a Navy destroyer and still bore some of the Navy Identification numbers.

While searching the bedroom we saw a Polaroid camera mounted on a tripod at the foot of the bed. There were several Polaroid negatives laying around the bedroom floor. A short search revealed a large stack of Polaroid pictures in a dresser drawer. The tripoded camera in the bedroom gave us a clue of what kind of photos we would find, and we were right. All the photos were of Kay and, or, Robert in various nude poses and sex acts. I would have hated to have their film bill. If they had bothered to buy any.

By the time we had loaded the truck it was early afternoon. We were just about to close up and leave the house when we decided to take one more look around. We returned to the utility area where we had removed the rheostat when we stopped to try to figure out what was wrong with the picture we were seeing.

We stood looking at the electrical panel for a full three minutes before we realized there was no meter. We looked up and saw the everpresent three wires leading into the power mast but no meter. A quick call to the power company told us that no power was being used at this address. We asked for a power crew to respond immediately.

When they arrived it took about three minutes for them to determine that Dickey had run his own power cables to a power pole about fifty yards down the hill and had bootlegged the power for his entire house operation. He had lived there for several years and had never paid a power bill.

After the power had been disconnected, we locked the premises and left, shaking our heads.

It took several days for us to return most of the property we had recovered. Some to our victims, some to West L.A. and some to Hollywood. Some had come from far flung areas of Los Angeles. Some of the heavier equipment had been missing for a couple of years. How the hell did they get that skip loader home?

It was hard to figure how Dickey had been so active for so long and had not been caught somewhere along the line.

During the several day process of returning the property, Kay had been arraigned on burglary and receiving stolen property charges. No decision had been made on the homicide charge. The flurry of activity had started to settle back to normal.

Interviews, reports, telephone calls, more reports, meetings, waiting for that "thing" that starts the spurt of adrenaline again. You are starting to get used to that feeling of smug satisfaction and starting to worry a little about it being too quiet.

Our surveillance group was lining up another target. We'd been 'invited' to work on a couple of residential burglars in Hollywood. It looked like we'd convinced some people.

Diana and I had just settled back to listen to some jazz after a nice meal of steak and Caesar salad. Diana was bringing in a couple of Plymouth Gin and tonics when the phone rang.

I wondered what I had been missing for the last few days. It was the phone. I leaned back in my chair as I answered.

"Hello."

"Hi Sgt., Fred Colford here."

Oh Damn, I felt my stomach start to flutter again.

"Yeah Fred, what is it, or do I really want to know?"

"Probably not, but it's going to be yours anyhow. We just took a burglary report from the Porter Washington family up on Doheny Rd. She's related to the Dohenys somehow. Anyway they returned from a dog show where they were showing some of their dogs and found their house burglarized. To the tune of over $100,000 dollars.

You're set for a follow-up at 9:00 AM tomorrow. They said their Insurance Adjuster would be there too. They seem like very nice people. Just thought you ought to know. Good Luck, Good Night." he hung up.

"Oh hell." There it is, the 'thing' that starts it . . .

CHAPTER 31

My interview with the Porter Washington family was set for 9:00 AM. I had enough time to read the reports and look over any physical evidence that the nightwatch detectives may have found during the preliminary investigation.

There wasn't much. The entry had apparently been gained through an open window in the den. The inside window sills were very wide and had numerous dog show trophies displayed throughout the room. The walls of the house were very thick and all the windows were recessed about 18 inches. The suspect had knocked over several trophies as he gained entry.

Although there had been servants in the house, no one had heard anything unusual. Because the servants were to be at home, the burglar alarm had not been set when the Washingtons had gone to the dog show.

The suspect had apparently proceeded into the hallway and up the open stairway to the bedroom level of the house. In getting to the stairway, he had to pass a walk-in closet which contained a large fur vault. The closet door and the vault door had been left open by the owner. All the stolen property had been removed from a couple of bedrooms and a bath on the second floor. The property list was to be ready for me when I did the follow-up.

I arrived early in order to talk to the victims before the arrival of the insurance adjuster. I also wanted to look around the grounds before talking with the victims. It didn't work. Miles Reece, an independent insurance adjuster, was already at the house when I arrived. Miles and I had worked together before on several cases and we got along well. It's just sometimes easier to talk to victims when the insurance angle is not a primary consideration. In talking with the Washingtons I found that insurance was certainly not their primary concern. Most of the property was not insured.

Mr. and Mrs. Washington were extremely concerned that their personal surroundings had been violated. That was not unusual. Sometimes that feeling of violation never wears off. Even if the culprit is caught and the property recovered, the outrage is still there.

In my first few sentences with the Washingtons I found that Miles had been expounding long and loud about his theories of who had pulled the job. Adjusters as well as Detectives become very familiar with the identities of burglars that specialize in certain types of burglaries. It seemed that Miles had been more than willing to toss the names of some well known, high profile, burglars around.

He had about convinced the Washingtons that it had to be Jimmy Pope, 'Jumpy' Calvert, or Jimmy Gould that had paid them a visit. They in turn asked me when I would be picking them up for questioning. It took me a while to impress on them that it would be beneficial for me to look over the premises first. Miles told me he had already surveyed the scene and was convinced that one of the infamous trio had done it. I managed to have Mr. Washington take Miles into the kitchen for coffee while Mrs. Washington showed me around the house.

We started in the den, where the suspect had apparently made entry through the window. The four trophies that he had knocked off the window sill were still on the floor. Mrs. Washington advised that the trophies were dusted at least every two days. I examined each one for fingerprints with no luck. Of course, if he knocked them to the floor, he needn't have touched them. I also checked the one remaining on the window sill. Nothing. The window and ledge revealed nothing.

Outside the window were two large rocks the suspect had apparently stood on the get in the window. Judging from the height of the window ledge from the ground, the suspect must not have been very tall or he would not have needed the rocks. There were no tracks or distinguishable shoe signs outside the window.

Mrs. Washington and I walked down the long driveway to the street without finding anything significant. She told me that the electric gate was closed when they had left and returned the night before. It was opened with the electric remote from their car.

The estate was surrounded with a wrought iron fence about 8 feet tall, interspersed every 10 feet with a brick column. The main entrance to the estate faces Doheny Road, with the driveway access controlled by an electrically controlled, 8 foot, wrought iron gate which was almost always closed. There was a service entrance on the east side of the house. Also with an electrically controlled gate. Both gates were equipped with an intercom system.

Back in the house Mrs. Washington guided me on a tour of the place, pointing out the fur vault in the downstairs, walk-in closet. She said the vault had been left open so she could replace the garment she had worn to the show. There had been four furs undisturbed in the vault. Upstairs, she pointed out the bedrooms, dressing rooms and baths.

They had left everything the way they had found it the night before. Going through the stolen property list and the locations it was taken from, she told me that a great many of the items taken had been purchased from and made by Ruser jewelers on Rodeo Drive. That was one piece of good news.

I knew from experience that Bill Ruser took photographs of all his designed merchandise and kept a file of each item sold to each client. I had only to ask him for the Washington file and it would have photos of all the items he had sold them. It would help greatly in the identification.

While she pointed out the places where the jewelry had been, she also pointed to many items that had not been disturbed. Very expensive items. Some items taken were part of a matched set. Yet the matching pieces were not taken even though they were laying next to the missing items. She noted that several items of costume jewelry had been taken while visible items of much greater value were untouched.

Incidents like this continued throughout our tour. Among

items taken was one walkie talkie, from a set of two. A small zippered gym bag had been removed from the closet shelf. Apparently to carry the merchandise. We returned to the dining room to join Miles and Mr. Washington.

They had been discussing the insurance coverage. It turned out that only about 50% of the missing merchandise was covered. When we had completed the major portion of the property list, Miles and I departed the premises.

We met about two blocks from the house to discuss the case. He was very insistent that one of his suspects had pulled the job and wanted me to locate them and question them. I tried very hard to explain to him that I had a strong feeling that this job had been pulled by some stumblebum that had accidently hit a big score. We had agreed that the loss would exceed a hundred thousand dollars. He became incensed when I wouldn't accept his theory. He refused to listen to my reasons for feeling the way I did. He drove off rapidly stating he would have to go to the Chief if I didn't start to pull in Calvert, Pope or Gould. He was upset.

When I got back to the office I began making the usual phone calls to alert my contemporaries to the burglary. And of course to keep their sources looking for any leads. I was on the phone to Bill Ruser when Capt. Hankins came into the office and interrupted my conversation by telling me the Chief wanted to see me. I closed with Bill and went to the Chief's office.

As I started into the Chief's office, his secretary, Vi Renquist, told me that Miles Reece had just left. By God, he had done it. He had actually gone in and complained. I knocked on the door, and the Chief called me in.

He motioned for me to take a chair and then settled back in his.

"Miles Reece just left. He says he doesn't think you are giving this case the attention it needs. He thinks it was pulled by some big timer because it is a large loss. What do you think ?"

"I think it's possible, but not very probable. I also think he's going way out of line."

"That may be, but tell me why you don't think it's probable."

"Well Chief, the location for one thing. The entire estate is surrounded with an eight foot fence and wall with only two gates. Both gates are clearly marked that the house is alarmed. The entry. Climbing through a window and knocking those trophies on the floor when the front door was unlocked. Bypassing the fur vault, that he would have certainly seen, and not taking anything. Hell there were two mink stoles, a full length mink, and a sable stole in there. Then he goes upstairs and takes only part of the loot that's available. Took some costume stuff and left valuable stuff in open view.

He took an emerald bracelet worth six thousand dollars and left the matching necklace and earrings that were laying right next to the bracelet. He even took one half of a walkie talkie set." I paused for a breath. "Now does that sound like one of our top guys? I'm not saying that I won't look into those guys but I just got a feeling it would be a waste of time."

"Well, do it your way. Just let him think he's having his way. He doesn't run this Department or any investigation. If we can, it's nice to maintain a good working relationship with the insurance people, but they need us more than we need them. O.K., go catch the guy."

By the time I've stood up, he was already on the telephone. I was fuming when I got back to my desk. Hankins came in and I told him what happened. He was not very happy with Miles either.

A few minutes later I was sitting in Bill Ruser's office on Rodeo as his secretary was getting us a cup of coffee and the Washington file. Bill was one of those people who knew he was good and didn't have to prove it or put on airs.

He was extremely helpful in supplying me with photos and descriptions of most of the missing items. Naturally it wasn't all bought from him. He also told me that Miles had called him wanting the pictures of the jewelry. Fat chance. I went back to the office to get out the obligatory teletype.

It was the middle of the afternoon when I handed the message to Sam Bottleman, for distribution. As I started back to the office I saw Pete Meaney of the FBI coming up the stairs. Pete was probably the only FBI Agent that was close to welcome in our building, let alone offices. We decided to go up to the jail kitchen for a cup of coffee and a talk. Funny, ours was the only Detective Bureau I knew that didn't have it's own coffee maker in the office. The Captain just didn't want to risk the Chief's wrath. Of course nobody had ever asked the Chief if he would mind. They just assumed he would.

There was more peace and quiet in the kitchen anyway. Al Grevelding, the jailer, poured us a cup of coffee and quietly disappeared. I filled Pete in on the events of the day and my theories about the perpetrator. He concurred, but as I, he didn't feel we could ignore the heavyweight burglars either.

We discussed the case from all angles and decided on our course of action. The high value of this case made it of special interest to the FBI. They took an interest in any burglary or robbery valued over five thousand dollars. Pete had several good sources in the criminal world and would tap those sources to see if any of the merchandise turned up in the normal channels. We finished our coffee and headed back to the office to conduct our other business.

The rest of the week was spent doing the things detectives do. Interview people. Question suspects arrested on other cases. Help the other detectives in making their arrests. There was never a shortage of things to do. All the time you're working on your cases too. Phone calls, meetings, checking addresses, trying to locate any possible leads.

Nothing clicks. No rumors. No hints. Not even any talk among the seedier element about the burglary itself. Sometimes when a big job is pulled, even if no one knows who did it, there is talk. What a nice score. What a neat job. Etc, etc. Not this time.

And during that time, at least two calls or messages a day from Miles Reece. It was getting hard to understand. He'd represented insurance companies on large losses before and never been this persistent. The insurance company's not even on the hook for the full amount. Miles was a hard working adjuster and was usually very cooperative with the Police. Maybe it was just me he was not comfortable with. Although we'd worked well together before. Whatever. We were headed into the weekend anyway so I wouldn't be bothered by him for a couple of days.

Early Sunday afternoon I got a phone call at home from Tom McCarthy. Tom was a former motor officer that had come into the Bureau a couple of months before. Tom was a jovial, hard working, redhead, about six feet tall or so. Like most of us are and were, he was very anxious to do a good job.

Tom told me that he'd seen a teletype from San Francisco describing some jewelry recovered with the arrest of an individual that was trying to pawn some of it. Tom read the description of an 18 karat gold elephant with one diamond and one ruby eye. A couple of other pieces also matched the Washington burglary. I told Tom to telephone San Francisco P.D. and place a hold on the suspect, one Edmund Chuski. I asked him to call me back when he got more information on Chuski and whether he could be released to us if the jewelry turned out to be from our job.

About twenty minutes later he called to tell me that a lot of the jewelry they have in custody matches the descriptions of the Washington loot. He also said that San Francisco has no other charges pending and that we can have the suspect whenever we come to get him. He also asked if I was going up to get Chuski, could he come along. I told him to stand by because I had to first get permission for me to go and then ask about him.

In a few minutes I called him back to tell him to get his traveling gear and the case file together because we were leaving as soon as we could get on the road. We arranged for him to bring a Detective car to pick me up and we would leave from my place in about an hour. I shaved, showered, shampooed, and shined, and was waiting on the stairs when Tom drove up. I looked back as we drove down the driveway to see Diana standing on the landing just shaking her head slowly.

The drive up old Highway 99 was a tedious one. Through the heart of every small town in the central valley. It was good and dark when we turned off 99 to head for San Francisco. Two hours later we were checking into the Travelodge on Lombard and looking for a place to eat before going to bed. The next couple of days were going to be long ones and we knew it.

By 8:30 the next morning we were waiting for Inspectors Lark and Peters to come into the General Works office of the SFPD. The unit covered the pawn shop detail and had responded to the call from the pawn shop when Chuski tried to sell the elephant.

The pawn shops in San Francisco were wired together with a buzzer intercom. When a suspicious person was trying to sell or pawn an item at one shop or another, the owner pressed the buzzer with his arranged signal. The men working the pawn shop detail would get the signal in any one of the shops they were covering and respond to the shop sounding the alarm. The system worked well for them.

Lark and Peters came into the office at about 10:00 AM. They had been in their pawn shop area when someone from the office told them we were waiting for them. It seemed they didn't usually come to the office except when they had an arrest or a meeting to attend. They rode the bus to the area of their pawnshops in the morning, and if nothing happened during the day, rode the bus home at night without reporting in to the Police Station. They were also permitted to show their badges as their fare on the bus system.

After introductions all around, we went to the property room to look at the recovered property. We took the property to an interrogation room and laid it on the table. I pulled out the file of photographs from Bill Ruser and immediately started to line up each piece with a photo. There was no doubt that this was the Washington loot. But less than half of it.

Lark and Peters told us that Chuski had attempted to sell the elephant pin to a local pawn shop for twenty dollars. The shopowner became suspicious when he looked at the elephant and valued it at over $700.00. He knew Chuski did not know what he had. When Lark and Peters picked him up he had a few pieces in his pockets, and the rest at the flea bag hotel room he was living in. Time to bring in Chuski and talk to him.

Chuski was a slightly built small man about 5'6" tall. He had the look of a whipped puppie. From all points of description, he was a typical ex-con. Head slightly bowed, eyes rapidly blinking, quick glances to both sides, on and on. Seated at the end of the table he glanced quickly at each one of us, then started around again.

Peters introduced Tom and I and told Chuski why we were there. I started by opening my file folder and handing him several photos of jewelry. He handed them right back without looking at them. Right away he was going to be a hard nose.

My turn.

"Mr Chuski, I'm going to start by telling you that I don't think you realize just what you accomplished when you pulled this job. Sure, it was a little sloppy, but even so, a hundred grand worth of merchandise is nothing to be sneezed at."

At the mention of the amount his head jerked ever so slightly and his eyes snapped in my direction. His head went down again.

"Do me a favor", I asked him, "Just take a look at those pictures. Take a look at the figures written on each one. Those are prices put there by the manufacturer of these items. He made them and sold them to the Washingtons. If anyone knows the value of the items he should."

"What the hell are you guys trying to pull on me. You're trying to hang some big job on me. I don't know what you're talking about."

This sparkling conversation went on for a full hour before we decided it was getting us nowhere. Chuski was put back in his cell to think about things while I tried to think of a new approach. In the meantime we were getting the paperwork together to return him to Beverly Hills the next day.

Chuski's rap sheet told it all. He had been arrested three times in his life, and had gone to prison each time. Not County jail time, not time and probation, but hard time each time. No arrests he hadn't been convicted on. His arrests started when he was barely 18 years old. He was now 44. This was his longest time out of jail between convictions, 6 weeks. This guy was definitely a loser.

We were taken to the shop where he tried to sell the pin. The owner said he may have bought the pin if Chuski had played his cards a little differently. Instead, Chuski presented the pin and immediately asked if he could sell it for $20.00. If he would have said, "how much will you give me for it?", the owner was about to offer him $75.00. The owner knew right away the Chuski didn't know what he had and called the police. He had only been shown one piece by Chuski. We thanked him and left.

We made arrangements to pick up Chuski the first thing next morning. Lark and Peters left us on Market St. as they got on their bus and headed for home. Tom and I decided to have a good meal in North Beach and get a good nights sleep. The next day would be another long one.

We were at the Police Building at 8:00 AM. By nine, Lark and Peters had turned Chuski over to us. I presumed we would now pick up the jewelry. Wrong. They acted as if our business was concluded. They were escorting us toward the back door, where our car was parked. Puzzled, I asked,

"Hadn't we better go to the property room and pick up the evidence ?"

"Oh, have the insurance agent come and see us with a list of the missing property and we will release it to him."

It suddenly became very obvious what was happening. We had run into a City where recovery rewards were not only accepted but expected. After a few minutes of verbal sparring, I had to give them my word that I would refer the insurance adjuster directly to them. I explained to them we were not permitted to accept rewards and would not do so. They looked at me like I was lying but took my word anyway. I gave them Miles Reece' name and phone number. We finally left the building with our prisoner and the merchandise.

Once in the car and on our way, Tom and I both agreed that it would be a damned shame if we drove all the way back to Beverly Hills only to find that Chuski still had some loot stashed in San Francisco. I didn't want to have to call SFPD and have them go recover more jewelry then try to get it back. Less than half of the loot taken had been recovered with Chuski's arrest.

With Tom driving, and Chuski and I in the back seat, I decided that Chuski and I needed to have a very personal heart to heart talk. He still had not accepted the fact that he had pulled a hundred thousand dollar burglary. He couldn't explain why we would lie to him about it but he was sure we had some reason for trying to screw him. Prison mentality. It's tough to deal with sometimes. By the time we had reached Livermore I had exhausted all my nice guy approaches. Reason just did not register with him. He had acknowledged, not admitted, the burglary. But he just knew we were lying about the amount.

Just outside Livermore I asked Tom to find the next turn off up into the woods, which were about 300 yards from the highway. I had reached my limit of patience. I knew I certainly wasn't going to thump on this little man in any way, but I had to convince him I was not in the mood for any more delaying tactics. His internal amusement at dancing the cops around had to be brought to an end.

He started to ask nervously, "Why, why are you doing that ?" He'd started to fidget in the seat.

"What are you talking about? Why do you want to stop. What are you going to do?"

"Not a thing Edmund my boy, not a thing. It's just that you and I are going to have a complete meeting of the minds before we put another mile on this car. Can you imagine what kind of a laughing stock I would be if I got you all the way back to Beverly Hills and then found out that you had left some merchandise in San Francisco. Huh uh, I'm not about to be laughed out of the building. By the time we get back, I'm going to have the complete story about this burglary, where all the missing loot is, and all the help you can give us in finding it. Is that getting through to you?"

About that time, Tom was pulling off the highway and heading up a small dirt road to a patch of woods. Chuski was starting to get pale. We pulled off the road into a wide spot among the trees where Tom came to a stop. I got out of my side of the car and walked around to Chuski's side and opened his door. He didn't want to come out. I motioned for him to step out. Again he refused. I let out a deep sigh and reached into the car and put my hand on his shoulder.

"Wait a minute, wait a minute guys, lets talk", he said in a high squeaky voice. He slid to the center of the seat.

"I guess you're telling the truth about the amount of the job. I don't know why you would lie. It just startled me. I didn't think I had got anywhere near that amount. Come on guys, lets talk. You'll hear it all. Honest"

I sat on the seat beside him and for the next thirty minutes we heard him tell us all about his 'big score'.

He had only been out of prison for four weeks. Not on parole. He had done every day of his time. He was living in a fleabag motel on the lower end of Hollywood Blvd. when he was running out of money. With his last 35 cents he had boarded a bus on Sunset Blvd. and rode it as far as 35 cents would take him. Which happened to be Mountain and Sunset in Beverly Hills. He got off the bus at about 8:00 PM and wandered up to Doheny road looking for a place to make a score.

He walked until he noticed the house with a wall around it and a wrought iron gate. He figured it meant money. He climbed over the gate and walked up to the house. While he had paused on top of the gate he said a black and white police car drove by and didn't see him because he was so high up on the gate.

He looked in several windows and when he didn't see anyone, and found one window partially open, he decided to enter there. The window sill was too high for him to reach so he found a couple of rocks in the garden and put them under the window to help him get in.

I asked him why he didn't use the unlocked front door. He said he hadn't gone that far around the house.

He really thought he had screwed up when he knocked the trophies off the window sill. "They made a hell of a racket"

When nobody came he felt for sure there was no one home. I would tell him later about the three servants that were in the other part of the house.

He wandered through the house to the stairway and went upstairs. He felt he had died and gone to heaven when he saw all the jewelry around. There was so much of it though, that he knew it must be costume stuff. He hadn't brought anything to carry the stuff in so he took a pillowcase out of a closet and started to fill it up. He said he only took the stuff he thought was worth something. He didn't know why he took the emerald bracelet and didn't take the earrings and necklace.

While he was going from one room to the other he found the gym bag and put the pillowcase in it. He found the walkie talkie and thought it was a small radio, so he took it. When he was done upstairs he went downstairs and back out the same way he had gone in. When he got to the gate, he was so tired and weak he couldn't climb over. He laid down and slid under, almost losing his bag. He walked down to Santa Monica Blvd. and using part of a few dollars he found on one of the dressers, caught a bus back to Hollywood.

While he was on the bus and looking through his loot, he decided to sell the "radio" to a man on the bus for $12.00. He took a check. The check was still in his property. He had another check in his property. He said it was for a wrist watch he sold to a guy from Seattle. He had gotten thirty dollars. When he got back to his room he spent the rest of the night sorting the good stuff from what he considered costume jewelry. Needing money quick he took seven rings to the bar he frequented and sold them to the bartender for $70.00. The next morning he tied the rest of the jewelry into the pillowcase and dropped it in the garbage can on the corner in front of his motel. He used the rest of the money to get to San Francisco where he thought he could dispose of the property more easily.

I began to show him photos of the jewelry again. He identified the watch he had sold to the man on the bus. I turned the picture over and showed him the value. It was $1200.00. He was now beginning to realize just how much he had taken. He picked out four of the seven rings he sold to the bartender for $70.00. Value over $5000.00. He was really getting upset with himself now. He was becoming more and more talkative. We felt it was safe to get on the road again. In a few minutes we were at the speed limit moving east toward Tracy.

I asked him to try to remember if the garbage can he threw the pillowcase in was full or empty. It would help to figure out if there was any chance of finding that property.

After giving it some deep thought he said he felt it was empty. He seemed to remember the 'clunk' the bag made when it hit the bottom of the can.

If that was the case, we may still have a chance to find the can there and not emptied yet. It'd been less than a week since he dumped the stuff and the cans are usually emptied once a week. Tom must have figured the same thing because his foot went farther down on the gas pedal. It was a damned long shot. We couldn't call the office and have them look because Chuski couldn't remember the name of the motel or the cross streets.

In the long drive back Edmund told us his life story. Before he was 18 years old he had been arrested for petty theft and gone to the juvenile hall for three months. Just after his 18th birthday he was arrested during the commission of a liquor store burglary and was convicted and sentenced to State Prison.

Within a month after he got out, no parole, he was again arrested for a residential burglary and again went to prison. Three weeks after his next release, the same thing. He swore to us he had been arrested for every crime he had ever committed, and had gone to jail for each one. He didn't feel bad about going back to jail for this burglary because he was now convinced jail was where he was supposed to be. He just couldn't cope with being out.

By the time we had reached Bakersfield he had offered us a deal. He would waive preliminary hearing, plead guilty at his arraignment, and ask for immediate sentencing. In turn we would not tell anyone he had not known how much his burglary was worth. He said he would be the laughing stock of the joint if they knew how he had screwed up. Otherwise he would have some measure of reputation or position if they thought he had pulled such a big score.

He knew he was going to go back inside anyhow and he wanted to do it with a little stature. Hell, why not. The poor guy was a flat loser. He needed some measure of pride. The way he told his story, you just had to believe him.

On the outskirts of town he asked for one more favor. He said the one thing he missed most in the joint was a glass of beer. Could we please get him a bottle of beer before he was put back in a cell. Tom pulled into the next market parking lot and we bought him a six pack of half quart cans. He immediately became our friend for life.

He had finished the six pack by the time we had come down the hill into the San Fernando Valley. He had a large smile on his face and a slight glow on. For a man going to jail, he was quite happy.

It was past 7:00 PM when we finished locking him in his cell. He was still thanking us profusely for our understanding. We told him we would see him in the morning to start tracing the rings and the motel he had used. He couldn't assure us enough that he would help.

After we had checked in the evidence, Tom and I went out the back door still smiling and shaking our heads.

"We'll have to get on him first thing in the morning if we want to locate that motel and the other jewelry", I said.

"O.K.", Tom said, "you want me to come in early ?"

"No, just so we start right away. We may not have a snowballs chance in hell of finding that other stuff anyhow. If it was in the bottom of the can we stand a better chance. No trash man worth his salt would empty a can and not look into a pillowcase that was knotted up on the bottom. It just wouldn't happen. The problem then becomes getting them to admit it."

We parted and I caught my ride home. I just remembered, I forgot to let Diana know when I would be home, Well, if she hadn't eaten yet I'd treat her to dinner.

She hadn't, but we decided to stay home and cook some bacon and eggs while I told her about Mr. Chuski and our day. For a while she thought I was pulling her leg. It took a while for her to believe it. She had heard me relate many stories about suspects but never anything like this. She was still skeptical when we went to bed.

By 7:45 AM the next morning Tom and I had filled in Capt. Hankins and Lt. Cork on the previous two days activities. They too began shaking their heads when we described Chuski for them. They were quite a bit more skeptical when we laid out our plan for recovering the rest of the property.

We were underway by 8:15 AM, with Chuski having a big smile on his face. He didn't think he'd get to see the outside again for a long time. He was very grateful for any taste of freedom, and for being treated well. Why not. A little decent treatment might mean someones life down the line. A prison guard, a policeman, who knows.

Within an hour we had located the motel, and the bar. Both were like he had described. The first thing we checked out was the garbage can. Empty. Completely. It had to have been collected within the last twelve hours. A few phone calls later we are headed to the rubbish transfer station on Pico Blvd. Tom sat with Edmund while I went in to talk to the Supervisor.

He told me that the trash had been emptied this morning at the corner we were interested in and that the truck and the employees were returning from their dump run. I explained to him what had happened and asked him to impress on his employees that we would be most happy to retrieve the merchandise without further inconvenience to either to us, or especially them. I also explained that should search warrants and surveillances on each suspect be necessary, it would probably result in upsetting a lot of police officers as well as some City fathers.

On the otherhand, immediate cooperation could result in a couple of hundred dollars reward from the insurance company and no further questions asked. Questions like, "why didn't you turn in this property when you first found it?" and "how much other stuff have you found that you neglected to turn in?", and "how many of your buddies are doing the same thing ?" Little things like that.

I was assured that he would talk to his crew and inform them of my desire to help them out of any embarrassing situation and secure some compensation for their public spirited efforts. I gave him our office phone number telling him I expected to hear from him before noon. We left and headed for the bar on Hollywood Blvd.

It was a typical lower end of Hollywood Blvd. dive. We parked on the street near the back door of the place. Chuski and Tom would go in the front door to see if the right bartender was there. I would be coming in the rear door just in case the bartender recognized Chuski, and made Tom as a cop, and decided he wanted to be somewhere else.

As they came in the front door the bartender nodded to Chuski. Maybe he knew him, maybe he didn't. We met and sat at a booth near the back of the joint. Chuski said "that's him".

"O.K. Ed, I'll want you to say that again when he comes over", I tell him.

The bartender came around the end of the bar to take our order, and I nodded O.K. to Edmund.

"This is the guy I sold the rings to for $70.00." Edmund said with a note of pride in his voice.

"What the hell are you talking about?", the bartender said with just the right amount of indignation.

"Mr. bartender", I said, "just think about what you've heard while you're bringing us three beers. Just think about it. You know we're cops and he's in custody, so just think about it for a minute while you bring the beers."

He headed back for the bar with his head hanging just a little. He didn't look up as he got the beers and came back to the table.

As he was setting down the beers I asked him to sit down for a minute. There was no one else in the place.

"Look Mr. bartender, I don't even want to know your name. I merely want to explain to you the way things are going to be. First, there's no doubt he identified you as buying the rings. Second, if you force us into it, I will arrest you now and my partner will go and get a search warrant for your bar and your residence. I have no doubt we'll find something hot there even if we don't find the rings. It looks like we have your attention now.

However, should you chose to acknowledge your unthinking act, and decide now to go get the rings and return them to us, we would be disposed to walk out of here and forget we ever saw you or this place. How's that sound?"

He started to look like he was going to either deny it or protest his innocence. His mouth is about half open when I hold up my finger and say,

"Hold it. Don't say anything rash. We have a very full day today and don't have any arguing time. We've given you the only options. Don't blow it."

"I can't leave now", he said as the wind goes out of him.

"Where do you have to go ?" Tom asked.

"My apartment is just down the block."

"Be gone my friend. We'll be happy to look after your premises while you're gone. I've done a little bartending in my time, and I don't tap the till." I told him jovially.

He's still trying to find some way to protest as he went out the door. I didn't have any work to do while he was gone. The place just didn't seem to be that popular.

Chuski genuinely enjoyed himself with the conversation that went on. He also enjoyed the beer he had. He couldn't stop thanking us for it. He said he didn't know cops could be nice guys. How about that.

The bartender returned in about 10 minutes. He had a wadded up handkerchief in his hand that he put on the table. As Tom opened it we saw seven beautiful rings. The bartender said, "My girlfriend is really pissed off, I had given her that one ring. She didn't want to give it back. I told her it was that or go to jail. She gave it to me." He seemed to be breathing easier.

"Is that all you want from me", he said as he got up.

"No," I say, "You can bring us one more round before we go."

When I had said no, you could see his back stiffen. It relaxed when I asked for the beer. Chuski brightened up when I placed the order. We drank up quickly and left. After paying for the drinks. The bartender had offered them on the house but we insisted we pay. He'd already lost $70.00, no sense rubbing it in.

When we got back to the station there was a phone call from the garbage supervisor. One of his crew wanted to talk to us. He would be at the office waiting for us. We put Chuski away and left immediately.

At the transfer station there was an older gentleman waiting for us. He didn't look like he felt well. The supervisor introduced us and said we could use his office. The gentleman started immediately to tell us he had not intended to steal anything. He thought the stuff in the bag was costume jewelry and he was going to give it to his nieces to play with. He would be glad to take us to the house and get it for us.

I ask him how it had gotten to his house so fast and he said he had dropped it off on the way to the dump site. We went to his house right away. He went to a closet just off the dining room and reached up on a shelf. He brought down a monogrammed, knotted pillowcase and put it on the table. When I opened it, it contained a large amount of jewelry. It looked like the Washington stuff. He brought a Zippo cigarette lighter out of his pocket and handed it to me saying, "Here, this was in there too."

I thanked him for his cooperation and explained to him that I would inform the insurance company of his cooperation and see if they could compensate him in some way. He seemed both relieved and pleased. We left him there and headed back to the office. Tom and I were smiling all the way. We both kept saying things like: "Do you know how unlikely that is, to find that stuff after it hit the trash cans?", and "What are the odds that we'd even find the right trash crew ?"

We were still laughing and smiling when we got back to the office. We went into Hankins office and emptied the bag on his desk. He could only say how lucky we were. Hell, we knew that.

There was just enough time to go to Santa Monica and get the complaint against Chuski. He could be arraigned tomorrow and be on his way to State Prison by Thursday. By the time we had explained the case to Chuck Weedman at the D.A.s office and gotten the complaint, it was time to go home. Chuski would be on his way tomorrow.

First thing next morning Chuski waived preliminary hearing and requested arraignment in Superior Court where he was to plead guilty. The judge questioned him to be sure he knew what he was doing, then bound him over to Superior Court. Fifteen minutes after getting the paper work from the court clerk, we were on our way to Superior Court. On our way to Santa Monica we stopped at a liquor store and Tom went in and got Chuski a quart of beer. He had a smile on his face all the way to court, even when the bottle was stuck in his mouth.

By 2:00 PM Chuski had been sentenced to State Prison for the term prescribed by law and was waiting for his transportation. He couldn't thank us enough. Here is a man going to prison for umpteen years and he's thanking the cops that put him there.

When we got back to the office Miles was sitting in Capt. Hankins office. He was very friendly and very effusive with his complements about the manner in which the case was handled. Nowhere during the conversation did we hear anything about his theories. I told him we still had a couple of pieces to try and get back but we had everything but the radio and a watch. Total value of the recovery, $104,000.

He continued to complement us on our work. I then brought up the subject of a small stipend for the rubbish collector. He immediately started to vacillate. He was hard to convince. He finally capitulated when he realized that the man had turned over about $50.000 worth of merchandise which we may not have gotten otherwise. He wasn't happy about it but he finally agreed to pay the man $300.00. The last of the big spenders and willing givers.

Tom and I ran down the guy who bought the radio and got that back. I had written Seattle P.D. and requested they contact the man who had bought the watch. After all, we had his check. They responded that he denied everything and there was nothing they could do. I wrote again, including a copy of the check, and their reply was the same.

By now I was getting upset. I secured his unlisted phone number from his bank and called him at home. He was irate. He wanted to know why he was still being bothered about the watch. He had turned it over to the first officers that contacted him and didn't want to be bothered anymore. I offered my apologies and called the original officers. They denied it and called him a liar.

I was at an impasse. Capt. Hankins suggested I talk it over with the Chief.

He suggested I prepare a letter for his signature to the Seattle Chief of Police and outline the matter and request his cooperation. This was done the next day and submitted to his office for signature and mailing.

I received no further word on the situation.

Aside from the watch, the only other thing we didn't get back was the gym bag. That watch still sticks in my craw.

CHAPTER 32

That vacation had been one of the better ones, even though it was almost over. We liked taking them early in May in order to avoid the summer rush as well as the summer raise in motel rates. We'd followed our usual pattern that year except that we'd added a new wrinkle. We were bringing Dianas' mother back with us from Seattle. We didn't have to do much convincing. She couldn't pass up the chance to be with our year old daughter, Linda.

We were on our way back to Beverly Hills now, our usual way, through South Lake Tahoe. Grandma was going to stay with Linda, while Mom and Pop went to the "Top of the Wheel" at Harvey's for a nice leisurely dinner and a quiet evening listening to some jazz at the piano bar. A few more days and the opportunity would be gone. That was Tuesday and I had to be in court the next Monday. A couple of days here and back to the grindstone. I had to admit though, I was still anxious to get back. I usually was.

That year though, I'd made a concession to my vacation. It was the first year that I hadn't brought along my collection of mug shots and case notes. I had made myself a pocket folder, like a wallet, in which I carried a wide variety of mug shots of active crooks as well as many case notes. Diana had asked me for some time to try to leave these things at home for once. This time I had. I felt naked at first but I got used to it. It was feeling pretty good.

We were just getting off the elevator from the "Top of the Wheel" and started toward the bar at the south end of the casino. I was holding Diana by the left elbow with my right hand when I saw him. I must have squeezed her arm with a lot of force because she let out a small yelp. I let go right away but never took my eyes off him.

"What's going on ? Who'd you see ?" she asked. We continued toward the bar but I was still looking back.

"Mike Blaustein just came in. He's sitting down at the five dollar blackjack table." I answered.

"Are you sure ?"

"Of course I'm sure. He's sitting right there. See him?"

She looked at where I had indicated and said, "That sure looks like him. What are you going to do ?" She had looked at my mug shot file so often she could recognize my suspects as well as I could.

"You just keep your eye on him while I get the hotel security and talk it over with them." I was gone before she could answer. I had seated her on a stool at the bar. She could see the whole Casino without seeming to be looking at anyone in particular. She was having a ball. She liked this work as much as I did. I headed for a security officer near the blackjack tables.

Close to a year ago Michael Blaustein had been arrested by Lt. Cork after a number of burglaries in several apartment houses. I don't remember exactly why, but I was not directly involved in his arrest even though my assignment was burglary. In any case Blaustein had been very active and after some excellent investigative work, Cork was able to locate his property stash and recover a large amount of property.

Blaustein had a good lawyer, Harry Weiss, who got him out on bail. Come time for his court appearance he was a no show.

A warrant was issued for his arrest and a couple of other jurisdictions were able to file complaints against him because of property recovered. His mere existence became a thorn in our side as well as other departments in the area.

He had been employed as a carpet cleaner and carpet layer before his latest arrest and it was presumed he would still be in that business. It gave him a good excuse for being around apartments, and offered him an excellent chance to case any apartment or house he was working in.

Although we had been very interested in locating him, we had to move on to other cases. He was always in the back of our minds as a sore spot, like an itch you can't scratch.

In the ensuing months we got word from some other departments that they were getting hit with his type of burglary. On one case in Pasadena a lady identified a mug shot of him as having been one of the workmen who had cleaned her carpets. She was later burglarized. We knew he was still operating but couldn't locate him. We had gotten word from the FBI and other agencies that he had left the country and gone to Canada, Israel, and Mexico.

He had claimed, when he was arrested, to have been a Hungarian Freedom Fighter and had been driven from his country by the Russians. Our investigation indicated he was just another damned burglar, with an accent.

His name became the needle we used to punch a hole in each other's balloon when we felt someone was getting too cockey. This went on for months. Finally we relegated him to the back burner. There were too many others to take stage front in our daily endeavors.

The Friday before I was to leave on my vacation, for some reason or other, Blaustein's name came up again. We had been good naturedly picking at each other about many things and his name came up. Just before I left the office I made the final stab. "Since you guys can't find him, I'll just have to bust his ass while I'm on vacation." I heard the cat calls all the way out the door.

Now here I was, 400 plus miles from home, and looking at Blaustein at the blackjack table. Now what are the odds of that. No one was going to believe it.

With my eyes still on Blaustein I had approached the security guard. I introduced myself and presented my badge and credentials. After quickly explaining the story of Blaustein the guard asked his partner to call the Douglas County Sheriff's Department for a deputy.

Deputy Sheriff Paul Delorey arrived shortly and I went over it again with him. Apparently I convinced him I knew what I was talking about because he and I, and the security guard approached Blaustein and asked him to accompany us to the office for a talk.

He agreed, with an innocent, questioning look. He was good. Not a flutter.

On the way to the office I asked him if he recognized me.

He looked right at me for the first time and there was a very slight spark of recognition in his eyes before he shook his head and said, "No, should I ?"

"Gosh my feelings are hurt now, Mike. I was one of the guys who took you to court in Beverly Hills the last time."

"I don't know what you're talking about. My name is Jerry and I've never been in Beverly Hills."

Once in the office he presented identification in the name of Jerry Brigandi. A drivers license less than a year old, and some miscellaneous identification. Also in his pocket was a pair of General Motors car keys. Although his story was pretty good, it had a few weak spots. Enough to cast a little doubt about my identification in the eyes of Paul Delorey. But only a little. Blaustein kept insisting he was Jerry Brigandi. I kept insisting he wasn't. It was decided we would go to the Zypher Cove sub-station and continue the inquiry.

On the way out the door Diana spotted me and waved indicating she would take the car and go to the motel. I waved back and nodded.

Once at the sub-station I met Sgt. Ralph Lovecchio and convinced him I knew what I was talking about. By that time I was beginning to feel a little crack in my own resolve that this was Blaustein. My God, what if it wasn't? Nah, no way.

We both took on Blaustein who kept insisting we had made a big mistake.

While all this was going on I placed a call to Pete Meaney of the FBI and asked that they place their Unlawful Flight warrant against Brigandi. Pete told me it hadn't worked it's way though the U.S. Attorney's Office yet. I called the Beverly Hills Police Department and told them I had arrested Blaustein at Tahoe and needed them to get a copy of Blausteins fingerprints and take them to the L.A. Airport and give them to the pilot of the first plane to

Reno. I would make arrangements to have them picked up and brought to Tahoe for positive identification.

They didn't believe me. It took a while to convince them I wasn't joking and Lt. Bob Bowers finally said they would do it. I must have convinced him. I called Cork at home and filled him in. He wasn't in the mood, at 2:30 AM, for any more jokes. Especially after my smart-assed parting remarks. It took a while to convince him I was serious. He said he would get to the office and take care of everything at his end.

Ralph, Paul and I were still working on Brigandi. His story got more and more holes in it but no matter how absurd it became, he wouldn't admit who he actually was. Or at least who I thought he was. In about an hour Cork called me and told me the prints were on a Western Airlines flight to Reno and would arrive in about two hours. He was on his way into the office and would wait there for my call.

Ralph made arrangements for the Douglas County fingerprint expert to pick up the prints and bring them to Zephyr Cove. Brigandi kept claiming he was Italian. Ralph then asked him to pronounce his name in Italian. He failed miserably. No one needed any more convincing.

We placed Brigandi in a cell while we waited for the fingerprints. We removed everything from his pockets, and found no car keys. He denied ever having a car. Even if I weren't a cop, I'd start to get suspicious now. We just couldn't find those keys. Which taught me another lesson. You never quit learning in this job.

We didn't have to long to wait. Just before daybreak the fingerprint man from Carson City arrived with the prints from the plane. He rolled Brigandi's prints and was sitting down to compare them.

Brigandi, still wiping the ink from his fingers, stepped to the table and said, "You don't have to bother, you got me. I'm Michael Blaustein. I thought you guys would give up before now."

I didn't know which one of us wanted to pop him in the mouth the most. The fingerprint man who got up in the middle of the night or Delorey or Lavecchio who were supposed to get off at midnight. Or me, who knew all along I was right and this jackass wasted all our time. The hotel security people called and told me that my wife had gone on back to the motel. What a night. And it wasn't over yet.

I called Cork right away and filled him in. He said he'd standby to see what else Blaustein would say.

We got back to questioning him and now he wanted to make a phone call. Supposedly to talk to his attorney, Harry Weiss. We set him up in a private room with a window in the door, and a telephone. While he was preparing to make his call, Ralph contacted the local operator, all long distance calls had to go through the operator, and advised her that we wanted to know what phone number he gave her to call. Once the call was connected he spoke only Hungarian. He certainly wasn't talking to Harry Weiss.

When the call was completed, I talked to the operator and got the telephone number he had called. I called Cork and gave him the number. We went back to talking to Blaustein, trying to locate the car. He maintained his denial about the car. We put him back in his cell and went to breakfast.

An hour or so later Cork called and told me he had located the address of the phone number and had talked to the man. He admitted Blaustein had called and given him several instructions. One being to go to Tahoe and retrieve his green Cadillac from the Harvey's parking lot and take it to his house. He had the license number. Ralph and I went to the lot and found the car in a few minutes. Not having any keys, we had it towed to the Sheriff's sub-station. We showed Blaustein the car and asked him for the keys, again. He finally took off his sock and removed the keys from the bottom of his foot. We opened the car and found several thousand dollars worth of jewelry and furs in the trunk.

Lesson one zillion: When you strip search a man, strip him all the way. I knew that. Why did I have to relearn it. In the meantime, two warrants had been teletyped to the Sheriff's office for holds on Blaustein. At 9:30 AM we went to the local Justice Court for a bail hearing. When the story was explained to the judge he inquired whether Blaustein would waive extradition. Mike seemed hesitant.

The judge then told him that the cell he had been using would be his permanent abode until the extradition hearing was held if he didn't want to waive. Mike agreed to waive extradition and signed it immediately.

By 11:30 AM Cork and Jack Mourning were on an airplane to the Lake Tahoe Airport to pick him up. I picked them up and took them to the Sheriff's Office where they arranged to take Blaustein back the next day. We had dinner at the "Top of the Wheel" that night. I started to get a full ration of razzing at that point. It was just too much coincidence that I had made my departing comment and then just "happened" to run into Mike. I wasn't sure they were ribbing me after a while. They sure sounded serious.

They were on their way back the next morning. Diana, her mom, Linda and I were planning to stay an extra night seeing as how we lost one whole day. Wrong. Cork called when he got back and told me I had to be in court on Friday to testify to the arrest of Blaustein. We packed and started home the next morning.

Diana in her usual resolute style took it in stride. Not a whimper, complaint or gripe. How did I get so lucky?

I took a real razzing when I walked into the office on Friday morning. No one would believe that I had accidently stumbled across Blaustein. They accused me of having gotten information that he would be there and I arranged to stop there by "accident". I think some people still believe that.

While I was walking to the courtroom I encountered the Chief returning to his office. His comment was, "About time you were doing some police work." A real Prince, that man.

I never did get my two days vacation back. And I paid the $16.00 telephone bill out of my pocket.

The last I heard of Blaustein he was headed for prison for "the term prescribed by law".

Whatever they want to believe, it was a great way to wind up a vacation.

CHAPTER 33

When I had returned from court I found the office empty. Unusual for that time of day. I went to the dispatcher and found out that a fur store robbery had taken place at Dutchess Furs, about a half hour before, and one of the customers had been shot.

It's not standard practice for us to have an armed robbery in town let alone someone getting shot. Since all our detectives were already on scene I decided to wait in the office and field any phone calls. A short time later Lt. Cork and Merv Pederson come back into the office, followed soon by Capt. Hankins. Cork and Pederson would be handling the investigation. The customer had been wounded in the thigh. The robbers had made away with a large number of mink stoles and full length mink coats.

The pressure was on from the start. An armed robbery is bad enough, but a shooting along with it, the heat was really on. We were all on the phones to every source we could think of. All the contacts in other departments were tapped. The first day seemed like we were going to run into a stone wall. On the second day, one of our associates in an L.A. Robbery Division contacted Cork and told him about some information he had received.

His informant told him a Joe Duchi and a guy nicknamed "Baldy" had pulled the robbery. He told Cork where Duchi could be found. Cork and Pederson left to join the L.A. officers and returned in a couple of hours with Joe Duchi in custody. It didn't seem to take long for them to break Duchi's story, and have him tell them all about the robbery. As usual, it's always the other guy who did the shooting. Joe apparently was cooperating but he swore he didn't know where "Baldy" lived.

The next day, the pressure was still on to find "Baldy", and get the property back. We were all scooping up the usual suspects and squeezing them. The same with other departments. Finally, on the evening of the second day Joe thought he may be able to point out the general area where "Baldy" lived. By that time only Cork, Mourning and I were left in the office. After all it was only six thirty. We decided that Cork would stay in the office to cover any calls we had to make from the field, and Mourning and I would drive Joe around and try to locate "Baldy's" pad.

We drove him around a formerly upper class neighborhood in the Westlake district for a couple of hours without results. He pointed out a couple of lookalike buildings but they didn't pan out. We had been on the phone with Cork several times to keep him up to date on our search. As we were giving up and heading for home, we got a radio call from Cork asking us to call him by phone. Our radio communication left much to be desired. Being a small town in area, we didn't really project a need for a radio repeater station. Therefore our radio range was pretty limited. Depending on the line of sight we could have good communication in some areas at some distance from our town and very poor in others.

On the phone, Cork told us he had just hung up from an anonymous call telling him that the stolen furs were located at the rear of a car wash on the corner of Highpoint and Pico. That was it. In less than a minute, Mourning and I were on our way. Once we got there we found a pretty deserted area. There was unusually little traffic on Pico for this hour, about 10:00 pm. Just to be sure, we cruised around the intersection for a couple of minutes. We stopped on the south side of Pico and staked out the station for a few minutes. This place was ripe for an ambush of some kind. It was enough to make your skin crawl.

The car wash took up the whole block on the north side of Pico. A couple of streetlights lit up the front of the place but there was no light on the alley side, which ran the entire length of the car wash on the back side. The rear seemed unusually dark, or at least it felt that way. I was starting to get the creepy crawlys up my back. Nothing to do but check it out.

We parked on Highpoint north of Pico and just south of the alley. Jack would stay with the car and our prisoner while I went to the back of the car wash to take a look. I took my flashlight and kept to the shadows. When I got next to the building I drew my gun. I got halfway down the wall of the building when I noticed a dark mass laying up against the building. At first I thought it was a body. I shined my light on the mass quickly and saw that it was a long blue bag, used to haul furs from one place to another. It was like a long duffle bag, with a long zipper on one side. I had turned the light off right away in case anyone may be watching the bag. I opened the zipper and felt inside. Furs. Many of them.

Now what was I going to do? It was a big bag and full of furs. I gave it a lift and found out is was very heavy. But I couldn't walk away and leave them while I went for the car. Now that we had found the furs I was not about to leave them unattended. I shoved my flashlight in my belt and holstered my gun. I found what was about the center of the bag and hoisted it up to my shoulder. It was clumsey and heavy.

As I started back to the car, I looked west in the alley and saw what looked like two people climbing over a wall at the next street, one block farther west. One was boosting the other up the wall. I didn't believe it for a few seconds. I quickened my pace and got to the car and dumped my load at the back.

Jack got out of the car with the keys and opened the trunk. We both were jabbering about the furs and our good fortune. I tried to tell him what I had seen and he thought I was trying to be funny. We closed the trunk after barely getting the bag inside. As he started around the side of the car I took him by the arm and said,

"Look Jack, dammit, I'm not kidding. There are two burglars getting into the back of that building on the next corner. Let's try to get our office on the radio and call for some L.A. units. We are in L.A."

We got the car started and tried to radio our office. Radio communications were bad at best. After a couple of tries, we moved our location about a half block and could barely receive our dispatcher. Another half block and we got our message through. We then pulled the car into the end of the alley, handcuffed Joe to the doorframe of the car, and crept toward the back of the building where the suspects had climbed over the fence. We wanted to keep the place under surveillance until the L.A. cars arrived.

Apparently we had not been as quiet as we thought. As we got close to Pointview St. and the alleyway we heard a lot of noise coming from the street side of the building. Jack had been about 10 feet ahead of me, and was right at the corner of the building. He stepped to his right away from the building and raised his gun arm. He shouted "stop, police". A split second later I heard a gun shot. Jack leveled his gun and fired two shots. I heard another shot and Jack was again moving slightly to his right. I had reached the corner at that time and saw one suspect running from my left to my right across the alley entrance. At that same instant Jack went down, hard.

My only thought was "that son of a bitch shot him". I raised my gun and fired two shots as the suspect crossed the alley, heading north. Damn, missed. As I moved to Jack I caught sight of another subject running south along the west side of the building, toward Pico.

As I got next to Jack he was starting to get up.

"Where are you hit ?" I asked him.

"I'm not hit, damn it, I slipped on that gravel."

With that, I ran back to the car and broadcast to our office for immediate assistance, shots fired. We had finally gotten to a good location because our dispatcher acknowledged right away. A few seconds later I heard sirens start to wind up a few blocks away. Within seconds we were surrounded by L.A. units. We give them a description of our two suspects and they fanned out in the area.

While they are searching, their patrol sergeant decided that we hadn't played the game according to his rules. He began to read us chapter and verse about jurisdictions, cooperation, etc. He was starting to get irritating. We had just been shot at and had done some shooting. We didn't need a lecture. We had tried to follow procedure but the crooks changed the rules on us. He kept it up.

During this harangue, one of the patrol cars pulled up with a man in the back seat. The driver came to us as his partner turned on the rear seat light. They had captured one of our suspects. We I.D. him and they departed for the station. He didn't have the gun.

I hadn't noticed, but Sgt. Howard, one of our close friends from Wilshire Division Detectives had shown up at the scene. He was working nights. The patrol sergeant started in again.

"Hold it Sergeant", Howard said, "I know these guys. They wouldn't pull anything to cause any problems between departments. Besides, they stopped a damned burglary for you and even helped you capture the suspect. That's enough of your bullshit." He took Jack and I by the arm and lead us toward our car.

"You know Howard, we did try to stay out of it but I guess the burglars spotted us and took off."

"Don't worry about it. That sergeant is an asshole anyhow. He thinks he wants to get into the detective bureau but he isn't going to make it. Take your prisoner and go on, I'll take care of it here. Thanks guys. See ya."

We were unhooking Joe from the window frame as Howard left. When we got into the car and started out Joe remarked,

"Jeez, this cops and robbers shit is great. That's what I should have been, a cop."

Mourning and I about split a gut. It took about 10 minutes to get to our office. Cork met us on the ramp and helped get the furs and Joe up to the jail floor. After Joe was put away we got the furs out and checked them against the list of stolen ones. They were all there. Whoever had them had decided they were just to hot to handle.

Baldy was picked up a few days later and the case was wrapped up. While we were all sitting around discussing the case, we also suggested that Jack quit wearing those damned leather heeled shoes.

That wasn't the first time they had caused him to fall on his ass, and you could hear him coming for a block.

Just a few weeks later Jack and I were in the office when the department got a silent alarm bank robbery call. We both took off for the cars on a dead run. When we got to the parking ramp I ran to the drivers side and Jack went straight ahead to the passengers door. As he tried to slow down to grab the door handle his leather heels and soles started to slide and he went on his tail again. I knew better than say anything. He was not a happy camper. But, the last I heard, he was still wearing leather soles and heels.

CHAPTER 34

It had been quiet enough that previous week to consider getting our surveillance group at it again. The same group that most of Central Burglary and several other Divisions virtually laughed out of the building when we suggested the concept.

"Takes too much time", "Waste of manpower", "Can't you guys find something productive to do?" A few of the more repeatable comments we took when we first got started.

After our first two unqualified successes the comments were sticking in some peoples throats. Chief of Detectives Thad Brown was extolling the virtues of our operation to anyone that would listen. He's even suggesting that some of the other divisions follow our lead. And, rubbing salt in the wound, suggested that they go along with us to see how it was done.

Thad Brown was known world wide as a "cop's cop". He knew what it was like to work the streets and backed his detectives, "til their chests caved in". Not really. He was no one to try to put anything over on. He had been there and done that. He respected initiative and a job well done. He had even been on the other end, as a victim. His gun collection had been stolen from his house during a burglary. One of our Beverly Hills detectives had gotten information that helped him recover his collection. He was pleasantly disposed toward Beverly Hills. He liked our surveillance operation and it showed.

We did our very best not to let our pride show.

This time we had convened at the request of Hollywood Division. They had reliable information that a residential burglar was very active in the Hollywood hills. It was certain that they were getting the hell beat out of them on daytime burglaries in that area. It was a tough place to expect anyone to see what was going on around them. Houses set back in the brush, or above or below the roadway. Many cars parked on the narrow streets. Neighbors didn't know each other so they couldn't tell who was supposed to be there and who was not.

Our group had talked it over and decided we really wanted to do this one if only to validate our theory. Hence, we were at Hollywood Division getting a briefing from the Detectives handling this particular case, Robinson and Reed.

Our suspect was Jimmy Swan. He had a history for burglary and armed robbery, and was known to carry a weapon on some of his jobs. We were given his picture, his address, his vehicle description, and our discretion on how to handle him.

The other information indicated he was in his late twenties, didn't work anywhere, was popular with the Hollywood girls, and spent way to much money.

When we hit the street there were five cars of us. Frank and Andy in one car, two Intelligence Division cars, One Hollywood car, all from L.A., and me in my Beverly Hills car. In a few minutes we were all in position and staked out around a large, very nice, apartment house on Franklin at the corner of Gardener. It was a four story building with a semi-subterranean garage. The garage itself had about two feet of open space between the garage walls and the lower part of the building itself. From anywhere in the garage you could see the street around the place.

One of our group had made a quick trip through the garage to verify that the suspect vehicle was still there. It was. Then to settle back and wait. Also begin the "what if" games again. Your head's on a swivel, your eyes are constantly moving, but you still have time to play "what if".

After a couple of hours of waiting, our guy was on the move. Just when everyone had to go to the bathroom. It never fails. Now we hope he heads for the hills and not downtown. He headed straight for the restaurant on Hollywood and Curson.

He parked, went inside and sat at the counter. Very generous of him. Maybe we could all parade through the place and go to the bathroom. And that's what it looked like, a parade. He couldn't have missed us if he had been paying any attention. Makes you realize he was to damned sure of himself. We'd have to drop sand in his crankcase on that one. No way any burglar should be so damned sure of himself that he doesn't look over his shoulder frequently. There are too many victims out there, and too damned many parasites making them that way.

He had his breakfast and we had our pit stop so it was time to move on. He was out of the restaurant and standing near his car with a cigarette in his mouth. In a couple of minutes a girl wearing a waitres's uniform came out the back door of the restaurant and got in the car with him. Hell, it looked like romance time.

They took off out the rear of the lot and drove right to his apartment house where she got out of the car and went into the building. He drove to the Hollywood hills and started slowly cruising. Because of the narrow and short streets we had to stay back quite a ways to avoid running over him. We decided to leapfrog from one intersection to another, looking down the side streets, to keep him in sight.

After a half hour of this, he seemed to have roosted somewhere. We sent our female unit down the street we last saw him. Halfway down the street they spotted his empty car parked in a carport. If he was burglarizing that place he's got a lot of balls. One of our group got out of their car and walked to the next street above the cars location. He got there in time to see Swan putting an armload of property in the back of his convertible. A few seconds later he was on his way again.

Expecting him to head back to his pad, one of our units headed directly there to set up in the basement. Instead, he started to cruise the streets again. We started our leapfrog operation again. In a few minutes he'd found another victim.

No wonder Hollywood had been catching hell. He was a one man crime wave if he hit that often. This time one of our units could see the car. Our man Swan made two trips to the car then got in and drove away. This time it was my turn to make it back to the garage and wait for him.

Apparently he was satisfied with his score now. He was heading back to the apartment house. By this time I'd made it into the garage, parked, and gotten my shotgun out of the trunk. Swan was about two blocks away when Frank whipped into the garage rapidly and parked close to the elevator. A few seconds later our pigeon pulled into the garage and stopped in front of the elevator. He propped open the elevator door, and with his drivers door open he started loading property into the elevator. He loaded about half the car into the elevator, closed the car door and took the elevator up.

He stopped on the third floor and made three quick trips to his apartment. He was coming back down in the elevator when Frank, Andy and I moved in on each side of the car and elevator. Swan propped the door open again and opened the car door. Just as he reached into the car we all stepped from our places of concealment and the most deafening sound in the world was heard. Frank and Andy cocked their revolvers and I jacked a shotgun round into the chamber. In that concrete walled garage, those three simultaneous actions sounded like a bomb going off. I knew it was happening and even I got a shiver up my spine.

Swan had fallen or jumped across the front seat and was opening the glove box. Frank grabbed him by the back of his shirt and dragged him from the car. I reached into the glovebox and removed the Colt .38 caliber revolver that was in there.

"Hell Bob, we should have waited a couple of seconds longer," Frank says, "we could have saved the county a lot of money in court costs".

We closed the car door and all loaded onto the elevator. A couple of the others had joined us by this time. Swan was against the back wall of the elevator when Robinson got on the elevator and noticed the large wet area on the front of Swans' trousers.

"Must have been one hell of a party down here. Those shotguns have a way of scaring the piss out of the best of burglars", he said with no effort to hide the amusement in his voice.

Swan's face was red and he was getting very annoyed. He would like to think he had the guts to try to take any one of us on but even he had better sense. The ride was over and we all got off on the third floor.

Gusty Regan and her partner had gone up the stairs when the arrest started and were now waiting in the apartment. The girlfriend was seated on the couch and the first load of loot Swan had brought up was laying in the middle of the floor. As an act of compassion, just to show what nice guys we were, we dug out a pair of pants and shorts for Swan to put on. The girls had a tough time holding their snickers.

It took a couple of hours to search the apartment and secure the property in the car and apartment. Some had been identified as stolen in other Hollywood burglaries. At least two other burglaries were immediately identified from property recovered in the apartment. Robinson and Reed were pleased. So were we. Less than a full day on this one. We thought people would be happy that it was working out. We were wrong.

It seemed we were unintentionally embarrassing some people. Where did a pick up bunch of detectives get off thumbing their noses at established practice and policy. We certainly didn't think we were showing off. We were just happy we had found something that worked. At least for a while. Who knows, it may fall apart at anytime. That didn't matter. We had ruffled some feathers. Not big feathers, but noisy ones.

By the time I got all the information I needed for my absentee arrest reports it was nearly dinner time. I went back to my office and filed the activity report for our surveillance group. Frank was still keeping Thad Brown advised of our activities with these reports. My activity log was starting to get pretty thick.

The next two days were spent identifying property and talking to Swan. He cleared up numerous burglaries for Hollywood and North Hollywood but none for Beverly Hills or West L.A. There was some hint he was not happy with Frank or I because of the elevator episode and would not cop out to any of our crimes. We found none of our property in the recovered merchandise, and his method of operation didn't really fit any of our stuff anyhow.

He was out of business and on his way to the joint. His girlfriend was kicked loose because we really had nothing on her. He was charged with six counts and he pled guilty to the two we had watched him commit. Go straight to State Prison for the term prescribed by law.

Our surveillance team was now fielding requests for assistance from several different divisions. Our reputation was going to kill us if we weren't careful. We had to get together and work out some guidelines. It's always something.

There had been no formality in our operation. We made our rules as we went along. Now we had to start putting limits on who, what, and where we did what we did. As some in the group started to say "we've created our own monster . . . .and we love it."

During these weeks Lt. Phillips at L.A. Intelligence introduced us to a newly promoted Lieutenant who had just been assigned to the Intelligence Division. His name was Daryl Gates and was said to be a rising young star for the Department. He had been briefed on our surveillance operation and was reported to be very favorably impressed with it. We were to find out later that he was so impressed with it that he proposed the establishment of a permanent unit to conduct such surveillances. We also were to find out that our own Sgt. Frank Gravante had been asked to transfer downtown and head up the formation of the unit. To our great relief he turned it down.

Over the next few months a surveillance unit was formed and became a permanent part of the department. While the unit was in its infancy it experienced great success and was greatly hailed. As with many effective operations it began to draw criticism because of its effectiveness. Mostly from the bums and their attorneys who were being stifled in their pursuits.

As is often the case, these misunderstood miscreants, were convincing some well meaning and not so well meaning do-gooders that the activities of the surveillance unit were invading their privacy and entraping them when they were committing their crimes.

They were being taken unfair advantage of. I have never been able to figure out why they would complain about someone following them if they were not going to commit any crime. In any event the criticism of the SIU continues to this day.

CHAPTER 35

I had just finished the final reports on the Swan surveillance and recovery for distribution to anyone who was interested when the Captain called. I walked across the hall into his office.

"Yes Captain, you wanted to see me ?"

"Yes Downey, if you're interested, we have a special job for tomorrow night. Tony Curtis and Janet Leigh are having their 10th wedding anniversary party at their house and have asked for two plain clothes officers for security. Would you be interested ?"

"Sure Captain. Since I worked that threat against her after that "Physco" movie, I haven't been back to the house. It might be interesting. What time is it, and who else is working it ?"

"Well, I thought maybe I'd work it with you. I haven't worked a special job for a long time. There's going to be a couple of hundred guests. It will be interesting to see who's there."

That was an answer that threw me. I knew the Captain was a little star struck but to work a special job party just seemed to be a little beneath a Captain of Detectives. I don't know why I felt that way, it just seemed a little out of the norm.

"Why don't you go up and talk to them this afternoon and get the details. You already know the house and grounds, just see if there is anything that may have changed. What special precautions they expect. You know the routine."

"O.K. Captain. I'll go, and let you know if there is anything unusual. I'll see if they have an extra guest list available. There will be a hell of a traffic jam up on that narrow street.

I parked in the Curtis' driveway about two PM. The door bell was answered by the same housekeeper I had met on my first visit. She recognized me and took me into the den. I was joined shortly by Tony Curtis. He was dressed casually, and well. He was anxious to get all the details straight and make sure nothing was left to chance. He supplied me with a guest list. Parking would be handled by a professional valet service.

We discussed the usual security desired at such an occasion and the things they didn't want to happen. Like people roaming through the upper floor of the house. There were ample accommodations in the lower portions of the house and most of their expensive paintings and art objects were displayed on or in the upper balcony, hallways, and sitting rooms. I made a few suggestions about moving some of the other valuables upstairs. He agreed.

The caterers were working in the side and backyards setting up the tents and tables and bars. Tony introduced me to the manager of the catering firm and left me to get what other information I needed from the caterer. His staff would consist of himself and 18 long time employees. No temporary help. There would be two tents, and a stage. His personnel would be briefed to notify us of anyone on the premises that didn't seem to belong there. It was after all, a big estate. The details seemed to have been covered.

When I got back to the office I filled in Capt Hankins. We would have to be there by 5:30 PM. The guests would start arriving at 7:00 PM. At least they were supposed to. It would be interesting to see who got there first. The same Watch Commander working tonight would be working tomorrow night. I briefed him on the party and the parking arrangements. He would expect some noise complaints. Probably not too many though. People in this area were pretty tolerant of their neighbors. A good many of them were in the entertainment industry and aware of the necessity to entertain ones contemporaries. It also didn't hurt to invite your neighbors.

"Pickfair" estate was right across the street. The home of Mary Pickford and Buddy Rogers. Fred Astaire was a half block down the hill. Etc, Etc. Nice neighborhood.

The next day Hankins and I cheated a little. We left the office at 5:00 pm in order to change clothes and clean up for the evening. It felt like we were playing hookey. We had a patrol car take us to the party to conserve parking spaces. They would need it.

We had enough time to see and become acquainted with the

valet staff, and the catering staff. The delivery people were coming and going and were hard to keep track of. I had to make several rounds of the interior of the house to be sure no workers got "lost". I missed the first arrivals because of this. It didn't make any difference, I didn't recognize them when Hankins pointed them out. Things started to get hectic about 7:30. Everyone must have decided that was the time to be fashionably late.

Ernie Kovac and his Rolls Royce arrived. The valet was very careful. Jack Lemmon and Felicia Farr arrived at about the same time as Shirley McClain. Sammy Davis Jr. brought a lot of life to the party. Rock Hudson came with Marilyn Maxwell. The conversation buzzed among the catering staff about who they would go home with. The entire evening was filled with luminaries, great and small. Once dinner was over the music and dancing started. And the drinking, for real.

Some of the guests drifted away fairly early, leaving the real party people. Sammy Davis joined the band on the drums, and sang a few songs. Great entertainer. Kovacs and his cigar were having fun. On one occasion he spilled a drink down the back of Shirley McClain, then picked up a bar towel, lifted the back of her dress and proceeded to try to towel her off. She deftly avoided most of this maneuver. He had given it a good try though.

The party settled into a mellow mood about midnight. The band was playing dance music and the temporary floor was pretty full. Little by little the party died. A peaceful death. The remarks of the people leaving indicated that everyone had had a good time. The caterers were cleaning up the food and drinks and we were on our way home by 2:00 AM.

It had been a good night for cops to practice their stock in trade, people watching. The night had passed without incident. But it was going to be a short night. The only blemish on the experience was that a few months later Janet and Tony separated and subsequently divorced. All is not what it appears in the film capital.

CHAPTER 36

For a while that morning we were tripping over each other in the office. Since lunch however, everyone seemed to be disappearing one by one. Capt. Hankins, Jack Egger and I were the only ones left in the office. With a day as pretty as that one you just wished you had a follow-up to do or an errand to run instead of paperwork.

Hankins must not have had much to do either because the phone only half rang before he picked it up. A very short time later Egger and I were on our way into the Chief's office. He had placed his order for a command performance through Captain Hankins. Hankins told us he didn't know what it was about. You could tell he was as curious as we were, but just as happy not to be going. We had to wait a couple of minutes at the Chief's door until he got off the phone. Just enough time to add more pressure. You never could tell what was on his mind. Jack and I had worked a couple of check cases together lately, maybe that was what it was about. Who knows? We'd find out pretty soon.

We heard a grunt after the sound of the phone hanging up. We had to assume he was calling us in.

You didn't have to stand at attention when you went into his office but you always felt like you should. You had to make a conscious effort not to.

He wasted no time on small talk.

"You two go up to the Beverly Hills Hotel and round up this guy Marshal Caifano. He's part of the mob out of Chicago and got to the hotel yesterday. Have a talk with him. Convince him we don't need his type in this town. Suggest to him if he must stay around, that the Ambassador or the Hollywood Roosevelt are comfortable and need the business."

That was it. No hesitation. He went right back to the paperwork on his desk. Jack and I took a quick look at each other and went back out the door.

"You think maybe we should get some more background on this guy before we jack him up by the short hairs ?" Jack asked as we got back into our office. We both had heard of Caifano and had mug shots of him in our gangster file. Jack dug out the picture as I called Lt. Phillips at L.A. Intelligence and filled him in while getting an update from him of Caifano's action. They hadn't known he was in town and thanked us for the call.

"We're on our way to the hotel and persuade him that he would be more comfortable at some hotel out of town."

"You're going to tell him what? Well, maybe in your town you can still get away with that. Let me know if it works." I can still hear him chuckling as he hung up the phone. I filled Jack in as we headed out the door.

Capt. Hankins stopped us and got his briefing. When we finished he looked uncomfortable. He headed back for his office slowly shaking his head. He would rather not have known.

In a few minutes we were parked at the front door of the "Pink Palace", the Beverly Hills Hotel. There always seemed to be room for a police car at the front of the place. And the doormen and valets always seemed to know which cars are police cars. So much for plain cars.

We checked at the desk for Caifano's room number and any messages or calls made from the room. Not surprising that he hadn't made any calls from the room. Those bums were getting smarter every day. We determined that he was not in his room so we started checking the various restaurants and bars in the place. Nothing. Well, it's waiting time again. Something we're not happy about but quite used to. God knows when he'll get back to the hotel.

Jack and I headed for the front entrance lobby when we both looked through the window to the right of the doorway. Coming up the walkway from the gardens to the right of the entrance was our man. Impeccably dressed and seemingly without a worry in the world. Who knows? Maybe he didn't have any. We intercepted him about 40 feet from the doorway. Jack stood to his right and I took up a spot slightly to his left.

He looked us right in the eye and knew without doubt that we were bad news. The hotel staff had silently disappeared from the front of the doorway.

"All right, what's wrong ?" he said with just a hint of irritation in his voice.

"Mr. Caifano, we're from the Beverly Hills Police Department and . . ." Jack is interrupted, rudely.

"Don't bother, I know you're cops, what the hell do you want?"

He was not being nice. Darn. You hate to start out that way. I looked at Jack and we both shook our heads and took a half step toward him. He leaned back slightly.

"You know Mr. Caifano," I said quietly, "it's hard to get angry with someone who's stupid. The last thing you need right now is for us to get pissed off."

"Suppose you just shut your mouth and listen to what we have to say, politely." Jack used his more conciliatory tone of voice. "We like for our visitors to be comfortable and we have decided that you would be much more comfortable in some other hotel."

"Yes, preferably out of town. Some place like the Hollywood Roosevelt or the Ambassador seeing as how you obviously like comfort." I added to Jack's invitation.

"You can't run me out of town. I haven't done anything."

"Who said we were running you out of town. We're interested in your comfort. So much so that we've informed the desk that you'd probably be checking out this afternoon. They'll have your bill ready. We hope you won't make it necessary to contact you again. Have we properly impressed you with our interest in your welfare ?"

"Yeah I get the picture. I'm still going to talk to an attorney about this." as he turned toward the door.

"You do that sir, if it'll make you feel better." we imparted as we headed for our car. The desk knew to call us if he had not left by six PM.

When we got back to the office the hotel had already left us a message that Caifano had requested his bill and a bellman to take his bag out. Now to wait for a call from the doorman to let us know what cab he had taken and to what hotel. An hour later he was ensconced in the Hollywood Roosevelt. We let L.A. Intelligence know that they had a visitor in their town. They thanked us. Oh Yeah. Sure.

We filled in the Captain who filled in the Chief. In another half hour our report was done and filed. Just another day in the big city. That's one of the things that make this job so great. You never, never, can anticipate what's going to happen at any given time.

Not too long after this incident, Lt. Phillips called to inform us that Marshal Caifano had been shotgunned to death in the driveway of his home in Chicago. To my knowledge no one has ever been charged with this execution. Not unusual.

For several weeks the activity around the Beverly Wilshire Pharmacy at night slacked off significantly.

The usual appearances of Mickey Cohen, Joe DeCarlo, Doc Stacher and Phil Packer and their entourages were noticable by their absences.

You began to wonder what went through their minds when one of their contemporaries was terminated like that. We had several known "associates" of organized crime living in town but most of them kept a very low profile and appeared to conduct their meetings and businesses out of town. You would still write down any license numbers you saw in their driveways or parked close but for the most part you had no overt problems from them.

It was the same with the hookers in town. The ones that lived there. As soon as we had gotten word someone was apparently active we would pay a them a call and extend an invitation to ply their trade elsewhere. It usually worked. We had some "weekend warriors" that would work some of the local bars on the weekends but they were few and far between.

Those that tried to work the hotels were short lived because the bellman or consierge would report them immediately. It cut into their operation too much. All in all it worked pretty well.

At one time the Chief said we had no active bookmakers in town. So it must have been true. The periodic reports we got must have been meant for L.A.

CHAPTER 37

Late one evening Howard called me to tell me that Sgt. Johnny Meyers, L.A. Sheriff's Office Safe Burglary detail had called him and was discussing a safe burglary that had occurred in our town recently. Meyers and his partner, Sully, had been working on an accomplished safe burglar named Rudy Privett, who they felt could very well be responsible. Johnny said they had a warrant for Rudy and had located a house for him in the Valley. They wanted to know if we would care to join them when they arrested him the next day. How could you refuse such an invitation ?

Bright and early the next morning we met John and Sully at a coffee shop in the valley. After a quick coffee and a short discussion of how we'd proceed, we headed for our cars. John would come with me and we would take the back of the house. Howard and Sully would take the front.

Just as we were about to get into the cars, John and Sully got into a tiff about whose turn it was to bring the guns. Being a greenhorn in that I had not worked much with them, I damn near believed them.

We got to our relative positions about eight a.m. John and I climbed over the rear fence and headed for the back door of the single story ranch style house. We were supposed to make our entry when we heard Sully and Howard hit the front door. The back of the house had a covered patio stretching to the right from an ell shaped kitchen extension. The kitchen door was to the left of the patio and had a nine paneled window in the upper part of the door. There was a sliding glass door to the right, on the patio, leading to the living room/den of the house. The drapes were open.

John and I had taken up positions at the back door just as the front door was being hit. John immediately raised his right foot and kicked the door just above the knob. His foot slipped and went through one of the panes of glass just next to the knob. There he was dancing on his left leg, with his gun raised in the air, and with his right leg thrust up to his calf into the kitchen.

I was trying to reach in through the broken window to unlock the door when we both looked toward the sliding glass door. Standing inside the house were two small kids, eyes as big as baseballs, pointing at us.

Once we got John's leg out of the window, we reached in and unlocked the door. We raced toward the bedroom area just in time to join Howard and Sully stopped at a doorway. As we looked over their shoulders we could see what stopped them. There was our suspect deeply engaged in an act of intercourse with his wife. He looked at us and said,

"Oh no guys, not now. God, just a second, just a second." We complied. He was right, it was just a second.

He grabbed his pants and came into the hallway while his wife put on a robe. John told him why he was being arrested and got the rest of his clothes for him. The wife took the kids into the kitchen for some breakfast.

Rudy had said as soon as he heard the door go down he knew he was going back to jail and would be the last time he could be with his wife for a long time. Seeing as how he had already started, he might as well finish. Both he and his wife, as well as the kids, were very nice people. Except for his profession.

We did a search of his house and garage and recovered some equipment that we seized as evidence. We were on our way back to our respective offices by ten A.M. This was one of those nice arrests. The suspects and evidence are in custody and you don't have any of the paper work that goes with it. No hours of booking, listing evidence, questioning, filing complaints. Would that they were all like this.

As it turned out Rudy said he didn't have anything to do with the jewelry store safe burglary in Beverly Hills. We had a tendency to believe him. None of his prior burglaries involved nitroglycerine. We had recovered a small amount of what the lab said was homemade nitro in a small glass vial at the scene. We never did wrap anyone up for that burglary. We had a few good hunches but never enough to lock anyone up.

CHAPTER 38

I had gotten a phone call from 'Nathan' that morning. Not something I normally would look forward to. He was one of the sources of information I'd developed during the years. One that I never really felt comfortable with. He was the type of guy who never did anything for nothing. He always had an angle for himself somewhere. I knew that he would like to get me compromised some way or other but I couldn't turn down the kind of information he was feeding me. Dealing with informants, especially like him, is not one of the more pleasant aspects of the job. I knew I had to be on my toes at every turn so he could never put me in a negative position. I got damned tired of watching my back around him but when he wanted to feed me something it was usually very good.

I began to find out that a lot of the people he was handing me, he wanted to either get rid of or get even with them for some transgression, either real or imagined. I could live with this as long as they weren't set ups. I quickly learned to check every angle of any situation he told me about. No blind actions. He got a little fiesty sometimes when I didn't act right away but I think he finally got the message that I didn't quite trust him. No, not even a little bit.

I had learned pretty early in my career, the only thing you really had going for you was your reputation for keeping your word, and the trust of the people that worked with you.

'Nathan' operated a popular nightclub on the fringes of Hollywood which attracted the more shady element. He was in a position to be offered stolen merchandise quite frequently, and to overhear many plans and conversations. Our independent information was that he did indeed buy stolen property. We tried to keep a close eye on him but we couldn't live with him.

He had called me one day to tell me about a major burglary in Atherton, CA. He said the burglar was from the L.A. area and wanted to sell him the merchandise or let him handle the sale for him. He gave me the name of the burglar and I checked his pretty extensive record. I also contacted the Atherton P.D. to ask if they had had such a burglary. They had, and were very anxious to get their hands on the guy and the jewelry. I told them I would get back to them.

My man, 'Nathan', said he would set up a viewing of the property for me. He would then give the property back to the burglar and I could arrest him when he left the bar. I had to agree to set it up to look like a routine traffic stop that escalated into an arrest. Since it was going to happen in Los Angeles, I got together with Frank Gravante, so we could coordinate everything.

In the meantime the Atherton P.D. had notified the victims insurance company that we were working on recovering the jewelry and arresting the suspect. The insurance company had notified a local independent adjuster to contact us. When he did, Frank and I explained just what was going to happen. He was not happy with the situation. He felt that it smacked too much of a 'buy back'. A 'buy back' was a definite no-no as far as we were concerned.

The intent was that the 'informant', Nathan, was to be paid a finders fee after we recovered the jewelry and arrested the burglar. The adjuster flat said no. In the interim, our plans were being set up to nail the burglar.

On the night everything was supposed to happen, Frank and I were set up in our separate cars waiting for the burglar to show at Nathan's club. We also had an L.A. patrol unit standing by to make the 'routine' stop and subsequently find the jewelry. The appointed time came and went with no call from 'Nathan'. I began to get pissed. He was playing games again. We let the uniformed car go and I went into the club to brace 'Nathan', while Frank waited outside, just in case. In case of what, I don't know. Just in case.

'Nathan' gave me a line of crap that the guy had showed up early and left, and that he had tried to get in touch with me.

"Bull shit. You're trying to pull another one of your slick tricks for some reason or other. I don't know why yet but I will sooner or later."

"No, Bob, no. He left some of the stuff here for me to show to buyers and said he would call me about when to pick it up. Come into the office and look at it." I followed him into his office where he opened the safe and laid out several pieces of jewelry. I pulled my Minox camera out of my pocket and took pictures. After I chewed his ass about trying to screw me around I left with his assurance that he would call me whenever the guy was coming back, or when he found out where the guy was staying.

I went back out and met with Frank.

"He's trying to pull some bull shit play but I can't figure out just what yet." I said.

"Well Bob, you know snitches, they always have some kind of angle. The worst part is, they always think we're stupid. That's the part that makes me madder than anything."

"If I get the chance on this one or any other, I'll jerk him up by the short hairs in a minute. I guess we can call it a night for this one. I have some pictures of the jewelry in my camera. I'll get them developed tomorrow. I'll see you."

"O.K. I'll talk to you tomorrow."

A few days later, 'Nathan' called and told me that the burglar had come by to pick up the jewelry he had. He said he couldn't stall, and gave him the stuff then because he was in a hurry. I told him there wasn't much I can do about it. He'd have to play it the best way he could. For all intents and purposes we had lost the jewelry. I was sure of one thing though. Knowing Nathan, he had done a turn around. He had figured out some way to make a better deal by playing along with the burglar rather than his getting arrested. These people were slippery.

A short time later I told Atherton P.D. the circumstances and that the insurance adjuster was not about to cooperate in recovery of the jewelry. They were not happy. They were happy to know the identity of the burglar and would be glad to get the pictures of what jewelry I had seen.

A few days later the insurance adjuster came into the office madder than hell, saying I had ruined his reputation. It seemed the insurance company had gotten the story from Atherton P.D. and was upset that they would have to pay out close to a hundred thousand dollars without a recovery. After we discussed the matter further, he began to claim that he hadn't been aware of the whole situation and would have cooperated with our efforts if he had been better informed. What a crock. He had known everything we knew. His hard nosed attitude had just jumped up and bit him. He knew he had lost that insurance company as a client and that information got around the industry very fast.

Some time later another adjuster told me that some adjusters say they paid out several thousand in rewards when actually they were pocketing the money themselves. He felt that's what may have happened in this case.

About a week later I got another call from 'Nathan'. He wanted to meet me at Highland and Fountain as soon as I could make it. He didn't want to tell me over the phone what he had for me. He sounded scared. I agreed, and asked Cork to cover my back during the meeting. We left right away and parked about a block away. I approached on foot while Cork tailed me from across the street.

He was waiting at the corner, as nervous as a cat. Now what? He saw me coming and virtually ran up to me. I damned near drew my gun the way he was coming at me. He stopped and started to look around like he was expecting someone to come out of the trees and grab him or something. If he's putting on an act, he was good.

"What the hell are you so nervous about ? Stand still. What have you got that's so important?"

"You'll know why I'm nervous when I tell you what I've got. "You'll know."

"O.K., what is it ? Here, step over here closer to this tree. You stay next to the tree so no one can see you if it makes you feel better."

"Yeah, yeah it will. You know that big robbery at that Vegas hotel last week ? You know, at the El Cortez hotel? Well, one of the guys that pulled that job is in town. He's shacking up with a hooker I know. They're at her apartment on the corner of Franklin and Vista."

"O.K., but why are you so shook up. And what's in it for you?" There had to be something in it for him.

"These guys are bad. They jumped the counter into the cashier's cage and held guns on the cashiers in broad daylight. They've got to be crazy to knock over a Casino in Vegas. How many times have you heard that happen. You got to be nuts to do that."

"How'd you find out about this guy. What's your interest in this. There's got to be something. You and I both know it. Just what is it ?" My voice is starting to show my irritation at his efforts to convince me of his sincerity. He's just no good at "sincere".

"The guy's name is John Ardelyen. He's supposed to be a bad dude. The girl's a friend of mine and I don't want her to get hurt. Besides, (here it comes), I got a call from a friend in Vegas who is connected with the hotel. He said it could mean a few bucks for me if I could find this guy."

"Why the hell didn't you say so. We both know you don't do anything for nothing. How about the girl ? Are you going to cut her in? After all, she's the one who gave him to you. It would be a good idea don't you think ?"

I didn't want him cutting her out. He knew she couldn't tell anyone she had ratted on the guy so he didn't have to worry about anyone finding out he had shorted her. He just had too damn many angles.

"Sure, I'm going to take care of her. She's taking a hell of a chance. If he finds out he'll blow her head off. He sleeps with a gun under the pillow. I had to come to you because I had to have someone I could trust not to burn me or the girl. These guys are scarey. He usually sleeps till about 10:00 am. What do you think, can you take him without tipping him off where it came from?"

"Of course. But don't say anything to the girl. We don't want her acting any different than she is right now. He may get wise and take off. Which apartment house is it ?"

"It's on the northwest corner. She lives in 603. It's a nice place. She must make good bread to afford to live there. When are you going to do it?"

"After I check out a few facts. I have to talk to Vegas first and see what they can tell me. Maybe they can give me enough to cover your trail on this end. We'll see. Is that all?"

"Jesus, how much do you want ?" He started to act like I hurt his feelings. Hell, I knew he had no feelings.

"O.K., I'll check it out and be in touch this afternoon"

"O.K., I'll see ya." He headed out down the street with his head lowered, as if no one could see him. He'd make a terrible spy.

I went back to the car and joined Cork. As we headed back to the station I relayed all the information to him.

"God", Cork says, "he acted like he was standing on a hot skillet. Do you think he's that worried about this guy being so tough? I guess he should be worried. He's burned a lot of people in his time. Someone may just figure it out someday and really get to him."

"Naw, he's only worried that someone else will pop this guy before we do and he won't get his cut from whoever in Vegas he's dealing with. The money is his goal, and that's it."

Back at the office I called Las Vegas and talked with the robbery detectives. They were quite anxious to hear from me. It seemed they had a warrant for John Ardelyen and were more than happy to have us put him away. They had an informant who laid out all the robbers just after it happened and they had the other two in jail already. They wanted to know when they could come over and get Ardelyen.

I asked them to teletype an abstract of their warrant and I'd keep them advised. It was to late to get him today because he would be on the move around town right now. Probably tomorrow morning, Saturday. They hung up telling me they will be close to the phones.

Cork and I got in touch with Frank Gravante to go along with us. Because we trust him, and this operation will take place in L.A. Trust being the main thing. When you're going up against an armed suspect you need to know who you can depend on and where they will be. Vegas officers had told me that Ardelyen was known to be armed and dangerous.

The remainder of the afternoon I spent going to the apartment house and checking it out. It's always nice to know the lay of the land before you get there.

Frank met us at our office at seven AM the next morning. On the drive to the building we filled him in on the entire story and what we had found out up to then. He'd heard about the robbery but didn't know anyone had been arrested. None of us believed anyone was damned fool enough to knock over a Vegas Casino. It just wasn't healthy. People have been known to disappear forever for just talking about doing it. Things had changed since then.

We parked discreetly at the apartment house and made it to the managers apartment. He told us there was such a girl living in 603, and that she'd had a male companion for several days. He also had a car parked in the garage. That was new information.

"Here, here is a pass key, and please try not to damage too much."

We got a "no thank you", when we asked him if he would like to observe from the corridor just to be sure we were being careful. After I went back to the car and got my short barreled shotgun, we took the elevator to the sixth floor. The door to 603 was just to the left of the elevator. It was just eight o'clock so there was not much movement in the building.

I took the left of the door, Frank the right, and Cork, with the key, the center. After a short listen at the door we were sure there was no one moving about the apartment. Cork slipped the key in the door ever so gently. The knob turned, and the door started to open. It stopped against the night chain. No hesitation now, Cork hit the door as Frank and I followed him through. The chain pieces were still ricocheting around the room when we had determined there was no one in the kitchen, dining room or living room.

The only other direction was down a short hallway to our left, passed what was probably a bathroom, and into a bedroom.

We glanced into the bath as we passed. I don't know how the three of us got down that hall at the same time, but that's the beauty of working with someone you know. You don't have to know how, you just know that it will happen. Those were the times when your hair was standing on end and every muscle was taught. "WHAT IF", time again.

Through the bedroom doorway we found we were standing at the foot of a queen sized bed with a sliding doored closet along the left wall, and a sliding glass door to a balcony along the opposite wall. I was in the center of the foot of the bed, Cork was to my left, and Frank was to my right.

The guy was laying face down, under a sheet, on the left side of the bed. The girl was on the right side, on her back under the sheet. She was awake. At least her eyes were the size of saucers. He still seemed to be asleep. We had made enough noise to wake the dead with our announcement of "police officer, we have a warrant", and the noise of the chain breaking. We weren't convinced he was asleep. Just no trust, I guess.

We motioned for her to slide out from under the sheet onto the floor, to the right. She complied very cautiously. As she came from under the sheet we saw that she was 'au natural' so to speak. She certainly was not armed.

We turned our attention to him. He was starting to stir and as he did, his right hand started to slide up under the pillow. As his fingers started to disappear, the loudest noise in the world broke the silence. Two revolvers being cocked and the shotgun safety being released, followed by a very low but firm, "DON'T MOVE".

He must have figured out what the noise was because he didn't move another muscle. Cork moved to the side of the bed and lifted the pillow. There on the mattress, about two inches from his fingers, was a .32 cal blue steel automatic.

With the gun secured, Frank pulled the sheet down. He wasn't hiding anymore weapons either. We let him lay there while we got a bathrobe for the girl and got her out of the room. We located his clothes and got him dressed in the bedroom. In a few minutes, and after a quick search of the apartment, we were ready to leave. We went to the basement and called for a tow truck after we had a quick look in the car.

When the tow truck arrived, we had it towed to Beverly Hills. We got all the identification information we needed from the girl and released her. The ride back to the station was a quiet but pleasant one. No problems, no mistakes, and no accidents. Ardelyen was congenial but not very communicative.

Once the booking process was done we turned our attention to notifying Las Vegas. They were right. They had stayed close to the phone. They were anxious to leave right away and pick up their prisoner. We had a conversation with Ardelyen and he had decided to waive extradition. He had signed a statement to that effect so Vegas could have him as soon as they wanted as far as we were concerned. They told us they were on their way. And, thanks, thanks, thanks.

Ardelyen sent word that he wanted to talk to us. Frank had gone home so Cork and I went up to see him. He didn't seem to want to put it into words but finally he came around. He wanted us to be sure to follow up on him to be sure he actually got back to Las Vegas. He wanted us to check to be sure the people picking him up were really police officers. He said he knew the magnitude of what he had done and had no illusions about what could happen to him.

We assured him we would check on him, and the officers, which seemed to satisfy him. Late in the afternoon the Las Vegas officers arrived. We checked their credentials, and told them why. They wanted to start right back so we turned our prisoner over to them after they had searched the car and took anything they felt would serve as evidence.

"Nathan" called shortly after they left and I told him that Ardelyen was on his way back to Vegas. He told me he knew we had arrested him and was waiting to find out when he was going back to Vegas. He had a giddiness in his voice. I never did find out how much he made out of the deal, or if he shared any with the girl. Like I said, he was a jerk to deal with but had to much good information to ignore.

That Monday, Cork and I got together with Frank over cup of coffee and discussed how quickly this had come together, been handled, and completed. It was a good feeling despite who we had to deal with.

One thing did bother us though. Considering the nature of the crime, none of us ever got called to testify about the arrest. Neither did we hear anything about the trial. Very Strange . . . ..

A few weeks later I checked and found that Ardelyn had been in court and was awaiting sentencing.

CHAPTER 39

Most of the guys were in court. Hankins, Cork and I were the only ones left in the office. It was shortly after nine o'clock and the phones had kept us all busy. It seemed people knew when you're shorthanded. That's when they want to call.

Between one of my calls I looked at Cork and he motioned for me to pick up on his call. After a few seconds he told the party on the other end that I was on the line too. He introduced us on the phone, "Bob Downey, Jack Williams from L.A. robbery on the line. He's telling me that he has good info that Paul Byron Wolfe is going to hit one of our penthouse apartments today. I've just offered him an invitation to join us."

"Sounds good to me", I said, "do we know which apartment house it will be ?"

"Yeah," Jack says, "411 No. Palm Dr., somebody named Silverman. The place is supposed to be empty after noon."

"What time can you be here Jack ?" Cork asked.

"In less than an hour if you can wait that long ?"

"No problem, make it as quick as you can though."

"Right, on my way. Bye."

We both hung up and headed for Hankins office and filled him in on our conversation. While we were talking I used the reverse directory to look up the occupants of 411 No. Palm Dr. There are two penthouse apartments at 411. One is occupied by a Mrs. Saul Silverman, P 401. Cork and I decided we'll take a quick ride past the building while we were waiting for Williams.

Paul Byron Wolfe had been known to us for sometime as a very good, and very active apartment house burglar. He was supposed to use a broad bladed screwdriver for entry and usually took only good jewelry, and sometimes a fur. He was in his mid-forties and had done prison time for burglary. He drove a blue Mercury Meteor. Other than that we didn't know to much about him.

The apartment house was a typical four story, stucco apartment building with a central tunneled entrance into a small gardened courtyard. No pool. To the right of the courtyard was the elevator and the mailboxes. It was a relatively new building and well maintained. Looking up from the courtyard you could see balconied walkways on each floor. We went back to the car and returned to the office.

Jack arrived a few minutes later. We gathered around Cork's desk as he filled us in.

"I have this informant whose close to Wolfe. The snitch owes me big time so he came to me last night and told me about this. He said Wolfe is going to hit this apartment today. He knows the place will be empty because the woman goes to her bridge club on Thursday and the maid is off. Wolfe's supposed to hit it around one o'clock. If he's challenged he poses as a sewing machine repairman. That's all I've got. What's the place look like ?"

"Typical four story courtyard apartment building. No pool, one elevator. Two inside stairways, one front and back, subterranean garage with a front entrance." I outlined for him.

"Let's go talk to the intended victim", Cork said as we got up to leave. A couple of minutes later we were ringing the bell of Penthouse 401.

The maid answered the door and ushered us in after we identified ourselves. We were seated in the living room when Mrs. Silverman joined us. In a few short minutes we explained our reasons for being there and the shock set in. She'd heard about people who had been victims but never considered that she might be one herself. When she settled down we went through the usual inquiry about her activities and habits that may have set her up for this burglary. She did not know anyone named Paul Byron Wolfe, and did not own a sewing machine. Her maid had been with her for twelve years and was beyond reproach.

The maid did not know anyone named Wolfe. They both recalled several "hang up" phone calls at different times during the last few days. Her phone number was not listed. She recalled no recent conflicts with anyone, nor any reason why anyone would want to target her for a burglary.

We explained that we wanted to stake out the apartment and that we would like her to leave as soon as possible. She explained that she and the maid were both scheduled to leave at the same time. That was their usual Thursday routine. In fact they were ready to leave now. While we were checking the apartment we found we could see the front courtyard and the mailboxes from the living room window.

As they were preparing for their departure Jack decided to stay in the apartment while Cork and I went back to the office and gathered some more help. The office was only five blocks away. We left the apartment at eleven thirty, a few minutes ahead of Mrs. Silverman.

Back at the office the only person we could round up for help was Jack Egger. He had just finished a preliminary hearing and was supposed to be headed for lunch. To late. Cork, Egger and I are heading down Palm Dr. and were about to pull into a parking place in front, as soon as this damned blue Meteor gets parked. WHOA. It's Wolfe !.. Luckily he was too busy trying to park to concentrate on us. I kept driving to the corner and parked on the next cross street.

Cork and I would take the front of the building and observe from the sub-garage across the street. Jack Egger would cover the back of the building from a garage across the alley. We had no way of warning Jack Williams that Wolfe had arrived early. We knew he would not answer the phone, thinking the burglar was stiffing in a test call. We certainly couldn't go up and knock on the door. From the garage we were in we could also see that Wolfe's car was not parked in front of the building. Where the hell had it gone so quickly? We waited, all we could do.

But not very long . . .

The sound of the first shot started us running across the street, guns drawn. Cork to the south side of the building, me to the north. Half way across the street the second shot went off. As I was nearing the alley, I heard a yell, "out the back!" Cork and I reached the alley at the same time, I saw him come into the alley as I did. He proceeded across the alley at top speed. As I went across I hesitated and noticed the blue Meteor parked at the rear of 411 No Palm.

I started to go between two garages across the alley when I caught a glimpse of a trouser leg coming from the walkway between the garages about twenty feet to the south of me. I turned and headed back to the alley. Wolfe was just getting into his car. I stopped at the corner of the garage and resting my gun against the corner of the garage I leveled it at his head.

"Don't move, You're under arrest Wolfe !!" As I said that, the starter was turning over in a very vain attempt to start the car. He had flooded it.

"Get out of the car or I'll shoot !" He was still trying to start the car. I took one step into the alley and pulled the hammer back on my revolver, and the starter noise stopped. The car door slowly opened and he started to step into the alley. At that point Cork stepped from between the same garages Wolfe had come from with his gun in firing position. I approached Wolfe, turned him around and put him over the hood of the car while I handcuffed him. That done, I stepped back and found my shirt and suit covered with blood.

Jack Williams had joined us and said,

"Huh, I didn't miss you after all, did I ?"

Wolfe then started to screech like a banshee.

"What do you mean ? Am I shot ? Where ? Oh my God, get me an ambulance." etc, etc, etc.

While he was yelling I was on my way to the caretakers apartment where I used his phone to call the office. John Wright, the dispatcher answered.

"John,,, Downey, we need an ambulance at the rear of 411 No. Palm Dr."

"Officer or suspect ?" was his reply.

"Suspect" I said and hung up. A few seconds later I could hear the sirens as they left the fire station. When they arrived Wolfe was lying in the alley. It seemed that he had also broken his foot in the rapid decent of the concrete stairway.

Wolfe was loaded into the ambulance and Jack Egger went to the hospital with him. We now had a chance to talk with Jack Williams.

He said he had been standing at the window not long after we left and had seen Wolfe come into the courtyard and approach the mailboxes. He knew we wouldn't have had time to come back yet so he moved back into the apartment to wait for Wolfe to make his entry. A short time later he heard noises from what seemed like the roof of the apartment. Then he heard noises from the front door.

He was trying to back into the bedroom when Wolfe came around the doorway into the hallway. Jack challenged him to stop but he took off running. When he didn't stop on the second challenge, Jack fired just as Wolfe was going out the door. He felt he couldn't have missed him but Wolfe kept running. He made it to the door of the back stairway and started down. Jack fired another shot at him as he was running down the stairs. Wolfe went outside when he reached the garage level. Jack was a couple of floors behind. He didn't have as much an incentive to run as Wolfe did.

He heard me shouting for Wolfe to get out of the car in the alley and came to join us.

We went back upstairs to check the door for marks and found pry marks at lock level. In the car we found a screwdriver that appeared to fit the marks. All in all, a pretty good day.

The trouble came later at the Superior Court trial.

At the preliminary hearing in Municipal Court, the D.A. had introduced as evidence, a slip of paper we had taken from Wolfe's pocket, which had the victims name address and phone number written on it.

In Superior Court the defense counsel contended that the "informant" had written the information and had given it to Wolfe. The defense contended that the "informant" had tipped off Williams in and effort to set up Wolfe for an arrest. They contended that Wolfe had been instructed by the "informant" to go there and pick up a sewing machine for repair. If that were the case, Jack was going to be very upset with the informant.

The judge ordered a handwriting exemplar from the now identified informant. His handwriting matched that on the note. The judge dismissed the case against Wolfe.

The judge apparently chose to disregard the fact that Wolfe pried open the front door to gain entry, refused to stop when ordered by a police officer, and the victim never owned a sewing machine.

We never did hear what Jack had to say to his informant when he finally caught up with him.

I told you they were a bitch to deal with.

CHAPTER 40

Our surveillance group was getting antsy. We'd all had to take some time to catch up on our paperwork and court appearances. There was nothing like sitting around in the hall of the courthouse waiting for your case to be called to make you yearn to get into the field and do some police work.

We had set and cancelled several meetings but now we'd finally been able to get everyone together at the same time. We were back at our usual meeting place at Santa Monica and La Cienega. That time we are all playing from the same deck of cards. We knew what we could do and so did many of our contemporaries. We'd made friends of some of the skeptics. Some still needed more convincing, but weren't nearly as vocal about it.

Our two Intelligence units, including the ladies, Frank Gravante, and I, had all received information about the same two burglars. Ronald Leon Powell and William Woodyard. Our information had come from independent sources so we were pretty sure it was reliable. Those guys were supposed to be active, and good for many upper class apartment house burglaries in West L.A., Beverly Hills, and the Hollywood/West Hollywood area.

They both had some criminal record connected primarily with burglary, but not lengthy. And no serious prison time. They had both been arrested, along with a couple of others, in connection with the burglary of actress Barbara Nichols residence where furs and jewelry were taken. Something sure seemed wrong with that case. After the suspects had been arrested and charges filed, she suddenly decided not to follow through on her complaint or appear in court. For whatever reason they missed their chance to go to the joint then. Maybe we could change that.

We were familiar with the kind of information we needed to begin our operation so we came to this meeting prepared. We each had some piece of information to contribute. Cars, residences, associates, employment, etc.

We could kick right into high gear immediately. I had to correlate our information and make a copy for each person, as well as mug shots of every person we knew to be associated with our subjects. What the hell, I had all afternoon. Our operation wouldn't start till eight A.M. the next morning.

Woodyard rented a small house on the corner of an estate owned by the actress, Ruta Lee. It was about two thirds of the way up Laurel Canyon, on the west side of the road. Powell shared a large house on a street off of Laurel Canyon. He worked as a bartender at an exclusive restaurant on LaCienega Blvd. just north of Wilshire. As far as we could tell, Woodyard had no regular job. The burglary business must have been good. Woodyard drove a new, grey, Buick Riviera. Powell rode with him and didn't seem to have a car of his own.

The first morning we had a hell of a time setting up on Woodyard. Laurel Canyon was a narrow winding street offering no place to observe his residence. We shifted locations a dozen times trying to get a lookout point. We had to know what he was doing at the house, and when he was leaving.

Finally, I had driven to the top of the Canyon, and took a dirt road back along the ridge. We had noticed three houses perched on the point of a hill above the Canyon which would afford a good look, if there was room to park, and stay inconspicuous. Sure enough, we had a lookout spot. The only trouble was, whoever had this spot could not join the surveillance for some time. It would take a while to get back out of here and on to the main street. We met at our usual rendezvous point to discuss the logistics of the situation.

"How long will it take you to get out of there, Bob?" Frank asked.

"I can't move 'til he gets out of his driveway or I'll give away my location. Even though I'm up pretty high above his house, any movement up there is very obvious. I'd say I'd be three minutes before I can join anything going south on Laurel. Going north I can probably join right in. It's a pretty straight shot out that road onto Laurel."

Jones chimed in, "O.K. then we'll have to set up so we can stay with him at least five minutes before we can rotate cars." No concern in his voice. No hesitation about how it will be done. Just, we have to do it, so we will. Positive thinking. It's great. Of course the confidence we've gotten in each other in the last few weeks helped a lot.

For three days we tailed Woodyard here and there. We'd loose him a couple of times only to find him at one of his haunts a little while later. We'd tailed him to a small house, actually part of a duplex, on Hayworth, just south of Sunset a couple of times. A little checking revealed this was where his girlfriend lived. We couldn't figure out just which one was his girlfriend. There was a good-looking woman about 30 to 35 years old, and a beautiful girl that looked about 15 or 16 years old. He fawned over both of them.

Woodyard and Powell were both good looking, well dressed men in their late twenties and early thirties. Powell didn't seem to have any particular lady friend and apparently because he worked, didn't pal around with anyone very often.

We spent a couple of days tailing Powell with no appreciable results. They were either laying low, or pulling jobs when we weren't around. Powell was scoring pretty well with the ladies at the bar where he worked. A different one would take him home almost every night. No wonder he didn't need a car.

After a week or so of futile gestures we decided to press all our sources of information again to get closer to our guys. In a couple of days we got information that Woodyard and Powell were going to be at a bar on South Robertson Blvd. to show several hot furs to a prospective buyer. They were to be there at one P.M. that afternoon. We had our first break. The bar was on the L.A. side of

Robertson and just a couple blocks south of Wilshire. We had barely two hours to gather and set up.

We made it. About one-ten P.M. Woodyard and Powell drove into the bar parking lot in Woodyard's Buick, and parked. We had four cars staked out in the area. Cork had accompanied me in mine, with his trusty little 8 mm movie camera, and little Andy was with Frank. The Intelligence unit which had dug up the information had the point position and eyeball on the Buick. They were describing everything going on in the parking lot. They told how our suspects had come back to the car with an unidentified subject and had opened the trunk and looked at what appeared to be furs. They closed the trunk and went back into the bar. Cork and I had moved into a position where Cork could film everything going on in the parking lot. He had gotten it all on film. All the probable cause we would need.

About a half hour later Woodyard and Powell returned to the car, got in, and drove out of the lot. We were on the move and Cork still had his camera going. They drove north on Robertson and turned east on Charleville. Just past Hamel they slowed slightly and appeared to start a turn into an apartment house parking garage. Cork and I were about three car lengths behind them. At the time they seemed to start their turn, Woodyard looked in his mirror, and straightened out the car when it seemed he had spotted us. He began to accelerate. We broadcast that information and decided to take them into custody. We turned on the red light and sounded the siren.

They pulled to the curb between Carson and Stanley. We pulled in behind, as the rest of the cars pulled in. They both got out of the car immediately and started back to us.

We herded everyone onto the sidewalk. Cork and I took Woodyard toward the rear of our car while Frank and Andy took Powell up next to Woodyards car. For the next few minutes we talked to them. It didn't take long to find out that Woodyard was the smart ass of the two. He had a bad mouth and attitude.

While we were talking the rest of the crew searched the car.

The trunk contained five mink stoles which Woodyard denied any knowledge of. Vehemently !! A continued search revealed a full set of Schlage pass keys concealed under the ash tray in the console of the car. As I held these keys up in front of Woodyard and asked him about them, he lunged toward me while raising his left knee toward my groin. Cork had been standing slightly to my left. Instantly his left arm came across in front of me, backhanded, and the heel of his fist caught Woodyard along the left jaw line. That blow would have felled an ox. Woodyard's body rose about three inches off the ground and he went over backward. There was a gut wrenching sound when his head hit the sidewalk. It hit before the rest of his body.

I was almost afraid to look at his head. I expected to see a large crack in the skull, with a grey matter leaking out. His head was harder than I thought. A minute or so later he was standing, shaking his eye rolling head, and mumbling unintelligible things. Powell kept asking "why'd he try to kick you ? What'd you say ? Why'd he do that?" That pretty much ended our street talk.

We had the car towed in as we transported the suspects to our jail for booking. After the booking we started the task of trying to identify the owners of the furs. In this case we had help. Three of the furs still had the initials and labels in the linings. By the next day we had them identified. In the meantime Woodyard and Powell had bailed out, on a writ. Not before Cork and I had a chance to talk with Powell.

He was the more cooperative of the two by far. Although he didn't actually confess to the burglaries, he didn't deny he had helped pull them. He also engaged in conversation about a guy called "the hat" who handled a lot of hot merchandise. He didn't know the guys real name, just that everyone called him "the hat" because he always wore a black felt hat with a black silk band. He was an older guy who hung around Sherry's and the deli at Sunset and Crescent Heights.

Powell was anxious to do what he could to help himself. He indicated he could let us know when Woodyard was holding merchandise, or was going to pull another job. If that would help him. He was told we would pass it on to the D.A. and see if it could help. This guy "the hat" was quite interesting to us. It was funny that none of us in the group had ever heard of him before. From what Ronny said he was pretty active and had been for some time. Unusual that none of us had known anything about him.

He also told us about a girl who comes into the bar on LaCienega and lives on Hamilton Drive in Beverly Hills. She had worn a large diamond ring on several occasions and became the victim of a burglary. She had reported the diamond ring was taken in the burglary but she actually had put it in her safety deposit box in the bank at Hamilton and Wilshire. The ring was supposed to be worth $10,000, and she had collected from the insurance company. She had been bragging about her good fortune.

Powell swore he had not pulled the job but was sore that she could clean up from the insurance company.

I checked our records and found the burglary report she had made. Sure enough, the ring was reported missing, among a few other items of jewelry. I contacted the insurance adjuster, Miles Reece, and he confirmed she had been paid for the loss of the ring. I briefed him on Powell's story and asked him to find out if the insurance company would prosecute if we filed a fraud report and got a search warrant to open the safety deposit box. After all, it was a significant fraud, and it would serve to get the attention of other people who were defrauding the insurance companies.

Reece called the next day to tell me the insurance company would not follow through with any action. They didn't want to appear overly harsh with their clients. Reece gave me the phone number of the claims manager and I spent the next half hour trying to convince him to follow through. He refused. It didn't impress him when I tried to tell him how tough it was to be busting our ass to recover property that had never been stolen. When we found an outright fraud case, it needed to be prosecuted. He still refused. I left him with the thought that we would very probably be crossing paths in the future on other significant losses.

Exasperated, Cork and I tried to figure out a way to at least shake up the alleged victim. We would keep that in the back of our mind as we worked on Woodyard and Powell.

In the next couple of weeks while we waited for their preliminary hearing, Powell kept calling us with small tidbits of useless information. The closer the preliminary hearing came the more frequent his calls. And the more suggestive. In the week or ten days before the hearing Powell began calling once or twice a day. During these calls he started suggesting that he could "set up" Woodyard by "planting" something in his car. I told him emphatically, No!. If he wasn't doing anything wrong we didn't want to waste our time with him.

I got some of the calls, and so did Cork. After a couple of calls each we put our heads together and decided Ronnie was trying to pull something. On us. We got the feeling he was trying to get us on tape agreeing to something illegal. The whole thing just had a stink to it.

That afternoon Ronnie called again. Cork was on the extension as I talked with him. He was again hinting strongly that he could do something to set up Woodyard.

"You know, I could put some marijuana in his car and he'd never know it. Then you guys could shake him down and find it. That would do it wouldn't it ?"

"Look Ronnie, there is no way we would go along with something like that. If you'd plant something in his car you would be the one to go to jail. We don't play that game."

"He'd never find out. And then you guys could help me with my problem."

"We said no, and we meant no. If he's going to do a job, or has hot merchandise, that's one thing. A set up is not legal and we want no part of it. If you hear or see anything we can use, call us. Otherwise, we'll see you in court."

As I hung up Cork came to my desk and said, "I've got a strong feeling he's trying to put us in a box someway."

"Yeah, so do I", I said. "We've still got that little old traffic warrant in file on him, why don't we take a quick ride up to his place and serve it. Now. I'd be interested to see what's hooked to his phone right now." I didn't need to finish my sentence. We had already headed out the door to the car, after picking up the warrant at the desk.

Twenty minutes later we had parked a half block away and were approaching the house on foot. We didn't want to drive into the driveway and let him know we were there. Cork and I both stood beside the door when Cork knocked. We didn't want him to see us outside. Ronnie opened the door and Cork took him by the wrist as he told him he was under arrest. I showed him the warrant. We followed him back into the house.

As we walked down the hallway we passed the telephone stand, and the tape recorder attached to the telephone.

"Ah, Ronnie, did you really think we were stupid enough to let you set Woodyard up ? What made you think we were crooked? You have really pissed us off now. You came to us wanting help and you try to trap us into doing something crooked. What a prick." I was really laying it on. I wanted him to know just how mad we were.

"Hey guys, it wasn't my idea. My attorney set it up. He said if you went along with it he could get us both off. It's his tape recorder. Bill (Woodyard) knew all about it. He was going to play along and let you search him and find something so he could prove entrapment. I didn't want to go along with it." He was really squirming. What a turd.

All the way to the office he tried to square himself by telling us things he thought we wanted to hear. He didn't seem to realize that nothing he said had any credibility now. We had seized the tape recorder and the tape as evidence in a possible federal wire tapping crime. His attorney was going to be very upset. When we explained this to Ronnie, he started to sweat even more. He really wanted to help us now.

"To late Ronnie," Cork said with conviction, "You're going to the joint, and with a snitch jacket. Oh you'll be very popular there."

Before we locked him in his cell we called a couple of our other detectives in while we played the tape. Almost all of his calls to us were on the recording. Each call had us telling him we wanted nothing to do with his plans to set Woodyard up. When the tape was over he sat in the corner and seemed to shrink in size. He knew without doubt he was gone.

We wrote up the report and directed a copy to Special Agent Peter Meaney of the FBI. They had long been interested in the activities of this particular attorney, as had several Police Departments in the area.

Powell bailed out on the traffic warrant and tried in vain to contact Cork or I. It didn't happen. He was dangling in the wind and he knew it. Their preliminary hearing was to be held in West L.A. Court next week. The furs we had identified had come from some of Frank's jobs. We hadn't cleared any cases but our apartment burglaries sure went down.

When it came time for court, Cork and I tossed a coin to see who would testify. I won, or lost, depending on your point of view. Woodyard had gotten another attorney, Max Soloman, who was known to be tough in court. Powell's attorney was known around town as a conniving corner cutter who'd sell any of his clients for a song, and sing it himself.

On the stand, Max really tried extra hard to discredit my testimony. I understood that. We were having fun with the give and take. He knew he wasn't going to do it, but he had to try. One of his questions involved my having seen the car start to turn into the underground garage at the apartment house.

"Wouldn't you say officer, actually, that if the wheels of the car did turn, it was only infinitesimal ?" Max asked with the sound of incredulity in his voice.

"No Counselor, if it had been infinitesimal I couldn't have seen the movement from my position. They turned enough for me to think they were going into the garage." We both were almost smiling at each other when I had finished my answer. He had no further questions.

Powell's lawyer however, attacked like a tiger. A paper tiger. I guess he thought bluster would carry him through. His main point became pretty obvious very shortly. He danced around the tape recording and recorder. He had worked himself into a position where my answer to one of his questions had to make him ask me if I still had the tape recorder. The judge then became interested.

"Sgt. Downey, do you still have the tape recorder ?" the judge asked, with a strong note of curiosity in his voice.

"Yes your Honor, As a matter of fact, I brought it to court with me and would be glad to play the recording for the court if you'd care to hear it."

I had hardly gotten that out of my mouth when Powell's attorney began to jump up and down and object on any of a half dozen grounds. He had already admitted that he had loaned the recorder to Powell. He wasn't sure just how far he was involved in a federal case. The judge was kind this day.

He declined to listen to the tape but advised the attorney that any further discussion of the tape or recorder would result in the court reviewing the tape to determine if there was any evidential value. The lawyer shut up and sat down.

Woodyard and Powell were held to answer in Superior Court for burglary.

During the subsequent weeks of investigation we had determined that Woodyards girlfriend was actually the 17 year old in the house on Hayworth. Powell then advised us that she was the Playmate of the Month for Playboy that coming month. The older woman was the girls mother. We took the juvenile officer, a police woman, and headed for the house at the D.A.'s direction.

Sharon Cintron answered our knock, with rollers in her hair. She was a very attractive girl. We asked to talk with her and she invited us into the house. When asked, she admitted she was only seventeen, and had posed for and was the Playmate of the Month for May. The issue was already in publication.

When she seated herself on a small stool in front of a dresser, three hand rolled cigarettes fell to the floor, from her hair rollers.

She was placed in custody for possession of marijuana and brought to the office for procession after a perfunctory search of the house. Her case was handled in the juvenile court system.

We danced around with Woodyard and Powell for months. On one occasion the court issued a warrant for Woodyard and notified us of it's issuance. We knew where he was living in Hollywood, with another very attractive young lady. That burglary business must hold some magnetic attraction for the pretty girls of Hollywood. When you talk to them though, they act like it's all a game. A game that goes on around them but never really touches them. That is until you arrest one of them for conspiracy, or receiving stolen property, or some other connected crime. All of a sudden, it's not so funny.

When we learned of the warrant, Jack Egger and I headed for the apartment, again located just south of Sunset, this time on Orange Grove. A very nice building. It was a Colonial style, two story building, with an arched entryway. There was a wide walkway into a nicely landscaped yard. On each side of the entryway was an apartment door. The front of the building, to the left and right of the entry, was fenced off with a bamboo fencing surrounding a concrete patio.

As Jack and I started into the entry we saw the apartment we were interested in on the left of the entry. Shortly after our knock, an attractive young lady opened the door a few inches. We asked her if Woodyard was there, and told her that we had a warrant for him. She immediately said no, and shut the door in our face. I stepped back into the front of the building and looked up at the second floor window of the apartment, and saw Woodyard looking out between the curtains.

I told Jack, "he's in there", and we charged the door with a vengeance. We needed a vengeance, and more. It was a solid oak door, with a throw bolt, and a dead bolt. When we both hit the door at the same time, it didn't budge. Not even shake. We got so frustrated and centered on that door we continued to kick and shoulder it with absolutely no success.

We must have looked like the Keystone Cops. During that fiasco a gentleman came to us from the back of the building with a four foot length of three inch pipe in his hand.

"Here", he said, "maybe this will help. Don't worry about it, I own the place. Go ahead." handing us the pipe and standing back. Three hearty blows with the pipe, directly at the lock, and the door opened.

Jack and I bolted upstairs and arrested Woodyard in one bedroom. After handcuffing him we went downstairs and talked briefly to the girl, trying to decide whether to arrest her for aiding and abetting. We started out the door, to be met by Woodyard's new attorney, and a bailbondsman. We had worked on that door so long that they had time to respond to his call. Talk about tunnel vision. We put Woodyard in the car and told his attorney and the bondsman to meet us at the Police Station.

We returned to talk with the apartment owner. He was not the least upset at the damage to the door. He understood our procedures but wondered why we had not merely stepped onto the patio and gone through the open sliding glass door into the apartment. I could feel the blood rushing to my face and started to hang my head. Jack and I both started to mumble our apologies about the damage, again. The owner assured us he well understood our frustration. We were all smiling when we parted.

Bail was being posted for Woodyard as we were booking him, and he was released immediately. Neither Jack nor I wanted to say too much to anyone else about the door. We had plenty to say to each other.

Woodyard's and Powell's cases dragged on for months. During that time Cork and I had occasion to talk to both of them in the interview room of our jail. They had decided to cooperate with us attempting to get us to put in a good word for them with the judge. They had agreed to help us identify the burglaries they had pulled in our city if we would not file any additional charges on them. We had discussed it with the D.A. and he agreed provided they did not lie to us. If we were to find any additional burglaries they had pulled we would be free to file more charges.

When everyone had reached an understanding on the ground rules we sat down to talk. When we got into the meat of our talks they were quite candid about the jobs they had pulled.

We were surprised at the sheer number of burglaries they finally admitted. We started to regret our deal not to file additional charges. We did get the satisfaction of driving a wedge in their "friendship". While we were talking about the items stolen in each of the crimes, Cork asked Woodyard, "what did you take on that job ?" Woodyard thought for a second and said, "oh, a diamond watch, 3 rings, and, oh yeah, $10,000 in cash was in a shoebox in the closet." With that Powell jumped up and said "you prick, you never told me about any ten grand." Woodyards face got red as a beet. The air was very tense in that room from then on.

We discussed the property taken in the burglaries and they reluctantly admitted they had dealt most of it to "John the Hat". We went through this process for a couple of days, finally bringing it to an end when we felt we had gotten everything we were going to get from them.

A couple of weeks later we came up with a traffic warrant on Woodyard. His little asshole attorney told us he was coming into Burbank airport from San Francisco that afternoon. Cork and I got to the airport just in time to arrest him as he was leaving the plane. As we were leaving the terminal with Woodyard, Powell walked in. As he did so Cork piped up, "Thanks Ronnie, we appreciate it. It would have been a pain in the ass to have to hunt for him again."

Powell, now as white as a sheet, stuttered out, "not me man, I never said anything." Honor among thieves. Sure.

We never were subpoenaed to testify at the trial so they must have pled guilty. In any event we had no further contact with then for a long time. They did leave us with a puzzle though. Who was "John the Hat"?

The girl with the diamond ring still didn't sit right with us. After some discussion Cork and I decided on an approach that we thought might work. I called her and set up an appointment for that afternoon. To discuss her case of course.

When we were seated in her apartment we began to go over the reported missing property. After a few minutes we asked her about the diamond ring. Her face changed colors slightly. It was then I asked her about her safe deposit box at the corner bank.

"Was it possible that the ring may have been placed in the box and she had forgotten it ? If that were the case then the insurance company would have no cause to file a fraud complaint."

The conversation continued in this vein for a few minutes. More and more she began to indicate that such a circumstance was possible. She was advised if that was the case then she could call the insurance company and explain it to them and everybody would be happy especially when they got their money back. We got the impression that paying back the money may pose some problems. She seized on the idea that her desire to do what was right would stand her in good stead when it came to making a deal with the insurance company to pay back the settlement. With a little help from us.

When we left she assured us that she would check her safe deposit box and if the ring was there she would be sure to notify the insurance company the next day. We left feeling our faith in mankind's honesty was not misplaced.

The next afternoon I took a call from the insurance company claims examiner telling me that the victim had located her ring and cancelled her claim and would return the money. He proceeded to tell me how his restraint in pursuing a fraud complaint had saved us both the embarassment of a false accusation. Yeah, sure.

CHAPTER 41

A few weeks later Cork, Polakov, and I had just returned from lunch after spending the morning in court. One of those memorable lunches at one of Howard's choice locations. A little place on Pico just outside the Beverly Hills City limits. It was one of those places that you pass every day and not take any general notice of it's existence. A small, neighborhood, storefront cafe with all the outward appeal of a hot dog stand. Although where Howard was concerned we should have known better. Once seated you got the feeling of a class operation. The decor was ordinary but the smell and feel of the place started you thinking of looks being deceiving. They certainly were.

The menu was intriguing. About as far from "cafe" fare as you could get. French dishes, German meals, a wide variety of European choices. It was all there. Howard suggested we try the Tuesday special, Swiss cheese and onion pie! What ? Thirty years later it would be quiche'. Who knew ? It was a truly memorable meal.

When we got back to the office Howard left for home and Cork and I met with a local resident who wanted to report some unusual activity in the vicinity of his home in the 200 block of South Doheny. He had gone to the Chief's office first and the Chief decided we should be assigned to solve this predicament.

It seemed the downstairs apartment at the next door south of our complainants apartment was receiving an unusual amount of traffic at all hours of the day and night. The apartment was apparently occupied by a young blonde woman and an older man.

The visitors were always men of different ages. Shortly after they arrived the male occupant of the apartment would leave and be gone up to an hour. Sometimes the blonde would leave with the visitor and be gone a couple of hours. There was no other unusual activity or noise coming from the place. We got the rest of the information from the complainant and started our preliminary investigation.

We directed the patrol units to maintain a special watch on the location and when possible interview some of the visitors when they left the place. A few days later we got several Field Interrogation cards from the patrol officers. It wasn't hard to figure out what was going on there. We took the information and our conclusions to the Chief and got our marching orders.

The Chief's direction always superseded logic, good judgement, or discretion. You could always be assured though, that if in following his directions you got into a bind, he would be there to back you. You would not be left to hang and twist in the wind. No sir. He would make sure someone held the rope so you wouldn't twist. More times than not his approach worked. His attitude and approach to such situations was always direct and confrontational. "You can live in this town if you behave yourself. You cannot ply your trade in this town and go undisturbed." One visit was usually enough.

On our way down to the 200 block South Doheny we decided our approach would be head on. What the hell, we weren't kidding anyone. We parked across the street and watched the place for a while. Seeing no activity we approached and knocked on the door. Our knock was answered by a blonde female who could have been in her mid-twenties. I say could have been. But it was going to be damned hard to tell by just looking. To classify her as less than attractive was being benevolent. Cork and I looked at each other and immediately began to rethink our prostitution angle.

The makeup would have to come off with a chisel. The hair was not what you could call blonde really, more of a canary yellow. It would be hard to conceive of this woman making money as a hooker let alone as much activity as was reported.

We introduced ourselves and she invited us in. She introduced herself as Sarah and once in the living room we were joined by an older man probably in his late forties. He was a small pale man of frail build and nearly bald. He seemed older and had the look in his eyes of a banty rooster getting ready for combat.

"We're from the Beverly Hills Police Department", Cork begins, "and we are responding to a complaint from your neighbors."

"Who's complaining about what ?" banty rooster asked in an antagonistic tone.

It was time to jerk this guys chain.

"What did you say your name was ?" I asked as I stood up and took a step towards him. "We were all talking when you came in and I didn't catch it." I tried to make my voice as nonchalant as possible. He got the point. So did Sarah. She got up and moved toward him.

"This is John, my boyfriend."

At the same time he says "my name is John, this is our home." This time a more friendly tone.

We asked them for enough information to file some Field Interrogation cards which further disturbed John.

"We might as well get to the point of our visit. We know what you're doing here and from here. Your neighbors have complained and we've had our patrol cars check out some of your visitors. Our visit is just that. A visit to impart some valuable information to you." Cork paused and I picked up the story.

"We're here to advise you that if you continue to engage in your profession, you will not do so in this City. We want you to know that we know you are here. We are not telling you to leave, merely advising you that you would probably be happier somewhere else."

With that John was on his feet.

"You can't run us out of town, we can live anywhere we want to. This isn't the old west." His voice is screeching now.

"You've misunderstood entirely", Cork says, "we're not running you out of town. We're merely providing you with information that we feel would be of benefit and interest to you. We presume that you would like to be happy wherever you live and just feel you would not be happy living here. If you will excuse us we'll be on our way. Nice to have met you."

We got up and headed for the door. Sarah got up and joined us. She had gotten the point. John was still blustering. As we went out the door she said, " Don't worry, we're moving anyway. Thank you and good bye."

We filled out our F.I. cards in the car. She is Sarah Umphrey, 23 yrs. old, he's John Vitolo, 48 yrs old. Both unemployed, no vehicle. He's got a short record for minor offenses, she, one arrest for prostitution. It figured.

Back at the office I filed the F.I. cards while Cork filled in the Chief. Hopefully that was the end of it. We left a memo for the patrol division to keep an eye on the place. Apparently everything had been taken care of. Fat chance.

Friday morning as I hit the top of the stairs in the business office the Watch Commander pointed me to the Chief's office with the comment, "Cork's already in there." God, it's only quarter after seven !

I stuck my head inside the lions den and was motioned to a seat beside Cork. Among a few mumbled phrases and a gesture or two I got the idea that our visit to Sarah's house was less successful than I had hoped. It seemed the neighbors were still complaining especially about the noisy fight the night before. Had we gotten in when the Chief did, (5:00 AM) we would have seen the entry on the activity blotter and known what was going to happen. Trumped again.

We got our marching orders, again . . . Take care of the problem with emphasis this time.

We left his office and stopped by the desk to read the blotter entry. Bob Bowers, the Watch Commander, had it in his hand waiting for us. We read it quickly and headed down the stairs to the car. Capt. Hankins was on his way in as we were going out. We explained briefly what was happening and he just ducked his head and started toward the stairs without a word. Guess who it would be that the Chief would pick to keep the rope from twisting ? Sound cynical ? Don't you believe it. I still loved the place.

It was too early to go calling so we stopped for a cup of coffee enroute. To go, that is. We spent the next half hour sipping coffee and watching our suspects apartment. Convinced now that if we were up, they should be up, we went to the door and knocked, loudly. It took several knocks for a bruised Sarah to open the door. This time we just stepped inside.

"Where's John ?", I asked.

"In the bedroom" she said in a very squeaky voice.

"Get him up and get your clothes on we're going to the office" Cork said as we headed for the bedroom just to make sure John understood the program. He was sitting on the edge of the bed when we got there.

"What's wrong ?, The cops were here last night and everything was settled then. What are you doing here ?" John asked as he was pulling on his pants.

"We're investigating an assault and we can do it better in our office, now get dressed. Or do you need help ?" I asked. He bent over to put on his shoes and mumbled something but not loudly enough to hear. Sarah had stepped into the closet to put on her clothes. After they made a quick trip to the bathroom we all left the apartment and headed for our office. It was a quiet ride.

Once back at the office we sat John in the business office and took Sarah to the interview room. We got her a cup of coffee and asked her about the night before. She was reluctant at first to say anything but started to come around in a few minutes. John had gotten physical when she didn't bring as much home as he expected her to from her last visitor. She had tried to explain to him that she couldn't very well beat any more out of him. John was going to teach her a lesson about not following his instructions to get the money up front. The neighbors heard the brawl and called the police. After the police left John got really upset but didn't dare beat on her anymore.

Sarah began to tell us a little about John and his customers. It seemed he sought out the weirdos for Sarah to have kinky sex with. His argument was that they paid better because of their quirks.

"I didn't think much about it till he started hitting on me for `golden showers'. That's when I found out he was as kinky as they were."

Cork and I looked at each other. We had both been around the block but 'golden shower' was new to us.

"What do you mean golden shower ?" we asked at the same time.

"Come on, you guys know." she said a note of incredulity in her voice.

"Maybe we know it by some other name but that one is new to me" I told her.

"He has me play with him till he gets a good hard on and then he jumps in the tub and I stand over him and pee on his chest. It seems to really get him off fast. He gets real mad if I run out of pee before he's done. I have to drink two or three bottles of beer sometimes before we do it. What do you guys call it?" she asked as she lit another cigarette.

"I have to admit it's new to me. Maybe I haven't been around as much as I thought." I stood up and left the room. I felt dirty. Yuck. Cork would have left too but I beat him to it.

When I went back in Sarah said she didn't want to make any trouble for John and wouldn't press any charges. We told her they would have to find some other place to live and soon. She agreed.

We brought John into the interrogation room and brought him up to date on our conversation with Sarah. Without the shower part. He had had some time to consider his position and didn't try to impress us with his savagery.

"John, we know what you did to her last night. We do not consider that behavior that can be overlooked in this City. Our last talk didn't seem to take so we'll put it more plainly."

Cork sat up in his chair and leaned across the desk toward John.

"There are three days till the end of the month. That is plenty of time for you two to find a place out of town to live and to move. In the meantime business will halt. We suggest you devote all your time to finding a place and moving." Corks voice had lowered and he had gotten very businesslike. He leaned back in his chair.

"Be advised that until you have moved you will become a career project for us." I told him. "Anytime you look outside your window one of our cars will be there. Business will not be good even if you decide not to move. But I'm sure that never entered your head. Did it?" I rose to open the door and escort them out. Sarah hadn't said a word.

John started to say something about not being enough time but Sarah whispered something to him and he shut up. When we got to the business office we asked the dispatcher to get them a ride home in a black and white. That would put a little icing on the cake for the neighbors. John again started to say something but thought better of it. The Chief had come out of his office to get a look at them before the patrol car took them home. After they left he asked if they were going to move and was told they would. The patrol units told us that they began moving that afternoon and were completely gone in two days. Another job well done.

While all this was going on Cork and I had been interviewing Woodyard and Powell, our apartment house burglars, in between other things. A few days after getting John and Sarah out of town I was in the L.A.P.D. Intelligence Division offices and talking to Lt. Marion Phillips. Phil was a walking encyclopedia of criminal intelligence information. Not only about L.A. but around the country. I had been telling him about the cases that Woodyard and Powell were clearing for us and some of the things they were saying.

"By the way Phil", I asked, "have you ever heard of a receiver by the name of "John the Hat" in the Hollywood area. They don't know his real name but say he's very active and handles a lot of their stuff."

Phil looked at me and says, “You’re joking, right?”

“No, not hardly. I’ve never heard of him.” I replied.

“You should have. You just ran him out of your town into ours. I meant to thank you for that but let it slip my mind. “John the Hat”, is John Vitolo. He’s moved into that big apartment house on the northwest corner of Crescent Heights and Franklin. With his girlfriend. Vice reported yesterday.”

“Ah bullshit. You’re jerking my chain. A pimp I can see but a receiver, hardly. This guy is supposed to be setting up some big jobs for burglars. Now that I think about it though, his girlfriends kinky customers are probably some of the victims. Damn.” So much for luck.

“Well he’s supposed to have some connections with organized crime but we think it’s more talk than anything else.” Phil said. He pulled out the most recent Vice Division report on John and Sarah. “She’s got the reputation of being the queen of kinky sex around town right now. Charges a bundle too. I wouldn’t be surprised if he was setting up her customers. Some of them are pretty prominent.”

When I told Cork what Phil had told me about John he expressed himself as I did. “Yeah, a pimp I can see. A setup man and receiver, damned hard to believe.”

We kept getting rumors about John but never got close enough to arrest him. Some months later L.A. did bag him for receiving stolen property, tried and convicted him and sent him to state prison at San Quentin. Word got back to us that John had a prison territorial dispute with one of our previous arrestees, Max Stern.

Max had been convicted for theft and extortion and had the reputation for being “BAD”. He and John apparently had a disagreement about who would run the “D” block of the prison. Max allegedly knocked John on his ass then dragged him into a workshop where he proceeded to clamp his little finger in a vise and saw it off with a hacksaw. That ended the dispute. Max had a pretty convincing argument. It’s a different world in there.

CHAPTER 42

"Hey Bob, Cork. Better meet me at the office as soon as you can make it."

"What's up ?"

"There's been a homicide and they have a guy in custody."

"On my way."

And that's the way it started. At five- thirty in the morning. A simple, quick, telephone call, and someone is dead.

"What's up ?" Diana asked as she turned over.

"That was Cork. There's been a homicide. He wants me to come in."

"O.K., I'll see you when you're done I guess." she purred.

Never any griping, just resignation and silent support.

A thousand scenarios ran through my head as I threw on some clothes. I called for a ride while I was pulling on my pants.

I had just tied my shoes when it rolled up the driveway. On the way to the station the officer told me what he knew of the case. It wasn't much. A north end resident dead from a gunshot wound, and a colored man found roaming in the area had been picked up.

I got more information when I got to the office. Cork and I sat down with the Watch Commander to find out that about four-thirty AM the desk got a call from a woman on North Linden Drive. She had heard what she thought was a shot and had come down from her bedroom to find her son bound and gagged, lying on the floor, partly in the closet, and in a pool of blood.

When the officers and ambulance arrived they determined that the man was dead, apparently from a gunshot wound to the back of the head.

Shortly before they got this call, the Beat Four officer had observed a colored man walking rapidly east on Elevado. Or at least as rapidly as he could. He was apparently highly disabled and walked with a very pronounced limp. When the officer stopped him he was very evasive and had no reason for being in the area. When he was searched for weapons, the officer found several pieces of expensive jewelry in his pockets. He was brought into the station a few minutes before the call about the body.

The Watch Commander said the house looked like it had been ransacked, and they showed the lady the jewelry they had found on the suspect. She identified it as belonging to her and her son. The suspect denied any knowledge of the burglary or the death. It was time for a long heart to heart talk with the guy.

We got him out of the cell block. They were right. He had a very pronounced limp. In fact his right leg seemed about five or six inches shorter than the left. He had to turn almost sideways and then swing his leg forward to walk. He was in his early thirties but the look in his eyes made him a lot older. He was short in stature, with rounded shoulders making him seem even shorter. He moved like a beaten man. Not particularly physically beaten, but internally and mentally beaten. He had some hard living wrapped up inside him.

We had brought his belongings, and the jewelry found in his pockets, to the interrogation room with us. It was spread out on the desk. We had also brought along a cup of coffee. He was very interested in that. It was gone quickly.

The conversation started pretty tensely. Sparring back and forth. He was being very defensive and antagonistic.

"You only arrested me because I'm black. Do you think every cripple is a thief ?"

"No, we don't. But this stuff on the table makes it look pretty bad don't you think ?" Cork ased.

He chose to ignore the jewelry that was found in his pockets. He would never directly answer any questions about where he had gotten the jewelry. We were bothered by the fact that the arresting officer had not found a gun on him. We shifted the conversation to his personal situation. How many times had he been arrested ?

How much time had he done in prison? Where was his family? How did he get his leg hurt? What kind of work did he do?

He wasn't about to give us too much information but would answer a few meaningless questions.

"Why were you walking on Elevado at four- thirty when the officer stopped you ?" I asked. He shifted to look right at me.

"What's the matter, can't a black man walk down a street in this town ?" He's got a real chip on his shoulder. Maybe if my body was as screwed up as his I may be testy too.

"Mister, the Pope would get stopped in Beverly Hills if he was walking around the streets of this town at that time in the morning." Cork responded to his comments.

This went on for about an hour. With several coffee refills, of course. By this time the jailer had come to work and had made a large pot of coffee. The Chief had come in and been filled in on the case by the Watch Commander. He wanted to know just what we were finding out from our suspect but he wasn't about to interrupt our interrogation.

We talked for a couple of hours just to find some common ground to talk with this man. He knew he had a big problem and he was scared. He was fighting hard not to show it. Eventually he started to answer some questions without the rancor in his voice. We were making some progress.

When we had gotten the overall atmosphere to a conversational tone, we started to suggest a polygraph exam. He immediately started to clam up again. He wasn't a believer in the polygraph. It was a trick to convict colored people. We backed off that subject. It took a while to get the calmness back. He was starting to loosen up enough to admit that he had come to town to find a house to burglarize. But he hadn't done it. While he was roaming around in the alleys, he found a small bundle laying in the alley. It was a handkerchief with some jewelry inside. The same jewelry that was found in his pocket. He figured someone had pulled a job and had dropped the handkerchief when he was getting away. It was starting to come, but very slowly.

We danced around with this prospect for a while. He saw that we were picking holes in his theory but he wasn't trying too hard to persuade us. He came up with half a dozen ways he had gotten into town. He was heading for a bus stop to leave town when he was picked up. We had sent the identification people to the house to gather any physical evidence and fingerprints they could find. They should be coming back anytime now, we informed him.

"When we match your prints to those found in the house, what are you going to tell us then ?" His head drooped a little and he looked at the floor for a second.

"Well I'll guess I have to tell you I was in the house, but I didn't hurt anyone."

We got the feeling he wanted to tell it all but just didn't know how to start it. It was going to take time. We resigned ourselves to that fact and just eased back a little. We arranged for some toast and coffee for us all and talked as we ate it. It was coming a little easier now. For some unknown reason he would clam up completely for a while and deny any connection with the burglary or jewelry. With a little gentle guidance, he returned to the subject, still not adding any details. It was starting to get frustrating. At one time he almost had us believing there may have been another person with him. But the story just didn't hang together.

We again brought up the polygraph. For his own benefit, of course. If he was innocent, it would clear him. But don't take it if you are guilty because it will show that too. He still wasn't having any. Not that he was guilty, of course. Just that he didn't trust those things. They didn't work right on colored people. He was convinced, or at least he said he was.

We finally had had enough. We started to change our attitude toward him. At least we gave him that impression. Cork and I had worked together enough to know each others signals. When to slack off. When to change course. Which one would talk while the other rested. When to feign surprise. When to jerk to attention. When to raise your voice. Now was the time to change our tack.

"Look, my friend. This has gone on far enough. Let's just take everything we have and line it out for you. Then you tell us what conclusion we should draw from this." Cork's voice had shown just the right amount of irritation, we hoped. We had both sat straight up in our chairs and were lining up the papers we had been taking notes on.

Between the two of us we took turns at pointing out each specific detail of his arrest, and the different stories he had told us. It was starting to pile up.

"Now," I said, "just what do you think you are going to say when your prints show up on the closet door and other places in the house? "Well ?" Cork asked.

It seemed like an hour that we sat there just looking at him. Finally his head moved up and he started looking at the wall.

"I couldn't help it. I didn't know how I was going to have enough time to get away if I just tied him up and put him in the closet." His voice was quivering. Wow, here it comes. Just like that. You may never know just what made him turn the corner, you're just glad he did.

"I got into the house O.K. but he must have heard me. He came downstairs and found me in the den. I stuck him up and made him get into the closet. I tied him up and gagged him. Then I went and got the rest of the jewelry. When I got back to him he had almost untied himself. You seen how I walk. I knew I wouldn't have enough time to get away if I just tied him up.

I put him in the closet and shot him so it wouldn't make to much noise. It sounded like a cannon going off. I got the hell out of there as fast as I could. About a block away I saw the cop car coming. I knew he was going to get me. There was no way a colored man could be in that part of Beverly Hills at that time of night and not get stopped. You know the rest."

He seemed to have had the air let out of him. But he also seemed at peace with himself. He looked like he felt more at ease. He seemed the perfect physical example of the expression, "confession is good for the sole". His whole demeanor had changed. His body was straighter, his speech clearer, and his eyes were alert and bright. Well, he did have an awful load on his mind. He may have felt better, but it still didn't do his victim any good.

"No my friend, not quite. Where did you put the gun ? That will wrap it all up. We need to find it before someone else does."

He hesitated, like that was the last secret and if he gave that up he had no more to hang on to.

"Right where the cop stopped me, maybe a few feet before, there is a tall hedge. I shoved the gun in the hedge, about shoulder high. It'll still be there. It's a thick hedge."

We had the Watch Commander send several officers to search the area. In fifteen minutes they had found the gun. A five inch barreled, .45 cal revolver, with one shot fired. It would have made one hell of a noise in that closet.

After we went over the whole thing again, we asked him to initial our notes, then put him back in the cell. The jailer was just now serving lunch.

Cork and I didn't say much to each other for several minutes. Cork filled the Chief in on the results of our interview, and then we decided to have a long lunch at Paul's Steak House.

We were on our second cocktail before we started really conversing.

"All he had to do was tie the guy up tighter. What the hell do you suppose gets into a guy to do something like that?" Cork was looking at the wall and shaking his head.

"I don't know, B.L. Why would you think executing someone for a few pieces of jewelry would be a solution to your problem. His only problem was escape. Why didn't he take one of the two cars in the driveway ? Do you suppose he thought about that ? Or do you think that maybe he can't drive ?"

"Maybe we can go back and ask him, but not before we get this bad taste out of our mouth. God I'm so glad something like this happens so seldom in this town."

We ate our sandwich and had our coffee in silence. The rest of the day we spent in a saddened haze. I had known before what one man could do to another. But every so often someone shows you again, just as a reminder.

We got our paperwork ready to go to the D.A's office the next morning and headed for home. Diana had beaten me home as usual. When I opened the door she took one look and said, "You look like you need a drink. Badly." With that she handed me the drink she had mixed when she saw the police car drive up the driveway.

"Was it a bad one ?"

"Yeah. No reason for it at all." I briefly filled her in the whole wretched mess.

"One person dead for a lousy 7 or 8 thousand dollars worth of jewelry. All he had to do was take one of the cars. Or tie the guy up tighter. I don't think I'll ever understand what goes through these guy's minds. And I'm not sure I want to." I said as I drained my drink and handed it to her for a refill.

"You understand all you need to to deal with them. I'm not sure how healthy it would be to know them too well." She said as she headed for the kitchen. She was back in a minute. This time with a short drink. She handed it to me and headed for the closet. Pulling out her coat she said,

"Come on. I'll let you treat me to dinner some place nice and quiet with a little music where you can come back from that hellish place you go when you have a case like this."

Not a bad idea at all. Saratoga here we come.

EPILOGUE

Now that you have finished this book, (I hope), I realize that you are left with some gnawing questions about what happened to various individuals. Well, I'll try to clear some of that up for you. You must first understand that quite often when you make a felony arrest you will probably have to go to court for the preliminary hearing. This hearing is to determine if a crime has been committed and if there is enough evidence to believe the defendant may have committed the crime. (Probable Cause) If the suspect is held to answer for trial in Superior Court, a date is set for arraignment in Superior Court.

If the suspect gets continuance after continuance, (not at all unusual) the investigating officer may never hear of the case again. Usually it happens if the defendant works out a plea bargain with the District Attorney. If the defendant is out on bail, the more postponments he gets, the better for him. (after all, he has to pay his attorney somehow) The case could drag out for a couple of years. The victims get upset, witness memories fade, the courts get more crowded so it puts pressure on the District Attorney to plead out as many cases as he can and not give away the store, so to speak. In the meantime you have gone on to several dozen other cases. You may or may not hear what finally happened to your defendant. I will attempt to fill you in on some of the people we have met in this book.

It doesn't help when you're doing your research to find out that the Police Department has purged most of their files before 1974.

No. 1 - The patrol sergeant. He survived, and eventually retired.

No. 2 - The peeper. He too survived and eventually retired. (He never did get caught where he could be prosecuted).

No. 3 - The officer on stake out on the window smash burglar and missed him with the shotgun, finally admitted he had been asleep and didn't wake up 'til he heard the window smash. A few months after that he was terminated due to drinking.

No. 4 - The Woodyard and Powell case dragged on for months. Eventually they reached a plea bargain with the D.A. and were sentenced to State Prison for an indeterminate time. Woodyard's seventeen year old girlfriend was handled by the juvenile justice system.

No. 5 - Michael Blaustein, (Lake Tahoe suspect) also dragged on for months. Eventually several cases from other jurisdictions were combined and he was sentenced to State Prison. At that time it was up to 15 years.

No. 6 - Pizzi, Despain, Kline, (Garfein & Soloman burglaries) were sent to State Prison. Their case was overturned on appeal and a new trial set. At their next arraignment in Superior Court, they pled guilty to a charge of grand larceny. The judge sentenced them to time served. They had spent a couple of years in prison.(It has always baffled me how a case could be reversed on appeal when the suspects had pled guilty in the first place).

No. 7 - The ladies that went to Santa Monica to view their property finally got some of it back. But not without the help of their lawyers.

No. 8 - Joe Duchy and 'Baldy' (Dutchess Furs) were sentenced to State Prison for five years.

No. 9 - The crippled suspect who 'executed' the burglary victim was sentenced to life in prison.

No.10 - Edmund Chuski (Washington Burglary) was sentenced to five to fifteen years. With his luck he'll do every day of it.

No.11 - The window smasher cooperated with the L.A. Auto Theft detectives and cleared several theft cases for them.

I have been asked about the high priced hookers that worked our town. Also about the bookmakers and "Mob" guys that lived and worked in town. To begin to understand the philosophy of enforcement in the "City" you must understand the "Chief". He said there were NO BOOKMAKERS in town. He also said that we ran all the prostitutes out of town. That was it. As far as unsavory characters living in town, yes, we had plenty. But there seemed to be an unwritten understanding that "you didn't crap in your own kitchen". And aside from "Bugsy" Seigel, it remained that way. Thank God.

JUST A THOUGHT

For years, many years, the law enforcement community as well as the general public, has been bombarded with the information that the criminal court system is clogged with the backlog of cases pending. This naturally has a ripple effect. Victims and witnesses move or die. Memories fade. After a while the defendants, who kept getting delays, now want a speedy trial knowing that the District Attorney's Office is backlogged. The defendants attorney uses this to coerce a less than desirable plea bargain (from a law enforcement point of view) for his client. The D.A. has to dispose of cases this way just to stay on top of the pile. The problem continues to grow.

BUT . . .

We are all aware of incidents where the defendant is guilty and yet pleads not guilty at arraignment. More delay. Now they have more time to negotiate. What if the system was changed. If the defendant pleads not guilty and requests a trial, when it is an absolute given that he is guilty or he has confessed and his confession is substantiated by physical evidence, then at the conclusion of his trial, and he is found guilty, his sentence is automatically doubled. I do not propose that we change our system for any other. A defendant should be represented by an attorney. The presumption of innocence should be maintained. But, we need some limitations on the ways the system can be manipulated to favor the criminal. If a defendant needs to enter information about extenuating circumstances that resulted in his committing this crime, he can plead "guilty, with mitigating circumstances", and then provide his mitigating factors to the judge. We all know from experience that criminals bargain for the least amount of time they can get away with. If they were to face double time for clogging up the courts while they make their deal, Things could change . . .

JUST A THOUGHT

588-DOWN

90000>
9 780738 807294